THE COLLECTED PAPERS
OF ROGER HARRISON

Titles available in the McGraw-Hill Developing Organizations Series

For further information on these titles and other forthcoming books please contact

The Product Manager, Professional Books, McGraw-Hill Book Company Europe, Shoppenhangers Road, Maidenhead, Berkshire, SL6 2QL, United Kingdom Telephone ++(0) 1628 23432 Fax ++ (0) 1628 770224

THE COLLECTED PAPERS OF ROGER HARRISON

Roger Harrison

Foreword by Edgar H. Schein

McGRAW-HILL BOOK COMPANY

London · New York · St Louis · San Francisco · Auckland
Bogotá · Caracas · Lisbon · Madrid · Mexico
Milan · Montreal · New Delhi · Panama · Paris · San Juan
São Paulo · Singapore · Sydney · Tokyo · Toronto

Published by McGraw-Hill Book Company Europe
Shoppenhangers Road, Maidenhead, Berkshire, SL6 2QL, England
Telephone 01628 23432
Fax 01628 770224

British Library Cataloguing in Publication Data

Harrison, Roger
    Collected Papers of Roger Harrison -
    (McGraw-Hill Developing Organizations
    Series)
    I. Title II. Series
    658
    ISBN 0-07-709090-X

Library of Congress Cataloging-in-Publication Data

The LOC data of this title is available from the Library of Congress, Washington DC, USA.

12345 CUP 998765

Printed and bound in Great Britain at the University Press, Cambridge.

Printed on permanent paper in compliance with ISO Standard 9706

CONTENTS

SERIES PREFACE

The McGraw-Hill *Developing Organizations* series is for people in the business of changing, developing and transforming their organizations. The books in the series bring together ideas and practice in the emerging field of organizational learning and development. Bridging theory and action, they contain new ideas, methods and models of how to get things done.

Organizational learning and development is the child of the organization development (OD) movement of the 1960s and 1970s. Then people like Schein, Beckhard, Bennis, Walton, Blake and Mouton *et al.* defined a *change technology*, which was exciting and revolutionary. Now the world has moved on.

The word "technology" goes with the organization-as-machine metaphor. OD emphasized the *outside-in* application of "behavioural science" which seems naive in the context of the power-broking, influence and leverage of today's language. Our dominant metaphor of organizations as organisms or collective living beings requires a balancing *inside-out* focus of development and transformation of what is already there.

Learning is the key to our current dilemmas. We are not just talking about change. Learning starts with me and you, with the person–and spreads to others–if we can organize in ways which encourage it.

Learning is at a premium because we are not so much masters of change as beset by it. There is no single formula or image for the excellent company. Even the idea of "progress" is problematic as companies stick to the knitting and go to the wall. Multiple possible futures, the need for discontinuity almost for the sake of it, means that we must be able to think imaginatively, to be able to develop ourselves and, in generative relationships with others, to organize and reorganize ourselves continuously.

Organizations are unique, with distinctive biographies, strengths, opportunities. Each creates its own future and finds its own development paths. The purpose of these books is not to offer ready-made tools, but to help you create your own tools from the best new ideas and practices around.

The authors in the series have been picked because they have something to say. You will find in all of the books the personal voice of the writer, and this reflects the voice which each of us needs in our own organizations to do the best we can.

The appearance of this Roger Harrison collection is a particular delight for me. Roger is one of those, mainly North Americans, who created the OD movement 25 years ago. However, he always struck me as different from many of his colleagues because he put learning at the centre of his endeavour. His 1967 paper The Design of Cross-cultural Training: An Alternative to the University Model *(with Richard Hopkins) was an inspiration for my colleagues and myself when we were struggling to find an alternative to our "systematic training" assumptions. Another paper that was seminal for me,* Defenses and the Need to Know, *goes to the heart of the matter of adult learning and self-development.*

It is not just the fecundity of his ideas – on organizational ideologies and cultures, on the depth of intervention in consultancy, on the feeding and care of infant systems, of role negotiation or New Age leadership – but the congenial and encouraging nature of his presentation that so appeals. From Roger you get, not only an idea that illuminates the very part of the world you have been searching darkly for years, but a method, an activity, a way of going forward in practice.

One of the minor puzzles of the age is that Roger has never before been published in book form. For this reason he is not as well known as he might be, although his work has filtered into the consultancy mainstream through the work of others. Happily this anomaly is now put right by this publication. I am pleased to have been part of the venture.

Mike Pedler

FOREWORD

It is a great pleasure to have the opportunity to introduce *The Collected Papers of Roger Harrison.* I have known Roger since 1960, when he first came to the National Training Labs at Bethel, Maine, to learn the mysteries of T-groups and Leadership Training. I had preceded him by one year, so we were learners together, and I had the pleasure of participating with him in many stimulating co-training sessions. Those were exciting times because we all participated in the birth of organization development—the application of experiential learning methods to managerial and organizational problems.

I remember Roger as one of the more seminal and critical thinkers in this emerging field. He was not swept up in the mystique of sensitivity training, and because of his background in industry, he always took a hard, analytical look at the relevance of what we were doing for organizational effectiveness and for the welfare of people in organizations. As the T-group "movement" evolved, it divided into two camps: those who saw sensitivity training as "therapy for normals," and those who continued to try to find applications to leadership, team building, and organization development. Clearly, Roger was in the latter camp, and therein lies the strength of his thinking and writing.

We continued to meet from time to time and occasionally even worked with the same companies. What always impressed me was Roger's courage in developing new concepts, new methodologies, and new applications in real organizational settings. When he wrote about what he was doing, he usually introduced a fresh way of looking at things and clarified areas that had been murky. For example, most of us working with organizations knew that we were intervening at various levels of "depth," but until Roger's clarifying paper on this subject (Harrison, 1970 [Chapter Two]), most of us were being intuitive and had few frame-works for analyzing when to do what. As we encountered various client systems, it was obvious that they differed in important ways; but until Roger wrote about organizational "character" (1972b [Chapter Ten]), we had only a few very ab-stract typologies drawn from anthropology and sociology to use in dealing with these differences. Roger's paper thus helped to open up the area of organizational culture. Through the sixties and seventies, we all changed our concepts of teach-ing and learning. We had all learned from our T-group experiences that people learn best when they are in charge of their own learning and when abstract ideas are closely linked to concrete concepts. Roger was one of the most active endorsers and developers of this "experiential" training philosophy, and he wrote articu-lately about its application in a variety of settings.

For the past decade or so, I had lost touch with Roger and with his work, so it was a welcome surprise to learn that his writings have been pulled together into one volume. One of the problems with the field of organization development (OD) has always been that it has had no conceptual core built out of a history of com-mon practice by OD practitioners. We have all gone our own way, loosely con-nected by a set of overarching values and a common set of process skills and insights, but we have not really thought about our history and what it all means. One way to begin to fill this gap is to develop some personal histories, and here Roger has done us a great service by providing us with his concepts and theories developed in a wide variety of contexts over thirty years. As I noted earlier, Roger has been one of the more creative and talented theoreticians and practitioners in the field, but until the publication of this book, many of his insights had been lost in various journals and books. Coming from a rich psychological background and experienced in a wide variety of organizational settings and cultures, he has been able to provide perspective on and insight into most of the critical issues that preoccupy organization development practitioners today.

I have identified five fundamental reasons why this collection is worth ex-ploring, browsing in, and reading in detail on selected topics:

1. The topics of the chapters are the central and important topics of OD: depth of intervention, role negotiation, power and influence, organizational charac-ter, psychological defenses, values, the learning organization, and leadership, to name just a few.
2. They are written from a personal perspective and include commentary by the author on the original papers, making them more vital and topical.
3. They are filled with useful analytical distinctions and typologies that organize complex phenomena into manageable units.
4. They also contain many practical examples and "how to's," so the practi-tioner can extrapolate from the concepts to the practice.
5. Perhaps of greatest importance, the entire collection is written from a strong values base. Roger's own philosophy and his vision for how organizations and

communities, if not the world, could be better places come through in virtually every one of his writings.

Roger's philosophy has a strong humanistic base. He is not afraid to advocate bringing love into organizational life. He points out that leaders can and often need to be stewards and servants. He reminds us again and again that learning does not really take place unless the learners have set their own goals and been provided with opportunities to experience what they are learning about. Organizations will never be fully effective unless they can figure out how to truly empower employees so that employee goals will be aligned with and attuned to organizational missions. The spiritual dimension belongs in organizational life, because it ultimately is part of our humanness, and organizations are, in the end, not abstract, impersonal structures, but human systems driven by human issues and concerns.

What gives these values potency is the degree to which they are woven into all of Roger's thinking, so that one can see their relevance whether one is reading about starting a new unit, developing a training program, gauging the depth of an intervention, deciding on a culture-change program, or building a community. This strong value orientation is what gives *The Collected Papers of Roger Harrison* its flavor; but the combining of these values with clearly thought-out typologies and analytical categories is the book's true contribution to the field. Readers will be richly rewarded by immersing themselves in the broad range of topics, ideas, and values that this book lays out for them.

March 1995   Edgar H. Schein
                                                    Sloan Fellows Professor of Management Emeritus
                                                    Senior Lecturer
                                                    MIT Sloan School of Management

PREFACE

I have been an organization development (OD) consultant for the better part of four decades, since before the term was coined in the mid sixties. I began my career with Procter & Gamble as an internal consultant, then taught organizational behavior at Yale University for a time, and became an independent consultant in 1967. I have participated in most of the developments in my profession that have come along during those years. I have invented one or two of the developments myself and have contributed in practice or in print to a good number of them, both in my work in the United States and in an eight-year period of living and working in Britain and Europe. Along the way, I have often been moved to write about my insights and discoveries, being a rather thoughtful and conceptual person by nature and through my training as an academic psychologist. I have scattered my work through a variety of outlets, depending on where I found myself geographically and what audience I wanted to reach. Until recently, however, I had never written a book. I have moved a little erratically, though with some speed, through the preoccupations and passions of my personal and professional search for truth and meaning. I have left my written work like the cairns of a cross-country explorer in the mountains I love, marking my way in case I should want to return. I have also seen myself as something of a dilettante, moving like a butterfly from flower to flower, tasting the sweetness or bitterness of each, but not alighting for long anywhere. If people wanted to read my work, they had to do a literature search or rely upon the "network" of kindred spirits who pass from hand to hand photocopies of what they find speaks to them.

Colleagues sometimes urged me to publish my collected papers. Until recently I refused, fearing that if I looked back too long, I would cease growing, perhaps turning into a pillar of salt, like Lot's wife, or into a monument to my own career, all motion frozen into a single form. One colleague who was especially persuasive was Graham Dawes when he was at the Roffey Park Institute in Britain. I am deeply grateful for his patient persistence and encouragement, without which I might never have come to the point of action.

Sometime in 1990, my attitude shifted. Suddenly, my concerns did not matter any more. I saw that the patterns in my life were circular, sometimes helical, but certainly not linear. My shifts of direction and vision were endless harmonic variations on a few basic themes. I was not going anywhere, except perhaps deeper into those melodies. I could continue that process or not, according to my needs and wishes. There was nothing to be superstitious about in looking back—maybe if I looked carefully enough, I would see my future!

Now I wanted to do the work, wanted to see the themes emerge from the mass of context, thought I had a few insights worth sharing. Some of these insights have to do with facing the darker side of those causes for which I have been a worker almost all my life: freedom, autonomy, empowerment, self-expression, and individuality. When these qualities are not balanced by compassion, empathy, and love, they become destructive to life. They tear apart the web of unseen connections and cooperative relationships among humans, and between humans and nature. We are now seeing that these relationships sustain life and must be healed if we are to continue on this planet.

The Time to Speak Is Now

I feel an increasing urgency to redress the balance, to heal the wounds, to reconnect people in their working lives with one another, and with their deepest resources of spirit. In these closing years of the millennium, it seems we have yet a little time while the fate of our planet hangs in the balance between evolution and disaster. At such a time, each of us counts for more than one, and our actions can have effects that will resound down the centuries ahead—for pain and darkness or for healing and light. The issue is not just making organizations more productive or even more humane places in which to work. It is living and acting in a way that reestablishes balance and harmony, both within our organizations and without. It means appreciating our oneness with all life and with the planet that nurtures us. It is no longer a question of making our human lives better, but of committing ourselves to sustainable life for all beings. In my own life and work, I have followed a path from rebellion to radical autonomy and self-expression through to cooperation and community. My path has been my own, and I have not arrived at the end, but it is a destination we must all choose to know if we are to leave the world better for our having walked upon it.

If the insights acquired along my way are to be useful to others, the time is now, if only because there seems so little time for anything we do to weigh upon the scales. But I have learned of late to appreciate more deeply what I have to offer. I am continually surprised by what I have learned along the way, and by what I am able to see and do as a consultant—especially by what I am able to see. I have always been drawn to the complexity of organizations, not because I am attracted to chaos itself but because I love to find the order in it, the deep structures. When we really *see*, we can use our intuition and our hearts to get where we want to go. We arrive more rested than when we use only our will and reason. As I have helped others to see what I see, I find I have, almost by accident, become a cartographer of a New World of organization culture and change. The maps I have drawn of the older continent of education and learning also contain some features whose exploration seems worth the journey, because I have been more interested in how people learn than in how they are to be taught.

Overview of the Contents

To put this collection together, I chose those of my articles and monographs that I and those advising me felt to have the most enduring value for leaders, managers, consultants, and members of organizations. They seemed to group themselves naturally into four categories, represented by the four parts of this volume: the theory and practice of organization development, understanding and working with (that is, changing) organization cultures, understanding the dynamics of communities, and designing and conducting experiential and self-directed education and learning for application in life and work.

I have chosen essays that at the time they were written expressed some insight, invention, or appreciation of connections and relationships, essays that I believe are worth rediscovering today. I have included the pieces that have become "classics" in the field, along with those that I think of as undiscovered treasures because they afforded me some measure of surprise and delight on rereading. As I applied this criterion of surprise and delight, I found that none of my more academic and empirical pieces were to be included. I chose well when I decided that the world of work, not the university, was where I could learn and create the most!

Within the four sections, the papers are arranged in roughly chronological order, although there are a few deviations to improve thematic flow. The publication dates do not necessarily reflect the order of creation. Some of my work was in the barrel for years before being bottled and sent out to the trade.

Each part begins with a general guide to the included essays, and in addition, I have supplied an introduction for each essay, giving the context in which it was written and my thoughts about its current significance. I have tried to keep the latter to the minimum, believing that if the work does not speak for itself, it is better left unsung. In several cases, I have appended material that extends the insights or experiences discussed in the article or brings them up to date.

Audience

These collected papers will of course be useful to students of organization development, organizational behavior, and the softer aspects of management and "human resources." It will also provide their teachers with a rich source of reading assignments. If we consider the organization from one perspective as a machine and from another as a living organism, then these essays touch upon most of the developments that derive from the organic side during the past forty years. It is doubtless in parts a fuzzy and distorted hologram, but I think the issues are all there in some form.

I believe this book will be of value to anyone who needs to understand, rather than simply suffer, the blooming, buzzing vortices of complexity we call organizations. Because I have always been interested in facilitating change and growth, it will be of most worth to those who want to do likewise: consultants, leaders of change, and leaders who are changing. It will encourage those who believe that we can trust organizations to heal and learn and grow without coercion. It will be of special value to those who wish to look before they leap, understand before they destroy, and keep to a minimum the harm they do the people and organizations in their care.

Those who are looking for prescriptions will find some comfort in my early work, written when I was caught up in the North American passion for social technology. Those looking for new technologies for organization transformation will initially be disappointed. However, I have told what I know about the organizational dynamics that determine the results obtained from such technologies. I have also pointed to recent developments in the techniques and methods of OD that I consider to be life enhancing for organizations, individuals, and the planet and I have said why I find them so.

How to Read This Book

I do not really presume to tell anyone how to read a book. It is an art that I have yet to master, for all the writing that I have done. Yet I have found useful a saying of Paramhansa Yogananda, which has been passed along by his disciple J. Donald Walters. Yogananda is reputed to have said, "Read for one hour; write for two; meditate for three."

It seems sound advice. I believe that all, or almost all, learning is remembering, in the sense of bringing forth what is already latent in us and giving it new form appropriate to the moment. If that is true, then a major purpose of reading is to stimulate one's own mental, emotional, or creative processes. One reads to catalyze remembering, and a little of the catalyst goes a long way. As a leader or practitioner, I would browse in a book such as this to stimulate my own creative powers, to remind me of connections forgotten or overlooked, and to evoke former insights and ideas that were discarded because they could not be acted upon at once. It would make me happy, too, if at least some readers would encounter here new hope for values once held dear, and dreams that have been misplaced under the grinding press of what passes for a full life.

March 1995   Roger Harrison
Clinton, Washington

THE AUTHOR

Roger Harrison is widely acknowledged as a pioneer practitioner in the field of organization development. He has participated in and contributed to nearly every phase of its growth—from survey research and team building to large-systems change and organization transformation. In addition to his successful career as a consultant, he is a leader in identifying emerging issues of theory and practice and crystallizing them in his writings and presentations. He has written numerous articles on learning, organization development, and organization culture, and several of these articles have become classics in the field. He was among the first to write about culture in organizations, and he has published (with Herb Stokes, 1986) a widely used instrument for assessing organization culture. His autobiography has recently been published by Jossey-Bass and McGraw-Hill. He has also designed a number of innovative training programs, including (with David Berlew) the Positive Power & Influence Program.

Harrison received his B.A. degree magna cum laude (1952) from Dartmouth College, and his doctorate in industrial psychology (1956) from the University of California at Berkeley. He began his consulting career with Procter & Gamble, then taught organizational psychology at Yale University until 1966. He was on the staff of the National Training Laboratories before moving to Europe in 1968. He practiced in Europe for eight years as an independent consultant, establishing an international reputation as a consultant and trainer of consultants with such multinational companies as Rank Xerox, Imperial Chemical Industries, Mobil, Esso Europe, Shell International, Norsk Hydro, and Volvo AB.

Harrison returned to the United States in 1976 and continues his consulting practice, now based in Clinton, Wasington. He is also a senior consultant with Innovation Associates of Framingham, Massachusetts. During recent years, he has focused on working with leaders to develop humane strategies for large-systems change, to implement learning, and to facilitate healing of the traumas of change. He is currently at work on a book exploring the relationship between healing and learning in organizations. He is also engaged in the practice and development of large-group methods for working with whole systems and in applications of dialogue to organizations.

Roger Harrison may be reached at:
3646 East Redtail Lane
Clinton, WA 98236
Phone: (360) 579–1805
Fax: (360) 579–1798

PART ONE

ON ORGANIZATION DEVELOPMENT

My early papers on organization development (OD) reflect the issues in that field as it was taking shape in the sixties and early seventies. OD had its roots in sensitivity training, and its initial underlying values were the same as those of T-groups: open and honest communication, trust, and power sharing. For the benefit of readers who do not have clear referents for *T-group* and *sensitivity training,* I should explain that these terms refer to a form of training that takes place in groups of ten to twelve members, usually meeting for a total of six hours a day, in two-hour segments, with a facilitator. The group has no agenda, other than to explore and understand its own processes, nor are structures and procedures imposed by the facilitator. The facilitator intervenes to help the group understand its process, sometimes making interpretations, sometimes suggesting activities the group can undertake to learn more. He or she also endeavors to keep the group's attention focused on the "here and now": the actions, events, and feelings that are occurring in present time within the group.

The T-group is designed to frustrate most of the ways people normally structure time and distribute power and influence in task-oriented groups and meetings. Strong feelings about the experience and about one another are generated as group members endeavor to cope with the ambiguity of the situation and to meet their needs for control, belonging, and positive regard. Group members are encouraged to express their feelings about what is happening in the group and about one another's behavior. It was through T-groups that the term *feedback* was borrowed from the field of electronics as a name for the process of sharing one's perceptions of and reactions to another member's behavior.

The facilitator discourages side trips into the "there and then": intellectual discussions, stories about events and people not present in the group, personal history, and the like. It is this strong focus on the here and now that distinguishes T-groups from encounter groups and therapy groups. If the experience goes well, and the group meets with some success in creating its own norms and making a life for itself, trust and good feeling build between the members. The trust fosters intimacy, deep self-disclosure, and increasingly honest and sensitive feedback.

A T-group "laboratory," as a set of sessions is called, may last a weekend, a week, or even longer. In 1960, when I began working with T-groups professionally, the sessions conducted by the National Training Laboratories (NTL) at Bethel, Maine, were three weeks long. Within a decade, however, the duration of a normal lab had shrunk to a week.

Following a T-group experience, group members usually report having learned a great deal about the ways in which their interpersonal styles and behaviors are perceived by others. They may also say that they have become more observant and aware of the subtleties of group and interpersonal dynamics. The heyday of T-groups was during the sixties. By the seventies, many T-group trainers were conducting *encounter groups,* which were designed to strip participants of their defenses and produce very deep and lasting personal transformation. While I did join encounter groups as a participant, I was not interested in leading them. I believed it was too easy to damage participants psychologically. By the mid seventies, T-groups and encounter groups were both on the wane. Their decline may have been helped by the notoriety they acquired through the excesses of some practitioners. There may also have been a

diminishing interest in deep personal exploration along with an increasing availability of alternative therapies and other ways of learning about the self. The NTL Institute continues to offer a diminished schedule of T-group laboratories, and the method is still applied in the training of organization development consultants. Much of what was learned by T-group and encounter group practitioners lives on in the technologies of group facilitation, in team development methods, and in new methods of group and individual therapy. For some time, it appeared to me that the *art form* of working with group dynamics was dying out, but it now seems to be having something of a renaissance in methods developed for working with whole systems, methods such as Future Search and the Technologies of Participation developed by the Institute for Cultural Affairs (ICA). For those interested in the practical application of these methods, Marvin Weisbord's recent publication is well worth reading (Weisbord and others, 1993), as is Laura Spencer's useful manual on the ICA approaches (Spencer, 1989).

T-groups evoked great missionary zeal among practitioners, including myself. As I experienced it, we became a movement dedicated to democratizing and humanizing the workplace, first through training leaders in *stranger labs,* which mixed people from different organizations, and later through bringing T-groups and their variations into organizations. It was evident from the first that in-company sensitivity training could be tricky and delicate. Participants were defensive and cautious in groups where what they did and said could have consequences for working relationships, and many group members were threatened by power differences within the groups.

I was deeply involved in the application of T-groups within organizations, most particularly in a project within Esso Research & Engineering in which I and a number of NTL associates trained Esso's internal consultants to conduct T-groups. From my work in Esso and elsewhere, I formed the opinion that T-groups were not safe interventions within business organizations. Too often, participants were seduced by the trusting atmosphere of the group into unwisely revealing inner thoughts and feelings that later came back to damage work relationships and sometimes their careers. Although business organizations today still have strong norms against the expression of feelings at work, the permitted range of emotional behavior was much narrower then. The groups were supposed to be confidential, but either the revelations found their way into performance evaluations or they were used as ammunition in the political infighting which is endemic in most organizations. By the end of the decade, the use of T-groups in organizations was rapidly dying out. Safer variations of the basic method lasted longer. The most popular was the managerial grid, developed by Robert Blake and his associates (Blake, Mouton, Barnes, and Greiner, 1964). But by the mid seventies, sensitivity training had such a bad reputation in business that many OD consultants had learned not to share with prospective clients that they had ever had anything to do with T-groups.

As it became clear that conducting sensitivity training with people who work together was a risky and often irresponsible adventure, many of us began to search for safer and more effective ways of fostering openness, trust, cooperation, and power sharing in work groups. For me, that search began in the mid sixties. My early papers in this section, "Choosing the Depth of Organizational Intervention" and "Role Negotiation," were a part of the search, which has continued to this day.

In the late sixties, I moved myself and my consulting practice to Europe, where I worked intensively for a while with new plant startups. However, I did not publish anything on my experiences until 1981, when I wrote "Startup: The Care and Feeding of Infant Systems." I also participated actively during the early seventies in training consultants in the United Kingdom, during the high tide of European interest and admiration for U.S. management methods. "Strategy Guidelines for an Internal Organization Development Unit" was a contribution to that work. Then, for about a decade, from the early seventies to the early eighties, I turned my attention from organization development consulting to management education and development. "Personal Power and Influence in Organization Development" was written during the latter part of that period, as I began to turn back to my earlier interest in OD. When I returned to consulting in the eighties, the climate for OD consultants' work had changed. Under the pressure of global competition, organizations were much more open to what we had to offer. I wrote "Empowerment in Organizations" during that period and followed it with "Implementing Transition to a More Responsive Organization." The latter paper reflects the expansive spirit of the eighties, when we were being given opportunities to attempt major changes in values, styles, and ways of working together in large systems.

At about the same time, I wrote "How to Focus Personal Energy with Organizational Mission Statements," which is about creating an organizational vision and mission statement. In it, I made a case for using the visioning exercise as a transformational experience for the top team, creating a "crucible" within which are forged the "ties that bind" people to one another and to their common purpose. In a sense, I returned to my T-group experiences for these ideas, and I have found the translation productive.

The first paper in this section, "Whither OD, and Other Fantasies," was written in 1993. It gives a condensed version of my professional history and of how I have seen the field of OD develop since its inception in the sixties. It reflects the philosophical mood that I have been in for several years as I survey how our profession has changed and what we have achieved, and consider where I want to put my own energies during the coming decades. In it, I make a case for our focusing our energies where I see the most urgent need: in bringing about changes in consciousness in organizations, changes that will support our relating to nature and to the Earth in ways that are sustainable and harmonious rather than destructive and competitive.

CHAPTER ONE

WHITHER OD, AND OTHER FANTASIES

I have been a consultant all my working life, and I have participated in almost all the processes and developments that have contributed to what is now thought of as "the state of the art" in organization development (OD). In this paper, I want to summarize the legacy of the past as it re-lates to the present, and I shall also put forward my view of the current existential issues in the field of OD. By *existential issues,* I mean those forces, events, and processes that impact the *experience and feeling* of being an OD consultant now, in the last decade of the twentieth century.

I attended my first sensitivity training session (T-group) in 1958, not long after finishing my formal training in psychology. The experience changed my life, as it did many another's. I experienced in those five days a depth of intimacy and heartfulness with the other men in my T-group that I had not known was possible outside of a love relationship. The experience brought to me a new vision of the potential of human relationships, and I soon became deeply involved in the study and practice of this work, which seemed to offer a way to humanize the workplace.

Source: Originally published as "A Consultant's Journey, 1956–1993," *Vision/Action,* 1994, *12*(4), 11–15. Reprinted here with permission of Roger Harrison.
Note: Citations of original papers reprinted here as chapters include the chapter numbers in brackets.

The Legacy of T-Groups

Learnings from T-groups addressed and awoke three issues that have continued to animate me during my career as a consultant. Those issues have been *empowerment, relationship,* and *learning.* Here are some of the things I and other consultants discovered about these issues during T-groups.

- Groups operating by consensus make better decisions than leaders do, because they use everyone's resources.
- Groups do not need a leader to tell them what to do—they can manage themselves.
- Intimacy depends on willingness to risk, not longevity of relationship.
- It is painful to see yourself as others see you, but it is bearable in a group where trust and support are high.
- Through sharing feelings, you can learn to love people you do not much like.
- Who risks and experiments more learns more.
- Who risks, experiments, *and reflects with others* learns most.
- You are not alone. If you feel strongly about something you see and everyone else denies it, some of the others are not owning up.
- Not everyone has the same experiences and assumptions as you; sharing your data as well as your conclusions saves time and conflict.

These learnings may not have been completely true, but for many of us, they became articles of faith and foundations of our consulting practice as the sensitivity training movement ripened into OD. Before that transition occurred, we learned bitter lessons as we brought T-groups into the workplace during the sixties. Our technology was more powerful than we were wise, and participants who were led by us to open themselves to colleagues were sometimes hurt later on when their openness was used against them in workplace politics.

OD came to life in the form of such innovations as "process consultation," "task-oriented team development," and "role negotiation," as we endeavored to bring what we had learned as T-group trainers into organizations and to make that learning safe for our clients. For me, the sixties and early seventies were a time of passionate commitment to the cause of empowerment for individuals in organizations, and I saw myself as a freedom fighter for that cause in most of my work. During this period, I developed the "autonomy laboratory" and (with David Berlew) the Positive Power & Influence Program, both of which were oriented to helping participants learn to make things happen in their lives and organizations. I became less optimistic, though not cynical, about the possibilities for openness and intimacy in organizations during those years, and it was a time when my own growth and development were oriented to personal autonomy and empowerment.

As I look back now, until about 1980, we OD consultants were knocking at the doors of organizations, asking for opportunities to contribute, but we were so strongly countercultural that we usually had to content ourselves with operating on the fringes, often concealing our true motives and objectives. There was no great felt need for change in organizations; they were "fat and happy" for the most part, and even when we could show them a better way, it was rare that the will existed to take advantage of it.

But things *were* changing in the wider society, and we in OD were a part of that change. People were expressing their individuality and a newfound freedom in many ways. During the sixties, it was the sexual revolution, the hippies, the communes, and "flower power." In the seventies, it was the emphasis on life-styles, the ethic of "doing your own thing," the continued questioning of authority, and the weakening of the nuclear family and of societal constraints on individual behavior. When I returned to the United States in 1976, after eight years in Europe, I found displayed on the airport newsstands a new America, one in which such books as *Power! How to Get It, How to Use It* (Korda, 1975), *Looking Out for Number One* (Ringer, 1977), and *Winning Through Intimidation* (Ringer, 1974) announced a swing from the relationship orientation of the sixties to a strong concern with personal power.

This trend gave me pause. I had begun by believing that empowerment *and* openness and cooperation were compatible and equally worthwhile objectives, and what I now saw about me in organizations was a world in which traditional authoritarian and bureaucratic cultures were giving way to an unbridled "Me First" competition in which the hand of each was raised against his or her fellows—empowerment *without* relationship. The ethic of this new organization culture has been well described by Michael Maccoby in *The Gamesman* (1976). It looked to me as though we were engaged in a reckless competition for the resources of our organizations and of society, with little care for the "ties that bind," the social fabric of cooperation and mutual responsibility that made possible the creation of those resources in the first place. The process was not confined to organizations and society; it also went on between our species and the Earth, where it was becoming clear that we could not go on exploiting our environment without destroying the delicate web of cooperative and nurturing processes that makes life here possible.

What I saw about me paralleled my own story. I went to Europe in 1968 as a freelance consultant seeking freedom, fame, and fortune, and I thought of myself as something of a freebooter. I lived by my wits; I was bound to no one; there was no one to catch me if I fell. It was a time for me of radical autonomy, self-reliance, and more than a little selfishness. It was also a time of marginality and loneliness. In 1976, I returned home longing for love, connection, and cooperation, and I found those things available to me within the Bay Area OD community. At the same time, I began working with client organizations in high technology and R&D, where people were more than ordinarily empowered and autonomous but where their ability to connect and cooperate left much to be desired. I saw in my clients what I had become and what I now saw as limiting to the human spirit.

I turned my attention to the relationship side of the empowerment/relationship frame and asked once again what we could do to make organizations safe for trust, cooperation, friendship, and love. In 1982, I wrote "Leadership and Strategy for a New Age" (Harrison, 1984 [Chapter Eleven]), in which I distinguished between *alignment* and *attunement* in organizations and first came out publicly for unleashing the power of love in organizations. I have been working that issue in one way or another ever since, not because love is the only thing I care about, but because it is too often suppressed in organizations. Missing love, we are also missing cooperation, mutual responsibility, appreciation of diversity, responsive service, and the ability to manage rapid change with grace and humanity.

During the sixties, there was a great deal of innovative ferment in OD, but it seemed to me that during the seventies not much changed. When I came back from time to time from England to attend a professional conference, I was relieved to find that I did not seem to have missed much by being in Europe. Consultants were putting their energies into being accepted as contributors; the problem was not to invent more powerful technology but rather to get a foot in the door. At that time, I was doing a good bit of training of consultants in Europe, and I remember saying somewhat ruefully to eager aspirants that as I saw it, the stages of consulting—Entry, Contracting, Diagnosis, and so on—collapsed down to Entry, Entry, Entry. In those years, one was seldom solidly in.

All that changed when the Japanese and others began to compete with high-quality products and advanced technology that began to take business away, not just from the weaker Western businesses but from the Western leaders as well. Then the doors on which we had been knocking swung open, and we stumbled across the threshold into the open arms of clients who were hoping for miracles from us—miracles that they hoped did not require fundamental change on their parts! This new enthusiasm on the part of clients was more than a little embarrassing to those of us who found ourselves asked to make good on the promise we had been making for years: "Only give us the time and resources, and we will bring you high performance and a more humane organization, too!" We got the time and the resources, but we frequently did not perform (or transform, either), partly because we did not know how and partly because the leadership in client organizations was either unwilling or unable to walk their talk.

I want to be clear in my assessment of our contribution as a profession that I cast no aspersions on the quality of work that we do nor the integrity with which it is undertaken. I have always felt myself in this work to be in the company of men and women of heart and goodwill, who frequently perform miracles through creativity, caring, and persistence. But the power of traditional organizational cultures lies like a dead hand on much of our work, and even where we succeed in liberating the human spirit, it is like opening Pandora's Box—what is released is not what we expected. So I have often said to consultants in training that, in this business, if you cannot live on hope, you had better find another way to make a living! We can all take satisfaction in the minds and hearts we have touched, and the learning we have stimulated, even while we continue seeking that perfect intervention or that perfect client organization that recedes like the pot of gold at the end of the rainbow.

As I experienced it and some of us wrote about it, the sixties were the decade of the T-group (Argyris, 1962; Schein and Bennis, 1965; Harrison, 1966; Harrison, 1963 [Chapter Eighteen]). That decade also saw the beginnings of our "technology" (Pfeiffer and Jones, 1969), the birth of OD (Clark, 1966; Schein, 1969), and significant contributions to organizational theory (Lawrence and Lorsch, 1967a). The seventies saw contributions to a theory of practice (Harrison, 1970 [Chapter Two]; Harrison, 1981b [Chapter Five]), team development (Kolb, Rubin, and McIntyre, 1971; Harrison, 1972c [Chapter Four]) and a proliferation of training approaches to personal growth and empowerment (Harrison, 1972a [Chapter Twenty-One]; Harrison and Oshry, 1972; Harrison, 1977 [Chapter Twenty-Two]). The eighties gave us visioning (Harrison, 1987a [Chapter Nine]; Harrison, 1988), organization culture (Harrison, 1972b [Chapter Ten]; Harrison, 1987b [Chapter Twelve]), systems thinking, and quality management. The nineties look like continuing the work on quality, and bringing forward the work of fostering systems thinking and organizational learning (Senge, 1990; Pedler, Burgoyne, and Boydell, 1991; Harrison, 1992; Weisbord and others, 1993). Of course, my own contributions were not nearly as prominent as they are in the above citations, which are meant to be suggestive rather than representative.

The Current Situation

Recently I have heard from a number of consultants, both here and in Europe, some of whom are experiencing a deep sense of disillusionment in their work, and some of whom are now convinced that the only change that is worthwhile to work on in organizations is radical change. I paraphrase some of their comments below.

- I have cut down my traditional work in organizations. My focus is on the personal/spiritual side of leadership and work life. For thousands of years, we have tried every possible kind of leadership and organization method, which has brought us to a situation where we seem to have bigger problems and deeper crises than ever. I have looked at what esoteric sources like *A Course in Miracles* and Krishnamurti have to say about leadership functions like strategic planning, problem solving, decision making, and the like. What they say is totally different from the way those functions are practiced today and have been throughout human history. Maybe such radical changes are the only "organizational healing" that has any lasting effect?
- I'm more and more doubting what I/we are doing. In my dark moments, I

think our work actually is like bandaging dead corpses. For a real shift to take place takes much more crisis, much more stepping into the unknown, than any of my clients are willing to experience. I question whether our work is not just making it possible for organizations to be efficient in an old mindset, and thereby prolonging the transition time. Even though my work is very rewarding from the point of view of the extraordinary results that happen, I question whether such results are enough.

- Something is different now. For the first time in my memory I have a sense that there is nothing much for me to do. It's not that I feel I have nothing to offer, or that I don't want to give what I have; it's more a feeling that there is a destructive process at work in our society, or perhaps it is a reconstructive process, that has to run its course before I can do anything. And I sense that as we move through this process, there will be new insights about how to be relevant. In this rather strange time, though, I don't believe in my own relevance.
- I feel my clients have so much on their plates that they don't have the resources to learn a better way. By taking their time I am becoming part of the problem, rather than helping.
- There are good people in the organizations I work with. I take satisfaction in helping them understand their interdependencies, and in gently leading them to look at the interdependencies that exist in the wider environment, but I cannot really believe in the value these organizations are bringing to mankind through their products.
- I enjoy the time between assignments more than when I have work.
- My *pro bono* assignments are more exciting and rewarding than my paid work.
- No matter how significantly I impact a system, it invariably falls back to the way it was before.
- I am finding myself unmotivated to seek new clients.

For these people there is a lack of *heart* in this work of being a consultant to organizations, a problem of *relevance*, a concern for *values* that are missing or distorted. For myself, I find that when I am in action, and particularly when I am immersed in the *skillful means* of my work, the designs and the technology, I become excited and involved. When I step back and ask myself the larger questions, I feel rather dispirited about what I am able to bring to organizations right now. I tend to agree with the consultants whose views I have just summarized, who feel that only radical changes will be beneficial in the long term.

In the present moment (1993), pressed by competition and struggling to outlast a severe economic downturn, most organizations are endeavoring to squeeze all they can out of the old Newtonian paradigm. Value is measured largely in material terms. Organizations are perceived as machines, and the goal is to obtain the greatest output with the least input of energy (in the form of money) and material. People are seen as parts of the machine, and the game is to get the most output from the fewest parts as fast as possible.

It sometimes seems as though organizations compete to see which can shed the most *parts* and work the remaining ones the hardest, and our social environment is becoming polluted with the anger, hopelessness, and bitterness of the rejected *parts*, who incidentally happen to be our neighbors and fellow citizens, people we grew up with and shared our dreams with. As a society, we seem unable to take a human stance toward these *parts*, viewing the problem in abstract terms of economics, rights, and law, and disowning the ties of love and responsibility that bind each of us to those whom organizations are treating as human waste.

For me, it is not the chaos of the world in which we live at the end of the twentieth century that is distressing. It is the denial of chaos and the extreme lengths to which we go to perceive our world as coherent and sane. Although I am hopeful about the long term, because we have to deal with reality sooner or later, I am a bit down about the present.

It is very painful to be a member of a self-organizing system which is, I hope and trust, preparing for a reorganization at a higher level of consciousness. Many organizations seem to me to be exhibiting a "fortress mentality" at present, and they are therefore not much fun to work with. However, I am optimistic for the long term. We are engaged in natural processes of perturbation which should, if the transformation goes well, provide the conditions for movement to a higher level of organization.

There is, of course, no guarantee that the transformation will go well, no assurance that our species will survive our current mindless destruction of the environment that supports us. The criteria by which our society currently evaluates the usefulness of its activities seem to me worse than irrelevant, for they are based on a notion of wealth creation that fosters the destruction of the ecosystems that nurture us—a paradigm that accepts the idea of taking from nature without giving back. Since our society operates on that paradigm, there are few organizations in which I can participate that are not operating on principles that I feel in my bones are wrong.

When I ask for guidance as to what contribution I can best make to the transformative process in organizations, I am directed to pay attention to what has heart and meaning for me, what activities I engage in that feel inspired by a higher purpose than gain, egoistic recognition, or technical fascination. There are still moments in organizations when I feel, "Yes, this is worth doing—this is what my life is about; this is what I came here to do." Sometimes they are moments when my heart is open, when I am able to give love, especially to those embattled warriors whose hearts may be armored against the pain of love or atrophied from long disuse. Sometimes they are moments of light, when I am able to *see* what feels like the truth and help others to see it as well. Sometimes they are moments of teamwork and camaraderie, when I and others experience true co-creation, or feel guided by our higher selves in the making of decisions that feel *right*. In those moments I feel the opposite of irrelevant; I feel myself to be taking part in the flow of an evolutionary stream which is moving us towards a higher level of participation in and with our universe.

For me there is no better guide than those intuitive feelings of *rightness*. I mistrust what passes for conventional wisdom and organizational values because I believe they are based on a misapprehension of our true relationship with nature. That does not mean that I have given up on the ideal of right action and right livelihood—rather it means that I have to take the responsibility for the value of what I do and for its consequences. It seems a heavy burden, but when I can bring myself to accept it, it makes for a meaningful and engaging personal and professional life.

CHAPTER TWO

CHOOSING THE DEPTH OF ORGANIZATIONAL INTERVENTION

I wrote "Choosing the Depth of Organizational Intervention" just before I left the United States in 1968 for a sojourn in Europe that was to last eight years. It was the first of my papers that went beyond my interest in T-groups and experiential learning. As I pointed out in the introduction to this section, during the middle and late sixties, many of us in OD consulting began to look for ways to bring openness and trust into work groups without exposing members to the risk of reprisals. Such inventions as process consultation (Schein, 1969) and task-oriented team development were part of the search. This paper, together with the one in Chapter Four ("Role Negotiation"), is the fruit of my own explorations into the subject.

I have always had an eye for the shadow side of our profession, and in my work with T-groups, I had seen the power of groups to damage members through pressure and attack. I had already written one paper advocating respect for people's fears and defenses (Chapter Eighteen) and in the present paper I extended that reasoning to what was to become the field of organization development (the reader will note that the term *organization development* is not mentioned in this paper as it was not then in common use). My reasoning was simple. Noticing the agitation and defensiveness that people displayed as a discussion became deeper and more personal, I came up with the idea of dealing with problems at the *shallowest* level at which they could be usefully addressed. This reversed the preferences and predilections of most of my colleagues, who were often imbued with the idea that truth lay

Source: Originally published in *Journal of Applied Behavioral Science*, 1970, *6*(2), 189–202. Reprinted here with permission of NTL Institute.

ever deeper and that accepting the client's definition of a problem was to collude with the client's defensiveness. That idea derived originally from psychoanalysis and was, in my experience, usually unquestioned by practitioners. I thought that by standing the conventional wisdom on its head, I might at least get my colleagues to question whether the push for depth was serving the clients' needs or their own.

If I have learned anything during my career as consultant, it is to respect the forces within an organization, and to work with them wherever possible. "Choosing the Depth of Organizational Intervention" reflects my dawning appreciation and respect for the power of organizational and personal defenses. For me, the basic principles first articulated here have become

stronger and more essential over time, although their mode of application is now very different from when I first wrote about them. (I have appended an afterword to the paper in order to share with readers how I am working with the principles now.)

This early paper seems to have traveled rather well. It has been reprinted several times and often photocopied. When I meet people who know me only through my writing, it is the one piece they most often refer to as having affected their thinking. I like to think that it may have helped them look for organizational interventions that are more homeopathic than allopathic, more oriented to wholeness and healing than to overcoming resistance to change.

Since World War II there has been a great proliferation of behavioral science-based methods by which consultants seek to facilitate growth and change in individuals, groups, and organizations. The methods range from operations analysis and manipulation of the organization chart, through the use of Grid Laboratories, T-groups, and nonverbal techniques. As was true in the development of clinical psychology and psychotherapy, the early stages of this developmental process tend to be accompanied by considerable competition, criticism, and argument about the relative merits of various approaches. It is my conviction that controversy over the relative goodness or badness, effectiveness or ineffectiveness, of various change strategies really accomplishes very little in the way of increased knowledge or unification of behavioral science. As long as we are arguing about what method is better than another, we tend to learn very little about how various approaches fit together or complement one another, and we certainly make more difficult and ambiguous the task of bringing these competing points of view within one overarching system of knowledge about human processes.

Note: In my earlier papers, the male pronoun was used extensively. After I returned to the United States in 1976, I changed my writing style, along with (more slowly!) my consciousness. I have chosen to leave the earlier papers as they were written, simply because the style used does reflect the state of my awareness at that time.

As our knowledge increases, it begins to be apparent that these competing change strategies are not really different ways of doing the same thing—some more effective and some less effective—but rather that they are different ways of doing *different* things. They touch the individual, the group, or the organization in different aspects of their functioning. They require differing kinds and amounts of commitment on the part of the client for them to be successful, and they demand different varieties and levels of skills and abilities on the part of the practitioner.

I believe that there is a real need for conceptual models which differentiate intervention strategies from one another in a way which permits rational matching of strategies to organizational change problems. The purpose of this paper is to present a modest beginning which I have made toward a conceptualization of strategies, and to derive from this conceptualization some criteria for choosing appropriate methods of intervention in particular applications.

The point of view of this paper is that the depth of individual emotional involvement in the change process can be a central concept for differentiating change strategies. In focusing on this dimension, we are concerned with the extent to which core areas of the personality or self are the focus of the change attempt. Strategies which touch the more deep, personal, private, and central aspects of the individual or his relationships with others fall toward the deeper end of this continuum. Strategies which deal with more external aspects of the individual and which focus upon the more formal and public aspects of role behavior tend to fall toward the surface end of the depth dimension. This dimension has the advantage that it is relatively easy to rank change strategies upon it and to get fairly close consensus as to the ranking. It is a widely discussed dimension of difference which has meaning and relevance to practitioners and their clients. I hope in this paper to promote greater flexibility and rationality in choosing appropriate depths of intervention. I shall approach this task by examining the effects of interventions at various depths. I shall also explore the ways in which two important organizational processes tend to make demands and to set limits upon the depth of intervention which can produce effective change in organizational functioning. These two processes are the autonomy of organization members and their own perception of their needs for help.

Before illustrating the concept by ranking five common intervention strategies along the dimension of depth, I should like to define the dimension somewhat more precisely. We are concerned essentially with how private, individual, and hidden are the issues and processes about which the consultant attempts directly to obtain information and which he seeks to influence. If, on the one hand, the consultant seeks information about relatively public and observable aspects of behavior and relationship and if he tries to influence directly only these relatively surface characteristics and processes, we would then categorize his intervention strategy as being closer to the surface. If, on the other hand, the consultant seeks information about very deep and private perceptions, attitudes, or feelings and if he intervenes in a way which directly affects these processes, then we would classify his intervention strategy as one of considerable depth. To illustrate the surface end of the dimension let us look first at operations research or operations analysis. This strategy is concerned with the roles and functions to be performed within the organization, generally with little regard to the individual characteristics of persons occupying the roles. The change strategy is to manipulate role relationships; in other words, to redistribute the tasks, the resources, and the relative power attached to various roles in the organization. This is essentially a process of rational analysis in which the tasks which need to be performed are determined and specified and then sliced up into role definitions for persons and groups in the organization. The operations analyst does not ordinarily need to know much about particular people. Indeed, his function is to design the organization in such a way that its successful operation does not depend too heavily upon any uniquely individual skills, abilities, values, or attitudes of persons in various roles. He may perform this function adequately without knowing in advance who the people are who will fill these slots. Persons are assumed to be moderately interchangeable, and in order to make this approach work it is necessary to design the organization so that the capacities, needs, and values of the individual which are relevant to role performance are relatively public and observable, and are possessed by a fairly large proportion of the population from which organization members are drawn. The approach is certainly one of very modest depth.

Somewhat deeper are those strategies which are based upon evaluating individual performance and attempting to manipulate it directly. Included in this approach is much of the industrial psychologist's work in selection, placement, appraisal, and counseling of employees. The intervener is concerned with what the individual is able and likely to do and achieve rather than with processes internal to the individual.

Direct attempts to influence performance may be made through the application of rewards and punishments such as promotions, salary increases, or transfers within the organization. An excellent illustration of this focus on end results is the practice of management by objectives. The intervention process is focused on establishing mutually agreed upon goals for performance between the individual and his supervisor. The practice is considered to be particularly advantageous because it permits the supervisor to avoid a focus on personal characteristics of the subordinate, particularly those deeper, more central characteristics which managers generally have difficulty in discussing with those who work under their supervision. The process is designed to limit information exchange to that which is public and observable, such as the setting of performance goals and the success or failure of the individual in attaining them.

Because of its focus on end results, rather than on the process by which those results are achieved, management by objectives must be considered less deep than the broad area of concern with work style which I shall term instrumental process analysis. We are concerned here not only with performance but with the processes by which that performance is achieved. However, we are primarily concerned with styles and processes of work rather than with the processes of interpersonal relationships which I would classify as being deeper on the basic dimension.

In instrumental process analysis we are concerned with how a person likes to organize and conduct his work and with the impact which this style of work has on others in the organization. Principally, we are concerned with how a person perceives his role, what he values and disvalues in it, and with what he works hard on and what he chooses to ignore. We are also interested in the instrumental acts which the individual directs toward others: delegating authority or reserving decisions to himself, communicating or withholding information, collaborating or competing with others on work-related issues. The focus on instrumentality means that we are interested in the person primarily as a doer of work or a performer of functions related to the goals of the organization. We are interested in what facilitates or inhibits his effective task performance.

We are not interested per se in whether his relationships with others are happy or unhappy, whether they perceive him as too warm or too cold, too authoritarian or too laissez-faire, or any other of the many interpersonal relationships which arise as people associate in organizations. However, I do not mean to imply that the line between instrumental relationships and interpersonal ones is an easy one to draw in action and practice, or even that it is desirable that this be done.

Depth Gauges: Level of Tasks and Feelings

What I am saying is that an intervention strategy can focus on instrumentality or it can focus on interpersonal relationships, and that there are important consequences of this difference in depth of intervention.

When we intervene at the level of instrumentality, it is to change work behavior and working relationships. Frequently this involves the process of bargaining or negotiation between groups and individuals. Diagnoses are made of the satisfactions or dissatisfactions of organization members with one another's work behavior. Reciprocal adjustments, bargains, and trade-offs can then be arranged in which each party gets some modification in the behavior of the other at the cost to him of some reciprocal accommodation. For example, Blake and Mouton's well-known Managerial Grid (Blake, Mouton, Barnes, and Greiner, 1964) works at the level of instrumentality, and it involves bargaining and negotiation of role behavior as an important change process.

At the deeper level of interpersonal relationships the focus is on feelings, attitudes, and perceptions which organization members have about others. At this level we are concerned with the quality of human relationships within the organization, with warmth and coldness of members to one another, and with the experiences of acceptance and rejection, love and hate, trust and suspicion among groups and individuals. At this level the consultant probes for normally hidden feelings, attitudes, and perceptions. He works to create relationships of openness about feelings and to help members to develop mutual understanding of one another as persons. Interventions are directed toward helping organization members to be more comfortable in being authentically themselves with one another, and the degree of mutual caring and concern is expected to increase. Sensitivity training using T-groups is a basic intervention strategy at this level. T-group educators emphasize increased personalization of relationships, the development of trust and openness, and the exchange of feelings. Interventions at this level deal directly and intensively with interpersonal emotionality. This is the first intervention strategy we have examined which is at a depth where the feelings of organization members about one another as persons are a direct focus of the intervention strategy. At the other levels, such feelings certainly exist and may be expressed, but they are not a direct concern of the intervention. The transition from the task orientation of instrumental process analysis to the feeling orientation of interpersonal process analysis seems, as I shall suggest later, to be a critical one for many organization members.

The deepest level of intervention which will be considered in this paper is that of intrapersonal analysis. Here the consultant uses a variety of methods to reveal the individual's deeper attitudes, values, and conflicts regarding his own functioning, identity, and existence. The focus is generally on increasing the range of experiences which the individual can bring into awareness and cope with. The material may be dealt with at the fantasy or symbolic level, and the intervention strategies include many which are non-interpersonal and nonverbal. Some examples of this approach are the use of marathon T-group sessions, the creative risk-taking laboratory approach of Byrd (1967), and some aspects of the task group therapy approach of Clark (1966). These approaches all tend to bring into focus very deep and intense feelings about one's own identity and one's relationships with significant others. Group dynamics conferences on the "Tavistock model," such as those offered by the A. K. Rice Institute, are also powerfully evocative of deep personal material.

Although I have characterized deeper interventions as dealing increasingly with the individual's affective life, I do not imply that issues at less deep levels may not be emotionally charged. Issues of role differentiation, reward distribution, ability and performance evaluation, for example, are frequently invested with strong feelings. The concept of depth is concerned more with the accessibility and individuality of attitudes, values, and perceptions than it is with their strength. This narrowing of the common usage of the term *depth* is necessary to avoid the contradictions which occur when strength and inaccessibility are confused. For instance, passionate value confrontation and bitter conflict have frequently occurred between labor and management over economic issues which are surely toward the surface end of my concept of depth.

In order to understand the importance of the concept of depth for choosing interventions in organizations, let us consider the effects upon organization members of working at different levels.

The first of the important concomitants of depth is the degree of dependence of the client on the special competence of the change agent. At the surface end of the depth dimension, the methods of intervention are easily communicated and made public. The client may reasonably expect to learn something of the change agent's skills, and the client can use these skills to improve his own practice. At the deeper levels, such as interpersonal and intrapersonal process analyses, it is more difficult for the client to understand the methods of intervention. The change agent is more likely to be seen as a person of special and unusual powers not found in ordinary men. Skills of intervention and change are less frequently learned by organization members, and the change process may tend to become personalized around the change agent as leader. Programs of change which are so dependent upon personal relationships and individual expertise are difficult to institutionalize. When the change agent leaves the system, he may not only take his expertise with him but the entire change process as well.

A second aspect of the change process which varies with depth is the extent to which the benefits of an intervention are transferable to members of the organization not originally participating in the change process. At surface levels of operations analysis and performance evaluation, the effects are institutionalized in the form of procedures, policies, and practices of the organization which may have considerable permanence beyond the tenure of individuals. At the level of instrumental behavior, the continuing effects of intervention are more likely to reside in the informal norms of groups within the organization regarding such matters as delegation, communication, decision making, competition and collaboration, and conflict resolution.

At the deepest levels of intervention, the target of change is the individual's inner life; and if the intervention is successful, the permanence of individual change should be greatest. There are indeed dramatic reports of cases in which persons have changed their careers and life goals as a result of such interventions, and the persistence of such change appears to be relatively high.

One consequence, then, of the level of intervention is that with greater depth of focus the individual increasingly becomes both the target and the carrier of change. In the light of this analysis, it is not surprising to observe that deeper levels of intervention are increasingly being used at higher organizational levels and in scientific and service organizations where the contribution of the individual has greatest impact.

An important concomitant of depth is that as the level of intervention becomes deeper, the information needed to intervene effectively becomes less available. At the less personal level of operations analysis, the information is often a matter of record. At the level of performance evaluation, it is a matter of observation. However, reactions of others to a person's work style are less likely to be discussed freely, and the more personal responses to his interpersonal style are even less likely to be readily given. At the deepest levels, important information may not be available to the individual himself. Thus, as we go deeper the consultant must use more of his time and skill uncovering information which is ordinarily private and hidden. This is one reason for the greater costs of interventions at deeper levels of focus.

Another aspect of the change process which varies with the depth of intervention is the personal risk and unpredictability of outcome for the individual. At deeper levels we deal with aspects of the individual's view of himself and his relationships with others which are relatively untested by exposure to the evaluations and emotional reactions of others. If in the change process the individual's self-perceptions are strongly disconfirmed, the resulting imbalance in internal forces may produce sudden changes in behavior, attitudes, and personality integration.

Because of the private and hidden nature of the processes into which we intervene at deeper levels, it is difficult to predict the individual impact of the change process in advance. The need for clinical sensitivity and skill on the part of the practitioner thus increases, since he must be prepared to diagnose and deal with developing situations involving considerable stress upon individuals.

Autonomy Increases Depth of Intervention

The foregoing analysis suggests a criterion by which to match intervention strategies to particular organizational problems. It is *to intervene at a level no deeper than that required to produce enduring solutions to the problems at hand.* This criterion derives directly from the observations above. The cost, skill demands, client dependency, and variability of outcome all increase with depth of intervention. Further, as the depth of intervention increases, the effects tend to locate more in the individual and less in the organization. The danger of losing the organization's investment in the change with the departure of the individual becomes a significant consideration. While this general criterion is simple and straightforward, its application is not. In particular, although the criterion should operate in the direction of less depth of intervention, there is a general trend in modern organizational life which tends to push the intervention level ever deeper. This trend is toward increased self-direction of organization members and increased independence of external pressures and incentives. I believe that there is a direct relationship between the autonomy of individuals and the depth of intervention needed to effect organizational change.

Before going on to discuss this relationship, I shall acknowledge freely that I cannot prove the existence of a trend toward a general increase in freedom of individuals within organizations. I intend only to assert the great importance of the degree of individual autonomy in determining the level of intervention which will be effective.

In order to understand the relationship between autonomy and depth of intervention, it is necessary to conceptualize a dimension which parallels and is implied by the depth dimension we have been discussing. This is the dimension of predictability and variability among persons in their responses to the different kinds of incentives which may be used to influence behavior in the organization. The key assumption in this analysis is that the more unpredictable and unique is the individual's response to the particular kinds of controls and incentives one can bring to bear upon him, the more one must know about that person in order to influence his behavior.

Most predictable and least individual is the response of the person to economic and bureaucratic controls when his needs for economic income and security are high. It is not necessary to delve very deeply into a person's inner processes in order to influence his behavior if we know that he badly needs his income and his position and if we are in a position to control his access to these rewards. Responses to economic and bureaucratic controls tend to be relatively simple and on the surface.

Independence of Economic Incentive

If for any reason organization members become relatively uninfluenceable through the manipulation of their income and economic security, the management of performance becomes strikingly more complex; and the need for more personal information about the individual increases. Except very generally, we do not know automatically or in advance what styles of instrumental or interpersonal interaction will be responded to as negative or positive incentives by the individual. One person may appreciate close supervision and direction; another may value independence of direction. One may prefer to work alone; another may function best when he is in close communication with others. One may thrive in close, intimate, personal interaction; while others are made uncomfortable by any but cool and distant relationships with colleagues.

What I am saying is that when bureaucratic and economic incentives lose their force for whatever reason, the improvement of performance must involve linking organization goals to the individual's attempts to meet his own needs for satisfying instrumental activities and interpersonal relationships. It is for this reason that I make the assertion that increases in personal autonomy dictate change interventions at deeper and more personal levels. In order to obtain the information necessary to link organizational needs to individual goals, one must probe fairly deeply into the attitudes, values, and emotions of the organization members.

If the need for deeper personal information becomes great when we intervene at the instrumental and interpersonal levels, it becomes even greater when one is dealing with organization members who are motivated less through their transactions with the environment and more in response to internal values and standards. An example is the researcher, engineer, or technical specialist whose work behavior may be influenced more by his own values and standards of creativity or professional excellence than by his relationships with others. The deepest organizational interventions at the intrapersonal level may be required in order to effect change when working with persons who are highly self-directed.

Let me summarize my position about the relationship among autonomy, influence, and level of intervention. As the individual becomes less subject to economic and bureaucratic pressures, he tends to seek more intangible rewards in the organization, which come from both the instrumental and interpersonal aspects of the system. I view this as a shift from greater external to more internal control and as an increase in autonomy. Further shifts in this direction may involve increased independence of rewards and punishments mediated by others, in favor of operation in accordance with internal values and standards.

I view organizations as systems of reciprocal influence. Achievement of organization goals is facilitated when individuals can seek their own satisfactions through activity which promotes the goals of the organization. As the satisfactions which are of most value to the individual change, so must the reciprocal influence systems, if the organization goals are to continue to be met.

If the individual changes are in the direction of increased independence of external incentives, then the influence systems must change to provide opportunities for individuals to achieve more intangible, self-determined satisfactions in their work. However, people are more differentiated, complex, and unique in their intangible goals and values than in their economic needs. In order to create systems which offer a wide variety of intangible satisfactions, much more private information about individuals is needed than is required to create and maintain systems based chiefly on economic and bureaucratic controls. For this reason, deeper interventions are called for when the system that the consultant and client want to change contains a high proportion of relatively autonomous individuals.

There are a number of factors promoting autonomy, all tending to free the individual from dependence upon economic and bureaucratic controls, which I have observed in my work with organizations. Wherever a number of these factors exist, it is probably an indication that deeper levels of intervention are required to effect lasting improvements in organizational functioning. I shall simply list these indicators briefly in categories to show what kinds of things might signify to the practitioner that deeper levels of intervention may be appropriate.

The first category includes anything which makes the evaluation of individual performance difficult:

- A long time span between the individual's actions and the results by which effectiveness of performance is to be judged.
- Nonrepetitive, unique tasks which cannot be evaluated by reference to the performance of others on similar tasks.
- Specialized skills and abilities possessed by an individual which cannot be evaluated by a supervisor who does not possess the skills or knowledge himself.

The second category concerns economic conditions:

- Arrangements which secure the job tenure and/or income of the individual.
- A market permitting easy transfer from one organization to another (such as engineers in the United States aerospace industry).
- Unique skills and knowledge of the individual which make him difficult to replace.

The third category includes characteristics of the system or its environment which lead to independence of the parts of the organization and decentralization of authority such as:

- An organization which works on a project basis instead of producing a standard line of products.
- An organization in which subparts must be given latitude to deal rapidly and flexibly with frequent environmental change.

The Ethics of Delving Deeper

I should like to conclude the discussion of this criterion for depth of intervention with a brief reference to the ethics of intervention, a problem which merits considerably more thorough treatment than I can give it here.

There is considerable concern in the United States about invasion of privacy by behavioral scientists. I would agree that such invasion of privacy is an actual as well as a fantasized concomitant of the use of organizational change strategies of greater depth. The recourse by organizations to such strategies has been widely viewed as an indication of greater organizational control over the most personal and private aspects of the lives of the members. The present analysis suggests, however, that recourse to these deeper interventions actually reflects the greater freedom of organization members from traditionally crude and impersonal means of organizational control. There is no reason to be concerned about a man's attitudes or values or interpersonal relationships when his job performance can be controlled by brute force, by economic coercion, or by bureaucratic rules and regulations. The "invasion of privacy" becomes worth the cost, bother, and uncertainty of outcome only when the individual has achieved relative independence from control by other means. Put another way, it makes organizational sense to try to get a man to want to do something only if you cannot make him do it. And regardless of what intervention strategy is used, the individual still retains considerably greater control over his own behavior than he had when he could be manipulated more crudely. As long as we can maintain a high degree of voluntarism regarding the nature and extent of an individual's participation in the deeper organizational change strategies, these strategies can work toward adapting the organization to the individual quite as much as they work the other way around. Only when an individual's participation in one of the deeper change strategies is coerced by economic or bureaucratic pressures do I feel that the ethics of the intervention clearly run counter to the values of a democratic society.

The Role of Client Norms and Values in Determining Depth

So far our attention to the choice of level of intervention has focused upon locating the depth at which the information exists which must be exchanged to facilitate system improvement. Unfortunately, it is not appropriate to base the choice of an intervention strategy on this criterion alone. Even if a correct diagnosis is made of the level at which the relevant information lies, we may not be able to work effectively at the desired depth because of client norms, values, resistances, and fears.

In an attempt to develop a second criterion for depth of intervention which takes such dispositions on the part of the client into account, I have considered two approaches which represent polarized orientations to the problem. One approach is based upon analyzing and overcoming client resistance; the other is based upon discovering and joining forces with the self-articulated wants or "felt needs" of the client.

There are several ways of characterizing these approaches. To me, the simplest is to point out that when the change agent is resistance-oriented he tends to lead or influence the client to work at a depth greater than that at which the latter feels comfortable. When resistance-oriented, the change agent tends to mistrust the client's statement of his problems and of the areas where he wants help. He suspects the client's presentation of being a smoke screen or defense against admission of his "real" problems and needs. The consultant works to expose the underlying processes and concerns and to influence the client to work at a deeper level. The resistance-oriented approach grows out of the work of clinicians and psychotherapists, and it characterizes much of the work of organizational consultants who specialize in sensitivity training and deeper intervention strategies.

Conversely, change agents may be oriented to the self-articulated needs of clients. When so oriented, the consultant tends more to follow and facilitate the client in working at whatever level the latter sets for himself. He may assist the client in defining problems and needs and in working on solutions, but he is inclined to try to anchor his work in the norms, values, and accepted standards of behavior of the organization.

I believe that there is a tendency for change agents working at the interpersonal and deeper levels to adopt a rather consistent resistance-oriented approach. Consultants so oriented seem to take a certain quixotic pride in dramatically and self-consciously violating organizational norms. Various techniques have been developed for pressuring or seducing organization members into departing from organizational norms in the service of change. The "marathon" T-group is a case in point, where the increased irritability and fatigue of prolonged contact and lack of sleep move participants to deal with one another more emotionally, personally, and spontaneously than they would normally be willing to do.

I suspect that unless such norm-violating intervention efforts actually succeed in changing organizational norms, their effects are relatively short-lived, because the social structures and interpersonal linkages have not been created which can utilize for day-to-day problem solving the deeper information produced by the intervention. It is true that the consultant may succeed in producing information, but he is less likely to succeed in creating social structures which can continue to work in his absence. The problem is directly analogous to that of the community developer who succeeds by virtue of his personal influence in getting villagers to build a school or a community center which falls into disuse as soon as he leaves because of the lack of any integration of these achievements into the social structure and day-to-day needs and desires of the community. Community developers have had to learn through bitter failure and frustration that ignoring or subverting the standards and norms of a social system often results in temporary success followed by a reactionary increase in resistance to the influence of the change agent. Conversely, felt needs embody those problems, issues, and difficulties which have a high conscious priority on the part of community or organization members. We can expect individuals and groups to be ready to invest time, energy, and resources in dealing with their felt needs, while they will be relatively passive or even resistant toward those who attempt to help them with externally defined needs. Community developers have found that attempts to help with felt needs are met with greater receptivity, support, and integration within the structure and life of the community than are intervention attempts which rely primarily upon the developer's value system for setting need priorities.

The emphasis of many organizational change agents on confronting and working through resistances was developed originally in the practice of individual psychoanalysis and psychotherapy, and it is also a central concept in the conduct of therapy groups and sensitivity training laboratories. In all of these situations, the change agent has a high degree of environmental control and is at least temporarily in a high-status position with respect to the client. To a degree that is frequently underestimated by practitioners, we manage to create a situation in which it is more unpleasant for the client to leave than to stay and submit to the pressure to confront and work through resistances. I believe that the tendency is for behavioral scientists to overplay their hands when they move from the clinical and training situations, where they have environmental control, to the organization consulting situation, where their control is sharply attenuated.

This attenuation derives only partially from the relative ease with which the client can terminate the relationship. Even if this most drastic step is not taken, the consultant can be tolerated, misled, and deceived in ways which are relatively difficult in the therapeutic or human relations training situations. He can also be openly defied and blocked if he runs afoul of strongly shared group norms; whereas when the consultant is dealing with a group of strangers, he can often utilize differences among the members to overcome this kind of resistance. I suspect that, in general, behavioral scientists underestimate their power in working with individuals and groups of strangers, and overestimate it when working with individuals and groups in organizations. I emphasize this point because I believe that a good many potentially fruitful and mutually satisfying consulting relationships are terminated early because of the consultant's taking the role of overcomer of resistance to change rather than that of collaborator in the client's attempts at solving his problems. It is these considerations which lead me to suggest my second criterion for the choice of organization intervention strategy: *to intervene at a level no deeper than that at which the energy and resources of the client can be committed to problem solving and to change.* These energies and resources can be mobilized through obtaining legitimation for the intervention in the norms of the organization and through devising intervention strategies which have clear relevance to consciously felt needs on the part of the organization members.

The Consultant's Dilemma: Felt Needs Versus Deeper Levels

Unfortunately, it is doubtless true that the forces which influence the conditions we desire to change often exist at deeper levels than can be dealt with by adhering to the criterion of working within organizational norms and meeting felt needs. The level at which an individual or group is willing and ready to invest energy and resources is probably always determined partly by a realistic assessment of the problems and partly by a defensive need to avoid confrontation and significant change. It is thus not likely that our two criteria for selection of intervention depth will result in the same decisions when practically applied. It is not the same to intervene at the level where behavior-determining forces are most potent as it is to work on felt needs as they are articulated by the client. This, it seems to me, is the consultant's dilemma. It always has been. We are continually faced with the choice between, on the one hand, leading the client into areas which are threatening, unfamiliar, and dependency-provoking for him (and where our own expertise shows up to best advantage) or, on the other hand, being guided by the client's own understanding of his problems and his willingness to invest resources in particular kinds of relatively familiar and nonthreatening strategies.

When time permits, this dilemma is ideally dealt with by intervening first at a level where there is good support from the norms, power structure, and felt needs of organization members. The consultant can then, over a period of time, develop trust, sophistication, and support within the organization to explore deeper levels at which particularly important forces may be operating. This would probably be agreed to, at least in principle, by most organization consultants. The point at which I feel I differ from a significant number of workers in this field is that I would advocate that interventions should always be limited to the depth of the client's felt needs and readiness to legitimize intervention. I believe we should always avoid moving deeper at a pace which outstrips a client system's willingness to subject it-self to exposure, dependency, and threat. What I am saying is that if the domi-nant response of organization members indicates that an intervention violates system norms regarding exposure, privacy, and confrontation, then one has in-tervened too deeply and should pull back to a level at which organization mem-bers are more ready to invest their own energy in the change process. This point of view is thus in opposition to that which sees negative reactions primarily as indications of resistances which are to be brought out into the open, confronted, and worked through as a central part of the intervention process. I believe that behavioral scientists acting as organization consultants have tended to place over-much emphasis on the overcoming of resistance to change and have under-emphasized the importance of enlisting in the service of change the energies and resources which the client can consciously direct and willingly devote to prob-lem solving.

What is advocated here is that we in general accept the client's felt needs or the problems he presents as real and that we work on them at a level at which he can serve as a competent and willing collaborator. This position is in opposition to the one which sees the presenting problem as more or less a smoke screen or barrier. I am not advocating this point of view because I value the right to privacy of organization members more highly than I value their growth and development or the solution of organizational problems. (This is an issue which concerns me, but it is enormously more complex than the ones with which I am dealing in this paper.) Rather, I place first priority on collaboration with the client, because I do not think we are frequently successful consultants without it.

In my own practice I have observed that the change in client response is fre-quently quite striking when I move from a resistance-oriented approach to an ac-ceptance of the client's norms and definitions of his own needs. With quite a few organizational clients in the United States, the line of legitimacy seems to lie somewhere between interventions at the instrumental level and those focused on interpersonal relationships. Members who exhibit hostility, passivity, and depen-dence when I initiate intervention at the interpersonal level may become dra-matically more active, collaborative, and involved when I shift the focus to the instrumental level.

If I intervene directly at the level of interpersonal relationships, I can be sure that at least some members, and often the whole group, will react with anxiety, passive resistance, and low or negative commitment to the change process. Fur-thermore, they express their resistance in terms of norms and values regarding the appropriateness or legitimacy of dealing at this level. They say things like, "It isn't right to force people's feelings about one another out into the open"; "I don't see what this has to do with improving organizational effectiveness"; "Peo-ple are being encouraged to say things which are better left unsaid."

If I then switch to a strategy which focuses on decision making, delegation of authority, information exchange, and other instrumental questions, these complaints about illegitimacy and the inappropriateness of the intervention are usually sharply reduced. This does not mean that the clients are necessarily comfortable or free from anxiety in the discussions, nor does it mean that strong feelings may not be expressed about one another's behavior. What is different is that the clients are more likely to work with instead of against me, to feel and express some sense of ownership in the change process, and to see many more possibilities for carrying it on among themselves in the absence of the consultant.

What I have found is that when I am resistance-oriented in my approach to the client, I am apt to feel rather uncomfortable in "letting sleeping dogs lie." But when I orient myself to the client's own assessment of his needs, I am uncomfortable when I feel I am leading or pushing the client to operate very far outside the shared norms of the organization. I have tried to indicate why I believe the latter orientation is more appropriate. I realize of course that many highly sophisticated and talented practitioners will not agree with me.

In summary, I have tried to show in this paper that the dimension of depth should be central to the conceptualization of intervention strategies. I have presented what I believe are the major consequences of intervening at greater or lesser depths, and from these consequences I have suggested two criteria for choosing the appropriate depth of intervention: first, to intervene at a level no deeper than that required to produce enduring solutions to the problems at hand; and second, to intervene at a level no deeper than that at which the energy and resources of the client can be committed to problem solving and to change.

I have analyzed the tendency for increases in individual autonomy in organizations to push the appropriate level of intervention deeper when the first criterion is followed. Opposed to this is the countervailing influence of the second criterion to work closer to the surface in order to enlist the energy and support of organization members in the change process. Arguments have been presented for resolving this dilemma in favor of the second, more conservative, criterion.

The dilemma remains, of course; the continuing tension under which the change agent works is between the desire to lead and push, or to collaborate and follow. The middle ground is never very stable, and I suspect we show our values and preferences by which criterion we choose to maximize when we are under the stress of difficult and ambiguous client-consultant relationships.

I have recently revisited the model I put forward in this paper some twenty-four years ago and have found it surprisingly viable and relevant. The issues are different, of course. We have become much more sophisticated about managing the level of stress and personal confrontation in team development sessions. Our clients have become more clear about what they want from us and what they will and will not tolerate.

Most recently, however, I have seen

the practice of organization transformation (OT), and also culture change, as raising once again the issues addressed in this paper. The ideals of empowerment, openness, trust, and concern for people are as important to me as they ever were—or even more so because of my conviction that these ideals are keys to ending our destructiveness as inhabitants of this planet. However, when we seek to lead our clients into areas that they have defined as personal and irrelevant to business, we can expect a great deal of resistance, and just plain incomprehension. Whatever the intrinsic worth of our current passions, if we cannot establish a clear link between what we do and the business purposes of our clients, we are in for lot of foot-dragging—and ultimate failure. In that regard, the caveats in this paper are as relevant and timely as they ever were. Since the paper was published, however, a great deal of ingenuity has been applied to create organization development technologies that combine both moderate depth and relevance to business issues. My own "Role Negotiation" (Chapter Four) was an early step in that direction. Future Search (Weisbord and others, 1993), technologies of participation (Spencer, 1989), appreciative inquiry (Cooperrider, 1990) and dialogue (Briggs and Bohm, 1993) are examples of recent methods that meet my criteria for appropriate depth and business relevance and that enable organizations to gain the deeper self-knowledge that they now need to heal themselves. (Figure 2.1 shows a scale of intervention together with typical interventions at each level.)

There is a larger sense in which the issues raised in this early paper are especially relevant now in working with organizations. Much of the change which is taking place in organizations today violates the basic principles underlying this paper: *First, do no harm!* and, *Intervene no more deeply than is necessary to create the desired business results!* For example, massive reorganizations and reductions in force are undertaken with little thought to the cost to the fabric of connections, relationships, values, and ways of working together that will be affected. What is going on today in organizations is similar to the huge urban redevelopment projects which were undertaken in the United States and Britain during the twenty years or so following World War II. In the cause of providing the most people with the most affordable housing, poor and rundown but established neighborhoods were razed and replaced by huge apartment buildings. Along with the old housing, the neighborhood cultures with their values, norms, and human connections were destroyed, and in their place grew crime, drugs, anomie, and despair. When we destroy the fabric that binds and connects people with one another, whether in neighborhoods or in organizations, we banish caring, loyalty, common purpose, compassion, and human love from people's lives. In their places grow selfishness, exploitation, intergroup strife, resentment, and anger. We are seeing just these results in organizations which have gone through massive reorganizations and wave after wave of downsizing.

Having devoted the better part of more than thirty-five years as a consultant to changing traditional organization cultures in one way or another, I would be the last to argue that they do not need to change. Evolution of values, styles, and ways of working based on the willing in-

FIGURE 2.1. INTERVENTIONS TYPICAL OF DIFFERENT LEVELS OF INTERVENTION DEPTH.

Level of Intervention	Example of Intervention	
		Low
Structures and systems	Reorganization	
Work design	Quality management sociotechnical systems	R E
Strategy planning and meeting management	Future search and the Participative Methods of the Institute for Cultural Affairs	S I S
Mutual role performance	Role negotiation and Management by Objectives (MBO)	T A
Interpersonal relations	Process consultation	N C
Personality dynamics, values, spirituality	Organization transformation (OT)	E
Identity, sense of self	Demotion, loss of work	
		High

The deeper we intervene, the more we impact core values and self-concepts.

Deeper values and concepts bind and channel high levels of group and individual energy.

terest of organization members in doing things better, faster, or more economically can be a positive change, building the new on the best of the past. More often, in the quest for immediate improvement in financial measures, organizations are destroying their cultures, not improving them. The executives who implement the changes are perhaps to be forgiven, for they often do not know the destruction they are wreaking on the unseen fabric of their organizations. Rebuilding that fabric will be far more costly than changing it from within, working *with* the interests, values, and ideals of the organization members.

In my recent work on organizational learning and the healing of organizations

(Harrison, 1992; Harrison and Dawes, 1994 [Chapter Twenty-Four]), I have looked at some other contemporary issues in working life to which the basic principles in the present paper apply. Chief among these is the bias for action which is so prevalent in business organizations, particularly in the United States. As this society enters the new millennium, managers live in such a complex and closely coupled world that the actions they take have rapid and unlooked for consequences at points far distant in time and space from where the actions are taken (Perrow, 1984). The passion for problem solving, action, and control that is so typical of U.S. leaders and managers has served them well in the past, but it is now a liability. Actions taken in haste to solve problems as soon as symptoms are observed lead to unintended consequences and additional problems. Jumping on new problems with quick solutions creates unintended consequences and more problems, and people in organizations find themselves running faster and faster just to stay even (see Senge, 1990, for a discussion of the system dynamics underlying these observations).

I believe there are alternatives to the infinite regression of hasty action that leads to ever greater imbalance in the systems we and others live and work in (Harrison, 1992). These alternatives are to be found in a gentler, more reflective approach to organization management, change, and problem solving. Figure 2.2 presents an outline of this approach, which begins with a balanced orientation between the basic values of the support and achievement cultures (see "Organization Culture and Quality of Service,"

Chapter Twelve). In this approach, we can value *both* purpose and achievement, on the one hand, *and* caring, connection, and appreciation, on the other. We can see the organization not only in instrumental terms, as a machine for material production, but also as an organism, with consciousness, with purposes and a life of its own, and with the capacity to grow, develop, and heal itself. Using this approach, we can see ourselves as healers, rather than change agents, and we can work *with* the forces in the organization, even, or especially, those that are in resistance to change. We can respect the organization culture and find within the current culture the seeds of its forward evolution. We can intervene delicately and noninvasively so as to preserve the capacity of the organization to perform as it changes.

In order to work *with* an organization in this way, a much deeper understanding of its dynamics are required than organization members and leaders normally possess. In a real sense, organization diagnosis *is itself* the intervention of choice when one is dealing with complex, closely coupled systems where hasty and ill-considered actions create powerful waves of unintended consequences. What is needed is for the organization to study and appreciate itself through deep reflection, involving all parts of the organization, because no group of leaders can know enough without input from the whole.

Thus, in my recent thinking, the principle of intervening no more deeply than we need to in order to achieve the desired results has metamorphosed into the idea of intervening in the least invasive ways

FIGURE 2.2. INTERVENING TO PRESERVE ORGANIZATIONAL BALANCE AND INTEGRITY.

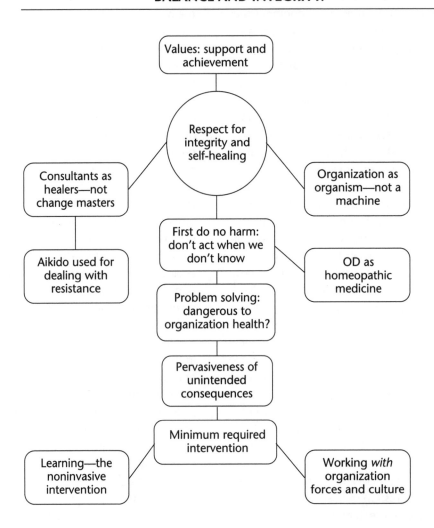

we can find so as to cause the least shock and damage to the organism. Paradoxically, that principle now means applying *deep* diagnosis, reflection, and appreciation, in advance of action. What is still the same is my sense of the importance of respecting the integrity of the organism, whether an individual or an organization, and working, so far as possible, with its own forces rather than against them.

CHAPTER THREE

STRATEGY GUIDELINES FOR AN INTERNAL ORGANIZATION DEVELOPMENT UNIT

"Strategy Guidelines for an Internal Organization Development Unit" was originally written as a discussion piece for a group of internal consultants I worked with in the early seventies during my sojourn as a freelance consultant based in London. The content was stimulated by a talk I had heard Herb Shepard give in a National Training Laboratories (NTL) program in Bethel, Maine, and I added some material of my own. In the paper can be seen the beginnings of an intervention theory for the practice of organization development. I have continued to work with the theory over the years, my most recent effort being an ambitious attempt to provide a comprehensive manual for planning and implementing large systems change

(Harrison, Cooper, and Dawes, 1991). I feel, however, that, "quick and dirty" as it is, this first effort captures in easily digested form much of what one needs to think about in starting out as an OD consultant, and indeed, the paper is much used today in training programs for organization development consultants.

I had worked for some months with the internal consulting group before I came to the conclusion that the members of the group were not serious in their commitment to making change happen in their organization, and I wrote the "Guidelines" as a kind of change manifesto. My (rather arrogant) idea was that if they embraced the document's precepts, then it was professionally correct for me to

Source: Originally published as "Strategy Guidelines for an Internal Organization Development Unit," *The OD Practitioner,* 1972, *4*(3), 1–4. Reprinted here with permission of OD Network.

continue working with them. If they did not, then I would know our relationship was a collusive one, in which their having me as an external consultant was a way of convincing themselves they were doing something about change, whereas what they really had was what they would have called a "talking shop," meaning much discussion but no real commitment to action.

Adapting to British ways was not easy for me, in spite of an Anglophilia that had its roots in childhood. When I came to live and work in England, it was the realization of a dream I had carried for many years. I found the quality of life in London in the late sixties to be almost everything I had hoped for, but work was another matter. It took me a long time to understand what the British really meant by what they said, and I perceived the pace of change in organizations to be just short of glacial. I sometimes described my experience of the pace of work and change in Britain as "walking in glue." It took me a long time to understand that we North Americans do not differ significantly from the British in the length of time it takes us to make important changes—it is our style and level of activity that are so strikingly different. We embrace change enthusiastically, talk it up,

and then often subtly sabotage it or change in outward forms only. The British are more apt to be skeptical of the new and to question and resist. Underneath, though, they may be covertly evaluating and comparing the old and the new and preparing to commit their time and resources to change.

My clients liked the paper, and passed it along to others, but their behavior did not change. I disengaged from them gracefully, having so far adopted British ways that I did not confront them with my real reasons for doing so.

During the early seventies, I was greatly engaged in training internal consultants in Britain. With some other U.S. consultants, notably Richard Beckhard, I took a role in the attempts to transplant the NTL Program for Specialists in Organization Development (PSOD) to Britain. The paper was useful as a handout in these programs and was recirculated widely among internal consultants, first in Britain and then in the United States. It migrated to North America via the PSODs NTL was running in Bethel, Maine, and some years later I published it in *The OD Practitioner.* I have appreciated the way it has held its relevance over the years, though much of what it says is common wisdom now.

These guidelines are intended as a kind of checklist or reminder, rather than as a comprehensive treatise on organization development (OD) strategy. My concern here is only with strategy, and not with the goals that the strategy is intended to achieve. These notes are relevant to OD means, not ends. I expect many of the points will be self-evident to experienced OD practitioners and hope that they will provoke thought and planning on the part of others.

Major Strategic Problems of an Internal OD Unit

1. To gain influence based on expertise and ability to help, rather than influence through channels of authority and power. To deploy limited economic and human resources in ways which maximize impact.

2. To develop the skills and knowledge of the internal agents of change in the organization.

3. To maintain the OD unit and to preserve the group and its members against the detrimental effects of pressure and stress. In so doing, to remain independent of organizational pressures for conformity of thought and action while maintaining confidence and trust on the part of organization members.

Guidelines for Gaining Appropriate Influence and Deploying Resources Effectively

1. Work *with* the forces in the organization which are supportive of change and improvement, rather than working *against* those who are defensive and resistant. It is better to find someone who wants help and work with him than it is to try to convince a skeptic that he has need of OD assistance. Wherever possible, follow the path of least organizational resistance to OD goals rather than confronting resistance. This implies *not* doing anything across the board: no mass training, no wholesale installation of management by objectives, no involvement of the entire organization in staff development programs and the like. The limited OD resources available are weakened and absorbed by the organization in such frontal assaults on problems, and the results are invariably disappointing.

2. Try to develop "critical mass" in each change project, a self-sustaining organizational improvement process which is motivated and powered from within the system which is changing. To do this, resources available to the OD unit must be concentrated on the target system for a time, to get the process underway. Organizations are self-stabilizing systems that can absorb a great deal of energy from the outside without changing very much. Investments of resources which are insufficient to stabilize the system in a new equilibrium are wasteful and unproductive.

3. When working with a given system, try to find multiple entry points into it: a variety of people, groups, processes, and problems with which contact can be made and to which help may be given. It is useful when approaching a particular organization or subsystem to brainstorm all the possible points of contact which might be used, and all the different ways in which the unit could offer useful help to the system. As many of these multiple entries as feasible can then be attempted.

4. Look for "felt needs," problems recognized by managers that can be dealt

with by OD techniques and processes. The best opportunities occur when there exist problems for which there is no "standard" procedural or bureaucratic solution, and where the managers involved are really bothered by their difficulty in coping. Look for these problems where new technology is being introduced (for example, computers); where a problem requires close collaboration and coordination across functional lines (for example, "strategic business units," or SBUs); where organizational boundaries are being changed (for example, mergers and takeovers); where organization restructuring of any kind is taking place; where physical locations are being changed or new plants and facilities being built and commissioned; or where the organization is expanding or contracting rapidly (for example, through redundancies).

5. Wherever possible, work with relatively healthy parts of the organization that have the will and the resources to improve. Avoid being seduced or pressured into working on "lost causes," individuals or groups which have lost the ability to cope with the situation as it is. Usually change requires additional energy and talent during the period of transition. Performance initially worsens even after the most beneficial changes until people learn how to make the changed organization work up to its potential. Persons or groups whose performance is substandard or barely adequate usually cannot afford and are not allowed the additional resources and period of further decreased performance which is required to change successfully. They are often unusually defensive in their reaction to outsiders offering "help."

Unfortunately, higher management may put great pressure on an OD unit to work with the more ineffective subsystems, sometimes on the assumption that the offending group is so far gone anyway that little harm can be done even by an incompetent intervention!

6. Work with individuals and groups which have as much freedom and discretion in managing their own operations as possible. It profits nothing to work out an agreed change with a manager who turns out not to have the latitude to carry it out. It is equally useless to work on a change with someone who *feels* dominated and controlled from above and who can therefore not muster the courage to risk experimenting on his own. These considerations cast great doubt on the wisdom of training in people management and staff development programs for lower levels of staff and supervisors unless the programs actively involve the management levels where effective control resides.

7. Try to obtain appropriate and realistic levels of involvement in the program of the OD unit on the part of top management. This does not mean that the highest levels of management must necessarily be "at the cutting edge of change." They are too often too personally identified with the status quo for this to be possible. Except in times of emergency the system tends to stabilize itself by placing people in the top positions whose values and styles perpetuate the accepted ways of doing things. Often the best supporters of an OD unit are among the ranks of management just below the top, where the personal commitment to the

present is less, and where the drive for achievement and advancement may be higher than at the very top.

There are three levels of commitment to OD objectives from top management which can be helpful. The minimum level is *giving permission for change to occur.* Top management sees the necessity of change, at least at an intellectual level, and allows it to occur without active opposition. The unspoken qualifier is usually "as long as *we* don't have to do anything differently."

The next level is that of *support and encouragement for change.* The involvement in change activities of other parts of the organization is facilitated, and higher management monitors and evaluates the changes achieved. As before, however, the actual changes in work and relationship patterns do not extend to the highest levels. The latter are insulated from actual change.

The third level is *participation in change,* in which higher management actively involves itself in the change process, often as a client for OD assistance. While this level is the most satisfactory, it is rarely achieved in practice. The failure to involve top management actively in the change process sets an upper limit on what can be accomplished, but the other levels of commitment still permit considerable useful work to be done. Unfortunately, in many change programs it is not clear that even the first level, *permission,* has been achieved, and such programs are usually rather ineffective.

8. Try to establish direct communication and contact with all levels of the organization. Try to develop customs and accepted practices of operating which exempt OD unit members from following normal bureaucratic channels or the "chain of command." OD practitioners cannot work effectively through formal authority or by using sources of coercive power. The only way they can influence anyone is through expertise, persuasion, and helpfulness. Direct contact and discussion with clients and with sources of information and support are vital, and reliance on intermediaries, no matter how well intentioned, hampers the work badly.

9. Develop confidence and credibility on the part of organization members through situations where the OD unit's unique expertise shows to best advantage. One good way for behaviorally oriented OD practitioners to develop trust and confidence on the part of potential clients is in the course of experiential, action-oriented training programs. In the atmosphere of openness and confrontation which often develops in such programs the client has a chance to size up the practitioner's ability to handle difficult situations effectively. Educational situations are a good way of allowing the client some low-risk opportunities to evaluate the potential contribution of the practitioners. Diagnostic studies also present chances to begin dialogue with a client. Many projects begin with a commitment to joint study of a problem, which commits neither client nor practitioner to go further.

10. Don't be afraid to ask to be involved in activities where you feel you may be able to make a contribution. Go directly to the potential client and tell him what you may be able to do to help. Since he probably does not know much about what you have to offer, he is unlikely to think of coming to the OD unit for help.

The worst the client can do is to say no. Proactive practitioners get many more opportunities to contribute than do passive ones.

11. Make known what the OD unit is doing, particularly when there are successes to report (but only with the client's permission, of course). A major failing of OD units is in not reporting widely enough their activities and achievements, perhaps out of modesty. The modesty may be commendable, but it does not advance the task to let the activities remain unknown. One good way is to hold a seminar for interested parties in which the client and the practitioner make a joint presentation of the change project, preferably with an honest description of the difficulties and drawbacks, as well as the successes.

12. Use outside consultants in ways which enhance, rather than compete with the credibility of OD unit members. For example, outsiders are often used to develop entry to top management, because OD unit members do not have high enough organizational status to be acceptable as consultants at that level. If at all possible, the outsider should pair up with someone from the unit who works as closely with him as the client will permit.

Similarly, when outsiders are asked in to give courses and seminars they should be paired with OD unit members as co-trainers. A clear understanding should be developed that the two will work in such a way as to permit increased visibility for the inside man's skills and talents, as well as to enable the insider to learn what the outside consultant has to teach.

Outsiders can sometimes also be used to gain acceptance for projects and to get them started. By involving the inside people from the beginning as coworkers, the latter can take over once the project is off the ground and run it with only occasional assistance from without.

13. Link together people who are working to improve organization functioning, so their activities reinforce and complement one another. People working in such areas as training, methods improvement, computer technology, and manpower planning are all working in areas related to organization development. Frequently they are in different functional lines and plan and conduct their work quite independently.

This splitting of resources reduces the likelihood of developing the "critical mass" referred to above, that self-sustaining change process which is the criterion of a really successful project. I feel strongly enough about the resulting wastage of resources to advocate combining these activities, either functionally or (perhaps as well) through some kind of matrix organizational structure similar to the concept of the "business area." At the least, there should be some policy commitment supported by appropriate structure to ensure joint planning and coordination of strategy and projects, so that the organizational improvement activities will all support one another.

One example of such coordination is the linking of training (especially in such attitudinal/style areas as people management, leadership, and effective group working) to follow-up activities in the work situation. Any such training should be built into some on-the-job change activity of the OD unit and should reinforce and in turn be reinforced by the work of the OD practitioner (for example, helping with problems of entry, diagnosis, team development, staff development, and the like). Attitudinal training and training in management style on an across-the-board basis should be avoided as a wasteful use of resources.

Training and OD activities can also be linked into technological, procedural, and structural changes stemming from application of management sciences to problems of rationalizing work. Such changes can be much more effectively implemented if there is adequate diagnosis of the readiness for and resistance to change, proper training of personnel who will be involved, and the establishment of ways of monitoring and dealing with human problems which develop during the change process. Activities which lend themselves to this sort of joint approach are the introduction of computer technology; the implementation of mergers, takeovers, and reorganizations; the starting up of new facilities; and the changing of work methods and procedures.

Guidelines for Developing the Skills and Knowledge of Internal Change Agents

1. A substantial proportion of the time of internal OD practitioners should be budgeted for their training and professional development. If they tend not to be professionally trained and to be relatively inexperienced, this should probably be on the order of 20 to 25 percent of their time. Most of this training should be practical and experiential. Some useful training and development activities are the following:

> *The pairing of less experienced people with more experienced ones or with outside consultants on projects.* The more experienced person advises and supports, but the less experienced one does the actual work of the project.
>
> *Regular project clinics led by an experienced practitioner in which participants share current problems and concerns they are experiencing in their work.* The other participants can then practice consulting and planning skills in helping with the presented problems. Such a group could include participants from outside the Division or Company as well as internal people.
>
> *Presentations and demonstrations of new techniques and processes by outsiders.*
>
> *Participation in some projects outside the company in which the practitioner takes the role of an external change agent.* These are most valuable, in my experience, for providing opportunities for taking increased responsibility and freedom

to take reasonable risks (a freedom which may be prevented at home by the exposed situation of the OD unit). Dramatic increases in confidence and competence can be achieved by the judicious use of such outside experiences.

Attendance at professional meetings and outside courses is also valuable, but less so, I think, than the other learning activities just mentioned.

2. Acquire a library of books and journals on OD and behavioral science applications. Make a special effort to retrieve techniques and instruments which have come into the hands of OD unit members through their work with outside consultants or by their own invention. Keep an up-to-date list of who has had experience with what different approaches and methods, so that unit personnel know where to go for practical help.

3. Arrange learning activities between the related areas of training, management sciences, and behavioral applications. In the process of teaching others people will become more competent in their own fields, and the cross-functional education will make it easier for them to work effectively together.

Guidelines for Protecting OD Practitioners from Undue Pressure and Stress

1. Arrange most of the work in teams and pairs for mutual learning and mutual support. People should not have to work alone in high-stress and high-risk situations until they are quite experienced.

2. Protect against premature evaluation of OD activities. Absorb a large proportion of the pressures from above and outside the unit in the senior manager(s) responsible. Management style in an OD unit should provide support and resources rather than direction, control, and evaluation. The clients may be depended upon for more than the optimum amounts of the latter.

3. Take special pains to build strong personal support relationships among OD unit members. Frequent team-building sessions and some T-group or group process work are helpful in achieving this. The use of an outside consultant to help build supportive internal relationships is frequently helpful.

4. Develop career paths within and through the OD unit. The policy and practice should make it desirable for some to develop professional careers in change facilitation and for others to advance their line or staff careers by doing well in shorter (two- to three-year) assignments in the OD unit.

One way of using this checklist might be to review the current organization of OD activities in the light of the guidelines. I am not so egoistic as to imagine that where the guidelines are different from current practice and policy it means the latter must be corrected; however, it may be that such discrepancies point to fruitful areas for discussion and decision.

Another way to use the guidelines is in planning particular change and development projects. The points can remind one of problems to be anticipated or resources which will be needed for a successful conclusion.

Similarly, it may help consultants to review these ideas when faced with a particularly difficult problem in a project, or when an activity seems to go along rather poorly for no obvious reason. The framework provided may help consultants to gain some perspective on the problem. Additionally, it may suggest diagnostic leads to the trouble or approaches to a solution.

CHAPTER FOUR

ROLE NEGOTIATION

R ole Negotiation" was written in Washington, D.C., during 1967, my first year as a freelance consultant. It continues the exploration of those issues of intervention depth and relevance to business issues that were introduced by me in "Choosing the Depth of Organizational Intervention." The content of the paper was stimulated by two quite different team development experiences. The first took place in a weekend team development workshop for administrators of a school district in Southern California. I was asked by Jim Clark of the Graduate School of Business at the University of California, Los Angeles, to fill in for another consultant in the second in the series of workshops, and everyone in the group except me had been present in the first event. In those days, I was always inclined to be a little critical of everyone's practice, including my own, and I was not too happy with the state of the group as we opened our weekend together. The members were edgy and ill at ease, and as we began, what came out was that they were nervous about repeating the "emotional bath" they had experienced during the first weekend. I saw in the situation an opportunity to practice what I had preached in "Choosing the Depth of Organizational Intervention," and I began endeavoring to make the group a little more comfortable by setting some norms around self-disclosure for our time together. I told them that I expected that they would be as open and honest about their work issues as possible, identifying the behaviors

Source: Originally published as "When Power Conflicts Trigger Team Spirit," *European Training,* 1972, 2, 57–65. Next published as "Role Negotiation: A Tough-Minded Approach to Team Development," in W. W. Burke and H. A. Hornstein (eds.), *The Social Technology of Organization Development* (La Jolla, Calif.: University Associates, 1972). Reprinted here with permission of *MCB University Press Ltd.*

and conditions that helped and hindered them in doing their jobs. Noting that they were uncomfortable about getting into interpersonal issues, and emotions, I said that as far as I was concerned, they need not express a feeling the whole weekend, if they did not want to. What we were there to work on was what people could do to improve their work effectiveness. If they wanted to express their feelings about that, it was all right with me, but it certainly was not required. After testing these ground rules a bit, the group settled down and worked constructively for the rest of the weekend. I went home feeling I was on to something important. It seemed to me that the participants in the workshop had settled down when I acknowledged and worked within their concept of what was *legitimate* in their organizational context: talking about the work and how it was done. When we started with work issues, feelings that came up around these issues were fairly freely expressed.

The next experience I had that influenced this paper was in Puerto Rico, working with a group of mental health professionals at the University of Puerto Rico. I had worked with the group on a previous occasion, and I knew that they freely and easily engaged with one another around feelings and interpersonal issues. However, with all their processing, nothing ever seemed to change in their working relationships. It seemed to me that they "escaped into depth," as a defense against upsetting the role and authority relationships in the group. I thought I would experiment a little to see if I could get the group to agree to adopt some real changes in the ways they worked together.

I began by sharing my observations with the group and asked if they really wanted to make some changes in their working relationships. They said they did, so I then took them through a rather elaborate process in which they charted their mutual responsibilities to one another: who is supposed to communicate what to whom, who decides, who has to be informed, who reports back—that sort of thing. I then asked each member of the group to identify any aspects of his or her task relationships that he or she wanted to change, and I suggested that the agreements group members made might be more likely to stick if they found some quid pro quo, such that each person got something of value in return for what he or she was contributing or giving up to the other(s). Group members spent the remainder of the time we had together in serious work on their agreements, and they were pleased and excited by what they achieved. Again, I left the session excited by what I had learned. I felt I had discovered an approach which worked with both "underpersonal" and "overpersonal" clients, calming the fears of the former and focusing the energy of the latter on the real work.

Before publishing my discovery, I experimented with role negotiation some more, and I also shared it with anyone who would listen, including participants in the NTL Program for Specialists in Organization Development. One of these was Uri Merry from Israel, who took the method back home with him and ingeniously adapted it for the *kibbutz* in which he lived. Unfortunately, by the time he shared his experiences with me, I had already published my article, so was unable to incorporate his findings in it. The most satisfying thing about having written this article is the large number of people who have used the role negotiation method in creative ways and then shared their experiences with me. Following the article, I have appended some thoughts about the method that have been stimulated by these experiences of others. I know the method continues to work for others, because I am constantly meeting people who tell me it has worked for them. I do not use it much myself because it does not fit my style of consulting very well. It feels a little mechanical.

The need for safeguards against consultants' tendencies to press teams inappropriately to "get into feelings" probably has passed long since. However, the method remains a useful tool in a consultant's kit whenever it is appropriate for one's clients to renegotiate their ways of working together. It is particularly useful now, when such emphasis is being placed on working in teams. For example, the method seems admirably suited to the needs of self-managing work groups. It is now, of course, much less radical to negotiate with colleagues, and even with authority figures, than it was when the method was developed. Now everyone negotiates everything, sometimes endlessly. It seems an inevitable result of the demystification of authority and the advent of more egalitarian organization cultures. In such a world, role negotiation should have a long and useful life!

G etting people to work together in harmony is no easy task. Modern management techniques abound with new approaches to improving the working relationship between employees. In the United States, sensitivity training has had quite a vogue, and various techniques such as the T-group or the managerial grid have been brought forth to encourage managers to abandon their competitiveness and to create mutual trust and egalitarian approaches to decision making.

Our managers have been urged to change their motivations from reliance upon monetary reward or punishment to more internal motivation based on intrinsic interest in the job and personal commitment to meeting work objectives. Examples are management by objectives (MBO) and programs of job enrichment. Still other practitioners have developed purely rational approaches to group problem solving (for example, Kepner Tregoe in the United States and Coverdale in Britain).

Running through these approaches is the tendency to ignore or explain away competition, conflict, and the struggle for power and influence. It is assumed that people will be cooperative and productive if they are taught how, or if the barriers to their so being are removed. These approaches may be called *tender minded* in that they see power struggles as a symptom of a managerial *mistake* rather than a basic and ubiquitous process in organizations.

The problem of organizational change is seen as one of *releasing* human potential for collaboration and productivity, rather than as one of controlling or checking competition for advantage and position.

However, consider the case of the production and engineering managers of a plant who had frequent disagreements over the work that was done by the latter for the former. The production manager complained that the engineering manager set maintenance priorities to meet his own convenience and reduce his own costs, rather than to make sure production targets were met. The engineering manager maintained that the production manager gave insufficient notice of jobs which could be anticipated, and the production operators caused unnecessary breakdowns by failure to carry out preventive maintenance procedures faithfully. The two men aired their dissatisfaction with one another's performance from time to time, but according to both parties, no significant change has occurred.

Or take the case of the scientist in a development department who complains of overly close supervision by his section manager. On the one hand, the scientist says the manager intervenes to change the priorities he assigns to work, or to interfere with his development of promising lines of inquiry, and to check up with insulting frequency to see whether the scientist is carrying out the manager's instructions.

The scientist is actively trying to get a transfer to another section because he feels he cannot do a proper job with so much hampering interference from above.

On the other hand, the section manager says the scientist does competent work but is secretive and unwilling to heed advice. He fails to let the manager know what he is doing and deviates without discussion from agreements the manager thought they had reached about how the work should be carried out. The manager feels he has to spend far too much time checking up on the scientist and is beginning to wonder whether his otherwise good work is worth the trouble required to manage him.

In both of these examples, the men are concerned with either gaining increased control over the actions of the other, reducing control by the other, or both. And they know it. A consultant talking to them about communication problems or target setting would no doubt be listened to politely, but in their hearts, these men would still feel it was a question of who was going to have the final say, who was going to be boss.

And, in a way, they are more intuitively right than any outside consultant could be. They know where the power and influence lie, whether people are on their side or against them. They are aware of those with whom they can be open and honest and those who will use information against them. And these concerns are much more accurate and real than an outsider's suggestions for openness and collaboration.

Knowing Where the Power and Coercion Lie

Does this mean that most behavioral science approaches to business are too optimistic? What is certain is that they fail to take into account the forces of power, competitiveness, and coercion. In this article, I shall propose a method that does work directly with these issues, a method that builds team spirit by requiring team members to face their differing interests head on.

The method is based on role negotiation. It changes the *role* that an individual or group performs in the organization through *negotiation* with other interested parties. By an individual's (or a group's) role, I mean what activities he is supposed to perform, what decisions he can make, to whom he reports and about what and how often, who can legitimately tell him what to do and under what circumstances, and so on. Some people would say that a man's *job* is the same as what I have called his *role*, and I would partially agree with this. But what I mean by role includes not only the formal job description but also all the informal understandings, agreements, expectations, and arrangements with others which determine the way one person's or group's work affects or fits in with another's.

Role negotiation intervenes directly in the relationships of power, authority, and influence within the group. The change effort is directed at the work relationships among members. It avoids probing into the likes and dislikes of members for one another and their personal feelings about one another. In this, it is more consonant with the task-oriented norms of business than are most other behavioral approaches.

The Fear of Touchy Emotional Confrontations

When I first developed the technique, I tried it out on members of a client group which was proving particularly hard to work with. They were suspicious and mistrustful of me and of each other, and said quite openly that talking about their relationships was both "irrelevant to our work problems" and "dangerous—it could split the group apart." When I introduced them to role negotiation, they saw ways they could deal with issues that were bothering them without getting into touchy emotional confrontations they could not handle. They dropped their resistance dramatically and turned to work with a will that surprised and delighted me.

I have used role negotiation successfully with top management groups, project teams, even between husbands and wives. The technique can be used with very small or quite large groups, although groups of over eight or ten should be broken down.

The technique makes one basic assumption: *most people prefer a fair negotiated settlement to a state of unresolved conflict,* and they are willing to invest some time and make some concessions in order to achieve a solution. To operate the program, a modest but significant risk is called for from the participants: they must be open about the changes in behavior, authority, responsibility, and the like that they wish to obtain from others in the situation.

If the participants are willing to specify concretely the changes they desire from others, then significant changes in work effectiveness can usually be obtained.

How does this program work in reality? First of all, the consultant must win the participants' confidence in his motives and competence so that they are willing at his behest to try something new and a bit strange. It also stands to reason that the consultant should know enough about the people, their work system, and their relationship problems to satisfy himself that the members of the group are ready to make a real effort toward improvement. No technique will work if the clients do not trust the consultant enough to give it a fair try or if the members of the group (particularly the high-influence members) devote most of their effort to maintaining the status quo. In the description that follows, I am assuming that this confidence and readiness to work have been established. Although this is a rather large assumption, these problems are universal in consulting and not peculiar to role negotiation. If anything, I have found that role negotiation requires somewhat less preparation than other team development techniques I have used.

Let us say we are working with a group of five to seven people, including a manager and his subordinates, two levels in the formal organization. Once basic assumptions of trust are established, I try to get at least a day with the group away from the job location to get the role negotiation process going. A two-day session with a commitment to follow up in three to four weeks is best. If the group is not felt to be quite prepared to undertake serious work, the session may be made longer with some trust-building and diagnostic activities in the beginning, working into the role negotiation when and if the group is ready for it.

No Probing into People's Feelings

The first step in the actual role negotiation is *contract setting*. Its purpose is to make it clear between the group and the consultant what each may expect from the other. This is a critical step in the change process. It controls and channels everything that happens afterwards.

My contract is usually based on the following provisions, which should be written down, if only as a first practice step in the formal way of working which I try to establish.

• It is not legitimate for the consultant to press or probe anyone's *feelings*. We are concerned about work: who does what, how, and with whom. How people *feel* about their work or about others in the group is their own business, to be introduced or not according to their own judgment and desire. The expression or nonexpression of feelings is not part of the contract.

• Openness and honesty about behavior are expected and essential for achieving results. The consultant will insist that people be specific and concrete in expressing their expectations and demands for the behavior of others. Each team member is expected to be open and specific about what he wants others to do *more* or *do better* or *do less* or maintain unchanged.

• No expectation or demand is adequately communicated until it has been *written down* and is clearly understood by both sender and receiver, nor will any change process be engaged in until this has been done.

• The full sharing of expectations and demands does not constitute a completed change process. It is only the precondition for change to be agreed upon through negotiation. It is unreasonable for anyone in the group, manager or subordinate, to expect that any change will take place merely as a result of communicating a demand or expectation. Unless a team member is willing to change his own behavior in order to get what he wants from the other(s), he is likely to waste his and the group's time talking about the issue. When a member makes a request or demand for changed behavior on the part of another, the consultant will always ask what quid pro quo (something for something) he is willing to give in order to get what he wants. This goes for the manager as well as for the subordinates. If the former can get what he wants simply by issuing orders or clarifying expectations from his position of authority, he probably does not need a consultant or a change process.

• The change process is essentially one of bargaining and negotiation in which two or more members each agree to change behavior in exchange for some desired change on the part of the other. This process is not complete until the agreement can be *written down* in terms which include the agreed changes in behavior and make clear what each party is expected to give in return.

• Threats and pressures are neither illegitimate nor excluded from the negotiation process. However, group members should realize that over-reliance on threats and punishment usually results in defensiveness, concealment, decreased communication, and retaliation, and may lead to breakdown of the negotiation. The consultant will do his best to help members accomplish their aims with positive incentives wherever possible.

The Process of Influence Bargaining

Each member has power and influence in the group, both positively to reward and collaborate with others, and negatively to resist, block, or punish. Each uses his power and influence to create a desirable and satisfying work situation for himself. Most of the time this process is gone about secretly. People use a lot of time and energy trying to figure out how to influence another person's behavior covertly, but since they rarely are aware of others' wants and needs, their attempts fail.

Although in stable organizations, employees can learn what works on others just through trial and error over long periods of time, nowadays the fast personnel turnover makes this primitive process obsolete.

Role negotiation tries to replace this old process with a more efficient one. If one person knows because it has been made public what another's wants or intentions are, he is bound to be more effective in trying to influence that person. In addition, when someone tries to influence him, the quid pro quo put forward is more likely to be one he really wants or needs. I try to show my clients that by sharing the information about desires and intentions, *role negotiation increases the total amount of influence group members have on one another.*

The next stage is *issue diagnosis.* Each member spends some time thinking about the way business is conducted between himself and the others in the group. What would he change if he could? What would he like to keep as is? Who and what would have to change in order to improve things? I ask the participants to focus especially on the things which might be changed to improve their *own effectiveness*, since these are the items to be discussed and negotiated.

After he has spent twenty minutes or so thinking about these matters and perhaps making a few notes, each member writes a message for each other member, listing those things he would like to see the other person:

1. Do more or do better.
2. Do less or stop doing.
3. Keep on doing, maintain unchanged.

All of these messages are intended to result in the sender's increasing his own effectiveness in his job.

These lists are exchanged so that each person has all the lists pertaining to his work behavior. Each member makes a master list for himself on a large piece of paper, itemizing the behavior which each other person desires him to do *more* or *better, less,* or *continue unchanged*. These are posted on individual flip charts so that the entire group can peruse and refer to each list. Each member is allowed to question the others who have sent messages about his behavior, querying the what, why, and how of their requests, *but no one is allowed a rebuttal, defense, or even a yes or no reply to the messages he has received.* The consultant must assure that only clarification is taking place; argument, discussion and decision making about issues must be engaged in at a later stage.

Controlling Defensive Responses

The purpose of the consultant's rather rigid and formal control on communication is to prevent the group from having a negative problem-solving experience and members from becoming polarized on issues or taking up extreme positions that they will feel impelled to defend just to save face. Communication is controlled to prevent escalation of actual or potential conflicts. Channeling the energy released by the sharing of demands and expectations into successful problem solving and mutual influence is the objective of this strategy of control.

The consultant intervenes to inhibit hostile and destructive expression at this point and later to facilitate constructive bargaining and negotiation of mutually beneficial agreements.

This initial sharing of desires and change goals among group members brings the team development process its most vulnerable point. If sufficient anger and defensiveness are generated by the problem sharing, the consultant will not be able to hold the negative processes in check long enough for the development of the positive problem-solving spiral on which the process depends for its effectiveness. It is true that such an uncontrollable breakthrough of hostility has not yet occurred in my experience with the method. Nevertheless, concern over the negative possibilities is in part responsible for my slow, deliberate, and rather formal development of the confrontation of issues within the group.

The Influence Trade

After each member has had an opportunity to clarify the messages he has received, the group selects the issues for negotiation. The consultant begins this phase by reemphasizing that unless a quid pro quo can be offered in return for a desired behavior change, there is little point in having a discussion about it. *Unless behavior changes on both sides, the most likely prediction is that the status quo will continue.*

If behavior changes merely as the result of an exchange of views between men of good will, all the better. However, one cannot count on it.

Each participant is asked to choose one or more issues on which he particularly wants to get some changes on the part of another. He is also asked to select one or more issues on which he feels it may be possible for him to move in the direction desired by others. He marks his high priority changes on the others' flip charts, and marks his own flip chart to indicate what behavior he is willing to consider changing. In effect, *each person indicates the issues upon which he most wants to exert influence and those on which he is most willing to accept influence.* With the help of the consultant, the group then goes through the lists to select the "most negotiable issues," those where there is a combination of a high desire for change on the part of an initiator and a willingness to negotiate on the part of the person whose behavior is the target of the change attempt. The consultant asks for two persons who are involved in one such issue to volunteer for a negotiation demonstration before the rest of the group. (It is quite feasible to have three-way negotiations or even more complex ones, but it is better to start with a pair.)

The negotiation process consists of the parties making contingent offers to one another such as "If you do X, I will do Y." The negotiation ends when all parties are satisfied that they will receive a reasonable return for whatever they are agreeing to give. The consultant asks that the agreement be formalized by writing down specifically and concretely what each party is going to give and receive in the bargain. He also asks the participants to discuss openly what sanctions can be applied in the case of nonfulfillment of the bargain by one or another party. Often this involves no more than reversion to the status quo, but it may involve the application of pressures and penalties as well.

After the negotiation demonstration, the members are asked to select other issues they wish to work on. A number of negotiations may go on simultaneously, the consultant's being involved at the request of any party to any negotiation. All agreements are published to the entire group, however, and questioned by the consultant and the other members to test the good faith and reality orientation of the parties in making them. Where agreement proves impossible, the consultant and other group members try to help the parties find further incentives (positive or, less desirably, coercive) which they may bring to bear to encourage agreement.

This process is, of course, not as simple as it sounds. All kinds of difficulties can occur, from bargaining in bad faith, to refusal to bargain at all, to escalation of conflict. In my experience, however, group members tend to be rather wise about the issues they can and cannot deal with, and I refrain from pushing them to negotiate issues they feel are unresolvable. My aim is to light the sparks of team development with a successful experience that group members can look on as a fruitful way of improving their effectiveness and satisfaction.

The Consultant Withers Away

The initial cycle ends here. Each group must then try living with its agreements. There is always, of course, the option to meet later with the consultant to work out new agreements or renegotiate old ones.

Ideally, the group should learn this process so thoroughly that the consultant's role withers away. To do this, though, group members must be so fully aware of the dangers and pitfalls involved in the negotiation process that a third party's arbitration is no longer needed.

So far this has not occurred in my experience. Groups seem to need the security of an independent stage manager or "referee." In between visits, however, there is less reversion to the old status quo than I tend to see in groups in which I have applied softer, more collaborative team development methods. Role negotiation agreements have real teeth in them, and they command more respect and compliance.

What are the advantages of role negotiation? First of all, participants seem more at home with problems of power and influence than with other interpersonal issues. They feel more competent and less dependent on the consultant in dealing with the problems, and so they are ready to work sooner and harder. Furthermore, the consultant's or "referee's" amount of skill and professional training that is required to conduct role negotiation is less than for more sensitive approaches.

That does not mean that role negotiation poses no threat to organization members. The consultant asks participants to be open about matters that are often kept secret in everyday life. This requires more than the normal amount of trust and confidence. If not, these matters would have been talked about before the group ever got to the role negotiation.

There also seems to be some additional discomfort involved in *writing down* the changes one would like to see another make in his work behavior. Several times, participants have questioned the necessity of doing this, because one feels so *exposed* when his concerns are written out for all to see, and there is the fear that others will think them silly, childish, or odd (though this never seems to happen). If the matter comes up, I point out that one need not write down *all* the concerns he has, but only those he would like to work on with others at this time.

Of course, role negotiation, like any other process that changes relationships, does pose a threat to the participants. The members are never sure they will personally be better off after the change than before. In the case of role negotiation, most of these fears arise around losing power and influence, or losing freedom and becoming more controlled by others. Resistance to talking openly about issues is especially likely to occur when someone is trying to manipulate another person to his own advantage, or when he feels that he might want to do this in the future. I think this is the main reason participants in role negotiation so often try to avoid the step of writing down their agreements. If things aren't down in black and white, they feel, it will be easier to ignore the agreement later on if it becomes inconvenient. Also, writing down agreements seems to dispel the aura of trust and good fellowship which some groups like to create on the surface and below which they engage in quite a lot of covert competition.

Role negotiation is of course no panacea for power struggles in groups and between people. People may bargain in bad faith; agreements once reached may be broken; circumstances and personnel may change so that the agreements reached become irrelevant. Of course, these problems can exist in any group or organization. What role negotiation *does* is deal with the problems directly and identify and use constructively those areas of *mutual* advantage in which both sides can benefit from discussion and agreement. These areas are almost always larger than people think they are, and when people find that they can achieve something for themselves by open negotiation which they could not achieve by covert competition, then the more constructive process can begin to grow.

Avoiding Consulting Fees

One other likely advantage of role negotiation is the ease and economy with which it can be introduced into the firm.

One disadvantage of most behavioral approaches to team development is that the consultant's level of skill and experience must be very high indeed. Managers themselves are not confident in dealing openly with conflict, and because they feel uneasy in this area, they reasonably want to have as much safety and skill as money can buy. The demand for skilled consultants on interpersonal and group processes has created a shortage and a meteoric rise in consulting fees. It seems unlikely that the supply will soon catch up with the demand.

The shortage of highly skilled practitioners argues for deskilling the requirements for effective consultant performance. I see role negotiation as a way of lowering the skill requirements for team development consultation. Preliminary results by internal consultants using the approach have been promising.

For example, one management development manager in a unit of IBM teamed up with a colleague to conduct a successful role negotiation with his own top management. He reported that his main problem was getting up enough confidence to take on the job. The role negotiation itself went smoothly. Although I cannot say whether this experience was typical, it does lead me to hope that role negotiation will prove to be practical for use by internal consultants without professional training in the behavioral sciences.

What then are the main points about role negotiation? First, role negotiation focuses on work relationships: what people do, and how they facilitate and inhibit one another in the performance of their jobs. It encourages participants to work with problems using words and concepts they are used to using in business. It avoids probing to the deeper levels of their feelings about one another unless this comes out naturally in the process.

Second, it deals directly with problems of power and influence that may be neglected by other behavioral approaches. It does not attempt to dethrone the authority in the group, but other members are helped to explore realistically the sources of power and influence available to them.

Also, unlike some other behavioral approaches to team development, role negotiation is highly action-oriented. Its aim is not just to expose and understand the issues in a group, but to achieve changed ways of working through mutually negotiated agreements. Changes brought about through role negotiation thus tend to be more stable and lasting than where such negotiated commitments are lacking.

In addition, all the procedures of role negotiation are clear and simple, if a bit mechanical, and can be described to participants in advance so they know what they are getting into. There is nothing mysterious about the technique, and this reduces participants' feelings of dependency upon the special skill of the consultant.

Furthermore, since role negotiation actually requires less skill from the consultant than some other behavioral approaches, internal consultants can suitably use the technique without lengthy special training in the behavioral sciences. It can therefore be a moderate cost approach to organizational change.

It is important to understand that role negotiation does not necessarily replace other "soft" behavioral approaches to organizational change. Work groups can be effective and achievement-oriented and at the same time allow open and deeply satisfying interpersonal relationships.

However, resolving conflict successfully at the interpersonal level can only be done by first attacking the ever-present issues of power and influence among members. Role negotiation does this and provides a sound and effective base upon which to build more satisfying relationships.

If role negotiation is an effective first or "basic" approach to team development, it goes without saying that further growth for individuals and groups means moving beyond this stage into a deeper exploration of how to integrate work and relationships.

Many of the innovations that others have made using role negotiation have been in the direction of putting more flexibility and openness into the process. For example, Uri Merry (personal communication) found that in a *kibbutz* in Israel, it was offensive to insist on a quid pro quo for everything, because people felt they should be motivated to contribute to the good of the community without thinking of a concrete return. In my own subsequent work with the method, I provided for each participant to indicate his or her response to a request for change by using the following hierarchy of symbols:

++ (double plus): "I'll be glad to do it—I didn't know you cared."

+ (single plus): "I will do as you request, if you can show me how it contributes to the whole."

O (open): "I am willing to negotiate a fair exchange for what you want."

- (negative): "What you ask is very difficult for me. I suggest we work on something else."

Role negotiation has been widely adapted, and it seems quite forgiving of mistakes. Clients sometimes refuse to play, but I have never had anyone tell me they used it and had a disaster. The most ambitious application I know of was a companywide project Richard Hill conducted for Diamond Shamrock, for which he developed a role negotiation workbook. His work is reported in Louis (1976). I found it interesting that in that project there was a strong emphasis placed on sanctions for failure to keep agreements.

CHAPTER FIVE

STARTUP: THE CARE AND FEEDING OF INFANT SYSTEMS

It can be exciting to revisit pieces I wrote years ago, and see in them deeper meanings than were apparent at the time. I did the work on which "Startup: The Care and Feeding of Infant Systems" is based in the late sixties and early seventies, and its conclusions and recommendations are taken from reports and client conferences of that era. However, I did not write the article itself until 1980, chiefly because I changed the focus of my work and became heavily involved in management education. In "Startup: The Care and Feeding of Infant Systems," I can now read both a prophecy and a critique of present-day organizations, where rapid changes in markets, technology, and business conditions have created what Peter Vaill has called "permanent white water" (1989, pp. 2–3).

In the fourteen years since I wrote the article, many organizations have come to be in a constant state of startup. The piece now presents itself to me as a set of prescriptions for organizing, managing, and maintaining (healing) any organization that is undergoing a process of rapid change in its business or technology. My proposals for the design of startup organizations were fairly radical when I first made them. Now, the structures, systems and team-based management that I proposed are, if not universal, at least not uncommon among leading technologically oriented organizations.

For me, the paradox is that as many organizations have become more like startups, consultants and managers have not yet very widely adopted the suggestions I make here for planning and managing the processes of change that are

Source: "Startup: The Care and Feeding of Infant Systems" was originally published in *Organizational Dynamics*, 1981, *10*(1), 5–29. Reprinted here with permission of *Organizational Dynamics*.

endemic to such organizations. The arts of preparation, planning, reflection, and learning that I advocate here to cope with the stress, fast pace, and confusion of startup are largely ignored. In this paper, I point to "task uncertainty" as a key variable in organizational design. I propose one way of designing an organization to function well in conditions of high task uncertainty, such as startups. I examine intergroup conflicts and individual stresses that come up when such designs are used. I believe that these ideas are as relevant to managing rapidly changing organizations as they were to managing startups. They apply to mergers and acquisitions, designing and developing new products and bringing them onstream, reorganizing or turning around a business, and redesigning or reengineering work processes. Yet with some shining exceptions, it seems to me that most organizations, even those greatly admired, still tend to muddle through these tasks and others that are high in uncertainty. It is as though excitement, chaos, challenge, and catch-as-catch-can management have some intrinsic addictive appeal that is very hard to let go of, even when there are promising ways to do so.

In the startups I facilitated, there were constant conflicts between planners and doers. The latter tended to ignore or sabotage the efforts of the former. Yet they acknowledged that "overkill" in contingency planning and preparation was beneficial to the startup. In my more recent work in the personal computer industry, I have found that same reluctance to take planning seriously.

I have read widely in the literature of the two World Wars, and have talked with people on both sides about their experiences in active service and in the underground. For many of them, it was a time when they felt more alive and more committed than at any time since. It was also a time of disorder, uncertainty, and constant change. It was truly "their finest hour," to which every work experience since is compared, and usually found wanting. For people who enjoy newness, challenge, and change, the startup of a new operation is the "moral equivalent of war." It is an opportunity to participate in what I have called the achievement culture (see Chapter Twelve). In such cultures, the goal is clear, the stakes are high, the need for each person's contribution is urgent, and there is a sense of camaraderie, even love, between "comrades in arms." Under the internalized pressure to achieve a desired result, awkward and perplexing questions about the ultimate desirability or goodness of the activity can be put aside. Reflection is an impossible luxury, or it seems to be, and when one is deeply involved in action, inner conflicts can be forgotten for a time. Perhaps there is something in us that loves chaos for its own sake, or for the sake of the relief it gives from other pains.

When I was involved in the most successful of the startups in which I participated, I pressed for planning out of mental conviction alone. My mind was made up, and it directed my will, but my heart was never in my proposals. Detailed planning has never been my way of approaching life or work. I have always seen myself as a startup kind of guy, loving to begin things, enjoying intuitive problem solving and decision making, but seldom staying around for the completion of the work.

Perhaps it is we who collude with the world "out there" to defeat our minds' attempts to bring order into our working lives. If that is so, then we shall do well to turn inward to know and embrace the wild man and woman within. Surely creativity, intuition, and spontaneity are not inevitably enemies of order and rationality but may be brought into relationship with them, perhaps through working with their cyclical alternation. However, that is for another time.

Not only are rationality and creativity at odds in the startups I studied and in present-day high-technology organizations, but the mind and the heart are in opposition as well. People in startup organizations are frequently in denial about the consequences of the willing self-exploitation that is characteristic of such systems, and the same is true in many present-day organizations engaged in constant change and innovation. I remain convinced that everything I said about the need to manage pressure and legislate rest and renewal in the startup is even more urgent today. While the startups of which I write in this article came to an end eventually, the stress and pressure of change in present-day organizations do not. Not knowing what to do about it, most leaders and managers endeavor to ignore, minimize, or rationalize it away. We urgently need to find ways to harmonize the mind and the heart so that the one need not oppress the other. I made some proposals in this article, but now they seem a bit inadequate and superficial for the magnitude of the task. The changes longed for in the inmost hearts of organization members are systemic and societal, and they will have to be rooted in a new appreciation of our own values and priorities as a species living a tenuous life on a fragile planet.

To put "Startup: The Care and Feeding of Infant Systems" in context in relation to my own development and that of OD consulting, in 1968, when I undertook my initial work with new plant startup, most organization development work was conducted in traditional hierarchical organizations. An implicit goal of the consultants was usually to shake up and loosen rigid bureaucratic structures and authority relationships, often by making it safe for people to speak their truth about what was really going on. Team development and process consultation (Schein, 1969) were the usual interventions of choice, and there was still a strong underlying assumption in team development sessions that what was really important was to "get down to feelings" and have team members give and receive personal feedback to and from one another. In fact, my involvement in the initial startup project began with such a team development session, conducted by myself and Jeffrey Atlas for a group of U.S. engineers who were soon to go overseas to provide technical consultation to the local management of a new chemical plant.

It was an unusually successful session, and following it, we were able to interest the team leader in the possibility of our facilitating the development of effective working relationships between his startup team and the local management of the new facility. Eventually, Jeff and I went overseas ourselves with a contract to help plan the development of the "human system" of the startup, to facilitate working relationships during the startup period, and to research the process of bringing the plant on-line, with a view to improving future startups. We arrived later than we had hoped, and our goal of helping to plan the system was submerged in the heat and pressure of what turned out to be a kind of war between the men and the machinery.

We had a tremendous learning experience about the limitations of our own behavioral technologies when, from the start, people saw our attempts to apply process consultation as "part of the problem" rather than as "part of the solution." We were attempting to apply a reflective process to situations that our clients believed cried out for immediate and continuous action. Our clients were impatient with the time we asked them to spend in meetings, and they were looking for quick solutions to the problems that were right in front of their faces. We were young and adaptable and inventive enough to find ways to be helpful when we understood what was wanted. We spent some of our time helping to facilitate problem-solving and coordination meetings and coaching team leaders in managing their meetings. We mediated interpersonal difficulties and role conflicts between members of the outside startup team and local management. We created a form of CBWA (consulting by walking around) in which we endeavored to spot difficulties in coordination, communication, and relationships in their early stages and bring help to bear. And we did our research. Each of the four consultant members of the startup team kept a daily log of important happenings and observations, and at the conclusion of the seven months we spent on the project, I sifted through these materials for clues to what had happened and why. The output was an analysis of the strengths and (mostly) weaknesses of the startup process as we had observed and participated in it, along with specific suggestions for planning and managing future startups.

Much to my chagrin, my report to the client was ignored at the time, and did not surface in any useful way for about fifteen years. Perhaps it was not written tactfully enough, but I suspect the major reason was that the startup was not considered successful, and the people involved just wanted to move on.

On leaving the project, I moved to England, where I practiced as an independent consultant for about eight years. I was sure I had acquired valuable knowledge that could provide a competitive advantage to any company willing to use it, and it was not long before I had another set of clients where I could test my ideas.

My new clients were eager to improve their startup planning and operations because they had been plagued with several difficult startups in the recent past. They were willing to invest in following my recommendations about bringing people on well in advance of the startup for training and planning and about carefully working out the interfaces and role relationships between the various groups involved in constructing, commissioning, and operating the new plant. We went through seemingly endless meetings to plan the startup and work through misunderstandings between the different teams as they developed. We did role negotiation to make sure everyone knew what he or she was supposed to do and everything was covered. We did contingency planning to prepare in advance for things that might go wrong. We trained everyone in a variant of the Kepner-Tregoe approach to problem solving. We constructed an elaborate, state-of-the-art planning process to make sure everything on the "critical path" was done when it needed to be.

I guess our planning paid off, because within four days of "lighting up," the plant was at 104 percent of capacity, and it stayed that way. As I point out in the article, economically, our overkill on planning and training had more than paid for itself, and everyone involved got credit for a job well done. Thus, in my experiences in startup, rationality and preparation have been the keys to high performance, even though they have not been much fun for me or for my clients.

As an applied behavioral scientist, I have enjoyed helping plan and execute large-scale plant startups. The experience is invariably exciting and poses a variety of problems of organization and management that differ from those of the "steady-state organization" in the same way that military leadership in the field differs from the management of a peacetime force. To me, the startup organization offers a kind of stress-testing laboratory for organizational structures and management practices. The startup organization grows quickly. In it we can observe the normal operating problems of organizations intensified many times, so that they move toward resolution or disaster at a much faster rate than ordinary.

From my observations of the startup of petrochemical installations, I have drawn some generalizations for the planning and management of a system startup. The generalizations concern the following: (1) designing the system (organization structure), (2) breathing life into the system (staffing, training, planning, and team development), (3) managing and maintaining the system (management style, conflict resolution, and stress reduction), (4) helping the system (the role of the internal or external organization consultant in a startup), and (5) managing the system's boundaries.

Designing the System

In his excellent book on organizational design, Jay Galbraith (1978) provides a model that is useful in understanding innovative startup organizations. He centers his model on the concept of task uncertainty, the unpredictability of events. In the startup of complex human/machine systems, the one thing we can be sure of in advance, whether we are consultants or managers, is that there will be many more problems and unexpected difficulties than we would expect in the same system when it is operating normally.

Task uncertainty requires us as consultants and managers to communicate, solve problems, and make decisions in organizations. If everything could be predicted in advance, we could bureaucratize the entire process, writing it all down in operating manuals, procedures, rules, and regulations. We would then need only to supervise operations to make sure that things were done as prescribed, and the system would manage itself. When we design productive systems, we try to minimize task uncertainty and provide decision-making rules and procedures. We also provide communication channels and problem-solving functions to take care of the degree of task uncertainty that we expect.

When we start up a complex system that has been designed to handle a normal amount of task uncertainty, we find that the provisions built into the organization for communication, problem solving, and decision making are inadequate to deal with the greatly increased uncertainty typical of the startup period. During startup, many things fail to go according to plan: equipment does not operate properly; roles and responsibilities are unclear or disputed; tasks are not carried out as expected; human and material resources are not available when needed or do not perform as expected; and so on. In short, the provisions made in a normal steady-state operation for communication, problem solving, and decision making are inadequate for startup operations; communication channels and management functions become overloaded and choked with data, problems, and requests for help, and the system does not perform very well. Anyone who has lived through a really difficult startup can supply the details.

We can deal with increased task uncertainty by providing additional resources, by reducing the need for information processing, or by redesigning the organization to increase its information-processing capacity. The first of these approaches appears to be by far the most common, chiefly because it can be done without any conscious decision or management action.

Providing Additional Resources

If we take no other action in response to the increased task uncertainty of a startup, we must provide additional resources. The most obvious of these are time, money, materials, and people. Since it takes longer to get things working properly under conditions of task uncertainty, we may try to reduce the time by providing material or human resources. When we see we are not going to make the schedule, we bring in additional technical and managerial resources, we work people longer hours, and we make expensive modifications to the physical plant. If the capital investment in the system is low, and the marginal value of the product is modest, then the cost of extending the time allotted for the startup may be the easiest cost to bear. In the complex petrochemical systems in which I gained my own startup experience, the cost of a day's production was reckoned in five figures, so it was less costly to add people and to spend money in ways that would reduce the startup time. Some of the ways in which this is done are to:

Add human resources. Typically, startups are overstaffed; additional technical personnel are made available, and extra maintenance people may be kept on call as well. Sometimes a "startup team" of highly qualified people will take over from the normal operating staff during startup, handing the system back to the latter when it is operating properly.

Add material resources. Extra parts may be kept on hand, along with complete units of critical pieces of equipment.

Add money. Budgetary restrictions and controls may be relaxed; procurement procedures may be streamlined and simplified so that operating and technical personnel may quickly order and obtain critically needed materials.

Add time. If all else fails, the startup will simply take longer to complete. Schedules will not be met, and projected targets will recede into the future. Time is the resource of last resort, and the one that requires the least planning and creativity to make available.

Reducing the Need for Information Processing

Whenever we can reduce interdependency between the parts of an organization, we reduce the need for information processing. In a continuous process operation this is difficult, but any time we can create a "holding" or buffer function between two interdependent parts, we can reduce the necessity for them to march precisely to the same drummer. Healthcare systems, providers of human services, and academic institutions are classic examples of organizations designed to reduce the interdependence of their parts and to cut down on joint decision making. This form of organization often produces an inferior product. In the case of the three examples, the value of their products and services is difficult to assess, and the organizational structure suits the needs of their professional members for autonomy.

In the startups in which I have participated, integrating the parts of the production process was a progressive function. During construction and early commissioning phases, the different parts of the plant were loosely linked by an overall schedule. As the different parts came closer to being onstream, it became more and more important to build and maintain joint decision-making and problem-solving links among them. If the changed requirements of a more interdependent system were not foreseen and consciously prepared for in advance, people often failed to make the shift when required, and the startup suffered accordingly.

Increasing Information Processing Capacity

My main point about organizational design is this: if we are unwilling to pay the costs of task uncertainty in missed schedules and lost production, then we must recognize that the ideal organization for startup does not have the same structure as does the optimum steady-state organization. The startup organization calls for additional problem-solving or learning capacity. This can be provided by both vertical and lateral alterations in the organization.

When we create lateral or cross-functional problem-solving relationships in an organization, we reduce the load on vertical channels. Day-to-day operating problems can be dealt with closer to the source, leaving higher management free to perform coordination and support functions. In a multiplant petrochemical startup, for example, the temporary startup organization was based on startup groups, one for each plant. Each consisted of the production and maintenance supervisors for the plant, relevant technical advisers, and vendors' representative(s). Each such startup group was responsible for planning and tracking the startup within its plant, solving operating and technical problems, and reporting on progress through the production supervisor to a startup steering committee. The latter consisted of the top site management, the heads of the various functions and advisory groups, and all the second-level production managers.

This modified matrix form of organization has a number of inherent advantages for rapid information processing during startup. It reduces information overload by shortening the linkage between the origin of a problem and the points at which a decision can be made and implemented. It thus reduces response time, permitting the organization to keep on top of a rapidly changing startup situation. Decisions are made in the field by those whose current experience and knowledge about the local situation are up to date and detailed. Therefore the organization's response is likely to be more appropriate and relevant than if the decision were being made at levels once or twice removed from the plant.

Other advantages are less obvious. When a modified matrix organization is operating well, it fosters cooperation, mutual influence, and cohesion between functions. People within the plant startup group are relatively free to work out their own roles and responsibilities to suit their differing styles and capacities, and they can develop a high degree of interdependence, teamwork, and team spirit. Because they feel jointly responsible for the success of the whole, they engage in less blaming and buck-passing than is typical of the normal functionally organized operation. Each individual has more authority and responsibility than he or she would normally have, so the jobs are more satisfying and fulfilling to ambitious, achievement-oriented people.

These advantages are not merely theoretical; the modified matrix works extremely well in practice. Unfortunately, it can also work very badly. The difference between effective and ineffective applications lies not in design of the organization, but in how it is implemented and managed. In most organizations there are potent forces that can work against the success of a modified matrix. These forces must be taken into account and dealt with if any such innovative organization form is to realize its promise.

If a modified matrix is temporarily superimposed on a normal functional organization, it is not at all unlikely that these two organizational forms will compete with each other. For one thing, rewards and discipline are meted out by the traditional functional organization, so functional managers have considerable power over their subordinates. If the functional managers are not committed to the matrix way of working, they will interfere with it and subvert it—and they often will not be aware that that is what they are doing.

In one startup, for example, the engineering manager kept pushing his people for progress on long-range planning projects. This conflicted with their day-to-day commitments to the plant startup group, but they did not confront him about this because they were new in the system and nervous about how he might react. As a result, they were always behind in work for their startup teams, and morale and cooperation within the plant startup groups suffered accordingly.

The functional organization offers its members relief from feelings of pressure and guilt. In the normal situation, a person can feel that he or she is doing all right so long as the boss is happy. In one startup for example, a technical adviser was asked for help by a vendor's representative in his area. There was nothing unreasonable about the request, but the adviser was hard pressed to cope with his workload. Instead of reevaluating his own priorities, he replied that the request would have to be routed through and approved by his functional manager. By the time this could be accomplished, the help would have been useless, so the vendor let it go. The adviser could be comfortable in feeling that he was "just doing his job," but the startup operation suffered.

In the matrix organization at its best, everyone from all functions is mutually responsible for the project's success. When the team's plant drops behind schedule, each team member feels pressure to perform better. The modified matrix requires that individuals be willing and able to exert a great deal of informal influence on their teammates across functional lines. Unless people accept this responsibility for influencing one another, the system works poorly.

Modified Matrix: A High Conflict Model

Trying to influence a peer to do his or her job better often results in stress and conflict, and many managers and engineers are not skillful in motivating and persuading without formal authority. The normal functional organization buffers the participants from this sort of confrontation, and when one's colleague fails to perform, it is comfortable to resort to blaming rather than exerting pressure for change. For example, a production supervisor constantly complained about the poor service he was getting from maintenance, but he would not confront the issue openly with the maintenance supervisor. To his functional way of thinking, it really was not up to him to get the maintenance people to do their jobs properly, and since he had many other things to worry about, it reduced stress on him to blame and complain rather than to accept responsibility for solving the problem.

Modified Matrix Styles and Staffing

In order to operate smoothly and effectively, the modified matrix organization requires a different staffing pattern and a different style of management from that of the normal functional organization. Most production organizations are organized in a fairly tight pyramid for close control of operations and maximum efficiency. At the organization's lower levels, the individual is neither expected nor encouraged to exercise initiative or to take on a great deal of responsibility. In the modified matrix organization, problem solving and decision making are pushed downward in the organization, so the people involved must be qualified and motivated to take a more proactive stance toward problems. Those who are used to a highly directive and controlling style of management often find this transition hard to make, and some are temperamentally disinclined to make it. Often, too, good individual contributors have difficulty working as group members in the team settings that the matrix organization always requires.

Higher management in production organizations tends to use a more directive and controlling role than is appropriate to the modified matrix organization advocated here. The whole thrust of the matrix design is to free higher management to focus on overall coordination, to provide both tangible support in the form of needed human and material resources and psychological support when the going is rough, and to manage the boundaries between the startup system and its environment. If higher management continues to direct and control the day-to-day details of the startup, these functions will be poorly covered. Furthermore, the problem-solving teams at lower levels of the organization will be demotivated and frustrated in the exercise of initiative and skill that the design was originally intended to release.

An example of this occurred when one plant startup group was behind schedule, and the site manager began attending the daily team meetings. Some of the team members who knew the day-to-day situation most intimately and should have been active participants in the discussions were intimidated by his presence, deferred to his authority, and hardly contributed when he was present. Their answers to my questions after the meetings made it clear that they had information and opinions that might have affected decisions made in the meeting, but they were reluctant to stick their necks out and be blamed later on if things went wrong. Later, when higher management was prevailed upon to stay away from these meetings, problem solving improved markedly.

This discussion may give the impression that the modified matrix organization is full of defects, or that making it work is more trouble than it is worth. As noted, it can work both superlatively well and agonizingly badly. It works well when people understand and are well prepared for their roles, and when higher management adopts the broadly facilitative and supportive style the startup team needs in order to take initiative and personal responsibility. It works badly when higher management's commitment is lacking, and when people do not really know how to work in a modified matrix. Some of the things that can go wrong have been noted; later sections on building, managing, and maintaining the startup system will discuss how to make them go right.

The modified matrix organization is an example of creating lateral relationships that improve problem solving and information processing. Vertical planning and tracking arrangements may also be designed to give decision makers quicker and more complete access to what is going on in the startup system. Higher management can use these planning and tracking systems either to control the startup process directly or to aid problem solving in the modified matrix system.

Critical path scheduling techniques may be used to plan startups. In one case, the plan was constructed in great detail by a planning section under the direction of a manager with considerable startup experience. The continuously updated plan was displayed on a number of large boards so that any member of the startup organization could immediately see how his own work related to the whole, and what parts of the operation were in danger of falling behind and holding up overall progress. Planning staff met twice each day with the plant startup group. The morning meeting dealt with overnight progress and problems and produced a revised action plan for the day shift. During that shift, the overall plan was updated by the planners. The overall plan was reviewed with the operating team in an afternoon meeting, and at that time, targets were established for the following twenty-four hours.

Management felt that this process gave a fine degree of control, but the favorable result was not achieved without difficulty, and the problems encountered illustrate some of the difficulties in implementing even the best-designed planning system: in the precommissioning and late construction phases of the project, the planners became immersed in the technical intricacies of the plan. The managers and engineers who were supposed to operate according to the plan tended to ignore it in favor of the ad hoc problem solving and decision making that suited their own strong bias for action. The plan became out of date because the operators were not very good about feeding information into it, and the planning manager became extremely frustrated over his inability to achieve his personal goal of managing the startup by means of the plan.

This difficulty with interactions was neither random nor caused by the personalities of the people involved. There is an inherent tension between doing and planning that is exacerbated under the heat and pressure of startup. The joy of battle that engineers and managers experience in their struggles to tame complex technical systems breeds distrust and disregard for the merely intellectual activities of the planners. Even if the interaction between doers and planners is carefully designed and managed, it will give trouble. If this inherent tension is ignored, then the best-laid plans will certainly go awry.

In starting up complex technical or sociotechnical systems, it is also useful to create special information-processing systems for problem identification and problem solving. Instead of waiting for problems to arise and coping with them on an impromptu basis, a set of roles and procedures can be agreed upon in advance that will greatly expedite problem solving in the heat of battle.

The simplest way of doing this is to engage in detailed advance contingency planning. Designers, vendors, technical experts, and those who will operate the equipment should meticulously go over the flowchart of the system before startup. They should identify possible trouble spots and agree on how these will be monitored, who will collect data on their functioning, and who will take what action if difficulties arise. This system of contingency agreements then serves as a blueprint for how the shape and functioning of the startup organization are to shift under emergency conditions. Help is ready to be activated at the first sign of need and without a lot of discussion about who is responsible for what.

Such contingency planning can trigger considerable resistance, reasonable though it may look on paper. Designers do not like to assume that their elegant creations will fail or function badly. The same goes for contractors and equipment vendors. Operating people prefer to deal with problems as they come up, rather than "borrow trouble" in advance. Nearly everyone has some reason for colluding in the false hope that everything will come out all right. I have found myself in a startup organization being at the same time the least technical person and the staunchest advocate of technical contingency planning. The fact is that people often have to be pushed pretty hard to engage in such advance planning.

In one startup, this initial resistance was turned into at least guarded enthusiasm after all those involved had gone through a form of problem-solving training (a variation on the Kepner-Tregoe approach) along with considerable work on problem solving in groups. The training heightened awareness and sensitivity to technical problem solving and gave everyone involved a common language and methodology with which to work. A system was designed that emphasized rapid spotting, evaluation, and assignment of technical problems through the medium of a central problem register managed by the engineers who had designed the plant.

It was also recognized that the problem-solving process itself could lead to difficulties if design changes and modifications to the plant were not carefully controlled. It is easy to upset the operation of a complex system by tinkering with one part of it. The problem-solving system that eventually evolved included stringent evaluation of all proposed modifications to the plant by designers, construction people, and operating management, and a procedure whereby accurate information on all design changes was used to update the line diagrams of the plant.

Planning from an Information-Processing Point of View

These rather homely examples illustrate that in talking about "organizational design," we are not necessarily involved in some grand restructuring of the organization. What is important is that we adapt and plan from an information-processing point of view when we deal with startup. We know in advance that startup problems and contingencies will overload the normal communication and decision-making capacities of the organization and its members. We can predict from experience and reason what kinds of trouble we are likely to run into. Designing the startup organization from the information-processing point of view means asking ourselves some simple questions:

- What sorts of problems, communications, and decisions are we likely to encounter during startup that are different from or more pressing than those encountered during normal operation of this system?
- In the normal organization, where does the information about these problems originate, and where does it have to be passed for decision and action?

- Can we shorten the communication pathways, reduce the number of levels involved, or bring the problem owners together with the problem solvers in such a way as to facilitate the speed and effectiveness of the startup?
- What procedures and systems can we invent to accomplish our information-processing tasks?
- What roles, responsibilities, and authorities must be assigned and accepted so that these procedures and systems will work?
- What kinds of training, briefing, team building, or intergroup negotiation must take place so that people will know and be motivated to perform their roles and responsibilities and make the system work?

Taken together, all of these questions except the last constitute the organizational design task. With a bit of consultation, most startup teams can do this work themselves. Designing an organization for startup does not require special knowledge and expertise beyond that possessed by managers experienced in startup. Rather, it is a matter of being willing to take the time and make the effort to think through the design of the organization, putting aside the model of the normal steady-state organization as an ideal, and asking ourselves, "What is the ideal organization for this, our unique startup situation?"

The answer to the last of the questions, however, is the one that transforms the startup organization from plan into reality, and I shall deal with it in depth in the next section.

Breathing Life into the System

The most cleverly and carefully designed startup organization is not worth the paper it is drawn upon, nor can it properly be said to exist, unless it is in the minds and hearts of the organization's members. "Breathing life into the system" is making the plan live through the attitudes, knowledge, and actions of people. This principle is more often than not ignored by those responsible for managing startups.

All of us know, from having worked for years in organizations, that they work well only when people know their roles, responsibilities, powers, and the ways in which their tasks fit with the tasks of those who interact with them. And, at least intuitively, we know that if people are not proud of their organization and if they do not believe in its purposes and ways of working, they will lack the energy needed to fuel a high-performing system. Building an organization is simply making sure that people will know their part in it and making sure that their hearts will be in their work.

The problem is that when we come to modify a work system or construct one from scratch, we usually overlook the organization building that has been required to give life to the organizations of which we are members or which we are helping. We underestimate the time and energy required to build an organization, partly because so much of the process is informal, implicit, and not under the control of management. To illustrate this, think back to some organizations you've joined as a new member, or some transfers you've made to a different part of your organization. Remember what your boss told you about what was expected of you and how to get along.

Now, remember how you *really* learned how to get on. You probably learned most from the peers and subordinates who gave you the word, either tactfully or frankly; from your own observations of how people did things and how they dealt with one another; and from the awkward trial-and-error process of learning how to get things done and how to get what you wanted. Remember how you learned which rules were meant to be observed and which you could safely ignore.

There was probably a period of time at the start during which you were not very effective; you may have felt you were not really earning the money you were being paid, and you felt a little guilty about it. All in all, however, it probably went fairly smoothly. After all, everyone else knew the ropes. You had only to keep your eyes and ears open and learn from observation and experience in order to play your part. After a while, you probably even learned to value and defend some of the old ways of doing things that you had thought were weird, inefficient, or downright stupid when you first arrived.

When you staff a startup system from the ground up, everyone is like you were when you first joined an organization or transferred to a new part of it—even the boss. That is, even the head of the startup organization does not know exactly how to use his or her authority to get things done and how to weld this collection of individuals into an organic and smoothly functioning whole. Everyone has expectations of everyone else, but each person's expectations are at least partly based on prior experiences that are not shared with the others. So everyone is continually being brought up short by the failure of the others to play their parts—to read their lines right. Roles and responsibilities are fuzzy and ill defined. Because people do not know exactly what the limits are, there is continual testing and jockeying for power and influence. A lot of energy gets drained away from the work into the confusion and competition over what the organization is and how it is to be operated.

These sorts of problems are impersonal in their root causes: people inevitably engage in a learning process when an organization is in the process of formation. It would not matter a great deal who the people were. The process would still be intense and difficult. Unfortunately for those who are in the situation, it is difficult to see it this way. Their experience is of other individuals who are uncooperative, competitive, uncomprehending, and dense. They take it all very personally indeed. Consequently, relationships fail to get off to a good start, and this can create a legacy of mistrust and bad feelings that gives trouble for a long time after the original causes have been forgotten.

When an organization is not completely new, and the startup puts people who already know one another into new roles and relationships, the situation is not so difficult. Much of the basic knowledge and behavioral norms that the individuals bring with them are still appropriate and useful. However, as the participants' roles change to meet the demands of a new technical system, their behavior must and will change as well, and this transition also calls for much learning about who is supposed to do what to whom. Some of this can be laid out in organization charts, but a surprising amount cannot be. It must be worked out by the participants themselves as they strive to build an organization that can cope with the increased stress, task uncertainty, and turbulence of the startup.

For some reason, those who manage startups often give little attention to programming the startup of the human system. They design the technical system to the nth degree, sometimes simulating its operation with computer models. They provide for exhaustive quality checks on the construction, and for cleaning and testing each of the parts before they are brought onstream to function together as a system. In contrast to the care and attention to detail that are given to complex technical equipment, the people who will make this system work or allow it to fail are given a quick briefing on the organization, trained in the technical parts of their work if they are not already qualified, and plugged into the system. If the system then does not work very well, the tendency is to blame the people who do not seem to be doing their jobs properly. The job itself, including its interfaces with other jobs, is much less often looked at as the root cause for poor system performance. This is so in spite of the fact that usually the best and brightest individuals in the organization are given key startup roles; startups are seldom staffed with "dead wood."

In my experience, the most serious causes of poor startup performance are poor fit between adjacent roles (jobs that require their incumbents to work closely together) and a lack of shared understanding between the incumbents on how they are going to manage the interface between their jobs. These problems are what bringing an organization to life is about. Once the overall design has been set up, its parts (roles) have to be carefully shaped to fit together without too much overlap or too many gaps, and the members have to learn how to operate those parts for which they are responsible (their jobs) in a way that harmonizes with the whole.

Building an effective startup organization is a bit like putting on a modern dance performance. First an overall structure is designed, and the movements that each dancer will make are specified and integrated with the movements of others (the choreography). Then the dancers have to be rehearsed in their parts. Even though each dancer may be well qualified for his or her part, each will be stronger in some aspects and weaker in others. As rehearsals progress, opportunities will occur to strengthen the entire piece by redesigning the parts to make better use of the talents of individual dancers, and the dancers themselves will learn how to coordinate their movements and how to compensate for one's weaknesses with another's strengths.

If the dancers have been well rehearsed, the first performance (startup) will be a good one, but it will not be flawless. The dancers will respond in differing ways to the stress of opening night, and their operating characteristics will change somewhat from what they were during rehearsal. Further mutual adjustments will be required under this new load of performance in front of a live audience before the company's artistry reaches its ultimate peak.

This analogy may seem fanciful to the reader, but to one who views an organization as an intricate pattern of continually moving human relationships, it is appropriate in all but one respect. The director of a dance company would not consider performing without rehearsal, but managers of startups frequently do call upon their performers to play their parts with only the most cursory briefing. And it is the star performers, the key managers and technical people, who are given the least rehearsal of all. At least the operators are generally given fairly thorough job training.

The reason usually given for bringing people into a startup with little lead time is that good people are expensive and their resources are needed elsewhere in the organization until the startup begins. I am not convinced that this is really the reason involved. People who design and build complex plants are pretty intelligent when it comes to figuring out cost/benefit ratios, and a few minutes with a calculator could convince anyone that where capital cost and product value are high, the cost of bringing people in early to save just a few days in startup time is small by comparison. I believe, rather, that managers are unaware or unconvinced that startup time and costs can be substantially reduced by bringing people in early and rehearsing them in their startup roles. When people do arrive early, their work is not ready for them, and though we can simulate the behavior of technical systems on a computer, no one has yet produced a program that simulates all the technical, logistical, and human problems in managing a startup. People who arrive early for a startup often complain that they have too little to do and a lack of direction and structure.

Doing It Well: A Case in Point

I shall present an alternative to this state of affairs, based on a very successful startup I helped plan for a British chemical company. Organization building by bringing people in early was judged by local management to be a major key to the success of this project. Here is what the commissioning manager, Dr. J. B. Horsley (Horsley, 1973), said about the project:

> There was a clear notion that the people and the organization were just as important as the technology. . . . The equality of people and technology was expressed via the People Plan, . . . a controlled way of bringing people on to the project in advance of the tasks they were required to do. . . . The Plan appeared as a huge bar chart which indicated the dates people would arrive and the things they would be doing prior to their "real" tasks—the aim was to cre-

ate situations in advance and train people so that the startup would not create any surprises.

In addition to the job training and technical planning that the management and technical staff engaged in to prepare for the startup, all exempt staff engaged in organization building. A key aspect of this process was an activity called "role negotiation." This began with a plan for the organization drawn up by the project manager. Each person in the team then made a detailed specification of his tasks and of the work relationships with others that were required to achieve good performance on his own job. These role and relationship specifications were exchanged and reviewed for overlap and gaps between roles, and for disagreements about who was responsible for what.

In a series of team meetings, the people then negotiated modifications in their tasks, responsibilities, and authority until all were satisfied that they had a system that would work under the demands of the startup. The results of the negotiations were written down in the form of "contracts" specifying the reciprocal duties and responsibilities that people agreed to carry out during different phases of the startup process. If a person's role was to change from one part of the startup to another, that change was negotiated and detailed in writing in advance. If the "ownership" or responsibility for a piece of equipment or task was to change, this too was determined beforehand. If it appeared that workloads would be especially high for a person or group during one phase of the startup, an arrangement for sharing that workload was negotiated.

The use of role negotiation permitted an orderly development that elicited this further comment from Horsley (1973): "The whole organization evolved because it just seemed to fit the people, the tasks, and the problems. Because the organization was developed from within, there was a high degree of commitment to it. Even if it wasn't perfect, people had a will to make it work."

People were committed because they themselves had built the organization and because it fitted them. During role negotiation, questions of personal preference and of individual suitability for particular tasks and responsibilities were openly (though uncomfortably) discussed and provided for. These considerations took precedence over what was considered "normal" in the organization. People took pride in the unique structure and way of operating they had developed, and when arrangements failed to work as expected, they worked to adjust the system instead of blaming a mythical "them" for their problems.

In my experience, such an "organic" approach to organization building is effective in producing a cohesive and determined team whose members know what is expected of them and who work together unusually well. It is important, however, to be clear about the costs and demands that must be met to achieve a positive result. The most important of these is the provision by higher management of lead time—that is, bringing people into the organization far enough in advance that the organization-building process can be accomplished before the startup begins.

This is only partly a question of the amount of time it takes to define roles and to go through the mechanical process of negotiating them. The role negotiation process is moderately demanding on the individuals involved. It requires people to confront one another openly about both task issues and personal preferences. It takes time to develop the trust and confidence to do this, and doing it may be somewhat stressful. It is a process that cannot be effectively accomplished when the startup is imminent or under way. When the participants are already under high pressure and stress, they will find the personal demands of role negotiation threatening and stressful, and they will reject the process or only participate at a superficial level. In such circumstances, the likelihood is that differences and conflicts will be inadequately worked through, and some work relationships will be strained rather than strengthened.

Success also depends on higher management's understanding the constraints it is placing on its own prerogatives by delegating some aspects of organization building and detailed organizational design. There is nothing more demotivating and discouraging to participants in this demanding and difficult work than to be told that the decisions they and their teammates have made have been changed by the hierarchy.

Finally, although team-building processes like role negotiation are not technically complex, it is useful to have someone with experience help the people who are carrying it out. When people first engage in these processes, they tend to feel a little timid and uncertain; the support of someone who knows it works and knows how to make it work is comforting and saves time.

In summary, the process of organization building fleshes out the bony skeleton of an organization chart with detailed roles and with formal and informal understandings among members as to how they are to work together. It brings the organization to life. Without attention to this process, the major startup problems will often turn out to be human and managerial, rather than technical. The use of some team-building process such as role negotiation can provide experience in working together in advance of the startup. This gives key personnel a rehearsal in working together under moderate pressure. They learn one another's "operating characteristics," establish mutual expectations, and find their places in the social network and pecking order of the new organization. When the startup begins they have built their own organization, and they are committed to make it work. They have also established and practiced ways of changing the organization when the need arises.

I regard the organization-building process as a key to startup success. For it to proceed effectively, key participants must have enough lead time on the project to engage in team-building activities. It is really impossible to plan the organization once the startup is under way. The best that can be done is muddle through. Unfortunately, because breathing life into the new organization is an organic process rather than a tangible task, it is usually overlooked and underresourced by "pragmatic" engineers and managers.

Managing and Maintaining the System

The traditional, steady-state production organization is characterized by the drive for efficiency—that is, producing the greatest economic output from the least input. To achieve this ideal, procedures are specified in detail. Operations are closely controlled and monitored; deviations are quickly detected and corrected. Such organizations tend to be hierarchical, pyramidal, and managed from the top.

The task uncertainty and change faced by the startup organization dictates that it be managed for learning and adaptation, not solely for efficiency. As pointed out above, this ideal learning organization is flatter, with more lateral communication and more overlap between roles. Practice is guided more by overall principles and the communication of experience, and less by specific rules and procedures. To avoid overload at the top, problem solving is pushed down in the organization, and higher management is therefore less closely in touch with day-to-day details of the operation.

As the focus of the organization shifts from efficiency to learning, the appropriate management style moves from directive toward facilitative management. Facilitative management styles differ from directive management not in being softer or less ultimately demanding of results, but in the ways in which high performance is fostered. Facilitative management focuses on providing the conditions under which people will be motivated and enabled to perform well. Instead of managing the startup from the top, higher management's energy is devoted to selecting and developing people, inspiring them to their best efforts, planning the organization and the startup process, assuring the flow of needed resources into the startup, managing boundaries with the parent organization, and monitoring performance against targets.

At levels below the top, a directive, "take charge" management style may still be most appropriate during the action phases of the startup; the managers who do well in operating roles in a startup are often dynamic, powerful people who enjoy the excitement, drama, and the personal responsibility of operating under emergency conditions. When such an operating style is applied from the highest level, however, it can cause trouble.

One difficult startup was made more difficult by the needs of the site manager to take personal control when things went wrong. Because the system was too complicated and fast moving for him both to stay abreast of daily events and also to perform his overall coordination job, he succeeded well at neither. The active presence of his dynamic personality and authority in the control room and in team meetings paralyzed those who had current information and expertise, and the coordination, resourcing, and boundary management functions suffered from his neglect.

By contrast, a very successful job of startup management was done by another manager who might well have been overlooked for this role because of his thoughtful, introspective, and somewhat slow-moving style. This manager consulted all interested parties before making difficult decisions. He insisted on detailed planning of the organization and of the startup procedures. He spent what his subordinates thought was an inordinate amount of time in group meetings, making sure everyone was informed and committed, and working to resolve or smooth out disagreements and conflicts between key actors. He was so receptive and attentive to advice as almost to appear insecure. His subordinates were busy with the many details of the startup, but he always seemed to have time to talk with people.

This manager facilitated the operation instead of directing it. That does not mean he was weak or soft. When conflicts surfaced, he faced them head-on and got the parties together to resolve the issues. When a key subordinate failed to produce, he replaced him. But he clearly saw his role as creating the conditions for others to get on with the job, rather than doing it himself. Thus he was able to create an effective team.

If this facilitative style is to be effective, it needs time to become the accepted norm within the startup organization. Most of the staff will probably come from production organizations that are directed and controlled from the top, and they will tend to maintain their normal habits of looking to the top for solutions and restricting communication and cooperation with their peers. But when managed closely from the top, the modified matrix will not produce the benefits claimed for it. It is vital that if such a structure is chosen, members of top management be willing and able to learn to use a more facilitative style than they normally do. Otherwise, it is probably better to try to muddle through with a more traditional organizational structure that is managed in the way most people know and expect.

An important aspect of management style in any organization is how conflicts are managed and settled. It acquires great importance in the startup organization because the nature of the work creates conflict. The normal steady-state organization has an answer for most operating problems that come up, so usually the only task conflicts that arise are those that concern proposed changes. The startup organization, operating under much greater task uncertainty, calls for first-time solutions of a correspondingly greater number of problems. The more new problems there are to be solved, the more opportunities there are for disagreement and conflict. As Horsley (1973) put it: "The ideal organization for a project . . . produces a fairly high degree of conflict over work issues. People therefore need some understanding of the nature of task conflict and personal conflict plus skills in handling each so that they might tolerate moderate amounts of conflict."

In traditional organizations, a good deal of task conflict is handled by *forcing* or by *smoothing*. *Forcing* occurs when a difference of opinion is handled by someone's using organizational authority or personal power to require others to go along with his or her decision whether they agree or not. *Smoothing*, or covering up conflict, occurs when people act as though they have no difference of opinion; they avoid actions and discussions that are certain to bring their differences into the open.

Forcing works all right when the person with the power has the best answer, or when the quality of the decision is less important than getting everyone lined up and headed in the same direction. But it should be used in moderation; otherwise, people become resentful and begin to hang back, or they sabotage decisions they disagree with.

Similarly, smoothing is an acceptable way to reduce personal wear and tear when the matter at issue does not affect the quality of system operation much, or when there is a lot of time available to work things out in indirect, roundabout ways.

However, if people are trying to come up with really good problem solutions, and if several people hold important pieces of the puzzle, then some method of conflict resolution that is both more direct and more participative than smoothing or forcing must be used. People need to learn to confront conflict: they must learn to be open about their ideas and objectives, listen to each other's ideas and talk them over, and agree to some action on the basis of a reasonable weighing up of the alternatives.

Unfortunately, in the pressure cooker of a difficult startup, many people are found wanting in the listening and reasonable weighing-up parts of this equation. They become passionately committed to their own ideas, and the high stress involved narrows their vision. It becomes difficult for them to expand their thinking to take in unfamiliar alternatives. Conflicts that began as mere differences of opinion become bitter and personal as individuals react to one another's apparent stubbornness and unwillingness to listen. After a while, relationships deteriorate, and everyone seems to become irritable and touchy. When those involved cannot find ways to solve their problems together, they either withdraw into smoothing, or they resort to forcing those issues on which they can muster enough clout to get their way. Either way, problem solving suffers.

Probably the best remedy for this condition is organization building before the startup begins, so that people establish good working relationships and personal bonds strong enough to keep them trying to solve problems openly when the pressure is on. Training in formal methods of problem solving also helps, because people get to know one another's ways of working, and because it gives them a common language and approach that can be invoked to depersonalize the disagreements that inevitably arise. Training in meeting management and in confrontative problem-solving approaches to conflict resolution are also worth considering.

When conflicts do become personal and those on both sides become stubborn and irrational, it helps for someone to intervene to bring them together. One of the functions that evolved for me in one startup was to take pairs or triads offsite for lunch to discuss their differences. The neutral ground, the healing process of eating together, and the nonpartisan concern of a third party were frequently enough to break the deadlock. It did not matter that I had no understanding of the technical issues. My ignorance made it easier for me not to be seen as taking sides.

Startup and Stress

Startups are stressful because they create a high degree of pressure for success, and they involve high costs of failure and considerable task uncertainty. Up to a point, the pressures actually enhance performance. We all perform better when the job is important and we are anxious enough about the outcome to pay attention, stay alert, and give our best. Under long continuous pressure, however, depressive reactions set in as individuals run out of reserves and the body demands withdrawal for recuperation. When high pressure becomes chronic in an organization, a pattern of stress-reducing behaviors develops that helps members cope but is dysfunctional for organizational performance. Readers familiar with startup will recognize most of them.

Activity levels remain high, but problem solving decreases. Productivity remains high on simple, routine activities, but the quality of thinking and learning deteriorates.

Time perspective decreases. People go for short-term solutions that will alleviate current pressures without taking long-term costs into account.

Perception narrows. There is a noticeable decrease in the number and variety of solutions to problems that people consider before acting. They deal with individual problems as isolated entities, without taking other, related problems into account. Problem solvers resist the introduction of new data and stop their investigations too soon.

Cooperation and helping decrease. People have enough problems of their own without worrying about someone else's.

Blaming and avoidance of responsibility increase. It becomes easier and more satisfying to criticize others than to take the risk of doing something about the problem. When risks are taken, they are more likely to be impulsive and economically unjustified. The impulsive act becomes a release from pressure and uncertainty. Even if it fails, it lowers the pressure.

Stress symptoms increase and withdrawal occurs. Some people become apathetic or discouraged; some may develop mild to severe emotional upsets or psychosomatic disorders that cause them to stay away from work.

A counterbalancing factor is the strong commitment to organizational goals and the high team spirit that frequently develop during startup. People willingly endure long hours and unpleasant working conditions, sacrificing family life and other outside interests to meet the needs of the startup. In fact, a norm of loyalty and commitment that causes people to make unnecessary sacrifices may develop. People stay on the job when they are not needed because they want to "be a part of it all." People come to feel that if they are not overworked, they are not doing their job. They refuse rest, and they show up on the job even when they are not needed—when both they and the work would benefit from their taking some time off.

The costs of stress are consistently underestimated in managers' thinking about startup. Except in a few dramatic instances—for example, when one manager began hallucinating and pushed the wrong button, or when another succumbed to a heart attack—I have not been able to convince managers of the high cost of stress. Such stress-related behaviors as slow problem solving, indecision, impulsive risk taking, and avoidance of planning tend to be typical of poor management anywhere, and who can say what is stress related and what is due to incompetence and lack of experience? But then, incompetent managers are not usually selected for key startup roles. So my money is on stress as the root cause of startlingly poor management performance in startup.

Here are some suggestions for controlling stress in startups:

Plan to the point of "overkill" in startup preparation. The best way to control stress is to prevent it from happening. The entire system and the people in it will work best if they are well prepared. The cost of exhaustive contingency planning—providing reserve human and material resources, doing a thorough job of training, and organization building—is modest compared with that of a few days saved in a highly complex and capital intensive system. Such systems probably start up best if, during preparation, they are treated as though they were "moonshots." (In a moonshot, you only get one chance to succeed!)

Use selective management pressure. Paradoxically, pressure and directive control during startup can actually reduce stress. Where there is good structure—that is, clear plans, directives, rules, and procedures—performance can be enhanced, and the stress on the individuals involved may actually be reduced. It makes people feel secure and confident to have a boss who knows exactly what to do in a tense situation (such as in the startup and testing of high-pressure systems or high-speed rotating equipment), and who makes sure that everything is done just right. By reducing the number of alternatives, providing people with the certainty that what they are doing is correct, and reducing their personal responsibility, a directive manager can lower stress levels.

However, the choice to apply directive pressure must be based on an accurate diagnosis of the problem situation. As mentioned above, in situations where structure is unclear and cannot be made clear, high pressure for performance has a negative effect. Situations that call for painstaking diagnosis and insightful problem solving, and in which the solution is needed yesterday, are exacerbated by management pressure to produce. The participants are usually highly motivated and doing their best to start with, and their problem-solving capacity is already reduced by their own sense of urgency and the knowledge that everyone is waiting for them to come up with the answer. What is needed here are support, calmness, and management action to shield the problem solvers from outside pressure and interference. Of course, if the problem does not yield, it may be necessary to provide more help or different problem solvers. But up to the point where such action is required, added pressure is unlikely to be constructive.

Provide for social support. Stress and pressure disrupt performance most when one has to bear them alone. During a startup, people are frequently brought in as spare resources, advisers, and consultants with little thought given to their integration into the organization. In my experience, people who have not been integrated into some kind of group demonstrate lower morale and effectiveness than those who belong to an organizational "home." This is another argument for bringing people in early and building teams at the outset.

Counterbalance the "commitment culture." In order to feel accepted, people work long hours and endure fatigue uncomplainingly. The norms about sacrificing personal time are probably inevitable in a cohesive startup team, but they need checks and balances. Some fairly high-status person or staff group should be given responsibility for monitoring fatigue and visible signs of stress, for directing people to take time off, and for delegating some of their work to subordinates. Members of a medical department would seem logical choices for this role, if they have enough credibility and clout. Organization consultants can also influence management in this direction.

Know techniques for reducing one's own stress. There are many relaxation and meditation techniques that people can use to reduce their own stress, and there are effective programs that teach these. Like any training that deals with deeply ingrained habits and personality patterns, however, these programs are most likely to be effective when the individual participant is highly motivated. It is also important that there be a long enough lapse of time between the training and the need for its application to enable the person to develop the new skills and habits to the point where they will work for him or her. There is of course little point in giving people training that cannot be applied because organizational norms are strongly opposed to it.

Career Development and Startup

Startups are stressful tests of persons and organizations. In any such test, some people fail to function well in the roles they have been given, either because the role was not well conceived or because the individual is not suited to its demands. Each startup probably has its share of career casualties resulting from poor planning, bad luck, or personal inadequacy.

When a person performs badly during startup, management has few options. Normally, the individual might be given additional training and/or brought along through a combination of counseling and closer supervision. Unfortunately, training with a developmental orientation (as opposed to informational or technical skills training) is not effective when the individual who receives it is under high stress. Under pressure, individuals tend to cling to familiar ways of dealing with people and problems, even though they may know those ways are dysfunctional. One chooses the "devil one knows" even if it leads to sure disaster.

In a startup, we are much more likely to be able to salvage the situation by restructuring the role or reassigning individuals than we are by developing the person. There are often some roles in a startup that hardly anyone could perform effectively, and it is much more economical (and certainly more humane) to change the role than it is to waste two or three managers before deciding that we are demanding too much of them. If we prepared for the startup by some kind of team building around mutual role definition, we would be less likely to have such "killer roles" in the organization—and even if they should crop up, we would have accepted processes and skills in place to renegotiate and modify the organization to better fit people's capacities.

The process of changing the responsibilities attached to a role is made much less traumatic and damaging to the career of an individual who is not performing well if the startup roles are defined as temporary and somewhat fluid in the first place. The more rigid the role and the more formal its definition, the greater opprobrium will be attached to having it changed. Leaving the roles somewhat flexible and open to change and renegotiation permits management to avoid black marks on the performance record of otherwise competent managers who have the bad luck to be given unpredictably punishing assignments. Because most organizations have a long memory for failure, we can keep valuable careers alive by being vague in defining startup roles.

Caveat

I must comment on one paradox about human and organizational performance during startup. Such an operation brings out team spirit, a sense of excitement and dedication, and a commitment to high organizational ideals that are often missing in the daily life of most organization members. Indeed, a difficult startup can give its participants a sense of living life to the full.

By contrast, consider what Horsley (1973) has to say about the factors important to the highly successful startup cited earlier. He identifies "overkill and control" as the "two main attributes of the startup," followed by overmanning, team building, organization development, bringing people onto the project early, contingency planning, and problem-solving training. He concludes: "In retrospect, many of these activities are bureaucratic, boring, and expensive, but not as costly as failures or delays. It is also evident that the fun and personal satisfaction of being in the thick of things, having a tremendous degree of responsibility, working long hours, and so on, are not efficient ways to start up a plant. The paradox is that, in fact, an efficient startup, without the emergence of numerous challenging technical problems will probably be slightly dull and disappointing to technologists and experts."

Could it be that so many startups are confusing, difficult, prodigal of human and material resources, frustrating, exciting, stimulating, and enjoyable because managers and engineers really like it that way?

Helping the System

Some managers call upon consultants to advise and help them in managing start-ups. I want to offer some guidelines on how consultants may be used effectively during startup, and offer some wisdom acquired from painful experience about the inappropriateness to startup of certain organization development activities that are often used with normal, steady-state organizations.

I referred earlier to production-oriented organizations as tending toward rigidity and resistance to needed change. Accordingly, many consulting techniques and methods are oriented toward "unfreezing" rigid systems, humanizing them, and making room for individual creativity and personal fulfillment. In my early startup consulting work, I carried this tool kit with me and quickly learned that it was easy to overuse it. Interventions designed to loosen or shake up rigid structures are not generally useful during a startup.

Startup consultants need skills in helping managers design, build, and manage effective structures, because the startup organization is often inadequately structured. It needs building up, not weakening. In my first startup, as my colleagues and I became more attuned to the organization's needs, we found ourselves helping the managers clarify their procedures, resolve boundary disputes, strengthen role definitions, and run meetings more crisply so that they would be able to arrive at clear-cut decisions.

Helping managers run meetings effectively is a decided contribution, because many of the managers and engineers who are attracted to startup see themselves as rugged individual contributors rather than as team members. But they can learn to run much more effective meetings if coached on such matters as building an agenda, drawing out the quiet members, testing for consensus, and delegating responsibility for implementation.

Consultants are well advised to focus on task rather than interpersonal issues during startups. Under the pressure of startup people are not very interested in interpersonal issues unless they get seriously in the way of doing the job. The technical system is too exciting, too demanding, and too threatening.

We learned a few other things that can help managers and consultants deal constructively with each other. For instance, we found that the stress of startup greatly increases managers' sensitivity to criticism, so consultants need to be less confronting and more supportive than in a more typical client/consultant relationship. They need to make finer judgments about the level of stress the system and its people are under, and match their contributions to their clients' "felt needs." When this occurs, the perceptions of the managers involved may shift—from an initial view of the consultant as "part of the problem" to a view of him or her as a problem solver.

This is not to say that startup managers do not need any help with interpersonal relationships. They do, especially where there are mismatched styles, misunderstandings, power conflicts, and petty irritations. But unless people really feel themselves seriously frustrated, and their work is suffering because of interpersonal difficulties, they are usually willing to put up with such minor inconveniences. The tendency is to shelve interpersonal concerns "for the duration," just as a nation at war ignores its internal squabbles to make common cause against the enemy.

Instead of drawing attention to interpersonal issues, the consultants' best approach is to offer services in a quiet way to those in conflict to help them resolve boundary disputes between their roles, to negotiate settlements around authority and responsibility, and to help them learn to live with others' abrasive personal styles. Whenever possible, the focus should be on the task component of a conflict, leaving the interpersonal aspect to work itself out. Thus many interpersonal conflicts are not so much resolved as they are lubricated. Such lubrication can do much to help the organization and its members get through some stressful times. I have never thought of myself as oriented to quick fixes, but after a startup begins in earnest, that is the way I tend to operate.

Last, my colleagues and I found that once a startup has begun, you are more or less stuck with the organization structure you have. You can tinker with the roles and change the people around, but any major changes in concept will seriously disrupt performance.

Managing the System's Boundaries

I have discussed the startup system as though it were more or less independent of the larger organization of which it is a part. This is a dangerous oversimplification. Relationships with that larger system are always important, and they may make or break the startup effort.

The subsystem that is starting up is often culturally deviant from the larger organization. It has high task uncertainty and is undergoing rapid change compared with the relative stability of the larger organization's long-established operations. Its members develop a short time perspective: planning deals only with the next few days, or hours, while the rest of the organization continues to think in terms of months and years. Roles and relationships are fluid and temporary in the startup: people move in, do their jobs, and move on. Often, the pressure under which people operate is much greater than that which they could or would tolerate in a job with a longer time frame. To members of the larger organization, a startup system organized according to the principles of a modified matrix and dealing with one crisis after another appears disorderly, inefficient, and difficult to control. To the startup people, the larger system may appear bureaucratic, rigid, and oriented toward tight control at the expense of high performance.

Cultural differences lead to conflict; conflict and misunderstanding often occur between a startup system and the larger organization. These are further exacerbated by the unclear role boundaries between the new or temporary startup organization and the larger system. There is seldom a consensus about the demarcation of each group's responsibility and authority, and considerable confusion develops about who is supposed to do what to whom.

When things are going well, the differences between the startup system and its organizational parent may be no more than annoying. When the startup is difficult, the conflicts become serious. They often center on needs for information and control. The parent organization needs to know what is going on, how its money is being spent, and why things are not progressing according to schedule. If the startup slips badly, it needs to know who is responsible and to determine whether additional help is needed, and whether key personnel should be replaced.

The startup organization needs the freedom to adapt, to learn from its mistakes, and to change its plan with the rapidly changing shape of its problems. It needs to protect its members from undue pressure and fear of failure so that they will be able to direct their energies to problem solving and away from a defensive protection of their positions and careers. These differing needs can create enormous conflict and misunderstanding.

Because the startup and parent organizations are different cultures and have such different needs, they perceive and react to events differently. For example, startup teams normally make quite a few mistakes. The mistakes can be regarded as experiments necessary to the process of learning. From the point of view of the parent organization, however, they are more likely to be seen as signs of incompetence and failure.

The parent organization naturally wants to help. When things are going badly, it will frequently send specialists and advisers to provide assistance. However, startup team members are often unable to use the help because they are already overloaded. Their information-processing capacity cannot cope with additional advice, suggestions, problem diagnoses, and so forth, without neglecting something they are already doing. The outsiders are viewed as "part of the problem" unless they are adept at fitting their help unobtrusively into what is already going on.

The parent organization wants to know how things are going so that it can provide help, update production plans, and make management changes, if necessary. The startup organization may tend to restrict communication, tell the parent organization what it wants to hear, and become unresponsive to requests for more information. This is partly because people are simply so busy *doing* that they can't be bothered with *reporting*. Partly it is fear of evaluation and interference. It is a major source of tension between startup and parent organizations, especially when the startup is located far from the home office. When the people at home get nervous about the lack of information, they may send emissaries; the emissaries may be treated as spies, and the cycle of mistrust escalates.

These sources of conflict cannot be eliminated, but they can be planned for and managed. Some suggestions for doing so are given below.

Select a person who has credibility in both the startup and the parent organization to act as a liaison between them. Both organizations should perceive that the liaison person has competence in and knowledge about the task at hand and is not being sent in merely because of his or her position and power. This person's role and career path should be such that he or she is strongly motivated to contribute to the success of the startup, but is not too strongly identified with the people in the startup organization. The person will have to be an effective communicator, able to influence through negotiation, persuasion, and problem solving, rather than through the use of formal authority.

Equalize authority between the connecting roles. Have the startup organization report to a manager in the parent organization who is at a level equivalent to or not much higher than that of the startup manager.

Formalize contacts with the startup organization. Negotiate in advance who will control access to the startup site and what procedures visitors must go through in order to be admitted. Legitimize the startup organization's resistance to unwanted help, and specify the conditions under which "help" will be imposed.

Clarify in advance what the tolerances are in target dates and budgets. Let startup managers know how much maneuvering room they have to get themselves out of trouble before the roof falls in. (I am sure this guideline will be strongly resisted by managers who feel that any "give" in the targets is an invitation to schedule slippage and cost overruns. Their attitude underestimates the team spirit and drive that are typical of startups.)

Establish a norm of resolving conflicts and disagreements between startup and parent organizations through confrontation, problem solving, and negotiation. Establish how and by whom differences will be resolved. Avoid the use of naked power and authority except as a last resort. This will contribute to more open communication and to mutual learning between the two systems.

Establish in advance how progress is to be communicated and by whom. Respect the channels established, and use informal communications sparingly and with discretion.

These guidelines will not totally eliminate conflict between startup and parent organizations, because such conflict is built into the cultural differences between them. However, it is important to recognize the causes of the conflict and to plan in advance to manage it through structure, systems, and management attention. Those involved in such endeavors should recognize that conflict is not primarily a function of personalities, and they should avoid finding scapegoats for everything that goes wrong.

Startups Are Learning Organizations

There is one central message in these various threads of reflection, experience, and speculation about startups. It is that the complex startup of a new organization is a special task that requires its own organizational structure, systems, staffing, and management style. Starting up a complex production or service delivery system is not simply a slightly more difficult case of running that type of system. It is a qualitatively different task.

That fundamentally different quality has to do with learning. In a complex startup the need for everyone to learn a great deal very fast hangs over and presses in upon each operation and management decision. The startup differs from the normal steady-state organization in that it is a "learning system." Its central purpose is to learn to operate, in contrast to the steady-state organization that is oriented toward control and efficiency.

Because managers are not used to thinking of production or service delivery organizations as learning systems, the accumulated experience of startup participants tends not to be fully understood or well used to improve future startup efforts. This experience does not fit well into the "mind maps" that managers have about relatively steady-state organizations. When the startup is viewed as a producing system, its values and costs are seen very differently from what they are when interpreted as part of a learning process. For example, mistakes and failures in a producing system are taken as a sign of lack of skill, ability, or judgment. A failure during a learning process is more likely to be seen as a trial or experiment. The one is judged on what it cost; the other is evaluated on the knowledge gained, *and* what the learning cost.

Learning is a qualitative endeavor; production is more quantitative. These differences in point of view can be very great indeed. Seeing a complex startup from the point of view of production can be like looking at an archeological dig from the point of view of a construction foreman: "Why are they using those little spades and brushes when we could just get a power shovel in here and clear this whole area in about half a day?" The production orientation leads to overpowering the startup problem with resources; the learning orientation leads to studying the system until the key is found that will unlock it.

Of course, neither caricature represents a balanced approach to startup. The object of the exercise is, at the end of the day, to produce, and the startup is not simply a laboratory for specialists to study technical problems. My point is simply that if the management decisions that must be made about the structure, systems, staffing, and management style of a startup are made from the point of view of creating the most productive learning system consistent with cost, then startups will progress better.

Furthermore, the organization will begin to accumulate a body of principles, knowledge, and experience about how to create and manage effective learning systems, and it can apply this to other startups. The experience acquired on each startup will be retrieved and retained because it will fit meaningfully into the developing "mind maps" managers have about building temporary learning systems. Events and processes that are not categorized crudely as "bad luck," "poor judgment," "incompetence," and the like may be understood in the light of their part in the pattern of learning and problem solving. Instead of being discarded and forgotten, these data will be used to redesign, fine tune, and operate future startup learning systems that will become much more sophisticated and powerful than those we use today. It is in the hope of stimulating the creation of these more powerful systems that this article is offered.

CHAPTER SIX

PERSONAL POWER AND INFLUENCE IN ORGANIZATION DEVELOPMENT

During most of the seventies, I was deeply involved in a project which I undertook with David Berlew to develop, refine, and deliver a training product, the Positive Power & Influence Program. During that time, my capacity for writing was almost entirely absorbed by that program and its successors, the Positive Negotiation Program and a program for training people in "long-cycle selling." I was frustrated that we were learning so much about personal power and influence and that none of it was available outside of our proprietary programs. Finally, late in the period of my involvement with the Positive Power & Influence Program, I wrote, with the assistance of my colleague and fellow "power trainer" Jim Kouzes, the piece printed here. The paper was intended to be a handout in a version of the program that I was developing for use in a workshop for consultants, and I also created my Consulting Styles Questionnaire and a set of exercises to go along with it.

I gave the workshop once or twice, but I knew by that time that running a training business was diverting me from my true path of service. I was beginning to move on to other things, and I did not publish the program. However, the American Society of Training and Development published a shortened version of the paper in *Training and Development Journal,* and it now stands as the sole public monument to a decade of my life. The energy model presented in the paper derives from work by psychoanalyst Karen Horney. I must have read her work years before, in

Source: A shortened version of this paper was coauthored with J. M. Kouzes and published as "The Power Potential of Organization Development," *Training and Development Journal,* Apr. 1980, 43–47. Reprinted here with the permission of the American Society for Training and Development.

graduate school, but I remembered nothing of it until I attended a national conference of the Association for Humanistic Psychology at Princeton in the late seventies. There, Robert Semple conducted an experiential session to demonstrate Horney's theory on how people use energy in relating to others, and I was thrilled with the model, instantly seeing how I could use it to improve on the one my colleagues and I were then using in our training programs. It was the first time I used the metaphor of *energy* to help myself and others understand interpersonal processes, and energy has been an increasingly useful and central theme in my thought and work ever since. As we leave the Age of Matter, in which our preoccupations were largely with the material world, and work more and more with mental and even spiritual powers, our mental models need to shift accordingly. The model presented in "Personal Power and Influence in Organization Development" is appropriate to our new ways of thinking and perceiving as we enter the Age of Energy (or the Age of Information, which I see as *encoded energy*).

We live in a world in which many people are chronically confused and upset about issues of power and influence. In more settled times, the stable structures of organizations and social institutions provided reliable road maps to how to get what we wanted in the world. Sometimes the road maps showed that we could not get where we wanted to go from where we started if we lacked advantages of birth, education, and connections, but at least we knew where we stood. More recently, the rapid pace of social, political, and technological changes has blocked some paths to our heart's desire and opened others up, and the map changes with bewildering rapidity. In the city where I live, Berkeley, California, a place of exquisite cultural fluidity, it is said that "everything is possible, but nothing is especially likely." I think this aphorism epitomizes a society in which people become very preoccupied with power and influence, the art of getting what we need and want from other people. Certainly this preoccupation is both recent and pervasive.

When I left the United States in 1968 to live and work in Europe, books full of hope and peace, like *The Greening of America*, were spinning messages of love to optimistic Americans. When I returned in 1976, the airport newsstands offered *Power! How to Get It, How to Use It; Winning Through Intimidation;* and *Looking Out for Number One*. Clearly, something had changed in our culture, rapidly and radically. Professionally, that change suited me well enough, for I was engaged in attempting to interest clients in the Positive Power & Influence Program which David Berlew and I had recently developed and the signs pointed to a ready market for our efforts. Personally, I was saddened, and I wished for the good old days of hope and love.

Those ambivalent feelings persist, and as I have watched both consultants and managers go through our programs, I frequently see in other OD practitioners a similar tension between a professional interest in power and a personal longing for a gentler world. I have come to suspect that, like others, I create for my clients those educational experiences that I need myself for working through my conflicts and uncertainties. I have spent an enormous amount of time during the past six or seven years in helping all kinds of people to use their personal power more effectively, and in the process, I have learned lots of fascinating things about myself and about face-to-face influence processes. The doubts and questions persist, however, and what I should like to share with colleagues is more a framework for considering the professional and personal issues around power and influence that arise for OD practitioners than a set of conclusions. Let me say at the outset that I believe part of the problem to be the tendency many of us have to limit our implicit understanding of the meaning of the word *power* in a way that makes the concept negative, causes us to experience guilt and discomfort over our own power needs and motives, and weakens us in dealing with strong clients and tough organizational issues.

Personal Versus Positional Power

We are taught to associate power with authority and position. According to the balance of our dependent and counterdependent tendencies, we are impressed or offended by the authority that attaches to high political and organizational office. Like most others, we may personalize the office, attributing to the incumbents the system power that is located there, ignoring the checks and balances that may reduce their personal impact on the flow of events to a small fraction of what it appears to be.

These days, I think that more and more people are learning to differentiate this positional power from personal power, if for no other reason than that so often positional power is insufficient to get things done in organizations and in society. Increasingly, people at all levels in organizations are having to rely on their own skills of persuasion, negotiation, personal charisma, and trust building to get things done that used to yield to a word from the right source. Partly, this is because we are working more with matrix systems and other organization forms that are not strictly hierarchical. It also seems due to the proliferation of multiple power centers in organizations and in society at large. For example:

- Project and program managers must get support and cooperation from individuals and groups over whom they have some influence but no authority.
- Many more people are in staff roles where they must influence organizational policies and procedures through persuading and negotiating with line managers who carry the authority for implementation.
- Groups and categories of employees such as women, minorities, union mem-

bers, and youth increasingly question the good faith and the legitimacy of "legitimate" authority and have the legal or collective means to resist effectively.

Of course, as consultants, we have always relied on our personal influencing skills to get things done, rather than on our mostly nonexistent positional power. Most of us have developed considerable skill in doing this, and it ought to make us feel powerful. But with notable exceptions, we do not seem as a profession to consider ourselves to be terribly potent. We seem instead to define *power* as what our more prestigious clients have and to exclude our own interpersonal skills from that definition. We differentiate personal and positional power so sharply that we lose sight of their *mutual* participation in our ability to influence or control others' thoughts, feelings, and actions.

This failure to define interpersonal skill as power limits our experience of our own potency, and it weakens us in dealing with those who possess whatever it is we do accept as the signs and trappings of power. I believe this to be part of a process by which we deny our own power and magnify that of others.

Positive and Negative Power

We are a profession characterized by an emphasis on cooperation, caring, and the introduction of broadly humanistic values into the workplace. Most of us tend to be nice people personally. We are prone to deplore strife, bickering, and the selfish, destructive, and dehumanizing uses of political and organizational power that we see so frequently in client systems. Sometimes we come to see power as our enemy.

We are often a little envious, however. We usually occupy positions that are writ small on the informal "power maps" of our organizations, and we find ourselves dealing with clients whose understanding of power and ability to manipulate it are greater than ours. Their respect is sometimes reserved for those who are strong and assertive or politically astute. We do not allow ourselves to wish to dominate or bully others, but we have good ideas and worthwhile goals that we want to achieve. Often it does seem that nice guys like us finish last, even when our professional game is not overtly competitive. We define power as not quite nice, but we are still attracted by it. Somehow our power fantasies acquire the same guilty attractions that erotic ones did before we became so liberated in the sixties.

I invite you to explore for yourself some of your own ideas and values about personal power. Consider the following situations that an OD practitioner might run into. Ask yourself how you would go about trying to achieve your objectives in the situation, and how the other person might react to your approach.

- You have spent a lot of time working out the details of a project with a client, and she has agreed to go ahead. Now she informs you that she has asked another consultant to bid on the project, and has received a significantly lower bid. She has asked you if you want to do the job at the lower figure. You need the work, but you feel your figure is a fair one.

- Your client engaged you to conduct staff training, making it clear he expected to participate as co-trainer. After the first such experience, you have concluded that his heavy-handed and insensitive style seriously blocks the learning of the participants. Tactful attempts on your part to discuss the problem have been brushed aside. You feel you cannot be professionally responsible for the work if he participates.
- You have submitted your final report on a diagnostic study for a public agency, and you are to attend a meeting at which the report will be explained and discussed with those responsible for further funding. When you pick up your copy of the report at the meeting, you discover that without informing you, the agency head has deleted all the parts of your report that were in any way critical of the operation.
- Your colleague tends to become irritable and defensive when criticized in any way. Recently, he performed badly in an important presentation of your joint project. Another presentation is coming up, and he expects to take the lead as before. You believe you could do a much better job as presenter.
- Your client is an authoritarian manager with high needs for control. She keeps pressing you to reveal details of your conversations with subordinates. So far you have avoided a direct confrontation over this, but you feel it is time to get the matter straightened out.
- Your colleague on a project is enthusiastic and optimistic in selling services to the client, but lets you do most of the work behind the scenes. When you mention this, he is contrite and promises to do better, and praises the good job you have done covering for him. You are fed up with doing most of the work, and you want to get an agreement that will stick.

These situations are what George Peabody calls "power moments." They are critical points at which one's choice of an immediate response makes the difference between winning and losing, becoming weaker or stronger, succeeding or failing in one's purposes. These situations were chosen because they fit our stereotypes about power: there is some conflict of interest that must be resolved; there is considerable potential for conflict; one or both parties is likely to experience loss or defeat as a result; and a favorable economic or organizational position may give one party an advantage over the other.

In our programs on power and influence, my colleagues and I find that these kinds of situations create conflicts for many consultants and professional helpers. They have learned to value building trust and cooperation through being supportive and constructive. Conflict situations seem to offer only negative choices: being authoritarian, aggressive, or manipulative, or failing to achieve one's goals.

Let us contrast the foregoing situations with some others. Once again, ask yourself how you would handle the situation, and how the other person(s) might react.

- You are behind on an important project report. This has happened before, and your client is angry and upset. Although you cannot produce the report when she wants it, you want to maintain the relationship and keep the client.
- You are conducting a training exercise when one of the participants becomes very critical of your conduct of the meeting and abusive of your profession. You want to get that person "on board" and get on with the work.
- In discussing a project with a potential client, you have difficulty getting him to open up about his situation and needs. He keeps the conversation on *your* background, experience, and qualifications. While you are happy to answer these questions, you need more information from him if you are to come up with a pertinent proposal.
- Although your client has been an enthusiastic supporter of your work, manpower and budgetary problems are influencing her to cut back on the project just at the point where you feel a real payoff is imminent. You want to get her to commit the resources that are needed for the project to reach "critical mass" and become self-sustaining.
- You are working with two co-leaders to plan a workshop. The others show scant respect for one another's ideas, and their disagreements are seriously interfering with the work. You want to get them to submerge their differences in the common task of creating a worthwhile and exciting learning experience for the participants.
- When you presented the results of your diagnostic study to a client group, they became discouraged and defensive about the many problems revealed by your survey. You want them to see the positive opportunities that this survey opens up to create a better working environment and a more effective organization.

These situations, too, are power moments, in which the influencing skills we consultants have make the difference between succeeding and failing in our purposes. For most consultants, these situations are considerably less threatening than the first set. They seem to call for the skills we possess: active listening, trust building, generating enthusiasm. Equally important, they are situations in which a win-win outcome is easy to imagine, if not always to achieve. We can be comfortable exercising our personal power and take guilt-free satisfaction in succeeding in our aims.

We find in our workshops on power and influence that even when consultants possess formidable skills for dealing with situations like these, they often do not think of themselves as powerful people. Neither do they see the delight they take in their successful outcomes as "being into power." They seem to have a need to split or dissociate their helping skills from their idea of power. When they do include the helping abilities as part of the spectrum of power skills, there remains a strong tendency to see these softer skills as positive, and the pushing, confronting, and negotiating skills as not very nice.

A Model of Personal Power and Influence

A useful way to look at the influence process is to consider how people use *psychological energy* with each other. When a person tries to change or affect another, something analogous to physical energy or force is involved. It takes energy to overcome the inertia of the other person and to produce movement or change. We can identify four *energy modes* in interpersonal relationships on which to base a model of influencing behaviors, and we can identify a consultant power style that is associated with each. The reader may want to rank the four energy modes according to the frequency with which she or he uses each in his or her professional practice.

• *Pushing.* When we are pushing, we direct our energy toward others in order to get them to change in some way: to start or stop doing something, to believe or think in some new way, to adopt different attitudes, to perform according to certain standards, and so on. When we are pushing, we are attempting to move, induce, teach, or control the other person by the direct application of *suggestions, orders, information, criticism, arguments, pressures, threats,* and so on.

The consultant power style that is most closely associated with pushing is that of the *Expert.* In this style the consultant diagnoses, prescribes, and directs the client in an authoritative manner.

• *Attracting.* When we are attracting, we behave so that others are drawn to join or follow us. The others experience us, our ideas, or our energy as attractive, magnetic, or exciting. They are moved to join forces with us in our projects, go along with our ideas, and share our visions and ideals. We attract by *showing enthusiasm,* by *sharing dreams and ideals,* by appealing to *common values,* and by using colorful language to evoke *exciting possibilities.*

The consultant power style associated with attracting is that of the *Visionary.* In this style, the consultant inspires and energizes clients with hopes of a better world, and creates a sense of common purpose by appeals to deeply held values and ideals. David Berlew was, I think, the first to identify this as a management style (Berlew, 1974).

• *Joining.* When we join, we add our energy to that of others so as to increase or augment it. We join with others by *encouraging,* by *expressing empathy and understanding,* by *summarizing and reflecting* their ideas and feelings, and by *expressing our willingness to cooperate and reach agreement.* When we are criticized or attacked by others, the joining response is to *accept criticism* and to *admit our deficiencies and mistakes.* When used actively, joining influences the other by selectively augmenting behaviors and tendencies of the other, thus shaping behavior without pushing.

The consultant power style associated with joining is that of the *Facilitator.* The consultant builds an atmosphere of trust, support, and personal acceptance in which clients feel free to be themselves and to take personal risks with their ideas and feelings.

- *Disengaging.* When we disengage, we avoid or deflect others' energy. We diffuse or absorb energy and thus diminish its impact. We disengage by *withdrawing or failing to respond,* by *changing the subject,* and by *using humor* to lighten the atmosphere. We *postpone or refer* matters rather than dealing with them, and we *depersonalize conflicts* by reference to rules and regulations. In this way we avoid negative involvement and conserve energy.

The consultant power style associated with disengaging is that of the *System Worker.* In this style the consultant keeps a low profile and works within the system. He or she avoids confrontation and controversy by changes of direction and adroit timing, and strives to maintain an image of legitimacy for his or her activities.

In training OD consultants, a great deal of attention is given to the development of joining skills, and for many consultants and clients the image of the consultant's role is quite close to that of the Facilitator. In fact, the more successful among us usually possess and use substantial attracting skills as well, particularly those external consultants who command very high daily fees! And many successful internal consultants are adept at the use of disengaging in dealing with threatening uses of positional power by their detractors within the organization.

In spite of these actualities, the mystique and folklore of OD centers on joining as *the* valued cluster of influence behaviors, and on the Facilitator as the modal consultant power style. As a profession, consulting attracts relatively soft people in the first place, and the training we give further sharpens their soft power skills. We discourage the more active and forceful skills, such as pushing, and our literature and training tend to ignore attracting altogether.

To summarize this diagnosis: we members of the helping professions tend to think of *power* as referring to the exercise of skills of direction and control, negotiation and bargaining, and political manipulation. We tend to associate the possession of this power with positional authority in organizations. We tend not to think of ourselves as powerful people, and we do not include skills of facilitation and consultation in our definition of power. We tend to regard those influencing skills that we associate with our idea of power as inherently negative, and to value positively our own helping skills. At the same time, many of us are becoming fascinated with power. We are alternately attracted by what we imagine we could achieve if we had it and repelled by the corruption and exploitation that we associate with its irresponsible use. Although this diagnosis does not of course apply to all of us, I believe it is sufficiently pervasive to create some consequences for our profession. We find it hard to deal with the power of position, politics, and economic pressure in a way that commands the respect of those who feel at home with these currencies. We may thereby lose our access to the spectrum of "harder" power moments that have such important consequences for the organizations and individuals we serve, and for our own success.

We over-rely on our facilitating skills, and when we find ourselves in high-pressure, conflict-laden situations, we use our soft skills in manipulative and devious ways. Because we see our facilitative approach as essentially positive, we tend to be insensitive to the negative consequences we may create.

When we occasionally find ourselves cornered and finally resort to tougher means, our insecurity and lack of skill with them frequently result in destructive aggression and overkill. Because we become fearful in conflict situations, we are unable to be "firm but fair," or to be tough and straight without becoming judgmental.

We are unable to choose and use all the constructive tools that are available to us because we define some of them as *inherently* negative. We commit the reverse of the means-ends fallacy and reject the means without consideration of the likely outcomes. We thus impoverish ourselves of the personal power we need to do our work in situations in which the positional power scales are already loaded against us.

Against this background I shall offer several propositions about personal power that have guided the work my colleagues and I have been doing in helping both managers and consultants to increase their personal power:

• What makes an influence behavior positive or negative is not whether it is hard or soft, but whether it damages and weakens, or helps and strengthens the other person(s). The toughest behaviors can be used in ways that leave the other person whole and strong. We and others can endure the pain of confrontation, conflict, and occasional defeat without being damaged or weakened thereby.

• Both hard and soft influence behaviors can be used in ways that damage and weaken others. It is easy to see how this works with the tougher styles, less so with the softer ones. Softer styles often wreak their harm through dishonesty, deviousness, and deceit, and the buildup of debilitating tensions that occurs when confrontation is continuously blocked.

• When open conflict does occur and when authority must be used to compel compliance, people who feel strong and who are confident in their ability to use tougher influence styles are the least likely to damage or weaken others. People who are upset and fearful when facing conflict and using authority tend toward destructive aggression and overkill when finally provoked to show their strength.

• We all have lots of personal power and well-developed influencing skills, otherwise we would not be able to meet our basic needs. The crucial question is whether those skills are brought into play as a *reaction* to the behavior of others (they "push our buttons"), or whether we choose and use them *intentionally*. The purpose of personal power and influence training is to change oneself from a reactive robot into a proactive human being.

• Until we learn to *choose* our behavior, influencing skill is not a central issue. We react with the responses we have learned, in the way we have learned them. When we begin to choose among the possible responses to a situation, we find that we often do not have the skills to implement the approach we have chosen. We all start our lives with a broad spectrum of personal power potential, but our development is limited and channeled by environment, personal history, and received values.

• Consultants *must* have personal power to do their work, because positional power is not well suited to building the open, trusting, and cooperative relation ships that they strive to create with their clients. As consultants, we also need to be able to command respect for our strength and competence, and inspire confidence in our visions of the future. It is when we feel strong and potent in the exercise of the broad spectrum of influence behaviors that we are best able to achieve all of these objectives. To an ever increasing degree, this proposition applies to our clients as well as to ourselves. As positional power is diffused and eroded, personal power becomes more essential, and our clients become more like us in their needs for a wide range of influence skills.

Some of these propositions may be controversial; others are almost self-evident. Taken as a group, they provide a coherent foundation for an approach to building and managing consultant-client relationships. That approach is based on *style flexibility* as a consulting ideal. It argues that in educating consultants we should honor and teach all four energy modes in their positive manifestations.

This will require that we stretch both our own and our students' capacities to wield previously underused and avoided influence behaviors. Inevitably, this will require a stretching of our interpersonal values, as we confront the internal conflicts that these ventures into hitherto rejected uses of power will produce.

I have seen consultants reap rewards for themselves and their clients through increasing the range and depth of their personal power skills. I believe these benefits are available to all who accept the challenge The cost to be paid is that we must confront and overcome two basic and pervasive fears of our own power and the power of others.

The first is the fear that our own power needs will lead us to exploit others and damage our relationships with them. The second is that if we use our personal power freely and openly, we shall provoke competition and attack from powerful people in our environment

Neither of these fears is groundless. However, the alternative to dealing directly and actively with the complexities that they evoke is to remain relatively weak in influence and turn our backs on the opportunity to contribute much that is of value.

CHAPTER SEVEN

EMPOWERMENT IN ORGANIZATIONS

Empowerment in Organizations" was originally written as part of my attempt to ground my "New Age" thinking about organizations and their future. In the early eighties, I gave a number of talks to leaders and managers, mostly in Europe, on the material contained in "Leadership and Strategy for a New Age" (Chapter Eleven). At the end of each talk, people would come up to affirm the thoughts and feelings I had shared, and to question me about how I thought my precepts might best be put into practice. I had to say, frankly, that I did not know, that they knew as much about it as I did, or more. Then, once I was alone, I would ponder the questions they had raised, frustrated by my inability to see clearly the way ahead. I now know, or believe I know, that transformation begins with desire and is sustained by strongly held intentions that shape and inform all that we do. But I wanted very much to have something to offer these good-hearted pragmatic men and women who so hoped for a program for change that they could put their hearts into. And skillful means do count for something, too, when those means flow from an enlightened vision. Otherwise, much that we do in our attempts to transform organizations simply perpetuates the status quo, because it is grounded in the very consciousness that we are endeavoring to change.

I wrote "Empowerment in Organizations" in an attempt to differentiate power from empowerment and to broaden people's thinking about the latter. In the paper, I suggest that empowerment can come through liberation of the heart, not only the will and the mind, and I offer

Source: Originally published as a monograph (Clinton, Wash.: Harrison Associates, 1985). Reprinted here with permission of Roger Harrison.

some rudimentary thoughts about "empowering technologies." I also address for
the first time the crucial role of learning,
as distinct from problem solving, in
empowering organizations and their
members and in making it possible for organizations to work in harmony with their
environments.

This paper addresses itself to the ways in which organizations empower and disempower their members. We shall consider how current "traditional" ways of organizing and managing fail to empower organization members, and we shall examine three avenues to empowerment: knowledge, will, and love.

The empowerment of organization members is of special interest at this time, simply because business organizations need all the help they can get in coping with rapid change, turbulent environments, and competitive challenges. The hope is that we can empower individuals and, at the same time, link their interests with those of the organization, thus tapping into more powerful sources of motivation than we can through the application of external rewards and sanctions.

The Difference Between Power and Empowerment

We tend to think of *power* as the ability to affect others or cause them to act, regardless of their original intent. We tend to think of *empowerment* as enhancing the ability of individuals to act for themselves, following their own motives and intentions. Empowerment thus has a connotation of "letting go of power," of giving power to another. Thus, those who are especially interested in power may be disinclined to engage in empowerment of others. The study of empowerment is the study of how people can help and facilitate one another, rather than how they can motivate, manipulate, and control each other.

Aches and Pains of Traditional Management

There are many signs and signals that all is not well in traditionally managed organizations. We have sophisticated models for planning and strategizing, yet the environment seems more out of control than ever. We have better information systems, but we do not seem to make decisions more easily or better. We have learned a lot about human relations, and we are more skillful and sophisticated about relationships, but we do not seem to have committed and happy workers. It seems as though we have to work harder and control more closely just to keep even, and improved performance is hard to come by. Perhaps the reason is that the things we traditionally do to improve performance and solve problems are actually causing the troubles we face. Then, when we take action to improve the situation, we may actually be exacerbating our difficulties.

We tend to have illusions of autonomy and control, and these make us prone to overlook the fundamental connectedness of things. Because we share a mechanical, atomistic view of the world, it is hard to live our lives in appreciation of our dependence on others and theirs on us. Similarly, our approach to organizing involves a fundamentally atomistic way of viewing things. We break tasks down into their smallest parts; we analyze; we isolate in order to solve problems. When we see something wrong, we go to fix it, often heedless of the relationships between the part we are fixing and the many other parts that it affects. We suboptimize, striving to improve the performance of the part of the organization of which we are members, not knowing and often not caring that our improved performance may create a decrement in the functioning of other parts or, indeed, of the whole. We give lip service to the idea that the whole is greater than the sum of the parts, but we do not act in our organizational or public lives as though we believe it.

Because we do not know how things we endeavor to control are connected to other things, we do not really have control. We can interfere and tinker with things, but if the processes we are dealing with are even moderately complex, we cannot really be sure of our effects on them. We can make things happen, to the extent that we dispose of substantial resources and forces, but we do not control the outcomes of our actions.

In dealing with organizational problems, then, we need to empower ourselves, and we can do it by becoming more aware of the connectedness of the events and processes with which we deal. All the approaches to empowerment that I advocate here have in common that they attempt to redress our tendencies to analyze and isolate. They do this by helping organization members become more aware of connections and then actually connect themselves to others in empowering and satisfying ways. There are three ways in which we can come to learn the connectedness of events and processes and empower ourselves and others: through knowledge, through will, and through love.

Empowerment Through Knowledge

Of course, no organization is organized solely according to one of these organizing principles. Most traditional business organizations organize around knowledge in the service of will. That is, the organization is driven from the top by leaders who are motivated to succeed through action (will). The organization develops a strategy (knowledge) through which it pursues a position of advantage in the marketplace. Internally, tasks are defined and divided in a rational or bureaucratic way (knowledge) to implement the strategy. Organization members are motivated through the application of rewards and sanctions (will) to carry out the plans of higher management.

What would happen if we started seeing connections instead of trying to understand and control things by dividing them into parts? If we are in fact disempowered by our failure to apprehend the connections among events and therefore do not know the probable effects of our actions, then it must be empowering to learn the connections and, thus, to have things come out as we intend. As it turns out, however, learning connections among events is a task which cannot be undertaken from the top, by the top, and for the top of the organization. It requires the involvement and hence the empowerment of organization members at middle and lower levels as well.

Knowledge and Strategy

If we start seeing connections, our idea of strategy will change also. Traditionally, strategy is thought of as the search for advantage in the marketplace. That orientation tends to focus the gaze of the organization narrowly on markets and competitors, in a will-dominated thrust to overcome obstacles and achieve victory over opponents. Most business organizations are impatient of and unresponsive to unsolicited feedback from such stakeholders as government, stockholders, consumer and conservation groups, and the like, viewing their contributions as irrelevant at best, and interfering and obstructing at worst. Strategy is decided internally by the leaders of the organization and is a reflection of their perceptions and intentions, driven by their personal motivations.

An alternative point of view, however, is to consider the organization not as an individual entity, but as a part of a living system that includes all the environment whether considered "relevant" or not. According to such a view, living systems thrive when they are in balance with their environment, receiving what they need to live from it and giving back what is required to maintain the ecosystem. Living systems, living organizations, thrive only when they adapt and harmonize with their environment so that they are "in balance," nurtured and supported by the ecosystem and nurturing the larger whole in turn.

The consequence of an ecological view of strategy is not that a business organization with this view would avoid competition; it is rather that it would become much more sensitive to inputs and other messages from the environment, seeking those messages rather than endeavoring to screen them out. In becoming receptive to inputs, the organization would discover or "be given" its strategy by the larger system of which it is a part. Instead of strategy being a search for advantage, strategy becomes a search for meaning and purpose.

In other words, the focus of strategy formation shifts toward the interface between the organization and its environment, where the inputs and messages from the larger system are monitored and interpreted. Strategy thus comes to involve many more people at lower levels of the organization than the top. With participation in the strategy-making (or, as we should say, strategy-discovering) process comes an increase in participation and empowerment for many organization members.

Knowledge from Failure

When we seek to become empowered through knowledge we must recognize the value of failure and the poverty of success. In most business organizations, success (meeting goals, having intended results) is the signal to move on to something else. At most, we learn from our successes that such-and-such a series of actions led to a desired result. We are unlikely to learn the richer skein of connections that links our particular outcome to the circumstances surrounding our achievement. Conversely, when we fail, we are often punished, sometimes by being removed from the situation in which we failed. Naturally, we tend to conceal failure from others and to avoid looking at it ourselves.

Innovative organizations are beginning to encourage people to take risks and to fail, because failure is rich with opportunities for learning about connections. When something you try does not work, you go back and look harder at the situation, searching out influences which you may have overlooked and which may be creating your unintended results. If you look hard enough, you may end up completely reevaluating your understanding of the situation. To permit and encourage failure and to insist on its publication and examination by all concerned leads to increased knowledge of connections among events and processes, knowledge that empowers organization members in the performance of their tasks.

Knowledge and Organizational Objectives

Basically, there are two ways to integrate the activities of individuals in the service of organizational objectives: control systems and appreciation systems. In a control system, the people at the top get as much information as they can, decide what is to be done, and then tell those lower down what to do and how to do it. For example, such control systems as management information systems (MIS) are used by higher management in traditional organizations to serve the needs of top management in running the business. Each person (or group) is then responsible for optimizing his or her own performance of the received objectives, without regard to whether or not what he or she is doing optimizes the performance of the organization as a whole.

In an appreciation system, the organization members all have a good grasp of the mission and general direction which is desired, and they keep in close touch with each other as they do their work. The idea is then for each person (or group) to see how his or her efforts are meshing with the efforts of others and to adjust his or her behavior so as to optimize the performance of the whole. This more organic approach redistributes information, decision making, direction and control of performance much more widely in the organization, and is thus greatly empowering for organization members. For this more organic process a different kind of information system is used, which we may call the management appreciation system (MAS). The MAS collects information from all organization members and distributes it to all, permitting them to "appreciate" or understand what is happening to the system as a whole. Bulletin boards, teleconferencing, system flowcharts, and newspapers are all examples of more or less rudimentary management appreciation systems. They empower their users.*

Empowerment Through Will

There is currently a good deal of discussion of vision, values, and purpose as motivators of organization members. Visionary leadership exercised through charismatic leaders has the capacity to empower members through their identification with a (possibly noble) purpose larger than the self. In joining voluntarily with others in pursuit of a cherished vision, each experiences himself or herself as larger, stronger, and hence enhanced. The individual then willingly makes personal sacrifices for the good of the whole.

Organizational alignment, a process of developing a shared understanding and acceptance of the organization's purpose and a shared vision of the desired future, can result in self-motivation through commitment. Guided by the common vision, organization members are empowered to direct their own efforts. The role of higher management becomes that of facilitator rather than controller and director, providing resources to self-motivated people who are pursuing the common vision. The aligned organization has great power to evoke voluntary commitment, dedication, and sacrifice on the part of its members. Many businesses now pursue alignment, though relatively few yet achieve it. In all nations, aligned organizations have always arisen in the military during wartime, particularly among elite groups such as the U.S. Marines, the British Special Forces, or formerly, the Nazi SS units.

Empowerment Through Love

Most recent discussion regarding leadership and empowerment in organizations has centered on empowerment through will and knowledge, or more accurately, knowledge in the service of will. The current candidate for the most exciting new organizational concept appears to be the aligned organization, which I have just

---

*Since this paper was written, a number of management appreciation technologies have achieved prominence in organization development, notably, dialogue, appreciative inquiry, and future search.

described, or its nearly identical cousin, the high-performing system. I am some-what suspicious of the aligned organization because of its potential for exploiting, or "taking over," organization members, and because of its prevalence in war and the military. The aligned organization is not noted for its sensitivity to nuances of communication from its environment, nor for its harmony and adaptation to the ecosystems of which it is a part. Rather, it tends to be aggressive and "dai-monic" in its proclivity for expanding beyond all limits which are imposed from the outside. In other words, it appears to need checks and balances, and these are not provided from within.

Attunement

An alternative to alignment is attunement, which can provide empowerment through resonance and responsiveness. As organization alignment is the expression of knowledge in the service of will, so attunement may be thought of as the expression of knowledge in the service of love. Love is a powerful motivating force in people's lives, and anyone who has experienced love knows that it can be personally empowering in the sense that loving makes us feel larger, stronger, and more able to give to others. However, we tend to be suspicious of the workings of love in business organizations, and so it tends to go underground or stay in the closet. But by love, I simply mean the strong feelings of affection and positive value which people experience toward the work they do, the products they create, their organization, their co-workers, and the customers they serve.

When we experience love, we tend to become both responsive and responsible. We care, and we take care of the things, organizations, and people we love. We seek closeness, and we attune or harmonize ourselves with those to whom we feel close.

Egalitarian Networks

In the attuned organization, empowerment and integration of effort take place through communication and mutual responsiveness. People feel good when they are attuned or "in harmony," and so they seek to know others' needs and intentions and to come to agreement or consensus about what is to be done and how it is to be done. Attunement thus requires a good deal of personal face-to-face communication and discussion of values and needs at deeper levels than is common in many businesses. Such communication takes a lot of time but has the advantage that, after a while, people know each other very well and are able to act in harmony without discussion.

Support and Caring

The attuned organization tends to do a superb job of taking care of the people in it and of developing the "ties that bind." It is sensitive to people's personal needs and devotes time and resources to meeting them. People feel good about being part of the organization and are willing to give their time and energy to maintain and support it.

The downside of attunement is that people may become so concerned about one another's feelings that they cannot confront important differences. Such differences may have to do with policies and values or with ways and means. They may be differences in ability, motivation, and task contribution. Just as the aligned organization may exploit the individual and sacrifice him or her for the mission of the whole, so the attuned organization may sacrifice task performance for the needs of the individual through an inability to set limits and standards or to say no.

Clearly, alignment and attunement are in some ways polar opposites and need to be kept in balance for an organization and its members to get full value from both processes. Alignment gives a sense of external mission, of work to be done in the world, of purposes greater than any one person's individual concerns. Attunement keeps the individual safe and taken care of, maintains people and their relationships, and heals people and relationships when they are hurt. Both alignment and attunement are needed, but in most business organizations, we have far more conscious acceptance and valuing of alignment and of the power of will than we do of attunement and the workings of love.

Technologies for Empowerment

Most of the methods and techniques of modern management have been developed to run the bureaucracies in which most of us work. They are designed to permit those at the top of organizations to get the information, make the plans, and exercise the controls needed to run things. These methods and techniques are empowering for those at the top but not for organization members in general.

With the increasing turbulence and complexity of the environments in which most organizations exist, the rapid pace of change, and the difficulty of controlling a workforce that values its own autonomy, it is becoming harder and harder to run organizations from the top. It becomes necessary to empower the other ranks, and to find ways of integrating their semiautonomous activities. New and unusual techniques and methods are needed that can accomplish these purposes. Many such techniques are known but are not yet widely used. My colleague Juanita Brown calls them "transformational technologies." Some of them are listed in the paragraphs that follow.

Investigative technologies. By this term is meant a host of methods that have been devised in very expensive research and development activities, complex construction projects, plant startups, and the like, to help those involved understand and communicate the complex events and processes with which they are involved. Some of these methods are the following:

- Journal- and log-keeping of personal and technical events and changes
- System mapping, participated in by all members, not just the management
- Iterative decision making, to get everyone's input in reaching consensus
- Discussion arenas, in which conflicting parties can explain but not fight
- Debriefing, in which all participants try to figure out what happened
- "Premortems," in which we imagine what could possibly go wrong

Technologies of excellence. This term denotes the methods and techniques used by managers in the companies identified as "excellent" by Peters and Waterman in their now famous book, *In Search of Excellence* (1982). Many of the methods used by the managers they studied and interviewed are empowering for employees, such as the following:

- Making contact with customers; listening to customers; following up complaints
- Managing by walking around; listening to employees
- Dedicating top management to an overriding ideal: for example, quality
- Holding celebrations and rituals to recognize employees' achievements
- Building trust in place of controls
- Encouraging initiative and risk taking; rewarding failure
- Promoting informality and elimination of executive perks
- Using champions for implementation and "skunkworks" for innovation
- Choosing facilitative management: keeping bureaucrats off the backs of producers

Evocative technologies. This term refers to techniques and methods that may be thought by some to be a bit "way out," but that seem to offer promise if they can be introduced in ways that do not overly upset "the troops." The following are examples:

- Encouraging myths, legends, tales, and stories
- Using music in meetings to set mood and climate
- Joining in values clarification activities
- Holding visioning exercises: imaging the desired future
- Using "affirmations" to create desired results through "intentionality"
- Using group graphics to capture the feelings and values in meetings
- Engaging in group meditation, similar to Quaker meetings, for attunement
- Providing training in aikido, to learn harmonious ways of dealing with conflict

In my view, then, the now increasingly common notion of empowerment as alignment to common purpose is too limited. The vision of the aligned organization is too narrow, and its pursuit of success can be so frantic that it becomes disconnected from external reality and from human values. Balanced empowerment occurs not only at the level of will, but at the levels of knowledge and love. By learning together, we are all empowered, and not just to do more. The significant power of learning together is that it enables us to transcend the endless cycle of problem solving in which we are all caught in modern organizations, where each solution leads inevitably to a host of unintended consequences that become new problems.

When we add love to the equation and move beyond competition to cooperation, we empower one another through mutual support. We are stronger because we are no longer alone. We add to our skills and resources the talents of our compatriots. We do not have to protect ourselves from the political machinations of our co-workers. We can take more risks because we know there will be others to pick up the torch if we should stumble and fall. We experience less stress, and we stay healthier.

I strongly believe that in the future, organizations will find that empowerment through love and learning will provide the true competitive edge. It will not only be a time of achievement, but we shall reclaim our enjoyment of one another in the workplace.

CHAPTER EIGHT

IMPLEMENTING TRANSITION TO A MORE RESPONSIVE ORGANIZATION

In the mid eighties, I received a call from an internal consultant in an electric power utility who had read my paper, "Organization Culture and Quality of Service" (see Chapter Twelve). He told me the utility was about to engage in a major effort to become less bureaucratic, closer to its customers, and more service oriented. He was interested in knowing what I could do for the company and asked for a proposal right away. I normally have a bias against writing proposals, partly because they almost invariably require that one commit to a plan of action in advance of doing an adequate diagnosis. In my experience, they also tend to separate the client and the consultant, substituting a contract for the development of trust and joint planning. In this case, however, the project sounded like just the sort of thing I wanted to do, so I not only wrote the proposal but put a lot of work into it.

I did not know much about electric utilities, so I enlisted the aid of my friend Flo Hoylman, who was for many years an internal consultant with Pacific Gas & Electric Company. She and her colleagues had been conducting some very innovative work on reorganizing the delivery of service and empowering the service providers, and she generously made available to me much of their learning and experience. I borrowed liberally from what had worked for the Pacific Gas & Electric people, and after three days of very intensive work, I came up with the proposal which was to become "Implementing Transition to a More Responsive Organization." I wish I could say that I got the job and implemented the proposal as written,

---

Source: Originally published as *Managing Transition to a More Responsive Organization* (Clinton, Wash.: Harrison Associates, 1986). Reprinted here with permission of Roger Harrison.

with great success. All I can claim is that I got the job. The vicissitudes of the actual client engagement are described in *Consultant's Journey: A Dance of Work and Spirit* (1995).

What I still like about this piece is the way I was able to frame the work to be done within key dimensions that have to be worked with in any large-systems change process. I especially like it as a proposal, because it walks the line between giving vague generalities and irresponsibly committing oneself to concrete actions in advance of adequate diagnosis. I would reprint it here for its value as a model proposal alone.

In my subsequent work, I have carried forward the idea of employing a design team and a steering group (not, of course, my own invention). If I were redoing the proposal, I would emphasize even more strongly the importance of client involvement, and I would propose that a multi-level design team carry out a thorough diagnosis of the service issues prior to any further action. In this situation, as happens in many consulting situations, the clients

had already decided on an organizational solution to their customer service problems before inviting proposals from consultants. The clients' solution was to reorganize the customer service function, and they wanted help in implementing it. Had I a choice, I would much prefer to coach an internal team to carry out a diagnosis of the service delivery systems prior to making any decisions about reorganization. As part of the diagnosis, I would endeavor to conduct some large-group event (for example, future search; see Weisbord and others, 1993) which would involve all the stakeholders of the customer service function in assessing current functioning, working out an agreed strategic approach, and becoming part of the solutions. As time passes, I emphasize more and more strongly the importance of clients' assuming as much responsibility for doing as much of the actual work as possible. I place myself in the role of coach, expert adviser, and intuitive counselor. I am no longer interested in "running" change projects, instead preferring "running with" my clients.

This paper presents a point of view about and an approach to managing the transition to an organization dedicated to a higher degree of service and customer orientation. It was originally prepared for an organization that had made the decision to merge "customer service" and "operations" and was prepared to undertake a major systems change effort. The approach I proposed to that client may be of interest to others who are engaged in similar efforts.

Balancing Polarities: An Approach to Transition Management

The excellent organization is balanced between opposites: loose versus tight controls; the thrust for change versus the conservation of what we have; participation versus direction from the top. That balance is not a passive average but rather a dynamic tension between opposites. Each of the opposite poles is alive and in action in the thriving organization. It is when the tension is resolved that the organization becomes either lax and flabby, or rigid and constrained.

In approaching organization change, there are polarities to be managed, and we are most effective when we keep the opposites alive, strong, and in a dynamic rather than static equilibrium. Vitality does not come from "getting it right," but from being constantly aware of the imbalances and continually adjusting them.

Some polarities are particularly important and require special attention when an organization is undergoing major change:

Leadership from the transition team versus participation: articulating a vision from the center and keeping the effort on track, while remaining open and responsive to inputs on policy and practice from organization members at all levels.

Learning versus performing: keeping productivity and quality high, while embracing the risk and failure which lead to acquiring new competencies for the organization.

Planning versus experimenting: designing changes and charting the path ahead to reduce risk, while involving the organization in the action which tests concepts and expands experience.

Internal focus versus external focus: having confidence in the expertise and acquired wisdom of the organization in its business, while remaining open to needs and wants of customers which may challenge our experience and upset our priorities.

Embracing the future versus treasuring the past: improving the organization and reaching toward a vision of excellence while celebrating the achievements of the organization-as-it-is, and preserving its competencies and accumulated experience.

Doing it quickly versus doing it right: keeping up the momentum and energy of the vision while following a strategy of working in pace with the readiness of the organization and testing new concepts thoroughly before they are applied "across the board."

In any organization, especially one that is changing rapidly, there exists a tendency to move toward one pole or the other, and the art of managing change is that of finding the right balance for each stage of the process.

The most effective leaders are continuously "in touch" with their organizations, sensing and diagnosing the state of balance. During periods of change, when the complexity of the organization increases exponentially, and the demands on managers for decision and action become especially heavy, the sensing and diagnosing process needs to become more self-conscious. The consultant supplements the manager by providing an extra set of eyes and ears. The consultant brings a point of view which is attuned to the health and maintenance of the organization as a living system, while the manager may be more oriented to the organization as a producer of results.

Now that I have outlined some aspects of the change that may require particular attention to organizational balance during the transition, I will describe each one briefly, together with approaches to rebalancing. ("Transition team," in the following paragraphs, refers to the leaders responsible for the transition, plus their staff.)

Leadership from the Transition Team Versus Participation at All Levels

It is easy for the vision to become the sole property of the transition team, creating a "them-against-us" mentality. Other polarities which may well occur are: top management plus rank and file versus middle management and supervision and field managers versus central staff. Such polarities are natural and can be productive, but they need to be managed from the start by applying the "principle of over-inclusion" to the design of early events and activities.

For example, the transition team members need to get out and about early in the process, before they do their planning and before their vision of the process coalesces, listening actively to the views, advice, and concerns of others about service. Such informal contacts should be supplemented by more formal organization diagnosis, a process of "organizational mapping" in which the structures, procedures, and practices whereby service is currently delivered to the customer are carefully studied, along with the attitudes, values, and priorities that support current practice. Such an organizational map is essential to planning the change, and the process of building it permits the involvement and sampling of opinion of many people.

People learn and change best when they come to their own conclusions. Opportunities for managers to meet with panels of customers about service can be valuable both for anchoring the service plan in the real needs and wants of the customers and also for convincing the company's people of the urgency of the change. Similarly, visits to other companies in the industry to discover how they are improving service can be assigned to different teams, rather than confining this work to members of the transition team. The point is to include as many people as feasible in learning about service, and then to provide forums for them to talk service with others. Consultants can play a role in the design and in the facilitation of such "consciousness-raising" events and processes.

Learning Versus Performing

While change goes on, the organization needs to continue to produce and deliver products and services. "Business as usual" is as important as the change. The usual way of business is to focus on and reward results, to minimize risk and uncertainty, and in most organizations, to punish failure.

Maximizing learning, however, requires that experimentation and risk taking be encouraged and that failure be embraced for the learning that it brings. For example, most of us tend to downplay or even to cover up our failures. When we are learning, however, we need to follow the motto that "if a thing is worth doing, it's worth doing badly at first." Furthermore, we need publicly to discuss and diagnose our failures so that we and others may learn from them.

In order to foster the relatively sloppy, experimental processes of learning and still maintain a focus on productivity and results, it is useful to create a "parallel learning organization." All who are concerned with the change participate in the parallel organization, and they have concurrent roles in the business-as-usual system as well. The parallel organization consists of all the structures needed to plan, prepare for, and carry out the change: study groups; project teams; organization, systems, and work flow planning activities; steering and advisory committees; test sites; and so on.

The advantage of the self-conscious demarcation is that it lends itself to the creation of a dual standard, an arrangement whereby people play by the "transition rules" when they are in the parallel organization, and by the "operating rules" when they are back at their normal jobs.

The transition rules favor risk, experimentation, open discussion of failure, and putting understanding before action. The operating rules favor decisiveness, avoidance of risk and failure, and reliability of results. Conflict and confusion of priorities are reduced by clarifying the need for both ways of operating in an organization in transition, and making the differences explicit.

Planning Versus Experimenting

The task of maintaining the balance between planning and experimenting differs between technical and bureaucratic organizations. Groups that tend towards the bureaucratic side tend to plan forever and be reluctant to act. Those toward the technical side prefer to jump in without much debate and work things out as they go along (this is also true of market-oriented people).

In most organizations, the tendency is toward action, and people tend to become impatient with detailed organizational planning once the goal has been clearly identified. My stance is to endeavor to balance the action bias by invoking the same attention to detail in planning organizational changes that managers use in planning complex technical projects. The principles are the same (for example, contingency planning based on Murphy's Law). It is a case of applying the same rationality to organizational change that engineers apply to creating technical systems.

First and foremost, that means understanding the situation you are trying to change before you jump in. It means mapping the organization with respect to service, and it means updating the map as the change unfolds. It means sharing that map with the key players and making it real enough that it becomes a guide to thought and action. One way to do that, as mentioned above, is to involve organization members in the mapping process. Instead of doing the diagnostic work themselves, the consultants advise and train the organization members to carry out the work. Then the organization members own and believe the results.

Another way of maintaining the balance is to follow the adage of action research: "No research without action, and no action without research." Any action plan needs a way to retrieve and make sense of the results, and we need to plan how the results so obtained can become influential in the design of the next application.

Internal Versus External Focus

The balance here is between staying close to the customer and remaining responsive to the changing demands of the environment, on the one hand, and keeping the focus and thrust of one's own vision, on the other. The leaders of the company feel they have "got the message" from customers, and they feel good about their decision to take serious action to improve service. If, however, a company has over the years tended to decide what is good for its customers, it can easily fall into a paternal approach to service improvement. Having decided to make a change, the organization may come rather quickly to a decision as to what the customers need, and then proceed along those lines with relatively little continuing dialogue with those it is endeavoring to serve.

In such a situation, balancing means keeping open the dialogue with customers and accentuating it, even after change is underway. This can be done by means of relatively formal customer panels. It can also be done by instituting the retrieval of information that employees and managers collect informally in their interactions with people in the community. It can take the form of managers speaking at local groups, such as Rotary and the chamber of commerce, and reporting back on the reception they experienced.

The particular settings and processes are not crucial. What is important is to institute company-supported activities that emphasize service. Such activities should involve people at all levels in interacting with the customers and reporting back and discussing what they found out. Provision needs to be made for the information gained to be fed back into the ongoing decision-making processes of the transition, so that these processes continue to be in touch with changing attitudes and opinions in the communities served by the company.

Embracing the Future Versus Treasuring the Past

Some organizations remain encapsulated in dreams of past glory while they become more and more out of touch with current reality. Others innovate feverishly, obsessed by change for change's sake, and discarding the accumulated experience and wisdom of the past in favor of whatever fad or fancy catches their imagination or promises a quick fix. Maintaining balance means questioning current practice and experimenting with newer and better ways, while celebrating and cherishing the values and traditions that have led to past achievements. At times when there is a strong push for change in the organization, it is especially important not to focus exclusively on weaknesses, but to "grow from strength."

Put in a service context, the question becomes, "How can you expect people to give good service unless they feel good about themselves, and about the company they work for?" How can the skills, the experiences, and the wisdom of the past be turned to mastering the challenges of the future?

It is easy for people involved in serious efforts to improve things to come to believe that changing means giving up parts of themselves which they have previously treasured. For example, people might come to feel that instead of doing their jobs quickly, effectively, and at minimum cost, they are now going to be distracted from their work by the needs and demands of others in the name of "service."

It becomes important that people not see the change as "giving up" anything but rather as using their skills, abilities, and experience in new ways. The Japanese, for example, did not change from being producers of junk to being the best in the world in quality manufacture by giving up anything. Instead, they used their ability to learn from others. Formerly, that ability led to their producing inferior copies of others' products, but when the same ability was turned to learning from American engineers how to control quality, they quickly became winners.

In the same way, qualities of resourcefulness, technical inventiveness, and dedication to doing it right can be turned to the question, "How do we give the customers what they most want and need?" Success becomes a matter of defining the task in terms which the company's employees can see as using talents and resources they already have.

Managing this aspect of the change is partly a matter of the attitudes of the transition managers. In addition, it is possible to design and conduct activities and programs which make people feel good about themselves and focus their attention on the theme of service in a positive rather than a remedial way.

One such approach is to create a program based on the idea, "Catch Us Doing Something Right," from *The One Minute Manager* (Blanchard and Johnson, 1982). It would involve offering small rewards to customers and employees alike for "turning in" employees who have been "caught" giving particularly good service. Periodic celebrations would honor those employees. In addition, groups of employees and managers would study those examples in order to determine what sorts of behaviors are viewed by customers as good service.

They would then take the analysis one step further, asking: "How can we free ourselves and our fellow employees to do these things even more often than we do now? What kinds of systems, procedures, and more important, structures, would best release our natural inclinations to be of service?"

Such a study group becomes a more positive variation of the quality circle. Its orientation is described as "positive" because it is not problem oriented; instead, it is directed toward freeing people to do the good jobs and give the level of service which it is assumed they naturally want to do, but which they may not be free to do under the current arrangements.

Doing It Quickly Versus Doing It Right

This last balance issue has to do with the need to produce results balanced against the need of the organization and its people to learn from experience, to experiment, and to change their approach based on their failures and successes. The question of balance arises when managers have a good idea or have seen the results of a successful experiment, and they then decide to implement it across the organization. Often, the wider implementation spoils what was a promising beginning, turning what could have been a real change of purpose and values into just another bureaucratic exercise.

Such errors are made when managers regard the organization as more mechanically responsive than it is. Because the organization works well in its normal operating state, and because relatively small adjustments and improvements are well tolerated (what is called "first-order learning"), it is assumed that large changes involving attitudes, values, and that elusive "culture" will also yield to direction. In fact, organizations are not machines but living systems with a life of their own, a truth which it is easy to forget in large, somewhat impersonal systems. Consultants like myself often spend considerable time and energy trying to slow the change process, not because we do not like to see things change but because of the need for people to learn, and to experiment with and internalize, new ways of thinking, feeling, and doing. Usually, this effort to keep things moving at an "organic" rather than "mechanical" pace means proceeding by means of small steps, documenting and thoroughly analyzing new experiences, and planning ahead.

This is not to say that energy, determination, and a sense of urgency on the part of higher management are not of value to the change. Indeed, no major organizational changes can take place without strong leadership. But the encouraging leadership of a shepherd or teacher seems better suited to the learning process than that of the general officer, since it allows people the time and the space to find their own way toward the overall goal.

The Role of the External Consultant

The following are roles and services that a consultant (internal as well as external) can provide to help an organization make the transition to a service orientation.

Consult with Higher Management on the Strategy for Change

- Help design the structures and the special roles required, to the end that policy making, communication, and decision making about the change take place in timely fashion.
- Think through questions of participation: who should be consulted, and at what stages in the process; how the company can ensure that those with useful resources are involved and those whose commitment is required for success are on board.

Help Design and Implement Individual and Organizational Learning Processes

"Learning" here refers to all the changes in knowledge, attitudes, and understanding required to create and implement the change. To me, the concept of learning is at the heart of a successful transition. It is a much broader concept than "training," including:

- Creating a common vision and statement of purposes and goals
- Mapping in detail the current service delivery system
- Planning new work flow patterns and new patterns of cooperation between functional groupings
- Developing the attitudes and habits of thought characteristic of a "service culture"
- Designing, implementing, and researching organizational experiments, for example, test sites and service delivery systems

Consult to Change Managers on Their Leadership Roles and Styles

- Teach participative management, as opposed to isolating and/or authoritarian styles.
- Coach managers to manage by walking about (MBWA).
- Consult on how to invite feedback and handle it nondefensively.

Work with Groups Involved in the Transition

- Conduct team building: role negotiation, visioning, goal setting.
- Help with interface issues such as establishing coordination and communication, negotiating authority and responsibility, managing conflict.

Research and Document the Transition

- Retrieve and conceptualize what is learned; prepare reports and presentations to increase awareness and understanding of service delivery processes; communicate what such processes require of individuals and the organization in the way of resources, learning, and change.

- Help integrate new knowledge into the developing transition process: consult on modifying strategy, structures, and processes in accordance with experience.

Assist in Thinking Through Systems Changes Implied by the Change in Organizational Focus

- Reevaluate career paths.
- Redesign reward systems.
- Conduct management development and training.

Stay "Tuned In" on an Ongoing Basis

- Help transition managers diagnose the dynamic balance of the organization on the polarities described above.
- Help sense the state of health of the organization.

Structures and Activities for Change

When an organization plans a major change, a transition organization parallel to the normal organization must be designed, staffed, and managed. A skeleton description of such an organization, along with a sequence of transition activities, is given below. (Many of the ideas in this section derive from Flo Hoylman, of the Pacific Gas & Electric Company, and from Linda Ackerman, who generously made their experience and that of their colleagues available to me.)

Steering Group

Managers representing all the line and staff functions in the company are chosen to "advise and consent" to the activities of the transition team and the design team. The function of this steering group is to oversee the transition. It addresses policy regarding the relationship between the transition activities and the ongoing productive activities of the company, and it approves overall strategy for the transition.

As I conceive of the steering group, it reviews activities of the transition and design teams but does not carry out any project work itself. The members are active in using their contacts and their influence to assist and smooth the transition process.

The steering group will oversee policy and implementation issues in such areas as:

- Developing a statement of corporate purpose and values, which embodies the service concept and which can be embraced by all line and staff functions

- Selecting and recruiting of key transition team members, and getting them assigned to the transition team as a matter of high priority
- Formulating the philosophy of the change, particularly with regard to time and timing (for example, whether to focus on assessing needs and planning in advance, or to step into the change and work out the difficulties as they arise)
- Assessing resources needed by the transition team, and helping to free up those resources from the functions which own them
- Establishing of criteria for selection of test sites
- Planning and managing structural changes needed to support the service concept, particularly those changes which move the locus of decision making and control closer to the customer
- Educating functional management as to the changes in work flow, priorities, job descriptions, and rewards that are needed for the change to be more than just cosmetic
- Advising the transition team as to the politics of the change, and helping to ease the conflicts and dislocations of the change by using their influence
- Recognizing service-oriented achievements and publicizing them throughout the company.
- Helping to create a "service consciousness" by constantly talking about service

Transition Team

The transition team is the key planning and action group, led by the transition manager, a person respected not only in his or her own function but in those others with which he or she must deal. The transition manager will likely need the full-time help of a couple of first rate upper-middle managers (one highly experienced in field operations, and one with planning and organization design expertise) plus a couple of high-level clerical/secretarial people. Internal and external consultants complete the team.

Design Team

The design team is composed of respected and experienced managers representing the functions involved in the change. Where the steering group is concerned with policy and oversees the action, the design team actively works together with the transition team to develop the concepts, structures, and procedures needed to implement the change. Specifically, it is active in:

- Working with the steering group to create a statement of purpose and values, a mission statement that embodies the essence of the service concept.
- Developing the conceptual design of the field service organization: the structures, the linkages to the rest of the organization, the relationships to customers, the work flow concepts, the staffing patterns, the rewards.

Test Sites

These are field operations that are selected for early implementation of the service concept. There may be two or three, selected to represent different operating environments. The test sites are regarded as operating experiments, selected for their commitment as well as for their "face validity" (meaning that they would be seen by others as representative of the field organization as a whole).

Project Teams

Project teams assist the transition team in implementing the transition. They have overlapping membership with the design team, but add new faces, partly to bring specialized expertise to bear and partly to spread experience and commitment to the change throughout the organization. One project team will assist in implementing the test sites, and one will be active in implementing the redesign of the field organization.

A Transition Scenario

Phase 1: Orientation and Diagnosis (Four to Six Months)

The transition team studies the organization and its environment, working with customer panels and interviewing people at all levels, both in the field and in the central organization. A map of the organization is created, showing how the current organization delivers service and what facilitates or blocks optimum service to the customer.

Organization mapping also includes an assessment of the field and central organizations' readiness for change, with identification of nodes of support and indifference/resistance.

Visits are made to other companies in the industry in order to retrieve their experience in similar transitions.

The steering group is formed, and its members participate in the identification and recruitment of the design team.

Large-group meetings are held to publicize the service concept, and to recognize (celebrate) service achievements of the organization-as-it-is. A process is inaugurated for involving employees and customers in identifying examples of good service, for example, "Catch Us Doing Something Right." Employee study groups are formed to help in identifying aids and barriers to service in the current organization.

The design team is identified and briefed as to its responsibilities.

Phase 2: Service Concept Design (Three to Four Months)

The design team is educated on the information gathered during Phase 1. Using inputs from the meetings of management and employees conducted in Phase 1, the design team drafts a statement of purpose embodying the service concept. The draft statement is discussed with managers and employees in the field, so that when it is presented to the steering group for approval, the statement is broadly representative of the field organization.

Phase 3: Selection and Preparation of Test Sites (Three to Four Months)

The transition team visits the field to identify candidates for test sites. Interest and commitment are assessed on the part of key people in each potential site. The design team makes recommendations to the steering group; test sites are selected.

Phase 4: Test Site Planning (Six to Eight Months)

The test project team is selected, to link with the functions, help with planning the test, and facilitate needed changes in systems, procedures, work flow, and regulations during the test.

The transition team works with test sites, assisted by members of the test project team, to build commitment and understanding of the service concept. Together, they plan implementation, personnel changes and physical changes needed, work flow, and organization restructuring.

This is a time at which participation at all levels of the test sites is encouraged and heavy emphasis is laid on contingency planning: thinking through what can go wrong and planning how to cope.

Phase 5: Implementation of Test Sites (Nine to Twelve Months)

This is a time of tinkering with management systems, work simplification, linkages, and information flow. It is also a time of continuous documentation and evaluation of progress by the transition team together with the test project team. This phase is complete when the test sites are out of the startup phase, and enough has been learned to be confident of implementing further sites effectively.

During this phase, continuous feedback from the test sites informs and influences the ongoing design of the new field organization (Phase 5a).

Phase 5a: Designing the Field Organization (Five to Six Months)

This phase is concurrent with Phase 5. It involves the restructuring of the field organization in accordance with the service concept, so that at the conclusion of the test site implementation and evaluation phase, the remainder of the organization is ready to move toward implementation. The transition team, assisted by the field reorganization project team, works through the design process, under the eye of the steering group.

Continuous discussion and liaison with both the field and the functional organization is necessary during this phase, so that the planning process gains commitment and the planners do not become isolated from the rest of the organization.

Phase 6: Continuation and Consolidation

During the continuation phase, additional sites are converted to the new structures, systems, and procedures, using the experience of the test sites. Phase 6 lasts until the entire field organization is operating according to the new concepts.

A major task will be the reworking of job descriptions, job evaluations, and the compensation system. In order to fully implement the service concepts, it is necessary to embody them in the personnel systems. In most organizations, this takes much longer and is more difficult than expected. The process is facilitated by having made sure during previous phases that key personnel managers have been intimately involved in the work of the design team, the test project team, and the field reorganization project team.

A Transition Checklist

Here is a summary of guidelines or things to pay attention to in managing the transition process, put in the form of a checklist. This list owes a great deal to the contributions of Flo Hoylman and her colleagues.

1. The bringing together of different functions in the field in order to simplify the customer's relationships with the company will produce a need for more generalists in management, and for cross-training of present staff. In planning, give thought to designing a cross-functional development program in each unit affected by the change.

2. It is very important to get the design concept as clear as possible, and to continue to clarify and communicate the concept as the change develops. If people are clear about the concepts, they will know what to do. If not, they will have to use trial and error and will look "stupid" in the mistakes they make.

3. Review policy and practice on the delegation of authority: the more responsive organization is the one where authority is exercised at lower levels.

4. Plan and negotiate changes in line/staff relationships—staff will probably move more into an advising, consulting, and monitoring role as the line becomes more accountable and has more authority for their entire operation. Such changes

follow on the concept of a service culture because it is hard to be responsive if you do not have authority and accountability.

5. It is important to involve the personnel function early on in planning and advising about job changes. Personnel is often overlooked by line managers eager to get on with the work, and then things get difficult later when changes in job levels and reward structures become necessary.

6. There is a need to conceptualize and actively model the "customer advocacy" role and values. The active representing of the customer by the line from the bottom up is the only way that real changes in service will take place. The new priorities should impact the selection and promotion process. In particular, when selecting key field unit people, insist on demonstrated customer advocacy.

A customer advocacy attitude is also important in support services and administrative functions, and its development needs to be planned for among these persons who do not normally deal directly with customers.

7. Make a communication plan for each stage of the transition: what to communicate, when, and how. Give consideration to how to use the grapevine for communication! Remember that too much communication is better than too little because people usually do not "hear" a message until it begins to impact them.

8. Use two-way communication: give time for questions and discussion and, where feasible, employee input. But do not ask for employee input unless you intend to use it and do get back to employees with a response to input you asked for!

9. In designing each concrete change, prepare an impact analysis: a list of whom the change will affect, and how. This will turn up a list of obstacles and barriers to the change which can be planned for in advance. The impact analysis serves as contingency planning for the change.

10. In implementing new ways of working, each field unit should document (map) step-by-step processes for new business, before changing the work flow. This (a) assures that no critical steps are lost; (b) points the way to opportunities for streamlining; and (c) identifies where communication between functional specialties or work units need improvement.

11. The "mapping" process should document what customer contacts are made: who makes them and about what. Plan how to maintain customer contact during the transition. (In addition to the task benefits of the mapping process, it enhances work unit morale and commitment to implementation by involving the employees who know the current system and by recognizing and respecting their input.)

12. When a company undergoes a transition, the managers involved actually have two full-time jobs. Time management becomes critical, and the speed of the change will affect personal stress as well as the effectiveness of the business-as-usual part. Giving more time for the transition is beneficial in reducing stress and keeping the unit's performance up. There is little point in advertising a change towards greater service, and then reducing effectiveness by changing too rapidly.

13. The transition implies the building of new working teams. New teams

need to work self-consciously on their own startup (they can use help from consultants in this work). They should plan how people will work together: what each member needs from the others and needs to give to the others to get his or her job done in new or changed roles.

14. Team startup planning includes: managing the integration of the transition and the daily business; building an implementation plan that everyone understands and commits to; putting an early warning system in place and monitoring it; and learning more about leadership styles. Some useful activities are:

> Team startup meetings for planning, facilitated by a consultant.
>
> Role clarification: writing down each person's tasks, responsibilities and authority, and agreeing on them; renegotiating roles as experience is gained.

There is one last guideline, perhaps the most important of all. Expect the unexpected! Expect the change to take longer than you think it will, probably by a factor of two or three. You can plan for all the mechanical things that have to be done, but an organization is an organism, not a machine. It will grow and change at its own rate, just as a plant or tree does. You can water and fertilize the organism, but if the desired change is in the direction of empowerment and willing acceptance of responsibility, it cannot be forced.

Expect that performance and morale will become worse before they become better. The change will require upsetting systems and structures that people know and are able to make work, and it will take time to learn the new. No one knows how much learning has been involved in making the current system work, because it took place over a long period of time, slowly. Much that has been learned has to be unlearned, and unlearning is the hardest learning of all.

Expect that people will resist changes they said they wanted, because change is upsetting and because people in a bureaucratic organization have learned to be afraid of failure. People say that they want freedom, but most shrink from the freedom to make mistakes and be criticized for them.

Expect you will get little credit for what you have brought into being. When people really learn new ways of working and make them successful, they feel they have done it themselves. And they will have!

CHAPTER NINE

HOW TO FOCUS PERSONAL ENERGY WITH ORGANIZATIONAL MISSION STATEMENTS

How to Focus Personal Energy with Organizational Mission Statements" was originally written as a discussion piece for the design team in the electric utility project referred to in the introduction to "Implementing Transition to a More Responsive Organization" (Chapter Eight). The paper was written during three intensive days in the hotel room I was occupying in New York, having accompanied my wife, Diana, on one of her business trips to that city. (I wrote it on one of the first laptop computers to come on the market, a Radio Shack Model 100. It was immensely liberating to have this machine, which enabled me to write anywhere, any time!)

Like "Strategy Guidelines for an Internal Organization Development Unit" (Chapter Three) the present paper took form as a teaching intervention for a group of clients. In this case, I hoped to inspire the group to craft their own mission statement for the change project in which we were engaged, and then to energize the rest of the organization with their vision. The paper was read and understood, but the intervention was too little and too late. I consoled myself that at least I got a publishable paper out of the work and was paid for doing the writing—something that has been rare in my experience!

Much of the content of the paper derives from a long conversation I had with Bill Kutz, whom I met in San Diego in 1986 at a meeting of the Association for Humanistic Psychology. Bill had developed a new art form in the way he worked with clients to create a mission statement. He was very generous with his experiences and articulate about why he did what he

Source: Originally published as "Harnessing Personal Energy: How Companies Can Inspire Employees," in *Organizational Dynamics,* 1987, *16*(2), 4–20. Reprinted here with permission of Roger Harrison.

did, and I was eager to learn as much as I could from him. In my paper, I integrated my organization culture model into Bill's work on visioning and mission development, and I identified the criteria that need to be met for an organization to "manage by vision." I also described a key process by which differing goals, visions, and values become one amalgam under the heat and pressure of a mission development workshop. I call this process *alchemical,* because the heat and pressure of differences are applied to the group within the crucible of an intensive off-site meet-

ing. When the workshop is successful, and it often is, the bonding and commitment to the vision that takes place between members can be extremely strong. Unfortunately, as I later found in a major project with an R&D company (Harrison, 1995, Chapter Seven), this bonding can isolate the participants from the rest of the organization, and the vision can become a kind of living tomb.

I have since also incorporated my ideas into a workbook that teams can use to create a vision and a mission statement (Harrison, 1988).

In discussions of organizational productivity and high performance, great importance is often given to the development of vision, purpose, and a sense of mission. When leaders and consultants endeavor to focus the organization on a single mission, it quickly becomes apparent that the organization culture plays a central role in success or failure. Some organization cultures lend themselves to developing a sense of mission and purpose, while in others the effort seems to become enmeshed in political maneuvering and the conflicting claims of widely differing goals.

The purpose of this paper is to integrate current thinking and practice in helping organizations create effective mission statements with my work in conceptualizing and assessing organization cultures (Harrison, 1972b [Chapter Ten]; Harrison, 1975; Harrison and Stokes, 1986 [1992]; Harrison, 1987b [Chapter Twelve]). I will show how differing organization cultures handle a central issue that is fundamental to any design or redesign of an organization: How is each person's personal energy to be released, mobilized, and focused in the service of the organization and its stakeholders?

We shall see how certain organization cultures are able to release and access a greater proportion of their members' personal energy, and we shall explore the central role of a shared sense of mission and purpose in focusing this energy. We shall then set out some guidelines from experience in working with organizations to develop powerful and effective mission statements.

(My thinking about organizational missions and mission statements owes a great deal to the generosity of William Kutz in describing the work he and his partner, Dick Barnett, do with organizations.)

The Issue of Personal Energy

Why emphasize *personal energy*? Because that is the difference between a committed, high-energy organization and one where people do the minimum to get by. Personal energy is a shorthand term for all the capabilities which an individual brings to the workplace every day and which he or she can choose to commit or withhold.

A key to understanding organizational design is to be aware that each individual has complete control over the choice of whether and how much to commit his or her personal energy to the organization. That the choice may in some organizations be influenced by severe pressures and heavy coercion does not mean it ceases to be a choice. To see choice in action in any organization, simply compare the degree of effort and commitment put in by the highest and lowest performing members!

If the issue of personal energy is in fact so central in organizations, we may wonder why people are not talking about it all the time. I believe the issue is in fact at the heart of those interminable discussions of how to motivate employees, which are so often a part of conferences and management training courses. In daily organization life, the issue is less often addressed specifically, because the answers are implicit in the structures and processes of the organization. They are "the way things are around here."

When we want to change the way things are, the way we endeavor to tap into people's personal energy is critical to the success or failure of the change. We need to become much more aware, perceptive, and planful about this process than we normally are when we are doing business as usual. If we do not plan systematically how we will enlist the personal energy of organization members, our efforts will run into unexpected difficulties, and the cost of achieving our aims will be much greater than it should be.

This paper presents a way of thinking about how personal energy is accessed, channeled, and applied in traditional organizations, and compares it with how this is done in "high-performing" organizations. We shall see that the key to the difference is the development of a shared sense of mission and purpose, combined with unusually high trust between leaders and members of the organization.

Traditional Approaches to Accessing Personal Energy

The history of the development of modern business and industry is the story of creative managers and technical experts dedicated to minimizing the influence of workers' choices about committing their personal energy at work. The strategy for productivity improvement has been to develop technology and to design systems which require minimum personal contribution from workers, and then to ensure that they do put in that minimum by providing multiple layers of supervision and tight systems for controlling cost, quality, and output.

Like most good strategies, this one paid off handsomely at first, but the returns have diminished with continued application. Currently, most industries are engaged in self-defeating circular processes, both in the factory and in the office. Both white-collar and blue-collar workers respond to boring, repetitive tasks and close supervision by withdrawing effort and attention from the work. Quality and productivity suffer accordingly. Management responds by managing more closely and automating the work as much as possible. Because the workers feel more closely controlled and have less responsibility, they feel less committed, and they withdraw their commitment and attention from the work. And so the cycle goes around again.

Richard Walton, a pioneering student of the new approaches to productivity, says this "control strategy" to managing the workforce is obsolete. He asserts that any approach "that assumes low employee commitment and that is designed to produce reliable if not outstanding performance simply cannot match the standards of excellence set by world-class competitors" (Walton, 1985, p. 79).

The dilemma is that we cannot design work systems which compel outstanding performance. Systems which focus on control actually discourage outstanding performance by reducing opportunities for the exercise of initiative, creativity, and individual contributions to the work. These are qualities prized in our culture, and therefore they can be found in abundance in American workers. It is ironic that we increasingly design the exercise of those qualities out of our work systems.

As Jack Sherwood (1988, p. 8) has pointed out, our way of thinking about costs and resources leads us into the self-defeating circle of designing demotivating jobs. As he puts it, "If we think that people are principally a variable cost, which can almost always be reduced, then we are most likely to look to changes in technology or in work methods (resulting in less labor input) as ways to control costs." He goes on to say that in order to break the cycle, "the first step is to let go of the idea that our future lies exclusively in ever more highly developed technology. We need to accept modifications in technology which offer more central roles for people in using and managing the production process. . . . If we view people both as resources and as collaborators in the competitive marketplace, then the question becomes how can everyone's commitment, competence, and intelligence be aligned behind the company's purpose!"

This question is equivalent to asking, How can we release people's personal energy in the service of the organization? Sherwood, in common with other writers who have worked with the design and redesign of production plants, sees the answer in work design which balances the emphasis on technology with an emphasis on people.

In my own practice with R&D organizations, financial service companies, and customer service systems, I have tended to focus on the less tangible aspects of the question, addressing the culture change process involved in moving from high control/low commitment to its opposite, an organization culture dedicated to performance and service. I see the articulation of the organization's mission as a key to that culture change.

I want to construct a model that will explain the key role of the organization's mission in mobilizing personal energy. My concept was stimulated by the thinking of Robert Terry of the University of Minnesota (personal communication, 1986), but I have taken liberties with Terry's model that he would probably not accept. My version identifies three aspects of an organization which we can manage, manipulate, mess about with, or otherwise change:

MISSION

STRUCTURES

RESOURCES

Resources are the assets that are deployed to pursue the purposes of the organization: equipment, facilities, services, "headcount," and the money to acquire these things.

Structure consists of the organization's arrangements whereby its resources are deployed. Structure is seen in organization charts, job descriptions, work and information systems, budgets and accounting methods, regulations, policies, and operating manuals. Because structure controls access to resources and the ways they may be deployed, it is placed above resources in the hierarchy.

Mission refers to the aim of the organization, its purpose or reason for being. The mission leaves its tracks (but may not actually be present) in statements of organizational goals and in corporate philosophy statements. It may be more accurately inferred from the priorities and guidelines that organization members follow in their daily decision making. In a well-designed organization, the structures are subordinate to and are designed to achieve the mission, so we place it at the top of our hierarchy.

There is another universal element in organizations that I shall treat differently than Terry does. That final ingredient is *people*. It is not people considered as resources or headcount, however. I refer to people considered as human beings, possessed of those qualities of mind, heart, and spirit we think of as distinctively human when we talk about ourselves.

Organizations are people-pursuing-goals-together, and we can represent this connection between *people* and *mission* in a revised hierarchy.

PEOPLE ↔ MISSION

STRUCTURES

RESOURCES

To see what all this has to do with accessing personal energy in organizations, let us consider some typical, and some not so typical, organizations.

The Power-Oriented Organization: Using Resources to Control Personal Energy

A talented and energetic entrepreneur owns a business employing several other people. The employees serve as "hands, ears, and eyes" for the entrepreneur, doing his or her bidding in return for money. They serve at the entrepreneur's pleasure. They do what is required to keep their jobs, which basically means being useful to the boss, meeting his or her needs, and staying on his or her "good side." The organization's "mission" is whatever the boss wants, and that may change from day to day. Some of the more dependent employees who were hired in the early days of the firm develop deep loyalty to the person of the boss, identify with him or her, and serve faithfully. As the organization grows, those useful, loyal employees are given supervisory authority over others. With increasing size, few of the employees have a personal relationship with the founder but deal instead with his or her loyal lieutenants. Some of the employees try in their turn to be useful to their bosses and to put themselves in line for the best jobs and for eventual promotion. The majority do not compete. They do whatever is required to keep their jobs, and not much more. Some may resent being subject to "naked power," and they sometimes commit little acts of neglect or sabotage in retaliation. In public and on the surface, however, they are compliant and subservient to those above them in the hierarchy. Each level is kept "in line" by the control over resources exercised by the level above. Some of the resources used to control workers' behavior are pay, perquisites and privileges, the intrinsic interest and ease of the assigned work, the threat of being fired, praise and blame from the boss, and so on. Coordination and integration of individuals' efforts are the responsibility of the boss. Quality and output are managed by personal supervision and the application of appropriate rewards and punishments by the boss.

I have written elsewhere about this type of organization culture as "power oriented" (Harrison, 1972b [Chapter Ten]; Harrison and Stokes, 1986 [1992]; Harrison, 1987b [Chapter Twelve]). It is characterized by dependency and lack of initiative on the part of subordinates. Compliance is more highly valued than performance. The boss's resources are overused, and everyone else's are underused. People do what they are told, and when they are not told, they try to guess what the boss would want them to do. When they are not sure or are afraid of doing the wrong thing, they wait. At times of change, when unexpected or novel situations develop, the organization may become paralyzed. The boss is too busy to tell everyone what to do, and the people are too afraid, dependent, uninformed, or otherwise unwilling to take the initiative.

The power-oriented organization is good at multiplying the hands available to carry out the ideas of the boss, but it usually fails to mobilize more than a small fraction of the personal energy people have available for work.

Typically, the "pure" power-oriented organization does not outlast its entrepreneurial founder. However, the power orientation can be found in mixed or modified form in many organizations which are no longer entrepreneurial. Usually, the occasion for a change in such a culture is some crisis in the organization's life: rapid expansion, a merger, or a change in the technologies or markets with which the organization is involved. The next scenario shows how this might happen.

The Role-Oriented Organization: Using Structures to Channel Personal Energy

Eventually the founder/owner of the organization described above has a heart attack and sells the company to another firm in the same industry. The new owners want to manage the business at a distance, and they make this possible by setting up a system of regulations, guidelines, and policies which direct how the business is to be managed. Each position is minutely described and is evaluated according to the abilities and experience required to do the job. Criteria for determining the adequacy of job performance are specified, and systems are set up to monitor results. In the new organization, the scope of the work, the performance requirements, and the limits of one's authority are clearly defined. When one accepts a job in the new organization, one agrees to perform the prescribed duties, and the organization agrees that one can keep the job as long as one performs it adequately and as long as that job needs doing.

Instead of close personal supervision, the procedures for doing each job are now made part of a system in which the work is divided into a number of jobs that perform certain operations on materials or on information and pass them along to the next job in line. Everyone knows what they are supposed to do, so long as the system is working. They need only refer to supervision when an exception comes up, something which the system is not designed to handle. How high up in the organization the decision has to be made depends on the amount of money involved and the extent of the deviation from established policy which is required to solve the problem.

I have written about this type of organization culture as "role oriented" (Harrison, 1972b [Chapter Ten]; Harrison 1987b [Chapter Twelve]). We all recognize it as a bureaucracy, where personal control by the boss has been replaced by the impersonal control of structures and agreements. A job or position in the organization represents an agreement between the job holder and the organization, in which the employee undertakes to provide certain services and the organization agrees to certain levels of compensation and terms and conditions of work.

Instead of the bosses having to run around telling people what to do, people's behaviors and interactions are controlled by established structures, systems, and procedures which are written down in codes and manuals or made part of a computer program. The organization still must monitor performance to be sure that the agreements about the work are being kept, but once people know their work and get into the habit of doing it, it generally runs along pretty smoothly until the system has to be changed.

People are less dependent in such an organization. In a well-designed and professionally managed system, one has the security of knowing what is expected, and one is protected by established policies and procedures against abuse of authority by the boss. Of course, the system is ultimately backed up by the power to control resources, to reward for performance, and to punish for failure to perform. But the arbitrary exercise of power that can create a rule of fear and a hotbed of political intrigue in the power-oriented culture is at least limited and ameliorated. People have some rights; they know what they are; and they know where they stand.

Most of the organizations we know, live with, and work in are some combination of power oriented and role oriented, with the leaning in larger organizations being toward the bureaucratic mode. In such organizations, resources are controlled by the system, not by individuals. Even CEOs may be severely limited in the changes they can carry out. Each part of the organization has a sphere of influence and power which is embodied in the structure, and the structure cannot be changed without at least a measure of "due process."

In the role-oriented organization, jobs can be designed with varying degrees of latitude, so that differences in ability, expertise, and experience can be allowed for. People in our culture generally work more willingly under agreements than they do under capricious authority. At higher levels of the organization, the jobs are frequently designed to give considerable latitude and room for initiative, and this encourages people to bring a greater fraction of their personal energy to the job.

The trouble with the role-oriented organization is that it overuses the talents and personal energies of designers and underuses those of doers. Much management ingenuity and creativity go into the design and development of structures and systems, which then limit and frustrate the ingenuity and initiative of the people who are charged with carrying out the work. When the latter perceive the system as irrational, ineffectual, or just plain "stupid," their frustration eventually turns to resignation and apathy. They withdraw their personal energy from the work and become "nine to fivers" or "bureaucrats." When this happens, managers and technicians usually design the jobs into smaller units, install tighter controls, and generally reduce the scope and latitude which individuals have for making a unique contribution. Workers' frustrations with the system increase; they withdraw more of their personal energy; managers institute tighter controls; and the cycle continues.

The role-oriented organization thrives in stable situations, especially where its size, economic power, or favorable regulatory status permits it to control its markets and sources of supply to a high degree. Thus the railroads, airlines, banks, insurance companies, electric utilities, and the oil industry have all known periods which have favored their development as giant bureaucracies. During those periods, stability and economies of scale favor large, role-oriented organizations.

We are now in a period of turbulence in markets, technology, regulatory climate, and the world economic system, which places great strain on bureaucracies. Part of that strain stems from the structures, systems, and procedures that are assets during more stable periods.

Like any complex life form, the more specialized and rigid an organization is, the more vulnerable it is to "unusual" conditions. In the case of the role-oriented organization, the vulnerability arises from the way the organization processes information about exceptions to the rules.

Consider the typical pyramidal bureaucracy, divided into separate functions such as sales, distribution, production, and the like, and locating the authority to make exceptions to the rules at higher levels of the organization. When the environment of the organization undergoes rapid change, the information on which decisions have to be taken is generated at the "skin" of the organization (the base of the pyramid), where people are in contact with the environment: customers, suppliers, government inspectors, and so on.

In order to take account of changed environmental conditions, the information generated at the base of the pyramid has to travel up the chain of command. During times when systems are working fairly well and change is gradual, this is no great problem. When the pace of change heats up (for example, foreign competition, an energy crisis, the deregulation of an industry, an instability in world financial markets), then the number of exceptions moving up the chain of command and requiring attention from higher management increases rapidly. The pyramidal structure of bureaucratic organizations forces the information into narrower channels as it goes higher, so those who have the authority to change the rules and make decisions on exceptions quickly find themselves swamped with work.

The communication channels in a bureaucracy are easily overloaded because of this funnel effect, delaying needed changes in the design of the system. People at the bottom of the pyramid become frustrated and cynical; they can see the changes that are needed, and they cannot understand why their superiors do not act. People in middle management (those usually responsible for adjusting the system) are overworked and chronically behind in making the decisions and system changes that are required. In addition, because of the overloading of upward communication channels, the information decision makers receive and on which they base their actions is incomplete, out of date, and frequently distorted.

Members of higher management, seeing the mess, become in their turn frustrated with what appears to them to be the slow response and self-protective entrenchment of middle management and frequently move to bypass the middle and manage the workers directly. Since their information is also distorted and out of date, their assumption of control often fails to improve the situation markedly.

Thus, the rational structures and procedures, which serve the organization's purposes so well in stable times, become massive barriers to adaptation and change in more turbulent situations. Although it is in some ways an improvement over the power-oriented organization, the role-oriented organization also fails fully to release and apply the personal energy of its members for reasons which are inherent in its nature. In summary:

> People contribute more willingly by agreement than they do by fear. Contractual arrangements, however, not only set a lower limit on performance: they thrust forward the question, What's in it for me? when one considers contributing beyond the terms of the contract. Thus, for many organization members in bureaucracies, there seems little point in putting out more than the mediocre level of performance which we have come to think of as typical in most large organizations.

> The very structures and systems which are a strength in the organization in stable environments become barriers to change. When organization members are frustrated by the organization from making the contribution of which they are capable, they withdraw personal energy and become apathetic and cynical.

If we wish to release more fully the personal energy of organization members, we must consider not only how people in the organization are motivated (a common and constant concern in power- and role-oriented organizations) but how they motivate themselves. This is where the organization's sense of mission and purpose become important.

The Achievement Culture: Evoking Personal Energy Through Mission

Both the power-oriented and the role-oriented organization cultures foster external motivation. Organization members contribute their personal energy in return for rewards. In the case of the power culture, the rewards are administered personally, by more powerful individuals who control the organization's resources. In the role-oriented culture, the rewards come through transactions between the individual and the organization: so much salary for this or that job, opportunities for promotion linked to qualification and time in grade, and the like.

The relationship between the individual and the source of rewards is essentially dependent: the individual's behavior is manipulated by the combination of incentives and threats that the organization applies. The organization has available to it that fraction of each person's personal energy which he or she is willing to commit in return for such extrinsic rewards as the organization offers.

In fact, of course, many people like their work, believe they are making a worthwhile contribution to society, and enjoy their interactions with colleagues or customers. These are intrinsic rewards which are qualitative rather than quantitative and which arise from the nature of the work and its associations. For the most part, organizations are not designed to provide these intrinsic satisfactions. They arise incidentally, or through the occupational and job choices that people make on their own.

Some organizational situations seem to provide a positive climate for these intrinsic satisfactions. People who have worked in such diverse situations as new business and new plant startups, nuclear test shots, intensive care units, and political and community organizing campaigns, report that these work cultures can provide deep personal satisfactions and evoke personal commitment of a high order. These high-energy work situations are described by participants as follows:

- The work situation engages the total person.
- The values which people experience in the work transcend personal advantage. A quality of altruism is evoked which is personally satisfying to everyone involved. People feel they are working for something bigger than themselves.
- People give their all, working long hours without complaint. They may willingly sacrifice their family and social lives to the demands of the work.
- People supervise themselves, seeking out what needs to be done without direction from above.
- There is high morale and a sense of camaraderie, of "all for one and one for all." There is close teamwork, and the group frequently feels itself to be elite or special.
- There is a sense of urgency; people live "at the edge," putting out high energy for long periods of time. They may become addicted to stress.

Such high-energy experiences normally last for a few months, possibly a few years. Then people burn out, or the work system stabilizes and becomes more routine and bureaucratic. However, some organizations manage to maintain this "culture of commitment" over long periods of time. I have, for example, worked with an R&D organization which has operated in such a mode for more than forty years. People seem to burn out after about ten years in the really high intensity jobs. They then move to less stressful positions (management roles, for example!) and are replaced by "fresh troops."

Sparked initially by stories of high levels of worker commitment in Japanese companies, there has been a great deal of interest in the last few years in high-performing organizations, work systems in which some variant of the "commitment culture" can be created and sustained on an ongoing basis. Peters and Waterman's work on "excellent companies" (1982) has focused interest on the sense of mission that leaders of such companies are said to communicate to all levels of their organizations. Here are some of the qualities which seem to be characteristic of organizations which sustain high performance over a period of time:

- There is a clearly understood mission which is articulated at the highest level of the organization.
- The mission is emphasized and reinforced by everything members of higher management do: the decisions they make about where money is spent; the questions they ask; the topics they discuss in public presentations and meetings with employees; the amount of time spent in meetings on various topics; the reasons for rewarding, promoting, demoting, and firing people; where they make field visits and what they look at; and so on.
- The mission is stated in terms which are unambiguous, easy to understand, and difficult to argue about. There is a dominant value which is held to be more important than any other in the organization. People know that they cannot go far wrong so long as they are pursuing that value with sincerity and integrity.
- The value embedded in the mission is one which is larger than mere profit or growth. In pursuing it, organization members can experience themselves as making a contribution to society, as well as gaining something for the company.

There are additional qualities that seem to characterize organizations that are "mission driven," organizations whose cultures I call "achievement oriented," which have also been characterized as "aligned" (Harrison, 1987b [Chapter Twelve]; Kiefer and Senge, 1984).

- The organization is more egalitarian than most. Employees are treated like willing contributors. Those at lower levels are empowered to make decisions which in other organizations are reserved for those in supervision and middle management.
- Communication channels are open, both laterally and vertically. It is easy to be heard if you have an idea or suggestion.
- Failure is viewed as a learning experience, rather than as a sign of personal inadequacy. The organization empowers people to learn and innovate better ways to pursue the mission by making resources available, and by reducing the stigma and the career penalties for unsuccessful experiments.
- People do not argue much about the mission but only about how to achieve it. People who do not share the basic values and commitments of the organization are made to feel uncomfortable and usually leave.
- People do argue a lot about how best to achieve the mission. Positional authority does not shut off discussion or curb the expression of employees' ideas.
- People are given effective authority in accordance with their ability to contribute to the mission. Neither the red tape of the bureaucracy nor the privileges and status of a power elite count for as much as ability and contribution in making decisions about who does what.

In short, the achievement-oriented or aligned organization uses the mission to attract and release the personal energy of its members in pursuit of common goals. This is in marked contrast to the power- and role-oriented organizations which rely on the application of rewards and punishment and on impersonal systems and structures to control and constrain their members. The mission serves to focus the personal energy of individuals. Because contributions are freely given in response to commitment to a shared purpose, people willingly give more to the organization, and the whole prospers accordingly.

None of this means that structures and systems are not necessary in the achievement-oriented organization, or that the allocation and distribution of resources are not still problems to be solved. What it does mean is that the systems and structures serve the mission, rather than the reverse.

Such an organization begins with a sense of mission and purpose, clarifies that sense, and then goes on to create structures and assemble resources to make the mission manifest in the world. Thus, people know why they are there and what they are working for, and they know that anything which does not serve the mission is open to question.

In contrast, in the power-oriented organization, access to resources is the key to making things happen, and in such organizations, the "golden rule" is sometimes restated as, "he who has the gold, rules." In role-oriented organizations, the systems and structures are often more powerful than people, and certainly more powerful than the mission. In such organizations it is often true that "you can't beat the system." So, a mission-driven organization is far different in its character than the organizations that most of us have experienced during most of our working lives.

There is a downside to the achievement-oriented organization. Members of high-performing organizations with a strong sense of mission frequently exploit themselves in the service of the organization's purpose, to the detriment of their own quality of life. If the single-minded pursuit of achievement is not balanced by attention to taking care of the people, the people will suffer and may eventually burn out. Over time, even the most enthusiastic contributors may come to realize that they are valued only for their contribution to the organization's mission, as they see others used up and then cast aside.

The pure achievement-oriented organization has the deficiencies of its strengths. It is frequently under-organized for the work it has to do, relying on high motivation to overcome deficiencies in structures, systems, and planning. It evokes and directs enthusiasm and commitment, but it may not have a heart. The people and their needs are subordinate to the organization's mission and its needs. After a time, people realize this and may begin to mistrust the organization. At that point, they begin to look out for themselves, instead of giving their all to the task. Alternatively, the members may remain steadfast in their commitment, but they suffer high levels of stress, physically (for example, cardiovascular diseases) or socially (for example, high divorce rates).

Here are some quotations from interviews with people in a high-tech achievement-oriented organization where hard work and long hours substitute for planning and where the thrust for achievement has nearly completely driven out concern for people's needs. Many people still drive themselves willingly, but others are beginning to ask if it is worth it.

> "The lack of proper planning drives me nuts."
>
> "We're too busy doing to plan objectively."
>
> "There's bound to be organizational problems with tight resources and tight delivery schedules; things are bound to get tense. People who are attracted to our company like this climate—others would go loony here. Pressure is keen, and you have to compromise on quality sometimes."
>
> "People are beginning to burn out; you can't keep putting the pressure on people. We must turn down our expectations of the magic we can perform and do more realistic scheduling."
>
> "One of the craziest things about the company is the founders' ninety-hour weeks. My best people look like garbage only putting in sixty-hour weeks."
>
> "I'm worried about the health of some of the people; bad things are happening to the founders and old timers."
>
> "Everyone needs positive feedback; even those who show outside self-confidence still like to hear the words. It's hard for many to say those words; . . . it's easier to criticize than to stroke."

In the long term, you have to take care of the people if you expect them to take care of the organization's mission. This is a point frequently overlooked in discussions of high-performing organizations. It is why in outlining a hierarchy of organizational characteristics, I put People↔Mission at the top. Let us examine the qualities of an organization that gives a high priority to meeting the needs of its people.

The Support Culture: Evoking Personal Energy Through People

By the *support culture,* I mean to define a climate based on mutual trust between the individual and the organization. In such an organization, people believe that they are valued as human beings, not just as cogs in a machine or contributors to a task. In an organization characterized by the support culture, you can feel warmth and even love, not just driving enthusiasm. People like to come to work in the morning, not only because they like their work but because they care for the people they work with. Because they feel cared for, they are more human in their interactions with others: customers, suppliers, the public, fellow workers, subordinates.

The support organization is characterized as follows:

- People help each other beyond the formal demands of their jobs. Help is extended not only within one's own work group, but to other groups as well.
- People communicate a lot, not only about work, but about personal concerns. You can always find someone to listen to your ideas and problems.
- People like spending time together. They often see each other off the job as well as on.
- In hiring employees, weight is given to whether the person is caring and cooperative and will "fit in," as well as to whether he or she is competent.
- People are viewed as basically good. When things go wrong, they get a second chance.
- People know that the organization will look after them when they need it, beyond the requirements of the policy or the employment contract. In return, they go out of their way to take care of the organization. This may take the form of caring for the facilities and equipment, giving special attention to quality, conserving resources (turning the lights out!), or protecting the company's reputation in the community.
- People celebrate together. They not only take pride in their work achievements but they recognize one another's personal milestones: promotions, retirements, birthdays and anniversaries, and the like.
- People value harmony and avoid confrontation, sometimes to the point of leaving important issues unresolved.
- People "keep the faith." They do not let each other down. This does not just mean keeping their word; it also means doing one's share of the work, or coming in to work when one is not feeling well, in order not to overload others.

The support culture is the least visible in the United States of all those described in this paper. It is often hard to find because it is not valued by the dominant power- or role-oriented organizations, and so it goes underground. It can be seen in relatively small groups, where people know one another personally and interact face-to-face. It tends to develop in organizations where people work together for long enough periods of time to build personal relationships, work out their differences, and arrive at a degree of trust.

When not balanced by a thrust for success, the pure support culture tends to thrive only in not-for-profit organizations. In business, it makes its best contribution in dynamic tension with the achievement orientation. The latter releases and focuses the personal energy that is evoked for each of us by a love of doing and by a sense of high purpose and worthy mission. The support orientation taps into the personal energy present in the ties of love and trust that bind us to people, groups, and organizations for which we care.

There are two current issues in business where we can clearly see the benefits of a warm and caring organization climate: quality and service. It is no accident that successful approaches to quality improvement are usually based on small work teams or on "quality circles." There is, I believe, a close connection between loving one's work and wanting to do it well, and a sense of caring and trust with the people with whom one works. In quality circles, people develop both a love of quality and close ties with their co-workers. When assembly operators who had left their jobs at Honeywell and later reapplied for employment were asked why they decided to return, the most frequent reason given was, "I missed my quality circle!"

Service in organizations may be internal (for example, between staff groups and the line units they serve) or external, to customers or the public. Both are influenced by interpersonal relationships among organization members. I have written elsewhere of how the kind of service an organization gives flows naturally from its dominant cultural orientation (Harrison, 1987b). The power-oriented organization tends to respond to status, prestige, wealth, and power in differentiating who gets what kind of service. The role-oriented organization strives for equality and consistency of treatment. It creates complex, efficient service delivery systems which are economical to operate and which are experienced by customers as inhuman and inflexible. The achievement-oriented organization tends to be oriented to expertise: to providing the best, the latest, the most innovative products and services. Like experts anywhere, its members think they know what is good for the customer better than the customer does (firms of doctors, lawyers, and other professionals often exemplify this attitude; so do high-tech companies of all kinds).

Increasingly, people in our culture would like to be treated as individual human beings by those who provide them with service. This means caring and responsive service, not just efficiency and competence. Such service is given by people who themselves feel valued and cared for by their organization.

People do not always follow the golden rule in the sense of doing unto others as they would have others do unto them, but they usually do follow another, similar rule: they do unto others as they are done to. If love and mutual respect exist within the organization (whether or not they are self-consciously identified as such), then these qualities will be manifested outward into the world. Thus, if we would learn to make our service more responsive, we must learn to respond to the needs of those who serve.

When the enthusiasm of the mission-driven culture is balanced by mutual support and caring, then we have conditions where people will not only contribute their personal energy for the intrinsic satisfactions found in pursuing a common goal but will also contribute for the goodwill they bear each other. And they can feel safe in contributing fully of their personal energy, knowing that when they need a little extra support or consideration, it will be there for them.

This, then, is a model of a balanced organization culture. It is one where people are brought together by common goals and values, by a mission which is worth pursuing in its own right, and not simply because there are "bottom line" considerations to be met. It is one where people are bound together by mutual caring and loyalty. Because they feel good about one another, they are moved to do their work with care and to give caring and responsive service to customers and the public.

It is an organization culture in which structures, rules, systems, and procedures serve the mission and the people, rather than being experienced as tyrannous and frustrating. It is one in which resources are made available where they are needed by the mission and the people, and where access to the organization's resources is not an automatic and undeserved perquisite of power and position.

The Mission Statement: Catalyzing the Balanced Organization

How do we move toward such a balanced organization? For most organizations, the identification of the mission and the crafting of an agreed mission statement is a key to moving forward. The balance of this paper will address the considerations involved in framing a coherent, simple statement of the mission.

Most organization change efforts do focus on structure and the distribution of resources, which is why organization members become cynical about the possibility of "real change." When we experience real change we know it by the sense of excitement that always accompanies a significant shift in how we are choosing to direct our own personal energy. When we work with structure and resources and leave people and mission alone, it is as though we created an increasingly elegant piece of machinery, but gave no attention to its power source. When we move toward an organization which is animated by mission and bound together by trust, we increase the total personal energy or power which each organization member commits to the mission.

The organization's mission statement can be one key to increasing the amount of personal energy that people expend in work. An inspiring mission attracts personal energy like a magnet attracts iron filings. It energizes at the same time as it orients people to align themselves with the goals and values of the organization.

Of course, a mission statement may or may not reflect the true mission of the organization. The true mission is what people know and believe the organization stands for and strives toward, not a hopeful wish about what the goals and values of the organization may be at some unspecified date in the future. The mission is what energizes, aligns, and attracts people now. It reflects a present commitment of personal energy on the part of the people in the organization. Thus the real mission is an ongoing process, not a thing. Most organizations' real missions are real messes. They are hodgepodges of goals, values, and pious hopes, some of which support one another; some of which contradict and weaken others. This confusion is reflected in mission statements that are a compound of "motherhood" statements and qualifiers. They inspire nothing but cynicism among employees and managers.

In fact, this sort of mission statement is the product of a political process. Like most such products, it is a compromise and is neither focused nor exciting. William Kutz, a partner in the firm, Missions That Work, explains the difficulty in agreeing on a mission statement as a difference in the self-interest of the key players. He points out that in making decisions about where and how to commit personal energy in the organization, everyone, from the CEO on down, follows what he or she perceives to be his or her self-interest, his or her personal mission. When people are criticized for not doing their jobs, it is just that they have a different sense of their personal missions than those who are criticizing them.

It is possible, however, to create a mission statement which reflects and which can in turn influence the living process which is the organization's real mission: clarifying it, simplifying it, and focusing its direction. Bill Kutz has articulated guidelines for crafting an effective mission statement, although he says that it is more a matter of "impassioned struggle" than it is a question of technique!

Guidelines for Creating an Effective Mission Statement

- A good mission statement is short, clear, and unambiguous. It is less than fourteen words; six to eight words is even better! It "rolls off everyone's tongue."
- It evokes an emotional attachment which is bone deep. People have got to be able to have a sense of passion about it. Unless the mission statement connects with people's compelling interests, you do not have it.
- It differentiates your organization from everyone else's. It delineates what is unique about you; what value you add for customers or for the wider society.
- None of its terms should be subject to interpretive argument among organization members. It should be free of qualifiers and value modifiers (motherhood words like "creative" or "excellent") because people will argue endlessly about their meaning.
- It expresses what the organization intends to be now, rather than some wish for the future. Although the mission statement may not be totally realized in the present (and may never be completely manifest), it reflects the essence of what people consider themselves to be as an organization. Deviations from the mission statement are thus experienced as deviations from the true identity of the organization.

Examples of Good Mission Statements

- "Keep the lights on!" (an electric utility).
- "Provide service which brings guests back" (a hotel).
- "Satisfy each customer every time!"

- "Avis tries harder!"
- "Fix it right the first time!"
- "News that people want to read" (a newspaper).

Examples of Less Effective Mission Statements

- "Hertz is Number One." (Number one what? What do we do that makes us number one?)
- "Best quality for the money." (Pits quality against money—you never know whether you are there or not.)
- "Provide customers the best products and services, consistent with safety and cost." (Creates debates about how safe to be, what costs are "appropriate," what level of service is too costly.)
- "Maximum profit for stockholders, consistent with our responsibilities to employees, customers, suppliers and the community." (Profit for stockholders is not inspiring for employees; what the responsibilities are is arguable; pits employees, customers, and others against one another.)

It is not easy to come up with a mission statement that acts as a magnet to attract and align the personal energy of organization members. In some organizations, it is impossible, and its impossibility reflects the reality of the political struggles and power conflicts within the organization. Even within such an organization, however, it may be possible to energize a part of the organization with its own mission statement.

The process of agreeing on a mission statement among a group of managers or leaders can be difficult and conflictual because it involves each member's choosing to allow the organization to claim his or her personal energy. Individualistic as we Americans are, we will often settle for less than excellence rather than give up some of the autonomy that each of us has to choose how to spend our personal energy.

We each have, after all, our own personal missions. Unless the mission of the organization genuinely attracts us, appealing to deeper values or longings, we continue to pursue our more narrow interests. We resist the process of agreeing on the organization's mission, choosing to retain our own personal power, rather than trust in the increased collective power that a single unitary mission will give us as an organization.

Giving or withholding our personal energy is, for each of us, the one inalienable freedom we have. No matter how coercive the organization, its structures, or its leadership, no matter how dull and closely supervised our tasks, we make a choice at each moment in the work day as to how much of our own energy we devote to pursuit of the organization's goals. To genuinely adopt a mission is to accept, at least provisionally, a higher criterion for making that choice than our own wishes and preferences, and therefore voluntarily to surrender some of our autonomy.

Trust is thus the key to the creation of a unitary mission. Unless we trust that we shall receive value in return for the autonomy we surrender to the organization, we block or resist the clarification of the mission. This sense of trust (or mistrust) is built by the relationships between people and their leaders in the organization. It is a key part of what I have referred to above as the people side of the People↔Mission dimension.

The behavior of the group's leader is a key to the clarification of the organization's mission. Because he or she has the most (apparent) autonomy, he or she has the most to give up in establishing an agreed mission of the simple, unitary sort proposed here. The reason is that once the mission statement is agreed on and established as the "highest authority," it becomes the criterion by which every decision and every action may be judged, argued about, and influenced, including the decisions and actions of the leader. Since everyone in the organization has equal access to the power of the mission statement, everyone can legitimately dispute or question any decision or action of anyone else, including the CEO.

Many organizations tend to promote people who want power. For such people, the idea of having executive decision and privilege subject to question by the lowest organization member is not appealing! One would think the powerful people at the top of organizations stand to gain a lot from the alignment of everyone's energy with a simple, easily understood mission. In fact, they often seem to squabble interminably over the details of a proposed mission statement, coming out in the end with something so vague in its celebration of motherhood that it really enrolls no one and attracts little energy to it. In part, this is perhaps explained by the leaders' intuitive understanding that agreement on a unified, energy-focusing mission will give everyone in the organization a simple yardstick for assessing the leaders' dedication to the organization's greater good and the appropriateness of their choices and decisions to the ultimate goal.

Thus the willingness of leaders to accept and be guided by the same simple, unitary standard as everyone else in the organization is both a crucial test of their sincerity and commitment and a key to others becoming willing to trust the process and give their own hearts, minds, and energy to the mission.

The power of a clear, unitary mission is that, together with information, it can become a substitute for hands-on management. If each individual (1) knows and is committed to the goal (mission), and (2) understands the context and the situation (information), then people can manage themselves most of the time. What, after all, are the functions of management, other than to process information and control the behavior of those under them so that it supports the organization's goals?

New technology in production and data processing frequently provides sophisticated information systems that permit people at any level to have the same access to information as their bosses, and commitment of the members of the workforce to a clear mission allows them to direct their own personal energy in fulfillment of the organization's goals. It has been shown that when these conditions exist, it is possible to have far fewer levels and greater "span of control" than in organizations which lack these characteristics. (I have placed "span of control" in quotes, because in fact what is happening is that self-control is substituted for control by others.)

To recapitulate the reasons why agreeing on a simple, unitary mission statement can focus and release energy for the work of the organization:

- The mission organizes and releases the power which resides in individuals' choices over how they direct their personal energy.
- Organizational change efforts which ignore mission and personal energy may change the distribution of effort, but they do not release or focus large amounts of new energy.
- An effective statement of mission is less than fourteen words, and it articulates a single attractive, unambiguous goal which can be understood by anyone.
- The mission serves as a single standard against which each action and each decision can be evaluated. It "levels" ranks, in the sense that the actions of the CEO are evaluated against the same standard as those of the lowest clerk or worker.
- To embrace and be governed by the mission, each individual must be willing to subordinate control over his or her personal energy to the claims of the mission. This requires trust in the sincerity and goodwill of higher management and fellow workers, the people side of the People↔Mission dimension.
- People for whom the exercise of organizational power and authority is an important source of satisfaction have difficulty in accepting a clear and unambiguous mission because it subjects them to the same standards as everyone else.
- When combined with effective information systems, a clear, attractive, and unambiguous mission permits a flat organization with a large "span of control" because people become both capable of managing themselves in pursuit of the mission and motivated to do so.

Guidelines for Choosing a Mission

Understand that for most organizations, the choice of a mission is not simply a way of restating "business as usual." It is the making of a new choice—a refocusing of the activities, decisions, and energies of all the organization's people, from top to bottom.

Because the mission must be attractive to all the people, it must be free of bias towards the interests of one or another group of the organization's stakeholders. It needs to have an appeal above and beyond personal advantage and interests.

The mission should reflect the highest purpose of the organization—values people can identify with what they consider to be "good," not only for the organization but for the world beyond the organization's boundaries. Organizations that enlist the hearts and minds of all their people always seem to aim for something higher than material success. This is the ancient concept of "right livelihood"—making a living by being of service to others.

The most important thing is to tell the truth. The mission must be congruent with people's idea of what the organization is actually becoming. It is not necessary that the organization totally manifests its mission, but it is essential that the leadership is clearly seen to be moving in that direction.

Because few leaders are capable on their own of articulating a single unified vision of the mission with which their followers can all identify, choosing a mission needs to be a participative process, contributed to by more than just a few people at the top. If the mission does not come to be "owned" by all, it will be ineffective, so we may as well start as we mean to go on, with joint ownership during the creative part of the process.

The mission should be short, and "single-valued." It should identify one goal or value toward which the organization is to direct its energies, and it should not contain qualifying or balancing goals that modify that dominant value.

The mission should be stated in positive terms, not in terms of something which is to be avoided. It should be stated in the present tense, as befits a statement of the organization's true identity.

In Praise of Struggle: Using a Mission Workshop to Build a Support Culture

I have been pondering a dilemma which comes up when I work with top management groups to help them develop statements of their purpose and mission. I find that clients approach the task with a wish for clarity and structure, and I have noticed that consultants who do visioning work with organizations often provide a good deal of direction to their clients. A typical scenario might look something like this.

The consultant begins by leading the group members through an exploration of their individual values and operating styles, perhaps using the Meyers-Briggs Type Indicator. Then she or he moves the group members into some work that opens up their intuitive capabilities. They may do collages of the desired future, or bring in objects which symbolize that future. They may do some drawing or painting as a group. The consultant will perhaps also lead the group in a guided fantasy of the organization's future.

After loosening up the creative faculties, each individual may be asked to produce an individual vision of the future. Sometimes, the CEO is asked to write a vision which is then presented to the group for their reactions. The consultant facilitates the group members in resolving their differing visions and writing corporate statements of purpose and mission.

Scenarios such this one usually seem to work fairly well, if the individuals in the group are not too polarized in their values and interests, and if the organization is not overly political. For a long time, it was hard for me to know why I found working this way unsatisfying, since clients seemed happy enough.

I think I know the reason now, and that it is important. My discomfort has to do with the balance between the achievement and support orientations engendered by the process. In our interest in fostering alignment, and a sense of mission and purpose, we sometimes overlook the side of effective organizations which has to do with relationships and group dynamics, the support orientation. The sense of focus, direction, and purpose needs to be matched and balanced by a sense of commitment *to one another* in the top group in the company. The pursuit of an ambitious vision requires a very different kind of personal commitment than just doing your job and looking out for your own career. The implementation of a vision requires a lot more from people than business as usual. It also requires that they work together with a much higher degree of cooperation and coordinated effort than they are used to. Most high-level executives are highly ambitious; often they are more dedicated to their own careers than they are to the organization's welfare. I do not believe that in crafting our "technologies" of organization transformation, we have paid nearly enough attention to the question of building that sense of community and mutual support which must form the basis for any sustained effort toward real organization change.

I believe we can create the conditions for the development of an achievement/support orientation or, to define it another way, of mutual respect and love. However, when we provide well-planned and structured means for our clients to move toward agreement, we unwittingly frustrate or suboptimize the building of those "ties that bind" typical of the support orientation.

In a group of individuals, each with his or her own goals and interests, each with the intentions and the means of pursuing his or her own self-interest, the development of respect and love is fostered by any process which keeps the parties in contact and focused on their issues and which also prevents premature resolution of conflict through the exercise of power.

Ideal conditions for the development of the support orientation can occur in a group working on a task like visioning or developing a mission statement. Such a task requires the group to resolve differing interests and strongly held values, and there is no objective criterion for the "right" answer. The right conditions occur when neither the formal leader of the group (for example, the CEO) nor the consultant intervenes too actively to prevent the "floundering" or struggling together. The process of forming consensus on an ill-defined task is one of the most powerful ways commitment can be created in a group of managers who are highly differentiated in their outlooks, interests and values. The process is subtle, but the rationale is simple.

In the process of hammering out a mission statement, each member of the group has to take seriously, often for the first time, his or her colleagues' differing values, points of view, and priorities. If the process is not cut off by the intervention of an authority figure, and if the group does not give up in frustration, then coming together to consensus on a mission statement is a powerful process for bonding strong, disparate individuals into a cohesive group.

As the members hammer out differences in their visions of the future, the group becomes a kind of crucible in which are forged bonds of mutual respect, affection, and appreciation for one another's differing gifts and strengths. Such bonds make for a closely knit team. Such a team can work cooperatively together under the stresses and pressures that will surely be a concomitant of any serious effort to implement the mission.

When the CEO articulates the vision and "sells" it to the group, or when either the consultant or the CEO moves the consensus process to closure while the group is not substantially in agreement, this bonding process is interrupted prematurely. In that case, the group becomes dependent on the authority figure to resolve its differences. Compared to the members of a group that work through their differences without much intervention, the group members that have been "helped" to resolve their differences experience less commitment, less confidence in themselves and their colleagues, and more feelings of dependency. The price of "rescuing" the group is paid later when conflict among the members disrupts the implementation process. When the group members have not gone through the attunement process in which they learn to manage their own conflict, resolving their differences will require continued and repeated intervention on the part of CEO and perhaps also the consultant. The continued politicking and squabbling take energy from the positive leadership tasks which should be occupying the time of the top management group.

It is thus a delicate question when and how hard to push for agreement. If the conflict becomes too deep and polarized, the group will become frustrated, and the visioning process will lose its credibility. If, as is more often the case, the visioning process is structured in a way which keeps conflicts somewhat under wraps, or the consultant helps too much, or the CEO pushes too hard, then the process fails to bear the fruit of mutual respect and caring on the part of the team members.

As a consultant, what I try to do is keep the dialogue going and make sure that the points of view of minority members or those less articulate get a fair hearing. I insist, so far as I am able, that people listen to one another with as much respect as they can muster. I clarify the differences and the issues, and I try to uncover the positive motives which underlie seemingly stubborn obtuseness on the part of "deviant" members. In short, I try to keep people in contact and actively engaged with one another, even when they do not like it much.

When I provide conditions where clients can truly contend together in this way, they seem to develop really strong commitment to the vision and to one another. I want members of my client groups to develop bonds which will survive both adversity and success, without depending on the CEO to hold everything together. Those bonds will enable them to solve business problems creatively as a group, overcome differences, and reach much more rapid agreement on strategy and tactics than would be possible if each member of the group were bonded only to the leader and not to his or her colleagues as well.

That is why I tend to take more of a hands-off stance than some other consultants when I am present in a group of people who are working their issues. I aim for a process of fairly deep encounter with one another over personal goals and organizational values. My experience so far indicates that when I manage the process (as opposed to the outcomes) well (in the sense of keeping the level of energy high and avoiding deadlock), it ends by strengthening the top team a great deal.

My thinking about these matters goes back to my professional roots as a T-group trainer and to my work in the seventies in training leaders and managers in initiative, autonomy and risk taking (Harrison, 1972a [Chapter Twenty-One]). While the T-group has, for good reasons, lost its credibility as a team-building intervention, allowing a group to struggle over consensus in order to build trust and intimacy is still as good as gold. The practice of giving people "maximum feasible choice," which I developed in my work on self-directed learning (Harrison, 1977, p. 85 [Chapter Twenty-Two]), continues to enhance my effectiveness as a consultant. It just is not easy, and I have to put my credibility on the line to carry it through.

For example, I suspect I may look less competent at first to my clients than do some other consultants who stage-manage the process more actively. That can be uncomfortable for me initially. My way requires both more trust and more willingness to risk on the part of the clients than it would if I did more of the work for them. The outcomes, while I believe they are deeper, are less certain. The process is less controllable, and it is more likely to get stuck for periods of time. It is less comfortable for the clients and, because they are the ones who extricate themselves from their difficulties, there is less credit given the consultant for success.

On the positive side, there is enormous satisfaction for me in seeing a group of managers come through the crucible and move on confidently, having accepted personal responsibility for their organization and for one another. For me, that is worth the confusion and frustration, and the personal risks that I assume in taking a more hands-off stance to my work.

PART TWO

ON ORGANIZATION CULTURE

I have been interested in cross-cultural is-sues since my work in the sixties in the U.S. Peace Corps. That interest was inten-sified when I went overseas to live and work. It was then natural for my keen in-terest in cultural differences to expand into a concern for the differing cultures in organizations. "Understanding Your Orga-nization's Character" was, I think, among the first papers to be published on the subject.

Because few colleagues or clients seemed much interested in organization culture in the seventies, I went on to other things. My interest in organization culture was then rekindled by my response to the work of Tom Peters and his colleagues on excellent organizations. It seemed to me then, and does still, that Peters ignores or too readily accepts the dark side of high-performing organizations, and in 1982, I wrote "Leadership and Strategy for a New

Age" to provide a more balanced model of organizational values.

When it became fashionable to talk about organization culture in the eighties, I revamped the model I had put forward in "Understanding Your Organization's Character." I was motivated by my need for a way to talk with leaders and man-agers about love in a way they would find reasonable, if not totally agreeable. The two papers, *Organization Culture and Quality of Service: A Strategy for Releasing Love in the Workplace* (Harrison, 1987b) and *Culture and Levels of Consciousness in Organizations* (Harrison, 1990a) are the major fruits of that work. The culture model I developed in those papers be-came one of the foundations for the change model in my co-authored book on planning and implementing large-systems change (Harrison, Cooper, and Dawes, 1991).

CHAPTER TEN

UNDERSTANDING YOUR ORGANIZATION'S CHARACTER

Understanding Your Organization's Character" was published in 1972 in the *Harvard Business Review,* where it must have been one of the earliest contributions on the subject of organization culture. The model it presents was the outcome of a conversation with Charles Handy, then at the London Business School and now a famous British writer on work, business, and the future. Our talk took place under a tree in Bethel, Maine, at the National Training Laboratories' Program for Specialists in Organization Development in 1970. I was on the program staff and had volunteered to give a session on organization culture. I had been interested in such things since my involvement in cross-cultural issues in the Peace Corps in the sixties, and I was currently thinking a lot about my own awkward process of adaptation to living and working in Europe and Britain. Charles was a participant in the program. He had been very helpful to me during the previous year or two as I built a consulting practice in London, and struggled to come to grips with British business folkways. I enlisted his help in framing my talk, knowing that I could always count on him for conceptual clarity and stimulating ideas. The model we came up with was a modest success with the program participants, but we were thrilled with it because it seemed to encompass so much of what we saw in the changing face of business management. Charles went on to write a book on his version of the model (Handy, 1985). Perhaps due to his classical training, he used Greek gods to symbolize the four cultures. I prepared the following paper, which I hoped would put me on the map as a leading-edge thinker about organization culture. I also developed a quick-and-dirty little questionnaire which I used to help managers think about the culture of their own organizations. It evolved much later into a commercially published instrument for assessing organization culture (Harrison and Stokes, 1992).

In fact, the paper attracted virtually no attention at the time. It was to be nearly a decade before organization cultures began to shift radically enough that managers and consultants found a need to deal with culture as a differentiating quality of organizations. Until then, I believe, most inhabitants of organizations were not much more aware of their organizations' distinctive cultures than fish are of the properties of water.

The failure to recognize the ideological issues that underlie organizational conflict is common among managers and administrators. Usually the issues are recognized only when they are blatant and the lines of struggle are drawn, as in labor-management relationships. But by then, the conflict may well have developed to the point where a constructive resolution is virtually impossible.

Recognizing Ideological Issues

While the term *organization ideologies* is perhaps unfortunately ambiguous, it is the best name I can apply to the systems of thought that are central determinants of the character of organizations. An organization's ideology affects the behavior of its people, its ability to effectively meet their needs and demands, and the way it copes with the external environment. Furthermore, much of the conflict that surrounds organization change is really ideological struggle (an idea that is certainly not new to political science but one about which behavioral scientists have, until recently, been curiously quiet).

For example, during the commissioning and startup stages of a U.S. chemical plant in Europe, it became apparent that the Americans and local nationals involved had rather different ideas about decision making and commitment to decisions. Consider the approach of each group:

The Americans tended to operate within what I shall later describe as a task-oriented ideology. In problem-solving meetings they believed that everyone who had relevant ideas or information should contribute to the debates, and that in reaching a decision the greatest weight should be given to the best-informed and most knowledgeable people. They strove, moreover, for a clear-cut decision; and once the decision was made, they usually were committed to it even if they did not completely agree with it.

Some of the nationals, however, came to the project from very authoritarian organizations and tended to operate from a power-oriented ideological base (this will also be described later). Each individual seemed to be trying to exert as much control as possible and to accept as little influence from others as he could. If he was in a position of authority, he seemed to ignore the ideas of juniors and the advice of staff experts. If he was not in a position of authority, he kept rather quiet in meetings and seemed almost happy when there was an unclear decision or no decision at all. He could then proceed the way he had wanted to all along.

The task-oriented people regarded the foregoing behavior as uncooperative and, sometimes, as devious or dishonest. The power-oriented people, however, interpreted the task-oriented individuals' emphasis on communication and cooperation as evidence of softness and fear of taking responsibility.

Each group was engaging in what it regarded as normal and appropriate practice and tended to regard the other as difficult to work with or just plain wrong. The fact that the differences were ideological was dimly realized only by the more thoughtful participants. The remainder tended to react to each other as wrongheaded individuals rather than as adherents to a self-consistent and internally logical way of thinking and explaining their organizational world.

A Theory of Organization Ideologies

In this article, I shall present a theory that identifies four distinct, competing organization ideologies and their meaning for the businessman. But, first, let me attempt to further clarify the concept. Here are the most obvious functions that an organization ideology performs:

- Specifies the goals and values toward which the organization should be directed and by which its success and worth should be measured.
- Prescribes the appropriate relationships between individuals and the organization (that is, the "social contract" that legislates what the organization should be able to expect from its people, and vice versa).
- Indicates how behavior should be controlled in the organization and what kinds of control are legitimate and illegitimate.
- Depicts which qualities and characteristics of organization members should be valued or vilified, as well as how these should be rewarded or punished.
- Shows members how they should treat one another—competitively or collaboratively, honestly or dishonestly, closely or distantly.
- Establishes appropriate methods of dealing with the external environment— aggressive exploitation, responsible negotiation, proactive exploration.

Values and Ideologies

An organization ideology, however, is more than a set of prescriptions and prohibitions. It also establishes a rationale for these do's and don'ts. This rationale explains the behavior of an organization's members as well as the working of the external environment (in the latter case, by telling members how to expect other people and organization systems to behave).

The rationale of an organization ideology is similar to what behavioral scientists call "organization theory." The difference is that behavioral scientists try with varying degrees of success to keep their values from influencing their theories about organizations; people, for the most part, do not try to keep their values from influencing their organization ideologies. (This is one reason why education about organization behavior is likely to be so emotionally loaded; if you change a man's organization theory, he usually ends up questioning his values as well.)

Among people in organizations, ideas of "what is" and "what ought to be" merge into one another and are—or are made to appear—consistent. Here is an example:

The ideology of a large U.S. manufacturer of consumer products prescribed that work should be organized in the way that produced the most profit. If this meant that some organization members had boring jobs which offered little opportunity for satisfaction and pride in their work, then it was unfortunate but ideologically irrelevant. According to the rationale of this ideology, a majority of people did not have much aptitude or desire for responsibility and decision making, anyhow, and those who did would rise by natural selection to more responsible, satisfying jobs.

Some young managers, however, had rather more egalitarian personal values. They uneasily suspected that there were more boring jobs than there were apathetic people to fill them. They were very excited about a group of research studies which attempted to show that giving employees more responsibility and involvement in decision making actually led to improved performance. But in my discussions with the managers, I found that the studies' instrumental value in improving organization effectiveness was not the cause of their popularity; rather, they were welcomed because they helped the managers reconcile their personal values with the dictum of the prevailing ideology that work should, above all, be organized to produce the best economic result. (I have, in fact, found that behavioral research findings are usually accepted or rejected on such ideological grounds instead of on the probability of their being true.)

A Conceptual Framework for Understanding Organization Culture

In the remainder of this article, I shall present a conceptual framework for understanding organization culture. It postulates four organization ideologies: (1) power orientation, (2) role orientation, (3) task orientation, and (4) person orientation. These ideologies are seldom found in organizations as pure types, but most organizations tend to center on one or another of them. I shall describe and contrast them in their pure form to emphasize their differences, and then indicate what I believe to be the strengths and weaknesses of each. After this, I shall apply the conceptual model to some common conflicts in modern organizational life.

Power Orientation

An organization that is power-oriented attempts to dominate its environment and vanquish all opposition. It is unwilling to be subject to any external law or power. And within the organization those who are powerful strive to maintain absolute control over subordinates.

The power-oriented organization is competitive and jealous of its territory (whether this be markets, land area, product lines, or access to resources). It seeks to expand its control at the expense of others, often exploiting weaker organizations. Even a weak power-oriented organization takes satisfaction in being able to dominate others that are still weaker. Such organizations always attempt to bargain to their own advantage and readily find justification for abrogating agreements that are no longer self-serving.

Some modern conglomerates project images of power ideology. They buy and sell organizations and people as commodities, in apparent disregard of human values and the general welfare. They seem to have voracious appetites for growth, which is valued for its own sake. Competition to acquire other companies and properties is ruthless and sometimes outside the law. Within the organization, the law of the jungle often seems to prevail among executives as they struggle for personal advantage against their peers.

There is, however, a softer form of the power orientation that is often found among old established firms, particularly those with a background of family ownership. Here the employees may be cared for rather than exploited, especially those that are old and loyal. Externally, the proprietors may hold to a code of honor, especially when dealing with others like themselves. This is the power orientation with a velvet glove. But when the benevolent authority is crossed or challenged, from either within or without, the iron fist is very likely to appear again. In such cases, the test of power orientation is how hard a person or organization will fight for power and position when these are at issue.

Role Orientation

An organization that is role oriented aspires to be as rational and orderly as possible. In contrast to the willful autocracy of the power-oriented organization, there is a preoccupation with legality, legitimacy, and responsibility.

It is useful to see role orientation as having developed partly in reaction to power orientation. Competition and conflict, for example, are regulated or replaced by agreements, rules, and procedures. Rights and privileges are carefully defined and adhered to. While there is a strong emphasis on hierarchy and status, it is moderated by the commitment to legitimacy and legality.

The different attitudes of the power and role orientations toward authority might be likened to the differences between a dictatorship and a constitutional monarchy.

Predictability of behavior is high in the role-oriented organization, and stability and respectability are often valued as much as competence. The correct response tends to be more highly valued than the effective one. Procedures for change tend to be cumbersome; therefore the system is slow to adapt to change.

Most commercial organizations are too constricted by market demands to afford the extreme rigidity of a pure role orientation or the worst excesses of its tendency to place procedural correctness before task effectiveness. Some businesses, however, which either control their markets or operate in areas that are highly regulated by law, exhibit a considerable degree of role orientation. The rationality, impersonality, and adherence to procedure of many banks, insurance companies, public utilities, and social work organizations are cases in point. Their role orientation leaves the customer, the public, or the client with little alternate choice in dealing with them.

Task Orientation

In the organization that is task oriented, achievement of a superordinate goal is the highest value. The goal need not be economic: it could be winning a war, converting the heathen, reforming a government, or helping the poor. The important thing is that the organization's structure, functions, and activities are all evaluated in terms of their contribution to the superordinate goal.

Nothing is permitted to get in the way of accomplishing the task. If established authority impedes achievement, it is swept away. If outmoded roles, rules, and regulations hinder problem solving, they are changed. If individuals do not have the skills or technical knowledge to perform a task, they are retrained or replaced. And if personal needs and social considerations threaten to upset effective problem solving, they are suppressed in the interests of "getting on with the job."

There is no ideological commitment to authority, respectability, and order as such. Authority is considered legitimate only if it is based on appropriate knowledge and competence; it is not legitimate if it is based solely on power or position. And there is little hesitation to break rules and regulations if task accomplishment is furthered by doing so.

There is nothing inherently competitive about task orientation. The organization structure is shaped and changed to meet the requirements of the task or function to be performed. Emphasis is placed on rapid, flexible organization response to changed conditions. Collaboration is sought if it will advance the goal; allies are chosen on the basis of mutual goals and values; and there is little "advantage seeking" in relationships with other organizations.

The task orientation is most readily found in those small organizations whose members have come together because of some shared value, task, or goal. Examples are social service organizations, research teams, and high-risk businesses. Often, however, internal conflict and external stress drive these organizations toward power and role orientations.

Large organizations that operate in highly complex, shifting environments offer more durable examples. Companies involved with dynamic markets or fast-changing, complex technology frequently establish project teams or "task forces." These groups of specialists are selected to solve a particular problem and often operate in a very flexible and egalitarian manner until the problem is solved. The units are then disbanded, and the members join other teams to work on new problems. Although the larger organization in which it operates may be basically role or power oriented, the project team or task force often exhibits a relatively pure task orientation. Moreover, these groups have been so successful that some organizations are trying to install a task-oriented ideology throughout their operations.

Some of the aerospace industries have probably gone the furthest in this direction, TRW Systems being a notable example. Although I do not know of any large organization that could be classed as "pure" in its task orientation, the success of such task-oriented programs as management by objectives (MBO) is a sign of the growing interest among managers. Parenthetically, the most frequent reason for the failure of MBO is probably that task-oriented managers try to install it in power- or role-oriented organizations.

Person Orientation

Unlike the other three types, the person-oriented organization exists primarily to serve the needs of its members. The organization itself is a device through which the members can meet needs that they could not otherwise satisfy by themselves. Just as some organizations continually evaluate the worth of individual members as tools and accept or reject them accordingly, so the person-oriented organizations are evaluated as tools by their members. For this reason, some of these organizations may have a very short life; they are disposable when they cease to provide a system for members to "do their own thing."

Authority in the role- or power-oriented sense is discouraged. When it is absolutely necessary, authority may be assigned on the basis of task competence, but this practice is kept to the bare minimum. Instead, individuals are expected to influence each other through example, helpfulness, and caring.

Consensus methods of decision making are preferred; people are generally not expected to do things that are incongruent with their own goals and values. Thus rules are assigned on the basis of personal preference and the need for teaming and growth. Moreover, the burden of unrewarding and unpleasant tasks is shared equally.

Illustrations of person orientation are small groups of professionals who have joined together for research and development. Some consulting companies, too, seem to be designed primarily as vehicles for members. It is typical of such organizations that growth, expansion, and maximization of income and profit are not primary considerations. Rather, the organizations are conducted in the hope that they will make enough money to survive and provide their members with a reasonable living as well as an opportunity to do meaningful and enjoyable work with congenial people.

There seem to be increasing pressures from the members of modern industrial organizations to move toward person orientation. Young professionals are pushing their companies for opportunities to work on interesting, worthwhile (congruent with their own values) projects. Engineers and scientists, for example, have refused to work on projects for the military and have been successful in getting transfers to nondefense-related activities. Job recruiters find that college graduates are often more interested in opportunities to learn and grow than they are in their chances for organizational advancement. Such signs of social change illustrate why the person orientation must be considered an ideological force to be reckoned with, even though there are few contemporary organizations that operate in total congruence with their principles.

Strengths and Weaknesses of Each Ideology

An organization ideology obviously has a profound effect on organization effectiveness. It determines how (a) decisions are made, (b) human resources are used, and (c) the external environment is approached. An organization ideology tends to be internally viable when the people within the system want and need the prescribed incentives and satisfactions that reward good performance. It tends to be externally viable when the organization embodies it is a microcosm of the external environment and rewards the same skills, values, and motivations.

Information Processing

Usually, as an organization increases in size, its operational environment becomes more complex. The organization experiences conflicting messages and rapid change in many of the environmental domains in which it operates, and it is difficult to orchestrate an integrated response. Worldwide markets and rapidly changing technology, for example, make heavy demands on the information-processing and decision-making capabilities of organizations.

The power-oriented organization is not well adapted to flexible response and effective information processing in such environments. Since decisions are made at the top, the information has to pass through many people who screen out the "irrelevant" data. Moreover, some may distort the message to their own advantage (aggressive internal competition for advantage is part of the ideology). And when conditions change rapidly, the time lag introduced by the filtering process may unduly delay organization response.

The role-oriented organization is also insufficiently flexible to easily adapt to rapid external changes. In order to achieve the security that is one of its highest values, it must perpetuate rather rigid roles and reporting relationships. This gives stability but means that even the most powerful individuals may be unable to produce needed changes quickly.

In times of change, established procedures often do not apply, and the information channels become overloaded with problems that require higher-level decisions. Consider what happened in the commissioning and startup example referred to at the beginning of this article:

Because equipment was not working properly, many actions which ordinarily would have been dealt with by standard operating procedures required top-management decisions. But the ordinary channels would not carry the necessary volume of information, and the quality of decision making and problem solving suffered accordingly. However, when control was shifted to teams of experts clustered around each plant (a task-oriented system) the problems were handled much more smoothly.

Coping with Change

The task-oriented organization's greatest strength is dealing with complex and changing environments. Decentralized control shortens communication channels and reduces time lags, distortion, and attenuation of messages.

Both the power- and role-oriented organizations associate control with a *position* in the organization; neither provides for rapid and rational reassignment of appropriate persons to positions of influence. In contrast, the task-oriented ideology clears the way for a very flexible system of control—one that can shift rapidly over time as differing resources are required by external problems.

Probably the best example of this system in operation is the project team or task force that is formed to identify, diagnose, and solve a particular problem. Even some rather bureaucratic organizations make use of these temporary systems for emergency problem solving. The task force leader is selected for his combination of technical expertise and ability to manage a small group in an egalitarian manner.

The temporary work system is a particularly characteristic response of the task-oriented organization to environmental change. These temporary systems can be activated quickly, provided with the necessary mix of skills and abilities, and disbanded again when the need is past. Their use provides what is, in effect, a continuously variable organization structure.

The person-oriented organization, too, is well adapted to dealing with complexity and change. It also features a fluid structure and short lines of communication and control.

Coping with Threat

In a highly competitive environment where organizations are frequently confronted with overt threats and attacks, the strengths and weaknesses of ideological types form a different pattern.

For example, while the power-oriented organization is not well suited to handle complexity and change, its structure and decision-making processes are admirably suited for swift decision making and rapid follow-through under high-risk conditions. It tends to promote tough, aggressive people who can lead the organization in a dangerous, competitive environment.

The task-oriented organization usually takes longer to respond, but the response is more likely to be based on adequate data and planning. In contrast to the power-oriented structure, which is aggressively directed from the top, it tends to enlist the full commitment of organization members at all levels.

The role-oriented organization does not deal successfully with sudden increases in threat because it relies heavily on established operational procedures. Consequently, its structure is too cumbersome to react quickly in cases of overt threat.

The person-oriented organization has difficulty directing its members' activities in unison until the danger is so clear and present that it may be too late. The person-oriented structure, however, does offer some advantages—its members are committed and have a high concern for one another's welfare.

Probably the most viable organization in a hostile, threatening environment would have a combination of the power and task orientations. This is a difficult marriage, however, because the desire for personal power is often incompatible with the required willingness to relinquish control to those with the most knowledge and ability for the task at hand.

Internal Viability of Each Ideology

Internal Cohesion

The power-oriented organization is an excellent structure for attaching many eyes, ears, hands, and feet to one brain. It exercises tight internal control and integration. As mentioned earlier, the system works well when problems take the form of overt challenges that can be comprehended and solved by one or a few intelligent, courageous people at the top.

But when the power-oriented organization becomes large, and operates in complex environments, this control tends to break down. Under these conditions the role-oriented ideology is more effective. It provides rules and procedures that allow a high degree of internal integration with little active intervention from the top.

It is obviously more difficult to achieve internal cohesion under a task- or person-oriented ideology. For example, if the work is done by temporary project teams, how are their efforts to be coordinated to a common goal? When a problem-solving team comes up with a solution and then disbands, how is its work to be given impact and continuity in the rest of the organization? Some stable and central structure is needed to provide coordination, long-range planning, and continuity of effort. If it is too stable, however, it may become role oriented (rigid and hard to change) or power oriented (recentralizing control). The personal power and security needs of individual members may foster such developments.

New Forms of Coordination

These dilemmas of internal structure have led to various compromise solutions such as the *matrix organization*. The term *matrix* is used because the actual working groups *cut horizontally across* the normal functional-pyramidal organization, bringing together selected individuals from different functions and different levels to work in a relatively autonomous, egalitarian group. Structural stability is provided by a fixed role-oriented framework organized on functional lines. Personnel are readily detachable from the functions for varying periods of time during which they join a *task-oriented* work unit or project team. They are directed by the work unit; but their pay, career prospects, and promotions emanate from the role-oriented part of the system.

Matrix forms of organization have been used with success in highly technical businesses operating in a fast-changing environment. Again, TRW Systems is perhaps the oldest and most comprehensive example. Considerable experimentation with matrix forms has also taken place in the chemical industry, both in the United States and abroad.

Although the matrix system can be effective, it often suffers from attempts of the role-oriented functions to overcontrol the task-oriented functions. The resulting conflict is usually won by the former, which have greater permanence and more resources. One reason for this difficulty is that organizations try to operate partially task-oriented structures without commitment to the ideology. Role-oriented people cannot be plugged into a task-oriented system without conflict.

Effective Motivation

While the power-oriented organization provides a chance for a few aggressive people to fight their way to the top, it offers little security to the ordinary person. It is most viable in situations where people are deprived and powerless and have to accept a bad bargain as better than none. For example, the power-oriented organization thrives in underdeveloped countries.

The power-oriented organization also has the problem of using too much of its energy to police people. Reliance on rewards and punishments tends to produce surface compliance and covert rebellion. Where the quantity and quality of work can be observed (as on an assembly line), inspection and discipline may keep the system working. But if the power does not command loyalty as well, the system usually breaks down. A simple example is the sabotage of hard-to-test aspects of car assembly by disgruntled workers.

The role-oriented ideology tries to deal with the difficulty of supervising complex decision-making and problem-solving tasks by rationalization and simplification. Each job is broken into smaller elements, rules are established, and performance is observed. When conditions change, however, the members are likely to continue carrying out the same (now ineffective) procedures.

The power- and role-oriented organizations simply do not provide for the development and utilization of internal commitment, initiative, and independent judgment on the part of members at other than the highest levels. Nevertheless, in societies where most people's aspirations are just to get by, or at most to achieve a measure of economic security, the power- and role-oriented organizations are able to function adequately.

In affluent societies, however, where security is more widely assured, people begin to look for deeper satisfactions in their work. They attempt to change tightly controlled work assignments and rigid internal structures. When trends toward task orientation ("useful," "meaningful" work) and person orientation (interesting work, self-expression, and doing one's own thing) begin to develop in the wider society, internal pressures for change develop within power- and role-oriented organizations.

Unfortunately, not all people can function productively in a flexible and egalitarian structure. Some people are dependent, apathetic, or insecure. They do need external incentives to work and directives or rules to guide their activities.

Furthermore, the task-oriented ideology has its own ways of exploiting the individual. When his knowledge and skills become obsolete for the task at hand, an individual is expected to step gracefully aside to make room for someone who is better qualified. Status and recognition depend almost entirely on task contribution; if the problems facing the organization change suddenly, this can produce cruel reversals of an individual's personal fortune and work satisfaction.

The person-oriented organization seems to be specially created to fit the work situation to the motives and needs of the independent, self-directed individual. It is flexible to his demands, whereas the power-oriented organization is controlling; it gives scope for his individual expression, whereas the role-oriented organization programs every move; it is concerned about his personal needs, whereas the task-oriented organization uses people as instruments for "higher" ends. Unfortunately, as discussed above, the person-oriented organization is less likely to be effective in the external environment than organizations based on the other ideologies.

Resolving Ideological Conflicts in Organizations

One basic tension runs throughout the ideologies and organization types discussed thus far. It is the conflict between (a) the values and structural qualities that advance the interests of people and (b) the values and structural qualities that advance the interests of organizations.

I can identify six interests, all mentioned previously, which are currently the subject of ideological tension and struggle. Three of these are primarily interests of people, and three are primarily interests of organizations. The three interests of people are:

1. Security against economic, political, or psychological deprivation
2. Opportunities to voluntarily commit one's efforts to goals that are personally meaningful
3. The pursuit of one's own growth and development, even where this may conflict with the immediate needs of the organization

The three interests of organizations are:

1. Effective response to threatening and dangerous complex environments
2. Dealing rapidly and effectively with change and complex environments
3. Internal integration and coordination of effort toward organization needs and goals, including the subordination of individual needs to the needs of the organization

These are obviously not all the interests at issue, but in my opinion, they are among the most salient.

Table 10.1 shows the interests of people and how well they are met under each orientation. Table 10.2 shows the organization's interests and how well they are met by each orientation. The four ideologies have quite dissimilar profiles. Each ideology thus "fits" the needs of an organization and its members differently.

A couple of examples show how organizations with differing internal and external situations are best served by different cultural orientations. A small organization operating in a rapidly changing technical field and employing people who desire personal growth and autonomy might find its best fit with either the task or person orientation, depending on how competitive its markets are and how strong its finances are. A very large organization operating a slowly changing technology in a restricted market and employing people who desire stability and security might find that a role orientation would provide the best balance.

For most organizations, there is no perfect fit with any one of the four ideologies. The "ideal" ideology would possess some power orientation to deal smartly with the competition, a bit of role orientation for stability and internal integration, a charge of task orientation for good problem solving and rapid adaptation to change, and enough person orientation to meet the questions of the new recruit who wants to know why he should be involved at all unless his needs are met.

Unfortunately, on the one hand, this mixture of ideologies *and their consequences* for people and organizations will inevitably result in conflict and consequent wear and tear on organizations and their members. Trying to mix ideologies may also prevent each type from producing the advantages that are unique to it.

TABLE 10.1. INTERESTS OF PEOPLE UNDER FOUR ORIENTATIONS.

Organizational Orientation	Security Against Economic, Political, and Psychological Deprivation	Opportunities for Voluntary Commitment to Worthwhile Goals	Opportunities to Pursue One's Own Growth and Development Independently of Organizational Goals
Power Orientation	Low: at the pleasure of the autocrat.	Low: unless one is in a sufficiently high position to determine organizational goals.	Low: unless one is in a sufficiently high position to determine organizational goals.
Role Orientation	High: secured by law, custom, and procedure.	Low: at times even if one is in a high position.	Low: organizational goals are relatively rigid, and activities are closely prescribed.
Task Orientation	Moderate: psychological deprivation can occur when an individual's contributions are redundant.	High: a major basis of the individual's relationship to the organization.	Low: the individual should not be in the organization if he does not subscribe to its goals.
Person Orientation	High: the individual's welfare is the major concern.	High: but only if the individual is capable of generating his own goals.	High: organizational goals are determined by individual needs.

On the other hand, I do not think that the most viable organizations and the maximum satisfaction of human needs will result from monolithic structures that are ideologically homogeneous. It seems to me that we must learn to create and maintain organizations that contain within them the same diversity of ideologies and structures as are found in the complex environments in which the organizations must live and grow. This means that organizations may have to be composed of separate *parts* that are ideologically homogeneous within themselves yet still quite different from each other.

Such organizations will be very effective in dealing with complex environments and maximizing satisfactions for different types of people, but they will be subject to more internal conflict and ideological struggle than most current organizations could tolerate. For example, instead of a "company spirit" there will be several company spirits, all different and very likely antagonistic. In this environment of conflicting but mutually interdependent parts, the management—not the resolution—of conflict will be a task of the greatest importance. One can imagine, in fact, that as Lawrence and Lorsch have suggested, the most important job of top managers will not be directing the business but, instead, managing the integration of its parts (Lawrence and Lorsch, 1967b).

TABLE 10.2. INTERESTS OF THE ORGANIZATION UNDER FOUR ORIENTATIONS.

Organizational Orientation	Effective Response to Dangerous, Threatening Environments	Dealing Rapidly with Environmental Complexity and Change	Internal Integration and Coordination of Effort—if Necessary at the Expense of Individual Needs
Power Orientation	High: the organization tends to be perpetually ready for a fight.	Moderate to low: depends on size; pyramidal communication channels are easily overloaded.	High: effective control emanates from the top.
Role Orientation	Moderate to low: the organization is slow to mobilize to meet increases in threat.	Low: slow to change programmed procedures; communication channels are easily overloaded.	High: features a carefully planned rational system of work.
Task Orientation	Moderate to high: the organization may be slow to make decisions but produces highly competent responses.	High: flexible assignment of resources and short communication channels facilitate adaptation.	Moderate: integrated by common goal; but flexible, shifting structure may make coordination difficult.
Person Orientation	Low: the organization is slow to become aware of threat and slow to mobilize effort against it.	High: but response is erratic; assignment of resources to problems depends greatly on individual needs and interests.	Low: a common goal is difficult to achieve, and activities may shift with individual interests.

The Future of Organization Ideologies

Whether people confront or avoid them, ideological issues will continue to sharpen of their own accord, both inside and outside the organization. As long as we continue to raise and educate our children permissively, the pressure from younger members of the organization for greater person orientation will increase. As operational environments become more turbulent and more technical, the attractions of task orientation will make themselves felt. Yet every change in organizations means some degree of power redistribution and with it some shift in rewards—such shifts will always be resisted by those with the most to lose, usually the older members of the organization who have a higher status. Thus, I believe that ideological conflict will increase within organizations, whether that conflict is dealt with openly or not.

By dealing with such conflict openly, however, businessmen may find ways to manage it in the service of both the organization and its members and also to use tension creatively as well as competitively. Hidden conflict on the other hand, tends to eat away at the strength of an organization and then to erupt when it is most dangerous to organization health.

In writing this article, I have attempted to render these inevitable, ideological differences more conceptually clear. What is now needed is to develop a common language and set of norms that support both the open confrontation of such issues and the strategies for dealing with them in our organizations.

CHAPTER ELEVEN

LEADERSHIP AND STRATEGY FOR A NEW AGE

Writing "Leadership and Strategy for a New Age" took more courage than any other paper I have undertaken because in it I first spoke publicly about the importance of releasing the power of love in organizations. At the time I wrote the first version of the paper (1981), I had for several years been meeting with a group of fellow consultants to explore ways we might bring our practice more closely in tune with our personal and spiritual values. We met under the auspices of the Institute for Conscious Evolution, an organization established by Barry McWaters and Susan Campbell to foster the dissemination of the New Age thinking of people like Barbara Marx Hubbard and Willis Har-

man. One of the buzz words we used was *alignment,* by which we meant bringing actions into conformance with purpose and values. The concept of alignment had just received a big boost with the publication of *In Search of Excellence* (Peters and Waterman, 1982).

I was from the outset a little suspicious of the idea of alignment as an unalloyed virtue, because of my own experiences with highly aligned organizations. I had found in my work with plant startup in Europe (Harrison, 1981b [Chapter Five]) that the startup situation evoked such loyalty and commitment that people could not be trusted to take care of themselves, nor did the norms that developed

Source: Originally published as *Leadership and Strategy for a New Age: Lessons from Conscious Evolution,* Report to clients of the Values and Lifestyles Program (Palo Alto, Calif.: SRI International, 1982). Published next as "Strategies for a New Age," *Human Resource Management,* 1983, *22*(3), 209–234. Published next as "Leadership and Strategy for a New Age," in J. D. Adams (ed.), *Transforming Work* (Alexandria, Va.: Miles River Press, 1984).

encourage doing so. Startups are time limited, but I wondered what it would be like to work in an organization where such norms lasted for years. At the time *In Search of Excellence* was published, I was doing a good deal of work with one of the nation's National Laboratories, and I observed that the people in its Nuclear Weapons Program were about as aligned to purpose as people in an organization could be. Certainly they showed all the positive qualities claimed for such organizations. They voluntarily worked long hours for very modest pay; they had a strong sense of camaraderie; they made personal sacrifices to advance the work. But the dark side of alignment was evident, too. Although the antinuclear movement was swirling all about them, at times with protesters at the gate, I never heard any thoughtful discussion within the organization about the larger questions of value and policy evoked by members' work. By concentrating attention and intention so exclusively on their mission, people seemed able to keep their doubts and the awkward questions about greater purposes at bay.

It seemed to me that traditional authoritarian organizations were in retreat under the onslaught of the strongly self-oriented values that had begun to emerge during the sixties. These were individualistic values to which I and my colleagues had contributed our bit. Certainly, as I describe in my autobiography, in much of my early career I had cast myself in the role of a freedom fighter for the liberation of the individual in organizations (Harrison, 1995). I felt that what was missing in my own individualism and in that expressed in *In Search of Excellence* was an

appreciation of the needs of the whole. I suspected that in some ways the aligned organization would substitute the tyranny of purpose for the tyranny of the boss. I personally preferred an organization committed to purpose. However, when I thought of all the evil that has been done in the name of high purpose—for example, for God and Country—I was not sure the exchange would be as favorable as it seemed at first. What was missing, I felt, was the power of love as a balancing force to purpose.

These ideas of mine took shape through discussions in the Organization Alignment Group at the Institute for Conscious Evolution, and I wrote a short piece about them in the institute's journal (Harrison, 1981a). It was seen by Marie Spangler, who at that time directed the survey research staff in the Values and Lifestyles Program at SRI International. She asked me to write a longer treatment of the subject for distribution to the program's clients, most of whom were marketing departments in large consumer goods companies.

Faced with an invitation to go public with my ideas about love in organizations, I was both excited and nervous. I remember pacing the floor of my family's cabin in the woods, where I had gone to work on the paper, wondering out loud to my spouse, Diana, whether I was about to sacrifice my credibility as a rational, clear-thinking consultant by "coming out of the closet" about the importance of love in organizations. It felt enormously risky at that time, when U.S. businesses were becoming ever more strongly oriented to the "bottom line."

After the report went to the clients of

the Values and Lifestyles Program, it circulated by hand among consultants and interested managers, and I republished it twice (Harrison, 1983) and (Harrison, 1984). The version given here is the one that is closest to the original report. As I also described in my autobiography, the responses to this paper have been somewhat polarized, but I feel strongly that the encouragement my work has given to like-minded people in organizations has been well worth any risk I took. Subsequently, many others have written about the importance of releasing love in organizations. This paper was probably not the first, but it was one of the earliest.

During the last few of my twenty-five years as a management consultant, I have been impressed with the seeming intractability of organization problems. I ask myself why so many of our attempted solutions seem either to produce no effect or to exacerbate the problems they were designed to solve.

For example, why is it that decades of human relations training for supervisors and managers have not produced committed and happy workers? Is it only a coincidence that as information systems make more information available to managers, it becomes more difficult to make decisions? Why have incentive systems so often failed to keep productivity high, and why have more psychologically sound attempts to motivate workers had equally ambiguous outcomes? Is there any connection between the development of sophisticated planning systems and the increasingly unpredictable fluctuations in the environment? How is it that organizations seem so unmanageable just at the point when we have learned so much about the arts and sciences of management?

It seems to me that the processes by which leaders and consultants endeavor to fix organizations too often resemble eighteenth-century medical practices. They bleed and purge their patients, and when they become sicker and weaker, they bleed and purge them some more. When they do die, it is not clear whether they are carried off by the disease or the treatment. It would seem that all of us, leaders and consultants alike, would do well to heed the Hippocratic admonition, "First, do no harm." We seem impelled to action even when we may suspect that our interventions may be applying more of what caused our difficulties. To do nothing in the face of our problems would be painful, even though it might be as efficacious as the actions we do take.

Contemplating this state of affairs, I have slowly come to the conclusion that the tools and approaches that got us where we are today are not the ones we can use to advance to another level. I sense that like the drunk in the story, I have been looking for my lost keys under the streetlamp simply because there is more light there; the real answers to our dilemmas lie in the dark, beyond the circle of illumination given by our current concepts and methods.

Where to Look?

It is hard to venture out of our little circle of light into the vaster darkness without some guidance or sense of direction. Far easier to go busily over the ground again, hoping we may have missed our keys in the last circuit.

We may not yet be at the beginning of a New Age, but we do seem to be ending an old one, if that can be measured by the increasing unworkability of current form and by the failure of old beliefs and values to give peace, certainty, and satisfaction. It is a time when many varieties of heresy flourish, amid calls for a return to traditional virtues.

Return to the past has little heart for me, and as I contemplate the plethora of choices, the heresy that attracts me is a constellation of ideas that embodies that ancient admonition of gentle Hippocrates about doing no harm. We live in a troubled world, beset with forced changes. Surely the answers will not lie in ever more drastic intervention and frantic activity but rather in some organic approach that allows healing forces to emerge. In search of that approach, I find myself drawn toward an ideal of balance and harmony. For me, that ideal is best represented by the concepts of *alignment* and *attunement*.

Alignment: A New Age Conception of Leadership

Managers are fond of saying that people's attitudes toward work have changed, and the low productivity in the United States is often so explained in part. In place of a voluntary commitment to hard work and high quality, we manage with systems of rules, regulations, checks, and controls. This is not only costly, but the low trust and depersonalization that are engendered further reduce the motivation to contribute, and the system becomes self-perpetuating. In the effort to make up for the inadequacies of voluntary performance, more and more sophisticated systems are developed, often replacing humans with more reliable machines.

Of late, interest in leadership has been reawakening. The leader (as opposed to the mere manager) is seen as a source of vitality and vision who can articulate values that organization members can live by. Through his or her articulation of common purpose and exciting future possibilities, the leader lines up the organization members behind himself or herself, and the organization marches forward into a rosy new dawn. Indeed, in most arenas of contemporary life, we lament the lack of leadership and await its charismatic emergence, which we hope will lift us from our apathy. I believe it is true that most organization members hunger for some purpose higher than mere career success, a nobler vision in which they can enroll. The idea of alignment is about vision and purpose.

Alignment occurs when organization members act as parts of an integrated whole, each finding the opportunity to express his or her true purpose through the organization's purpose. According to Kiefer and Senge (1984), who have explored the concept in depth, the individual expands his or her individual purpose to include the organization's purpose. The authors point out that this concept differs from that where the individual sacrifices his or her own identity to the organization, a process that is said to achieve only "a degree of alignment." It is not quite clear what kinds of leaders and followers achieve the one result rather than the other, however.

There lies the difficulty. Most Americans mistrust, and rightly so I think, the easy giving over of one's will to any collectivity, whether it be the nation-state, one's employer, or even one's nuclear family. Even while we acknowledge the startling superiority of Japanese productivity to our own, most of us are unwilling to find our own fulfillment in the purposes, no matter how noble, of any business organization. And for the most part, our business organizations are indeed lacking the nobility of purpose that is attributed to the Japanese firms of whose productivity we have read so much.

Organizational alignment behind charismatic leadership must involve the merging of the individual's strength and will with that of the collectivity. In high-performing organizations animated by a noble purpose, this may not feel like much of a sacrifice. But even high-performing organizations have their inhumanities. They burn people out; they take over people's private lives; they ostracize or expel those who do not share their purposes; and they are frequently ruthless in their dealings with those outside the magic circle: competitors, suppliers, the public. It seems to me no accident that many of our most exciting tales of high-performing, closely aligned organizations are either literally or metaphorically "war stories." War is the ultimate expression of unbridled will in the pursuit of "noble" ends.

There are close parallels between the ideal of alignment and recent research and theory on high-performing groups and organizations. It seems to me that both tend to ignore the dark side of human nature, what Rollo May (1969) calls the *daimonic*. The daimonic is that aspect of humankind that seeks to express itself and to have impact on the world, no matter what the cost or consequences. It is amoral, and it tends to take over the whole person if unchecked. We find the daimonic in all sorts of obsessions, for there is hardly any human faculty that does not have the capacity, in some persons, to overcome and direct the personality. We find the daimonic in the passions of the social reformer, the libertine, the dictator, the actor, the artist, the evangelical preacher, the lover. We find it in the expansive dream of the entrepreneur, in the limitless personal ambition of the dedicated careerist, and in the dedicated money-making of the financial genius. Where it is checked and balanced by other parts of the personality, its energy fuels great achievements and contributions. Where it gets control of the person, it turns against nature and creates the tragedy of an Oedipus, an Othello, or a Julius Caesar.

People in groups seem to find one another's *daimons*. Mob scenes, sports stadiums, family quarrels, and battlefields are favorite haunts of the daimonic. Its power has always been with us, and I find it hard to conceive of any evolutionary leap that would rid us of it. New Age thinkers seldom write about the daimonic, and they tend to imply that it will wither away in the coming global transformation, as the state was supposed to under communism. I have my doubts.

Attunement

In New Age thought I find a powerful concept that is missing or understated in much contemporary writing about leadership and high-performing organizations. It is the concept of attunement, meaning a resonance or harmony among the parts of the system, and between the parts and the whole. As the concept of alignment speaks to us of *will*, so that of attunement summons up the mysterious operations of *love* in organizations: the sense of empathy, understanding, caring, nurturance, and mutual support.

Love. What a closet word it is in organizations! Far better to talk openly of those old shibboleths sex, money, and power than to speak of love. This is the true male chauvinism in business: the discrimination against women masks the deeper fear of love.

Yet love is far too powerful ever to be truly exorcised. We find it everywhere if we but look. Love is evoked by beauty and by quality in the products or services we produce. It is present in the comradeship of co-workers, in the relationship of mentor to protégé, in the loyalties between people that transcend personal advantage. Love is found in the high ideals of service and contribution that are articulated in the published values of many corporations. It speaks through our dedication to workmanship and excellence of performance.

There is a mystery in words. When we call the love we find in our organizations by other names than its own, it loses its power. I suspect we are reluctant to name love because to do so will release that power, and we do not have forms and processes with which to channel it. Love has its daimonic side too, and we are perhaps not wrong to be wary of it. We do speak, somewhat gingerly, about caring, open communication, consideration, and the like. Not about love.

When we do think about love and organizations, we are apt to see love as a disruptive force, destructive of order and good business judgment. Images come to mind of managers making personnel decisions on the basis of affinity and friendship, or setting prices based on the needs of the customer. Of course, people do sometimes make business decisions by consulting their hearts, but it is seldom admitted, and there are certainly no business school courses on how to do it more or better.

New Age organizations, by contrast, attempt more often than not to invoke the power of love in their decision making. They have developed forms and processes for effective decision making: group meditation to enable members to "go inside" and consult their hearts, asking themselves what they are "called" to do, and other similar approaches.

Alignment and attunement are both processes for achieving *integration* and unity of effort among the differentiated parts of a system. The idea of organizational alignment is getting a good press of late through the awakening interest in the role of superordinate values, top management leadership, and the characteristics of high-performing systems. I believe we also have much to learn of attunement. Alignment channels high energy and creates excitement and drive. It evokes the daimonic. Attunement is quieter, softer, receptive to the subtle energies that bind us to one another and to nature. It tames and balances the daimonic in alignment by opening us to one another's needs and to our own sense of what is fitting and right, what is the "path of the heart" that best expresses our higher selves.

Without attunement and without evoking the power of love in our organizational lives, I think we shall not find peace but only ceaseless striving. During the decades since World War II, we have unleashed in our organizations and in the world an enormous amount of personal power, through changes in expectations, aspirations, and values. Many of us learned to aim high in our careers and personal lives and to believe we could realize our dreams through our own efforts and the abundance that science, technology, and cheap energy brought us. We became net "takers," more concerned about what we could get and achieve for ourselves than what was needed to maintain our organizations and social institutions. In the process of doing our own thing, we became highly differentiated in our goals, values, tastes, and life-styles, and as we did so our differences and conflicts with others increased. In our efforts to get what we believed we deserved, we became increasingly issue oriented and litigious, careless of the fragile webs of relationship that bind any society together. We did indeed find "personal growth," but we pay an increasingly high price in conflict and stress for what we have achieved. We have created a world in which it is increasingly difficult to *compel* anyone to do anything. How shall we find order, peace, and harmony if we cannot learn to open our hearts to one another?

The "how" of attunement is beyond the scope of this paper, and indeed, the forms and processes that may work in business organizations are still unclear to me. I think we have something to learn from intentional communities, many of which have been extremely inventive in their search for noncoercive means of making and implementing group decisions. I believe that attunement begins in stillness, in some quieting or meditative process for connecting with our own higher purposes. As is true with any intuitive process, attunement can be facilitated by ritual, by music, and by the visual arts. I can imagine business meetings in which participants begin in an atmosphere of soft lights and meditative music, with a few minutes of silence in which they go inside to seek guidance as to the higher purposes to be achieved in the work of the meeting. When I think of my current clients engaging in such rituals, however, I am aware that there is some distance to be traveled between here and there!

The Leader as Steward

What does the foregoing imply about leadership? The picture of the leader that emerges looks remarkably like that which Michael Maccoby (1981) proposes, proceeding from a social psychological perspective. Maccoby looked at the emerging social character of the workforce and then projected the leadership traits that such a character would demand. The picture of the new leader that he draws has much in it of attunement. The new leader is seen as having a caring, respectful, and positive attitude toward people, and a willingness to share power. He or she is more open and nondefensive regarding his or her own faults and vulnerabilities than former leaders, and less likely to use fear, domination, or militant charisma than heretofore. The picture is one of a personally secure and mature individual who can articulate the values and high principles that give organizational life meaning but who is more humble and receptive than we normally expect visionary leaders to be. Perhaps this conception of leadership is best expressed as *stewardship*, that is, leadership as a trust that is exercised for the benefit of all: the leader serving the followers, guided by a vision of the higher purposes of the organization. Thus, the organization is seen as animated by a sense of its own higher purposes. The leader focuses the attention and consciousness of the members on those purposes. But the leader also knows that the individuals who are the parts of the organization have legitimate purposes of their own that are not completely expressed by the purposes of the whole, and he or she facilitates the attunement processes by means of which organization members can come to know, respect, and care for one another's needs and individual purposes. The flow of human energy is not one way, from the members to the organization, but the uniqueness of each individual is also preserved and nourished by the whole.

In the past, leaders we called "great" have generally been very strong, ruling through fear and respect, and/or very charismatic, releasing and focusing the daimonic for their followers. The concept of leadership described here is clearly different. The "new leader" avoids the use of fear and arbitrary authority, without being soft or avoiding conflict. He or she is a visionary, but the daimonic thrust that is implicit in the charismatic style is balanced and tamed by a nurturing receptivity. The leader brings healing and harmonizing influences that we can only call love into the organization.

We are clearly a long way from the point where we could imagine the majority of business organizations in this country as animated primarily by noble purposes and love. There are far too many situations that engender feelings of fear and weakness in organization members, and it is not possible to be truly loving when one is powerless and fearful. How could we ever get from here to there?

New Age thinking tells us where to start. We create reality with our thoughts. The events we experience as the world unfolds are actually manifestations of thought, having no existence independent of our willing and believing them into being. Thus, if we call love by its proper name, look for it in ourselves and others, and affirm its potency in our organizational lives, we shall summon it into being, much as Aladdin summoned up the genie from the lamp. At first glance, not an idea likely to appeal to most hard-headed business people.

Yet the idea of manifesting reality through thought has actually been around on the fringes of business for a long time, and it seems to be gaining currency. Motivational speakers such as Norman Vincent Peale on "the power of positive thinking" have never been more popular. Most of us (at least in California) have friends who practice the manifestation of money, career success, or love, and many tell remarkable tales indeed of the results of their efforts. (I manifest parking spaces myself, but I always make a joke of it when I mention it to others.)

We make jokes, too, about the stories we hear of the regimented inspirational group singing in Japanese companies like Matsushita and Toyota (or, closer to home, in IBM and Tupperware!). We may not respect their methods, but we certainly respect their success. In one way or another, mysterious or mundane, positive thinking in groups works for these organizations. Would they harmonize more sweetly at work if they sang of love? I do not know, and I know of only one way to find out.

Studies of high-performing people (athletes, managers, researchers) consistently turn up findings that suggest the power of thought. Successful people are prone to visualize the results they want in their lives and work and to affirm to themselves that they can accomplish their goals. They create a clear and conscious *intention* as to the desired outcomes and allow their actions to be guided by that frequently affirmed intention. Rather than planning in detail what they are going to do, they start by creating an intensely alive mental representation of the end state. That representation then works through the individual's intuition as he or she makes the multitude of everyday decisions that bring the goal ever nearer.

In fact, I have never in all my years as a consultant seen anyone change an organization in any fundamental way through rational planning. Plans have their place, of course, but the managers I have seen deeply influence their organizations' characters always operated by intuition, guided by strongly held intentions. They communicated their intentions verbally to others who could share their vision, and they communicated it daily to others through their real-time actions and decisions. In due course, enough people shared the vision/intention for it to reach critical mass, and the dream became reality. I guess if we are to have organizations that are animated by both love and will, it will be through the efforts of a few dedicated people who have a vision of what such an organization could be like, who share that vision with others, and who together *intend* it into becoming reality.

New Age Concepts of Strategic Thinking

We usually think of strategy as the art of predicting the future, and then planning how to change the organization so that it will perform well at the future time. It is a frustrating business for a number of reasons, not least because the organization is always defined as wanting when compared to the strategic ideal. Add to that the fact that the most dramatic aspects of the future are the ones that are least predictable from an analysis of the past (for example, the sudden increase in oil prices in 1973–1974) and it is little wonder that many managers have little taste for strategic planning.

We seem to do more planning in organizations as planning becomes less and less effective, in a desperate attempt to make the future behave. In fact, planning can only help us to deal with conditions and variables that we already know or suspect are important (Davis, 1982). Planning defines what we know and do not know within a given context. Any future changes in context (changes in variables not known or thought to be important when the planning was carried out) will invalidate our plans to a greater or lesser extent. Planning, for example, can estimate the risk of a downturn in the economy, based on known historical factors, and the probable impact of that downturn on, say, the launch of a new product. Planning cannot tell us anything about either the likelihood or the impact on our marketing plans of unforeseen events such as the sudden rise of a new religion or an epidemic of some new disease.

Most of us seem to be aware that unforeseen events are looming over our futures. We know that we do not know. We imagine wars, economic disasters, and cataclysmic natural events, but we do not believe we can predict their likelihood by reference to historical data trends, so we cannot plan for them. If we could assign a probability to these events, we would still find it difficult to plan, because the events we imagine are so sharply discontinuous with our current experience as to paralyze both mind and will. I think it is fair to say that because we cannot plan for the future we fear and imagine, we plan instead for the future we hope for, one in which even the projected negative events possess a comfortable familiarity.

Planning and Planetary Purposes

If we cannot plan for the future, how can we best prepare our organizations and ourselves for it? My suggestion is that we consider attuning our organizations to planetary purposes. This means moving out of the rational and analytical modes of thought typical of the planning process and into intuitive and intentional mental processes.

A radical leap is required to move from our normal habit of thinking of organizational purposes as defined internally to thinking of an organization in terms of planetary purpose. Seen from the planetary point of view, the organization exists only as part of a larger reality, supported and nurtured by the larger system on which it depends. Its purposes are not solely determined or decided by itself, but are "given" by its place in the larger system. Organizational purpose is not simply decided by its members but is rather to be *discovered*. The process of discovery is partly internal to the organization, involving an inner search for values and meaning. It also has an external aspect, that of discovering meaning through the transactions of the organization with its environment. Viewed in this way, a primary task of the organization is the discovery of its place and purpose in the larger system. Every event in its history can be viewed as part of a lesson, the meaning of which is to be intuited by the organization's members.

Adopting such a point of view requires a fundamental change in one's orientation to goals and to the success and failure of one's plans. We can begin, in Kipling's words, to "meet with Triumph and Disaster/And treat those two impostors just the same." If one's orientation is to learning, then failure carries just as much information as success. In fact, failure may be more valuable because in our failures are embedded nature's messages about required changes.

Most business organizations today strive to succeed and to win against their competitors, against the government, and sometimes against their suppliers and customers as well. The tougher conditions become, the harder they strive. Since conditions are increasingly tough, there are a lot of people out there striving. Because conditions are tough, those people experience a lot of failure and consequent blame from themselves and others. They are accordingly under a lot of stress, as can be seen from the ever increasing popularity of alcohol, tranquilizing drugs, and "stress management" courses.

When one is striving to achieve goals, one's learning is oriented to *means;* one learns more and more about what to do or not to do to achieve those particular goals. The excitement and stress are liable to blind us to the question of whether the goals themselves are worthy. Stepping back and taking the perspective of planetary needs forces us to ask the larger question: Are these goals in line with our higher purpose? Is the fact that they are becoming increasingly difficult to achieve perhaps a signal that they are no longer appropriate to this stage of our evolution? If we find on reflection that there is no longer joy in the struggle, that we are burning ourselves out in the effort, that we are no longer energized by what we do, then that may be a "signal from the universe" that it is time to move on to find a "path with heart."

Searching for Meaning

From a planetary point of view, strategic planning is a search for meaning rather than a search for advantage. It is an intuitive process in which the goals and activities of the organization are examined against the criteria of the heart: Does this task enliven the doer, giving value and meaning to life? Do we still experience satisfaction in the attainment of this goal? Do we strive joyously, or with desperation? Do we feel that we are net contributors of value in our work in the world?

As my colleague David Nicoll says, in approaching strategy from the point of view of purpose, our aim is definitional rather than positional in a market domain. Our endeavor is to forge a shared view of reality that will serve the organization members as a base for day-to-day decision making and that will direct the leadership thrust of the dominant coalition (Nicoll, personal communication, 1981).

The activity is definitional in that we are attempting to penetrate the forms the organization takes in its internal and external relationships in order to discover its essence. Our belief is that when the forms (systems and structures) and processes (doings) of the organization flow from its essential qualities (being), the organization will become energized and integrated and will be effective in dealing with its environment.

The questions we ask in order to determine the essential qualities of the organization are simple, though the process of answering them may be difficult.

First we may ask, Who are we and what are our gifts? What are our distinctive competences; What have we to contribute that is unique or different? What special knowledge do we have? What do we value? What do we believe in?

We may also ask of ourselves, What are we called to do? What needs do we see in the world that we are moved to meet? What activities have "heart" for us? What do we love doing?

We may examine our *core technology,* those processes we use to transform inputs into outputs. How does the core technology link us to those parts of the environment that supply us with our inputs and receive our outputs? What do these key domains in our environment need from us and what do we need from them?

We may ask ourselves what other messages we are receiving from the environment, from governments, publics, and special interest groups. Do these tell us more about our mission or calling in the world?

Of course, answering the questions can become extraordinarily complex when our organization is made up of many diverse constituent parts, each of which may produce markedly different answers to key questions. In heterogeneous organizations, it may be necessary for each part to go through the strategizing activity on its own. Then some integrating process is needed to attune the parts to one another and harmonize their differences. I am not underestimating the difficulty of this task, but it is one that must be faced by any strategizing activity in complex organizations. It is perhaps more difficult when we adopt the aim of preserving the essential integrity of each part, because then we forego the convenience of using authority simply to override the aims, values, and worldviews of those who disagree with us.

This strategizing process can embrace both alignment and attunement, as it searches deep within for values and turns outward to acknowledge the organization's connectedness with all of life. It results in a statement of the purposes of the organization, embedded in the larger purposes of its environment. The statement of purpose forms the basis for a projection of the organization into the future. This statement of intention, the "willed future," describes the organization's state of being and its relationship with its environment at a later point in time when its essence will have been realized in its forms and processes and it will be making its maximum contribution to the common good of the planet.

The statement of the willed future becomes the basic operating document of the organization, to which all plans and decisions are related and upon which the *intentions* of the organization members are focused. In this way, the power of thought to create reality is brought into play. By consulting the willed future at each point of uncertainty and endeavoring to keep plans and decisions in conformity with its statement of intentions, the organization aligns all its efforts with the strategy.

Evaluating the Approach

How shall we evaluate the usefulness of an approach to strategic planning that says, in effect, "Get your values right, listen for the call to serve, decide what you want, go for it with all your heart, and trust in the Lord"? Certainly, on the one hand, it has the advantage of simplicity in concept. It is consistent with the growing interest in leadership as a value-transmitting activity and a creator of meaning. Because of its comprehensiveness, it can have a unifying and stabilizing effect compared to strategies that are responsive to transitory changes in markets and competitive position.

On the other hand, there are real obstacles in modern organizations to the establishment of a common vision of purpose and a unified idea of the willed future. For one thing, most large and complex organizations are heterogeneous and highly differentiated. If it is difficult to keep a coordinated planning activity going between, for example, the production and marketing people, what shall we say of the chances of their agreeing on ultimate values and the meaning of life?

The idea of seeking consensus with one's business associates around values and the call to serve implies a high degree of mutual commitment between the individual and the organization. It is one thing to contract with the organization to give it control over our activities for a certain period each day. It is quite another for us to pledge to one another "our lives, our fortunes, and our sacred honor." Such deeper commitments to purpose are implicit in New Age strategizing. They are quite evidently not for everyone.

Then, too, I wonder why it is that so many nonprofit and grassroots organizations that are dedicated to the highest principles are badly managed, undisciplined, and prone to personal backbiting and political strife. Why, I ask myself, have I frequently found more kindness and human decency in organizations committed to commercial pursuits than I have in those espousing lofty ideals?

The answer to the paradox lies, I believe, in the operations of the daimonic. In many business organizations, the daimonic is repressed beneath layers of structure and impersonal systems, kept in check by authority and regulations, and bought off with financial rewards. It is as though the implicit contract is, "Leave your daimon at home, and we'll give you the wherewithal to indulge it during your off hours."

By contrast, many nonprofit organizations, and particularly the more activist ones, unleash the daimonic in the service of their ideals but fail to tame and channel it. It is easy for their members to fall into the tragic error of identifying their own egos with the ideals they serve, which results in their sometimes becoming self-righteous, arrogant, and quarrelsome. To me, the message seems clear. It is not sufficient simply to align oneself with high ideals and set off down the road in pursuit of lofty purpose. We need also to remain receptive to those we meet along the way, both companions and strangers. Through the heart-opening process of attunement and through the humility and reason that enable us to accept discipline in the service of order, we can keep the daimonic in check without losing its energy and vitality.

After due consideration, then, I remain basically optimistic about the possibility of introducing New Age thinking into business organizations. In the first place, the personal needs are there. There is a hunger for meaning, commitment, and service that is often not fulfilled in work. There is a reservoir of positive energy waiting to be tapped, if we can give people something to enroll in that is larger than their own careers.

At the same time, there exists in business organizations a willingness to be led, to accept discipline and to respect and follow rational authority. There is an ability to forego immediate ego gratification for the sake of getting a job done. I believe, in fact, that many business organizations are ripe for the transformation. Their members slumber uneasily, knowing there is something missing, that there should be more to working life than this. This energy and vitality wait to be released by a vision of purpose and love. At the same time, they fear the awakening, as we always fear powers that are unknown. We know that change is coming, for the signs and portents of change are all around us. It is hard to believe that the changes will be positive in the midst of increasing disorder, scarcity, and confusion. Thus, we cling to the past without really believing in it, and we distract ourselves with business as usual and with our personal careers. Even if the promises of the New Age are real, how shall we awaken ourselves and others to their messages?

The Processes of Paradigmatic Change

I said at the beginning of this paper that I am drawn toward a gentle stance on intervention and organizational change, one that seeks to release the organization's own vitality and healing energies. Are there organic approaches to transforming organizations in the rather fundamental ways discussed above?

In fact, I do not believe that organizations are changed much if at all by consultants like myself and my colleagues. They are occasionally changed by managers. They are mostly changed by markets, technology, economic cycles, and social and political developments. Managers and consultants can assist an organization to change in more productive and less painful ways, and that assistance may be decisive for its health and continued survival. Few of us, however, are given the opportunity to make history.

If events were going well, and we were all prosperous and expecting to become more so, no amount of intervention and management activity would be sufficient to accomplish significant changes in perceptions and values within business organizations. Crisis provides the stimulus and opportunity for change. The ingredients for transformation exist now in our organizations. We have to concern ourselves with what prevents change, not with how to create it.

Elizabeth Kübler-Ross (1969) and others have studied personal reactions to terminal illness and other traumatic losses. They have discovered that there is a predictable sequence through which individuals pass when they suffer major trauma or loss, such as impending death, loss of limb or crippling accident, death of a spouse, and the like. David Nicoll suggests and I believe that we may be going through a similar sequence as we face the death of our worldview, the concepts and values that have served us throughout our oil-fueled ride to prosperity and high technology (Nicoll, personal communication, 1981).

The early stages of this sequence are characterized by denial and rage; the later stages by depression and despair. These emotional reactions are followed by acceptance and a change in self-concept and worldview that is appropriate to the individual's new circumstances. With acceptance and reorientation, the individual experiences new energy for learning and coping with life as it is.

I do not think it is far-fetched to state that we are suffering just such reactions to traumatic loss as our dreams fade, our cherished institutions work less and less effectively, and scarcity takes the place of abundance. Since we are not one individual but a multitude, all of the emotional manifestations can be found at once, rather than in an ordered sequence.

Some resort to denial: "Reports of resource depletion and environmental damage are exaggerated. There is not really any scarcity. We have coal and oil resources for hundreds of years." "Concerns about nuclear pollution are overdrawn. Technology will take care of these problems, just as it has done before." "We will soon be able to feed the population of the Earth and provide ourselves with abundant nuclear power that will usher in the dawn of a New Age of global prosperity."

Some are angry: "It is the prophets of doom who are responsible for our doubt and uncertainty." "We have betrayed our traditional principles, and we're being drained of vitality by the freeloaders and the welfare cheats." "Our confidence is being undermined by a socialist conspiracy." "We are being exploited by the dominant military-industrial complex." "The youths of our nation are morally weak, dissolute, and unwilling to do an honest day's work."

Some are in despair and apathy: "War is inevitable." "We are headed for economic collapse." "The ecosystem is irreparably damaged." "We are headed for a new Dark Age. The Day of Judgment is upon us."

Depending upon whether we use denial, anger, or despair, we go on with our lives as if nothing crucial were happening or we strive to overcome or protect ourselves against the forces of change or we sink into a planless apathy and dread. Since the sequence is by no means irreversible, we may migrate between these positions, depending on how we are affected by events. I have certainly experienced all of them in myself at one time or another.

People who have worked with the dying and the severely traumatized know that explanations, arguments, and pressures are ineffective in moving the sufferer through these stages. Indeed, opposition tends to fix the individual in whatever stage he or she is at the moment or sometimes move the person back to an earlier and even less adaptive stage. Effective help consists first of all in offering empathy, understanding, and love. The helper neither forces unacceptable reality on the other, nor does he or she join into any delusions or distortions of reality. The unacceptable truth is offered without pressure. Acceptance of the person is offered too, and it is not contingent on the individual's readiness to deal with reality.

I think that in our organizational lives we are groping for ways to come to terms with the death of our paradigm: that complex of assumptions, values, and perceptual frames that constitutes our worldview. In the struggle to hold onto our dreams and beliefs, and in our attempts to deal with their demise, we have great need of one another's understanding and support. We also need new dreams and hopes, but we cannot use them until we have done some grieving for the world we have lost. In this process, we all stand in need of help, but instead, we tend to set off one another's defensive reactions with our differing interpretations of reality.

Against such an appreciation of our current dilemma, I have asked myself how managers and consultants can aid organizations in achieving a new, positive, energy-releasing worldview. As I have struggled with this question, I have come to understand more deeply my intuitive distrust of old-style charismatic leadership in this period. If the model I have outlined is correct and if most people have not yet accepted the changes that are in process, then they are in a state of denial or anger. That suggests a reason why great charismatic leaders are so notably lacking in our world: the new paradigm has not yet acquired enough vigor to be led.

If not charismatic leadership, then what? I have come to the ideas presented here too recently to have a program to propose for transforming organizations. What I am clear about is that the changes in consciousness that are required cannot be forced. The seeds of those changes are in all of us. We each need to experience conditions that support the growth of those seeds. One way to create those conditions is through discussion with others, discussion which goes beyond our day-to-day work and deals with our deeper hopes and fears for our work, our organizations, and our connections with others. I believe that in small discussion groups we can experience that combination of mutual support and gentle confrontation that we need in order to change. We need to be reminded that reality is changing, and we need to be understood and accepted in our struggles to come to terms with that change. I know that the properly managed small group can provide that balance of conditions, nudging people to change through exposure to different views of reality while creating a climate of mutual support that transcends differences of belief and opinion. (We all know that groups can be destructive, tyrannical, and intolerant as well, but we have learned a lot in the last three or four decades about how to create conditions for more positive outcomes.)

Concretely, what I would propose to those business leaders who wish to explore the relevance of New Age thinking to their work is that they meet regularly with a few others they trust and respect to share their concerns and thinking. Explore the issues outlined in this paper. Spend enough time at it that you can share your deeper hopes and fears. Open your hearts to one another a little at a time, as you test the others' willingness to accept you as you are. Here are some questions you might address:

- Can we see the daimonic at work in our organization? How does it express itself? If it is suppressed, what are the effects?
- Where do we see love at work in the organization? What stops us from talking about it? Does it matter?
- What does the idea of stewardship mean to us? What kind of leadership does our business need? What kind would we follow ourselves?
- Can we change reality with thought? What is the role of intention in bringing about the results we achieve? Do we visualize our desired results? What would happen if we visualized as a group?
- Do we use intuition to make decisions? For what kinds of decisions? How can reason and intuition work together?
- What kinds of future events do we ignore in our planning? What would happen if we allowed for them?
- What is our organization's purpose? What is its driving thrust, its distinctive competences, its values? How do these relate to our own purposes and values?
- Of what large purposive systems is our organization a part? How, if at all, does our organization's purpose become attuned to the larger system's purposes? If the planet had a purpose, how would our organization relate to it? How would we know?
- Does a focus on goal achievement block learning in our organization? How, and how well, does our organization learn?
- What messages do we receive from different parts of our environment? Are there some parts whose messages we consistently ignore? What would happen if we listened to them?
- With respect to goals, are we for the most part *pushed* by events or *pulled* by our vision of a desirable future outcome? Does it make a difference in the stress we experience in work?
- What is the relationship between our stated strategy and what we do? If our strategy does not determine our actions, what does?
- As an organization, can we identify a "willed future"? How does it focus our efforts? If we do not have one, would it make a difference if we did?

- What losses do we fear in the future? How do we deal with that fear? How do we react to people who have different fears? How can we help each other with our fears?

  Lastly, if the discussion of these issues in a small group of your peers has been a useful and productive experience, how might you offer such an experience to others in your organization? Is it possible that given the opportunity to open our hearts and minds to one another, we shall discover that we know our way home?

CHAPTER TWELVE

ORGANIZATION CULTURE AND QUALITY OF SERVICE

The publication of the paper in Chapter Eleven, "Leadership and Strategy for a New Age," marked a major shift in the focus of my public work, as distinct from my consulting work with clients. The latter continued to be a blend of the mundane and the ideal, depending on clients' needs and readiness. I had seen the dangers of "missionary work" during the sixties, when I and my colleagues thought to transform organizations through the application of T-groups. It had cost us dearly in credibility, and it had caused some unfortunate clients much pain. Although I was always alert for opportunities to bring more heart into the working lives of clients, and I endeavored to open my own heart in interactions with them, I confined my proselytizing to my lecturing and writing, speaking about my ideas to any group that would listen. However, I also spent quite a bit of time looking for ways that could bring hard-headed leaders and managers into dialogue on the subject of love in organizations, rather than turning them off. It was not until 1986 that I found what I was looking for in a return to my earlier interest in organization culture. In that year, I was invited to speak about my "New Age" ideas at the annual meeting of The Academy of Management. I arrived a little early at the room where the meeting was to be held, just as Tom Janz of the University of Calgary was finishing a presentation on a new measure of orga-

Source: Originally published as *Organization Culture and Quality of Service: A Strategy for Releasing Love in the Workplace*, I. Cunningham (ed.), (London: Association for Management Education and Development, 1987). Reprinted here with permission of Roger Harrison.

nization culture he had developed, using as a framework the ideas in *In Search of Excellence* (Peters and Waterman, 1982). Someone who had read my earlier work on organization culture saw me in the audience and suggested to Tom and me that we might have some interests in common. On looking over Janz's work, I saw that his carefully constructed and validated measure of organization culture was built on dimensions very similar to the model Charles Handy and I had come up with intuitively so many years before. I had not thought of that work for years, except to regret that it had been published so far ahead of its time, but now I saw it as an answer to my need for a way to discuss the place of love in organizations that would evoke interest and debate rather than defensiveness in audiences of business managers. Culture was a hot topic in the early eighties, and I thought I had something to say on the subject that could capture the interest of business leaders. My idea was that if I presented them with a model of organization culture in which a caring relationship-oriented culture was only one of the alternatives, it should not be hard to establish the need for balance among cultural extremes. I would revamp my old culture questionnaire to include a scale that assessed the levels of caring, support, and cooperation (love in action) in organizations. Then it should be easy to show people by their own data what desirable qualities were missing in their organization culture and get some discussion going about what should be changed and why.

I got to work on the reconstruction of my culture questionnaire, taking guidance

from Janz's statistical studies. Soon I had the help of Herb Stokes, who began using my new questionnaire in his consulting practice on work redesign and in his High Performing Systems workshops. Herb revised the items so they could be understood by everyone in an organization, from top to bottom of the hierarchy. I began using the questionnaire and the culture model in my talks and soon achieved my goal of being able to talk with managers about love in a balanced and thoughtful way.

In the mid eighties, U.S. companies began to take a belated interest in improving the quality of their service to customers, and I once again saw an opportunity to connect love with a current concern of managers. The result was the paper "Organization Culture and Quality of Service." In it, I show how differing organization cultures tend to produce differing styles of service, and I make a case for developing strong support cultures as a way of bringing caring and concern (love) into the service activities of an organization. The model of organization culture presented here is the same as that used in Herb Stokes's and my culture questionnaire, which has since been published commercially (Harrison and Stokes, 1992). Many of my speaking engagements at the time were in Europe and Britain, and the paper was published in Britain in 1987. Thus, it has not yet been widely read in the United States. I have revised this paper, "Organization Culture and Quality of Service," and the next one, "Culture and Levels of Consciousness in Organizations" (Chapter Thirteen), in order to minimize redundancy between the two pieces.

Like many of my consultant colleagues, and a good few of my clients, I have done a fair amount of "work" on myself. About ten years ago, the gap between what I thought and believed and what I was able to talk about and work with in business organizations began to bother me a lot. I felt that I could see a need for business managers to do less and to feel and imagine more. As their jobs became tougher under foreign competition, the cost squeezes brought on by the oil crisis, and the turbulence of financial markets, managers became more aggressive in changing their organizations. Believing that "when the going gets tough, the tough get going," they worked longer hours, reorganized their businesses, reduced the workforce, cut back on budgets, endeavored to shift from a production to a marketing orientation, and so on.

The Hazards of Short-Term Problem Solving

To me, much of what was done seemed to fall somewhere between marginally useful and counterproductive, especially when looked at from the perspective of the larger society or the planet. In reorganizing and in performing organization surgery, it seemed to me that people were intervening in very gross ways into complex living systems they did not understand very well. They would sometimes get the short-term benefits they were looking for, but they got a lot of long-term unintended consequences as well. Observe, for example, the performance decrements that almost always follow the acquisition of one organization by another.

From a societal perspective, we seem to have entered into a new cycle of environmental pollution. At the same time as we are cleaning up our rivers and our atmosphere, our businesses are discharging large amounts of garbage into the streets—human garbage! Every productive person who loses his or her job through forced early retirement or redundancy, every teenager or young adult who wants to work but cannot, becomes part of this stream of living effluent. The organizations that discharge the human "waste products" become tighter, leaner, more competitive and profitable; the larger society becomes poorer, more disorganized, more full of pain.

No one is really at fault. The sensitive and caring managers I talk to about these problems are as distressed as I am by the waste and the pain, but they see no viable alternatives to competing as hard as they can, by any legal means at hand. When they choose short-term solutions, it is not because they do not care: it is usually because the situations they deal with are too complex for them to understand the dynamics and predict the eventual consequences of their actions.

Part of the problem lies in how we see the world. In business, we learn to be competitive, action oriented, and autonomous and to think in "left-brained" ways:

analytically, concretely, and rationally. These are all qualities of behavior and thought which lend themselves to dealing with the physical world—and that includes organizations, when we think of them as machines.

New Ways to Think About Organization

Dealing effectively with complex living systems such as human beings, groups, organizations, markets, and the planet Earth requires habits of thought that are not widely distributed in business and not widely taught in schools and universities. I am talking about such "unbusinesslike" patterns and preoccupations as cooperation and appreciating interdependency. Associated modes of thought and feeling are "right-brained": intuitive, open to emotions as well as facts, and holistic.

Having begun life with every intention of becoming an engineer, I know the transition from the harder, more active pole to the softer, more receptive one is difficult and can be long. For me, that new understanding was forged in sensitivity training groups, in the experience of living and working in a foreign country, in psychotherapy, in meditation and spiritual seeking.

I do not fancy proposing such a regimen for my clients, but I am convinced that exploring what the world looks like from the softer side, from the *yin* as opposed to the *yang* point of view, offers my clients perspectives that can bring both power and healing into their organizations.

I have spent the last four or five years in efforts to bridge the gap between the softer disciplines and my tough-minded clients. In that time, I have encountered many others on the same path: managers and consultants, men and women, who share a vision of work as a healing and growthful experience, and organizations as healthy places for humans to become the best they can be. Through dialogue and experiment, I have evolved a theoretical framework and a strategy which I shall share in this paper. I believe my experiences can be useful to those others engaged in this work (sometimes called *organization transformation*) as well as to those who simply want to understand organizations and help them to be more effective (*organization development*).

Talking About Love—Alignment and Attunement

My vision, as I conceived it at the outset, was that I wanted to balance the powers of intellect and of human will in organizations with the powers of intuition and of love. For some time, I remained stuck in my vision, unable to imagine how to talk with managers about love, and doing a lot of compulsive dithering about risks to my professional reputation and future income! Then, screwing up my courage, in 1981 I began to write on organization alignment and attunement (Harrison, 1981a), (Harrison, 1984 [Chapter Eleven]). My earliest effort received very limited circulation. I sent it to some friends and colleagues in the United States and in Europe, and it was distributed to a small number of clients of SRI International. Then the feedback began to come in.

People who were "tuned in" to "New Age" ideas liked the paper all right and gave me some nice compliments. Outside of that inner circle, I got two kinds of strong feedback, both of which strengthened my belief that business organizations are not currently easy places in which to pursue the developments I had in mind. One kind of feedback came from professional friends and colleagues, people who have liked and respected my work and who wish me well. The following is a good example:

> You spoke of love at some length. After the initial shock of it my uneasiness did not go away. 'You keep talkin' about love, boy, and you gonna' get screwed royally,' remained my basic sentiment. I mean, 'love' in a high performance organization? That's tossing a hot potato into a cold/cool medium. Even if you do warm things up with attunement, can you ever warm it up to 'love' level and still keep an eye on business? . . . It seems to me, Roger, that using the term love for organization description stirs up people's deepest hurts and longings, and how you can meet their expectations and run a railroad at the same time is beyond me.

The second kind of feedback was from managers, people I did not know who had received the paper through the workings of the rather mysterious process that keeps putting like-minded people in touch with one another. The following quotation from a manager who had read the paper and then shared it with colleagues gives the flavor: "By the time I finished reading it, tears were streaming from my eyes. It is happening again, now as I write this note to you. For years, I have felt alone in thinking it was possible to work with people in such a caring atmosphere that the bottom line becomes a by product of that atmosphere. Now, thanks to your report, there are many people around me who share that seemingly impossible dream."

Both correspondents were focused on a basic truth: business organizations are tough places to nurture tender feelings. People who do harbor dreams of a more compassionate and responsive business world feel alone and unsupported, except when something occurs which brings their feelings out in the open. Then they find that others have also harbored these same, seemingly subversive thoughts and feelings.

The Need for an Alternative to the Competitive Paradigm

Seen through the lens of my vision, much of the business world is unbalanced and stuck. The strong and increasingly dominant values of action, competition, and strength mean that much of the energy and time expended in organizations goes into countering the actions and intentions of other people or organizations.

It is push against push, with lots of energy going out and not that much movement. There is too much "moving against" and not enough "moving toward" or "moving with."

The issue is not just one of educating individuals to be more caring and cooperative. People are already more caring and cooperative than their organizations allow them to be. Organizations block development of caring and compassion on the part of organization members, creating daily win-lose situations that channel people's energies into unproductive competition.

The behavior of organizations in society is also frozen into a competitive-exploitative orientation. Viable alternatives to competitive behavior cannot even be perceived from that vantage point. We shall continue stripping the world of natural resources; polluting our air and water; replacing people, who need work, with machines, which do not; manipulating one another into spending money we do not have for goods we do not need, so long as the development of the softer, responsive, compassionate side of people in business remains blocked. When we cannot allow ourselves to take care of one another in business, we certainly will not allow ourselves to take care of the larger society, let alone the planet.

Sometimes I wonder whether in shaping my practice around bringing love into the workplace I am not simply projecting my own needs onto a part of that world where they are inappropriate. I will never be sure until I have put the question to the test in the real world. I have decided that the best test of my thinking lies in committing myself to develop a strategy for helping organizations to open paths for their members to develop their compassionate, caring side in the conduct of business. If I am in fact sunk in some solipsistic dream, then I shall find few allies, and the strategy will fail for lack of an energetic response. In my profession, we live on our ability to attract the energy and commitment of our clients to projects which mean something to them personally, and the feedback is pretty swift if we are off in our assumptions about what they care about.

At present, the strategy has two parts: a model of organization culture and a focus on service. The idea is, first, to create a way of talking and thinking about organizations that provides a mental model of balance between hard and soft, competitive and caring. Then managers and leaders can see for themselves the extent to which their own organizations may be diminished because the powers of attunement, compassion, and love are missing.

Second, I have identified giving service as an organizational process or activity which most organizations are involved in and which is attracting increased management attention presently (see, for example, Albrecht and Zemke, 1985). Consider the following definition to see if it does not imply that service is love in action! "**Service.** n. 1. The action of serving, helping or benefiting; conduct tending to the welfare or advantage of another" (*The Shorter Oxford English Dictionary*, 1968).

In fact, as we experience service internally between different parts of our organizations and externally as customers, service is a lot of things that are neither supportive nor compassionate nor caring. Organizations and their customers experience the lack of caring most in service relationships, and it is in that area where performance improvement depends on opening the heart of the organization and its members. In attempting to understand the dynamic forces which influence the process of giving service, I have found it useful to focus on organization culture as a key variable. The model presented below identifies the varieties of service which we experience in practice, points up cultural barriers to giving service from the heart, and suggests directions that may be taken to remove those barriers.

Four Organization Cultures

Some years ago I wrote a paper on organization culture (Harrison, 1972b [Chapter Ten]) putting forward ideas originally developed by Charles Handy and myself and prompted by my experiences living and working as a consultant in Britain and Northern Europe. Later, I published an instrument (Harrison, 1975) which people could use to assess their organization's culture, and in the mid seventies, Charles Handy wrote a delightful book on the subject, a book that has since been republished (Handy, 1985).

Recent work by others on organization culture prompted me to take a fresh look at the concepts we developed. Tom Janz, in particular, has done interesting work on the factorial structure of organization members' perceptions of culture, the results of which are consistent with Handy's and my intuitive model (Janz, personal communication, 1986). On the basis of Janz's work and my own current thinking about organizations, I have revised my model and developed a new questionnaire (Harrison and Stokes, 1986 [1992]). Both the model and the questionnaire have found acceptance among managers and consultants engaged in new plant design and redesign, in which the quality of working relationships and of intergroup cooperation and service are prime considerations.

The Power Orientation

The power-oriented organization is based on inequality of access to resources. A *resource* can be anything one person controls that another person wants. In business, some "currencies" of power are money, privileges, job security, working conditions, and the ability to control others' access to these. The people in power use resources to satisfy or frustrate others' needs and thus to control others' behavior. Leadership resides in the persons of the leaders, and rests on their ability and willingness to administer rewards and punishments. People in power-oriented organizations are primarily motivated by external rewards and punishments and secondarily by the wish to be associated with a strong leader.

In the power organization at its best, leadership is based on strength, justice, and paternalistic benevolence on the part of the leaders. The leaders are firm, fair, and generous with loyal subordinates. They have a sense of obligation to their followers, and they exercise power according to their understanding of what is good for the organization and all its people. This orientation towards the use of responsible power seems to be typical of some of the best Japanese organizations. It rests on the acceptance of hierarchy and inequality as legitimate by all members of the organization. In more egalitarian societies, such as the United States, there is much less acceptance of hierarchy as being legitimate than in Japan, and there is not a strong tradition of benevolent power-oriented leadership.

At its worst, the power-oriented organization tends toward a rule by fear, with abuse of power for personal advantage on the part of the leaders, their friends and protégés. When the organization becomes large, or when the leaders struggle for dominance, it may degenerate into a hotbed of political intrigue.

The power orientation is well suited to entrepreneurial and startup situations where the leaders have the vision, intelligence, and will to manage the business and assume personal direction of the activities of its people. The other people in the organization extend the leaders' reach, leverage, and impact. There is a personal relationship between leaders and followers. The latter depend on their leaders for direction and security, and the leaders depend on followers for loyal service.

As the size and complexity of the business increases, the demands on the leadership of a power-oriented organization multiply exponentially. Large power-oriented organizations are frequently inefficient and full of fear and confusion, unless the power orientation is supplemented by good structures and systems for getting work done (role culture). As the distance between leaders and followers increases, effective control becomes more difficult. Because followers have been conditioned to be dependent, when power-oriented organizations expand, they often run short on leadership talent.

The Role Orientation

The role culture substitutes a system of structures and procedures for the naked power of the leaders. This gives protection to subordinates and stability to the organization. The struggle for power is moderated by the rule of law. The duties and the rewards of the members' roles are carefully defined, usually in writing, and are the subject of an explicit or implicit contract between the organization and the individual. Both the individual and the organization are expected to adhere to their part of the bargain.

The values of the role orientation are order, dependability, rationality, and consistency. Performance is organized by structure and procedures, rather than personally controlled by the leader. A well-designed system of roles (a bureaucracy) permits work to be reliably directed at a distance, so that large, complex organizations can be created and managed. Rather than the coalition at the top having all the power, authority and responsibility are delegated downward. Each level in the organization has a defined area of authority, and work can be controlled without direct supervision from the top.

At its best the role-oriented organization provides stability, justice, and efficient performance. Rules and "due process" give people protection from the arbitrary exercise of authority that is typical of the power orientation. They are able to spend less time "looking out for Number One" and thus they can devote more energy to the work.

A bureaucracy operating a stable technology in a slowly changing environment can be very efficient, because much of the routine work can be made subject to impersonal rules and a system of checks and balances. Well-designed systems, methods, and procedures maximize productivity and minimize error. Once an operating problem is solved, the solution gets built into the system. People know what is expected of them and are trained to do their jobs efficiently.

Role-oriented organizations require less direct supervision compared to the "hands-on" management typical of the power culture. Performance can be monitored by information systems, without much face-to-face contact with people who do the work. Routine work can be standardized and broken into small pieces that are learned quickly by relatively unskilled workers.

Traditional role-oriented organizations are best adapted to the more stable combinations of technology, supplies, and markets that characterized the century between 1850 and 1950. In rapidly changing situations, they have difficulty keeping up with circumstances. Nevertheless, most large organizations today have strong elements of the role culture. The advent of computer-aided data processing has possibly saved bureaucracy from a demise caused by information overload as the processes of change have speeded up dramatically. Our society is very "system dependent" and needs a strong role orientation to operate those complex systems reliably.

The weakness of role organizations is in the very impersonality which is their strength. They operate on the assumption that people are not much to be trusted, so they do not give individual autonomy or discretion to the members at lower levels. The system is designed to control people and prevent them from committing selfish and stupid acts. It also keeps people from being innovative, and from doing the right thing when the right thing is outside the rules. In the interests of rationality and order, it is made difficult to change or bend the rules, and it usually takes a long time to make needed changes.

In most of the Western business world, the development of systems and procedures has been strongly influenced by the ideas of *scientific management*. The assumption has been that there is "one best way," and that the best system is one which makes the fewest demands on the intelligence, initiative, and problem-solving ability of the worker. In order to prevent workers from "messing up" the system, the practice has been to leave them little discretion in how they do their work. Creative management thinkers are beginning to realize that these assumptions and practices are very limiting in a technologically changing world. In service industries, too, rigid systems make it difficult for workers to respond to the individual needs of customers.

In fact, good systems and procedures do not have to be inflexible or hard to change. They can be responsive as well as controlling, as the Japanese have demonstrated. The role culture as we experience it in most organizations is not only defined by an emphasis on rationality and well-designed systems. Its distinctive quality is its *unilateral control* of people's behavior by systems, rules, and regulations. The system controls the people rather than responding to their needs as workers.

New approaches to management, such as Employee Involvement and Total Quality Management, attempt to blend the role-orientation emphasis on well-designed and closely managed systems with the empowerment of employees typical of the achievement orientation. These approaches endeavor to make the system serve the workers, and thus to combine the economic effectiveness of the role orientation with the high energy of the achievement culture. However, their success depends on the extent to which genuine changes are made in the ways authority is distributed and work is organized. Without a significant degree of power sharing, the gains they bring are very limited.

The Achievement Orientation

Both the power-oriented and the role-oriented organization cultures depend on the use of external rewards and punishments to motivate people. Organization members are expected to contribute their personal energy in return for rewards. This means that the organization has available to it only that fraction of each person's energy that he or she is willing to commit in return for the extrinsic rewards the organization offers.

It is true, of course, that many people actually like their work, want to make a worthwhile contribution to society, and enjoy interacting with colleagues or customers. These are intrinsic rewards that are qualitative rather than quantitative and that arise from the nature of the work and/or the context in which it takes place. Traditional power- and role-oriented organizations are not designed to provide these intrinsic satisfactions, nor are they designed to harness the energy that people have for doing work they like to do in the way they like to do it.

In some work situations, intrinsic satisfactions arise naturally. People who have worked in such diverse situations as new business and new plant startups, nuclear test shots, intensive care units, and political- and community-organizing campaigns, report that these work cultures can provide deep personal satisfactions and evoke personal commitment of a high order. These "high energy" work situations are described by participants as having most of the following qualities:

- The work situation engages the total person.
- The values that people experience in the work transcend personal advantage.

The situation evokes altruism, which is satisfying to everyone involved. People feel they are working for something bigger than themselves.

- People give their all, working long hours without complaint. They may willingly sacrifice their family and social lives to the demands of the work.
- People supervise themselves, seeking out what needs to be done without direction from above.
- There is high morale, teamwork, and a sense of camaraderie. The group frequently feels itself to be elite or special.
- There is a sense of urgency; people live "on the edge," putting out high energy for long periods of time. They may become addicted to stress.
- There is a clearly understood mission that is articulated and supported at the highest level of the organization.
- The mission is emphasized and reinforced by everything upper managers do: the financial decisions they make; the questions they ask and the topics they pursue in meetings; the sorts of people they hire, fire, and promote; and the aspects of the operation they look at during field visits.
- The mission is stated in unambiguous terms. There are one or two dominant values that are more important than any others in the organization. People know that they cannot go far wrong as long as they pursue those values with sincerity and integrity.
- People do not argue much about the mission. People who do not share the organization's basic values and commitments are made to feel uncomfortable and usually leave.
- People do argue a lot about how best to achieve the mission. Positional authority does not shut off discussion or curb the expression of employees' ideas.
- The values embedded in the mission are larger than mere profit or growth. In pursuing the mission, organization members believe they are making a contribution to society, as well as gaining something for the company.
- The organization is more egalitarian than most. Employees are treated like willing contributors. Those at lower levels are empowered to make decisions that other organizations reserve for supervisors and middle managers.
- Communication channels are open, both laterally and vertically. It is easy to be heard if you have an idea or suggestion.
- Failure is viewed as something to learn from rather than as a sign of personal inadequacy.
- People are given effective authority in accordance with their ability to contribute to the mission. Neither the red tape of a bureaucracy, nor the privileges and status of a power elite count as much as ability and contribution in deciding who does what.

The achievement-oriented organization is an *aligned* organization. It "lines people up" behind a common vision or purpose. It uses the mission to attract and release the personal energy of its members in the pursuit of common goals. This is in marked contrast to the power- and role-oriented organizations that rely on the application of rewards and punishment and on impersonal systems and structures to control and constrain their members. The mission serves to focus the personal energy of individuals. Because members make their contributions freely in response to their commitment to a shared purpose, they willingly give more to the organization, and the whole prospers accordingly.

Of course, structures and systems are still necessary in the achievement-oriented organization, and the allocation and distribution of resources is still a problem. In the best such organizations, the systems and structures serve the mission and are changed when the mission requires it, rather than becoming laws unto themselves.

Power, too, has a place in such an organization. These organizations are not power oriented, but they use power. The people in power first establish the mission and then serve it. On a day-to-day basis, decisions are made by reference to the mission, not by reference to people in power. The actions of those in power are judged and criticized by the same standard as is applied to everyone else in the organization: Do they advance the mission?

Enthusiasm for the "hands-on, value-driven" approach said to be typical of "excellent companies" has been so great that a negative side to the achievement orientation may come as a surprise to some. The achievement culture has the deficiencies and distortions brought on by its strengths. The high energy and involvement which the achievement orientation generates are difficult to sustain, and organization members are subject to burnout and disillusionment. Such organizations may rely on the common vision to organize the work, rather than subjecting themselves to the discipline of systems and procedures. When the task is complex, and the vision takes on different forms for different parts of the organization, people lose focus and unity of effort. When different groups each "do their own thing," coordination suffers and resources are wasted.

Here are some actual quotes from interviews of veterans of achievement-oriented organizations where hard work and long hours substitute for planning, where the thrust for achievement has submerged concern for people's needs, and where elitism and competition have eroded cooperation.

- "We're too busy doing to plan objectively."
- "There's bound to be organizational problems with tight resources and tight delivery schedules; things are bound to get tense. People who are attracted to our company like this climate—others would go loony here. Pressure is keen, and you have to compromise on quality sometimes."
- "People are beginning to burn out; you can't keep putting the pressure on people. We must turn down our expectations of the magic we can perform and do more realistic scheduling."
- "One of the craziest things about the company is the founders' ninety-hour weeks. My best people look like garbage only putting in sixty-hour weeks."

- "I'm worried about the health of some of the people; bad things are happening to the founders and old timers."
- "Everyone needs positive feedback; even those who show outside self-confidence still like to hear the words. It's hard for many to say those words; . . . it's easier to criticize than to stroke."
- "We were team players inside and terribly competitive outside." People in other groups saw us as self-centered and uncooperative, and they were right. We really didn't care about anything but meeting our own objectives."
- "Our arrogance and elitism isolated us from the rest of the organization. When we did make some mistakes, they were glad to see us fail."
- We became intolerant. We couldn't accept criticism either from outside the group or from our own members.

The achievement-oriented organization is frequently underorganized; it relies on high motivation to overcome its deficiencies in structures, systems, and planning. Although it evokes enthusiasm and commitment, it may not have a heart. People's needs are subordinate to the organization's mission and its needs. After a time, people realize this and may begin to mistrust the organization—or they may remain committed but suffer high levels of emotional and physical stress. Under stress, organization members may withdraw into an idealistic fantasy world, losing touch with the realities of competition, customer needs, and the business environment (a fairly common phenomenon in R&D and high-tech organizations).

The Support Orientation

The support culture may be defined as an organization climate based on mutual trust between the individual and the organization. In such an organization, people believe that they are valued as human beings, not just as cogs in a machine or contributors to a task. A support culture fosters warmth and even love, not just driving enthusiasm. People like to come to work in the morning, not only because they like their work but because they care for the people they work with. Because they feel cared for, they are more human in their interactions with others: customers, suppliers, the public, and their fellow workers.

Support organizations show most of the following qualities:

- People help each other beyond the formal demands of their jobs. Help is extended not only within one's own work group but to other groups as well.
- People communicate a lot, not only about work, but also about personal concerns. They can always find someone to listen to their ideas and problems.
- People like spending time together. They often see each other off the job as well as at work.
- In hiring people, the organization gives special weight to whether the person is caring and cooperative and will fit in.

- People are viewed as basically good. When things go wrong, they get a second chance.
- People know that the organization will go beyond the requirements of the policy or the employment contract to look after them when they need it. In return, they go out of their way to take care of the organization, caring for the facilities and equipment, giving special attention to quality, conserving resources, and/or protecting the company's reputation in the community.
- People celebrate together. They not only take pride in their work achievements but they recognize such personal milestones as promotions, retirements, birthdays, and anniversaries.
- People value harmony and avoid confrontation, sometimes to the point of leaving important issues unresolved.
- People "keep the faith"; they do not let each other down. This does not merely mean keeping one's word; it also means doing one's share of the work, including coming in to work when one is not feeling quite up to par, in order not to overload others.

In Western societies, the support culture is the least typical of the four assessed by the questionnaire *Diagnosing Organization Culture* (Harrison and Stokes, 1986 [1992]). It is not valued by the leaders in power- or role-oriented organizations, and so it goes underground. It can be seen in relatively small groups, where people know one another personally and interact face to face. It tends to develop in organizations where people work together for long enough periods of time to build personal relationships, work out their differences, and arrive at a degree of trust.

When not balanced by a thrust for success, the pure support culture is seldom found in business; it is not results-oriented enough to enable a business to be competitive. It makes its best contribution when it is in dynamic tension with the achievement orientation. The latter releases and focuses the personal energy which is evoked for each of us by a love of doing and by a sense of high purpose and worthy mission. The support orientation taps into the personal energy present in the ties of love and trust which bind us to people, groups, and organizations for which we care.

There are two current issues in business where we can clearly see the benefits of a warm and caring organization climate: quality and service. It is no accident that successful approaches to quality improvement are often based on small work teams. There is a close connection between loving one's work and thus wanting to do it well and a sense of caring and trust with the people with whom one works. In teams dedicated to quality, people develop both a love of quality work and close ties with the others they work with. When assembly operators who had left their jobs at one Fortune 500 company and later reapplied for employment were asked why they decided to return, the most frequent reason given was, "I missed my quality circle!"

Like the achievement cultures, support-oriented organizations assume that people want to contribute. Rather than evoking their contribution through a common purpose or ideal (a *doing* culture), the support-oriented organization offers its members satisfactions which come from relationships: mutuality, belonging, and connection (a *being* culture). The assumption is that people will contribute out of a sense of commitment to a group or organization where they feel a real sense of belonging and in which they believe they have a personal stake.

The emphasis on human needs of the support culture balances and moderates the single-pointed task focus of the achievement orientation. Where the one may use people up and burn them out, the other binds up their wounds, restores their energy and vitality, and heals their relationships. The achievement culture unleashes and fuses the human will of organization members in the service of the organization's task. The support culture evokes human love for the nurturing of the organization's members and the maintenance of the organization's essential fabric of relationships.

The support culture can evoke extremely strong motivation in the service of the group. We see this motivation in the sacrifices which members of groups make for one another. The willingness of people to give their lives for those of their comrades is known not only in war but also in close-knit teams doing dangerous work such as polar exploration, police work, and fire fighting. In more mundane work situations, the effects of team loyalty on productivity, quality, and absenteeism are well publicized in recent writing on high-performing organizations.

The weaknesses of the support culture are the negative side of its strengths. Organizations in which the support culture is both strong and unbalanced tend to avoid conflict: in the interests of harmony, difficult issues are swept under the rug. Consensus may be overvalued, hampering the organization's ability to move decisively. Sometimes favoritism affects decisions about people, and injustice results. Differences in skill and ability may be ignored in the interests of 'equal treatment.' Tough decisions about people's performance may be postponed out of 'kindness,' negatively impacting the organization's effectiveness. In power- and role-oriented organizations, cohesive work teams may support their members in antimanagement behaviors such as rate restriction and rule breaking.

The support culture is more common in Scandinavia than it is in the United States or Britain. When I talk about culture to managers there, they report that cohesive groups often punish members who assert their own deviant opinions or take individual initiatives. They refer to it as "hammering down the nail whose head is sticking out."

Like everyone else, I have my own cultural biases. It would be easy to read a bias toward the achievement and support cultures into the way the cultures are described above and to see it also in the phrasing of the items in the questionnaire *Diagnosing Organization Culture* (Harrison and Stokes, 1986 [1992]). In fact, in constructing the questionnaire, I tried to write items which expressed the positive side of the power and role cultures and which would also be seen by people as descriptive of their organizational experiences. This task proved extraordinarily difficult. On reflection, that difficulty seems to me a reflection of the society in which we live, rather than some inherent negativity in the concepts of power and role.

Power has the capacity to enliven life in organizations, and to release the human spirit. There have been times in history when there has been a tradition of nobility and responsibility on the part of those who exercised power. In our own recent past, the concept of benevolent paternalism was much more prevalent than it is today. Although I have never worked in Japan, conversations with those who have suggest that responsible, caring power is much more common there than in the West. In fact, I suspect that one of the secrets of Japanese success is the acceptance of inequality on the part of Japanese employees, and the reciprocal acceptance of responsibility on the part of their leaders. The stability and mutual acceptance of one another's positions and prerogatives permits employees and leaders to work together without the power struggles that are such a frequent aspect of life in Western power-oriented organizations.

In the West, and particularly in America, we tend to have little love or respect for power or the people who wield it. Mirroring our negative attitudes, they often tend not to deserve our love or loyalty. Those who do are seen as individual exceptions to the rule rather than as examples of a socially valued tradition. We do not know how to make organizations work without power; at the same time, we do not know how to trust power or make it trustworthy.

The situation of the role-oriented organization is somewhat different. Traditionally, the systematic organization of work has been characterized by application of scientific management principles, top-down control and faceless bureaucracy. Those sorts of role-oriented organizations tend to squeeze the spirit out of working life, and the items in my and Stokes's questionnaire have some of this flavor.

Working rationally and systematically is not *inherently* soul deadening; it only becomes so when we elevate the system and the machine to the status of master and subordinate to that master our creativity, vision, and human values. That working to improve systems and procedures can be enlivening is demonstrated by some of the work in sociotechnical systems (STS) design, Total Quality Management (TQM), and Employee Involvement (EI), where the emphasis is on making systems more responsive to the needs of the task (achievement) and of the people who work in the organization (support).

If I have a bias, it is toward the release of the human spirit in work. With Kahlil Gibran, I believe that "work is love made manifest" and that our organizations will be richer materially and spiritually to the extent that we can realize that dream. In reaching toward that ideal, organizations will do well to avoid dominance by any one of the four cultures, preferring instead a dynamic balance in which each culture is expressed in its highest form, and the positive side of each balances the darker tendencies of the others. The ideal is not a compromise or average. It is a synthesis achieved by struggle and debate within the organization between differing views of what is good for the organization and good for its "stakeholders": employees, stockholders, customers, community, and the planet.

Frequent Patterns of Culture in Organizations

Although every organization is different, I have observed some patterns that come up frequently in the organizations with which I work.

Questionnaire scores on power are negatively correlated with those on achievement and support. This means that if a group has a high score on power it tends to have low scores on both achievement and support. The role scores tend to fluctuate fairly independently of the other scores.

The power culture has a potential for fear and manipulation. People in power-oriented cultures tend to be rather careful what they say and whom they say it to. The support and achievement cultures require a fairly high degree of openness and trust to flourish. Therefore, we should expect an organization high on power to be low on achievement and support, and vice versa. [For additional research on the instrument, see Harrison, 1990b, and Harrison, 1993.]

When people in an organization disagree about the culture they actually have, it is often because the culture looks and feels different from the perspectives of different parts of the organization. It feels different when you are at the top than it does when you are at the bottom. Upper managers see more of the achievement culture than do those lower down. The latter are more likely to see the organization as power oriented.

Often the kind of work people do and the way it is organized influences the culture of their group or department. Left to nature, research and development groups tend to be achievement oriented. Groups which keep track of and control money tend to be role oriented. Marketing groups tend to be achievement oriented, while sales organizations are more likely to lean toward the power culture. Production organizations tend toward a mix of power and role.

It is possible, however, to design organizations that have radically different cultures than those I have listed above as the norm. For example, I have seen sales organizations with achievement/support cultures that are as effective or more effective than power-oriented ones (and far more enjoyable for their members). (Tupperware and Mary Kay come to mind, although I have no personal experience of either.)

My experience is that in most organizations, differences between functions are less striking than is the overall organization culture. The departments within an organization are less differentiated in their cultures than we would expect, given the very different kinds of work the functions perform. Thus, in a strongly role-oriented organization (for example, a traditional insurance company) the marketing department would tend to be more role- and less achievement-oriented than it would in an organization with a dominant achievement culture (for example, some high-technology organizations).

Common Patterns in People's Preferred Cultures

Another observation I have made is that while people in different parts of the organization may disagree about what the culture actually is, they usually pretty much agree on how they would like it to be. Most people surveyed agree they prefer to work in a climate which is low on power, high on achievement, and middling on role. There is more disagreement about the degree to which people prefer the support culture, possibly because fewer people have fully experienced it than have experienced the other three.

Organization Culture and Styles of Service

My current strategy is based on the belief that as we move further into a service economy, organizations are coming under competitive pressures that will force consideration of the possibility that some version of the Golden Rule may actually be good business. As organizations respond to the demand of customers for more personal, individualized service, opportunities to operate from an open heart may increase. These developments are so far seen only in a rudimentary form which I hope heralds a growing trend. My strategy is rooted in the expectation of that change, and to help it along, I have determined to act as though it is already a reality.

Culture is the key to understanding service. An organization's cultural orientation has implications for every aspect of its operations and its internal and external relationships. Hence, each orientation tends to produce a typical attitude and style of customer service.

The effect of culture is quite aside from whether the service is "good" or "bad." Each produces a kind of service that is qualitatively different from the others, different in "taste" and "feel." Each may give "good" or "bad" service, and the definition of good service will differ from one culture to the other. I think this distinction is important, but I find that in much discussion and writing about service, the goodness of service is confused with its style. For example, warm, friendly, and relaxed service is not necessarily "better" than fast, efficient, and impersonal service, but it certainly feels different. The *style* of service that an organization offers, both internally and to its customers, is a reflection of that combination of values, preoccupations, social structure, norms, and mores which we call organization culture.

Power-Oriented Service

Power orientation is associated with a style of service which emphasizes status and prestige. When it is well done, it makes the customer "feel like a king." The hierarchical emphasis of the power orientation leads naturally to status differentiation in service. Different grades and classes of service are offered to customers based on their status, prestige, wealth, or the price of the goods or services consumed. On a recent flight to Europe I experienced very strongly the typical "feel" of power-oriented service. I was waited on hand and foot in the first-class cabin, with obsequious courtesy. The service was choreographed so as to make one feel like one of the elite, but it also managed to convey the impression that impostors would be found out. In the jeans and tennis shoes I usually wear for long-distance travel, I felt a bit like a tramp who had wandered into the Ritz. Nothing was said, of course, but I knew, and I knew that "they" knew that I knew!

Power-oriented service is typical of restaurants, hotels, resorts, casinos, and clothing establishments catering to the prestigious and affluent, particularly in Britain and Europe. It can be found in sales-oriented organizations that seek to influence purchases through lavish entertainment and gifts. A more aggressive and competitive variety of the power orientation can be found in the salesrooms of automobile dealerships, but there the energy is often devoted to making the customer feel inferior rather than royal!

If a strong leader becomes the champion of service, the power-oriented organization can be extremely service conscious. A classic example is the late J. W. Marriott, who was said to read every customer complaint personally, and who was fond of getting his subordinates up at 4:00 A.M. to make a surprise inspection tour of the kitchens. Such leaders make a strong impact on their organizations. If they are both strong and benevolent, then the quality of service they engender can be both willing and friendly. Often, however, there is more than a little motivation by fear in such leaders' style of management. The fear results in a degree of servility on the part of employees.

The power orientation at its best, and at its highest level of integrity, is often found today in relatively small, owner-managed businesses such as restaurants, hotels, summer camps, and resorts. Sometimes family operated, often with a family atmosphere, these organizations manage to combine the unity of direction that comes from a strong leader with the warmth and responsiveness to individuals' needs typical of the support culture. They are small enough for one person to exercise control over the details, and the employees are bonded to the owner by ties of affection, not just fear. Such organizations seem to be the last bastion of the benevolent autocracy which was such a prominent feature of the best business leadership in the nineteenth and early twentieth centuries.

Role-Oriented Service

Quality of service in the role-oriented organization tends to revolve around the *transaction* and around systems designed to make transactions faster, more efficient, and more profitable to the organization. The role orientation lends itself to the provision of goods and services on a large scale and to a focus on cost, price, and margins. Good service, for such organizations, means devising efficient service systems which meet the needs of the typical customer, and then managing the system so that the human components play their parts as designed.

In the United States, our ideas of service are often synonymous with fast, efficient systems designed to produce uniform and predictable outcomes. Such "excellent companies" as Federal Express and McDonald's have built reputations on the reliability of their systems in meeting customers' expectations. Their service is valued for cost benefit and uniformity rather than for making people feel warm and comfortable. Similarly, when we complain about service systems such as the U.S. Post Office or our local bank, we concern ourselves primarily with convenience (no long lines, no long waits on the phone, having the information we want), with reliability (not losing or delaying the mail, not inappropriately bouncing checks), and with whether we are getting value for our money (no continual rises in charges with diminished levels of service).

In accordance with their cultural priorities (order, system, predictability, costs, prices, and profits), role-oriented organizations tend to try to control variability in their environment. Their priorities are best met by having simple, hence reliable and cheap systems, which provide uniform goods and services to customers with uniform needs. During the last few decades, as our needs and wants have become more differentiated and unpredictable, systems have had to become more complex in the attempt to respond to customer wants, and they have predictably become less reliable as a result. When I compare the management in large bureaucratic organizations today with what it was thirty years ago when I began my own career, it is clear that both quality and effort are up but customer satisfaction is down. I believe that a major reason is the proliferating complexity of systems designed to offer variety and choice to customers. As Perrow has pointed out, complex, closely coupled systems are inherently unstable and unreliable, no matter how much human effort goes into trying to make them work (Perrow, 1984).

The public contact employees of large bureaucracies are often seen by the public to be excessively rigid, uncaring, and unresponsive to customers' needs. In my experience, these same employees feel themselves to be controlled and frustrated by the systems and structures under which they work. Most people, particularly those who choose work involving high contact with the public, enjoy being able to give service and satisfy people's needs. Often, their hands are tied.

Recently, the customer service people in an electric utility I work with got together the field supervisors in a series of meetings and asked, "What could we do in the short term to remove 'service inhibitors?'" Service inhibitors were defined as "anything which prevents our field crews and telephone contact people from giving customers the service they want, and which our people would like to give them." It had been expected that most of the ideas would involve additional manpower, money, and equipment. These commodities are in short supply in any cost-sensitive operation. In fact, people enthusiastically contributed over fifty suggestions for short-term service improvements, only one of which required additional resources. The rest were matters of changing current practices and policies or giving field people additional discretion to decide which requests from customers were reasonable.

Role-oriented organizations also tend to be inward turning in their preoccupations and their priorities. They are often large and centralized, and what this means in systems terms is that contact with the environment is limited to the thin, often stretched and overworked "skin" of the organization. The vast preponderance of organization members are busy responding to one another, and to the requirements of the systems that control their daily activities.

Thus, today, large bureaucratic organizations are in trouble as customers demand more variety, and particularly as they demand more responsiveness to their individual needs. The dilemma which exists for such organizations when they want to improve customer service is that they are in trouble because of their size, their systems, their structures, and their associated culture. The difficulty is not, I think, because of any inherent incapacity, personality traits, or unwillingness to respond on the part of their managers or the people who do the work.

Of course, with our penchant for finding the closest and most obvious culprit for anything that goes wrong, it is the employees who usually are fingered as responsible for service failures. Then the need for improved service is addressed by providing training and closer supervision and perhaps by introducing incentives and awards (for example, "employee of the month"). It is typical of the role (and the power) orientation to assume that it is the employees who need to be fixed and not the conditions under which they work.

Achievement-Oriented Service

The achievement-oriented organization marches to its own drum, and its concept of service derives from its own sense of purpose and mission. The mission may or may not include a focus on service, but in any event, the definition of good service is based on internal values and standards. The standards sometimes bear scant resemblance to customers' ideas of what they want.

The world of high technology abounds with examples of unilateral definition of customers' needs. Apple Computer under Steve Jobs was a classic example of the achievement culture. Asked what was Apple's mission, Jobs is reported to have said, "To change the world!" He decided that the Macintosh computer was what computer users needed to change the world, and he focused the energies of the organization on that product. Meanwhile, fanatically loyal users of earlier Apple products languished, fretted, and eventually became disaffected as their requests for product information and service were ignored.

Scientists, engineers, professionals, and staff specialists of all kinds who love their work and believe they are making a contribution tend to share the achievement culture's implicit assumption that what the customer (or the organization or the world) needs is what they offer. In consulting with these professionals on how they can be more effective in dealing with their clients, I find that difficulties in giving service are nearly always framed as problems in influencing others. "How can we get the line managers to see that our new performance appraisal program is a real improvement over what they're doing?" "How can we get the refineries to adopt our new catalyst?" "How can I get my patients to take their medicine as prescribed?" "How can we get the program managers to cooperate with our improved budgeting process?"

Thus, service is seen as *doing* something *to* someone. The customer becomes the target or object of the service activity. Individuals and organizations that are highly oriented to achievement tend to define the service relationship unilaterally, and "good customers" are those who respect the service provider's expertise and cooperate in their own treatment. In other words, good customers are "good patients."

The strength of the achievement orientation in service is its dedication to excellence, to innovation, and to professional integrity. Achievement-oriented organizations will often spare no time, money, or expense to get it right, make it work, solve the problem. Because their people are dedicated to their work and believe in what they are doing, they tend to be self-motivated, and to drive themselves and others to high levels of personal performance.

Achievement-oriented people like challenges. If an achievement-oriented organization has a concept of service as central to its mission, it will put the same energy into achieving high standards of service as it would put into any other activity. Although I am not familiar firsthand with Jan Carlzon of SAS, I have read reports of his drive to improve customer service in that organization. They read like a classic example of the passionate striving for excellence which is typical of the achievement orientation. A few quotes from *Service America!* give the flavor:

> "With the help of his key executives, Carlzon began to preach and teach this gospel of customer orientation energetically and persistently throughout the organization."

> "According to Olle Stiwenius, director of the internal SAS management consultants, 'Jan Carlzon really masterminded the turnabout maneuver. He . . . himself supplied the vision to get it going and the energy to see it through.'"

> "Carlzon's approach was characterized by an almost obsessive commitment to managing the customer's experience at all points in the cycle of service" (Albrecht and Zemke, 1985).

This is visionary leadership at its best: thrusting for excellence, preaching the message, inspiring the troops, energizing the organization from the top. Doubtless, the strategy called for sampling customer opinion, responding swiftly to complaints, and the like. But the accounts one reads do not convey that the customer was in the driver's seat. Carlzon was in the driver's seat, and the organization was responding to his vision. The idea of service in the achievement culture is active—shaping, building, creative—rather than receptive or responsive. For the latter, we must look to the support orientation.

Support-Oriented Service

The support orientation is in important ways the other side of the coin from the achievement culture. Both are internally motivated. In the power and role cultures, people are controlled by the application of external rewards and punishments: for example, fear of losing their jobs or hope of monetary rewards and promotions. In contrast, it is intrinsically fulfilling for most people to perform and participate in the support and achievement cultures.

The support culture emphasizes "being" values of cooperation, belonging, caring, responsiveness, and receptivity. These are opposite from the "doing" values of achievement: action, autonomy, performance, innovation, and building and shaping the environment.

Thus, the idea of service in the support culture is much more oriented to listening to customers or clients, empathizing with their needs, and responding to their concerns. Rather than actively shaping the environment, the support culture endeavors to flow with external forces and work with them.

Comparing Service Styles

For example, the achievement response to a problem is to attack and overcome it. The support response is like the martial art of aikido. One joins with the forces of the others, working with them in a kind of dance, the outcome of which is not a victory but is more likely to be learning for all parties and mutual appreciation.

Where the strategy of the achievement orientation is to offer or sell something new or better to the customer, the support strategy is to ask, "What can we do for you?"

Staff-line relationships within an organization are often an interesting study in the contrast between active and responsive orientations on the part of staff when they are serving the line. Some staff groups have high standards of professionalism and are oriented to excellence in the practice of their professions. They spend a great deal of time in their own offices, thinking up ways to help the line: new technology, better systems, innovative ways to solve problems. They have well-articulated visions of how the application of their expertise can make their organizations better. When they invent or discover something particularly exciting, they venture out with great enthusiasm to "sell" line managers on adopting it. When they do not make a sale, they interpret it as a failure on the part of the line to comprehend the benefits which are being offered. They characterize the line as "resistant to change," or "conservative." These staff groups are behaving in a typically achievement-oriented way.

Other groups conceive of themselves as identifying and responding to the needs of line managers. They spend a lot of time in line managers' offices, talking with them about their operations and their problems. They look for ways to be useful to their "clients." They get to know them personally, often building close relationships that are over and above what is required to do the work. They are often so busy putting out fires and performing other services for the line that they do not have time to think and be creative. Their way of giving service is typically support oriented.

An Example of the Difference Between Support and Achievement Service

I have spent quite a lot of time with training and management development people in organizations, and there the contrast between support and achievement orientations is marked. I remember particularly one extremely competent and creative training manager who devoted his time primarily to finding and bringing into the organization the best and latest in "experience-based" training. He spent a lot of company money on outside consultants, and he put on some of the best-designed and best-conducted training it has been my pleasure to see within a company.

Most of the executives in the company were engineers. They did not understand or share my friend's passion for interpersonal process. It was a very "bottom line"–oriented company, and these managers could not see a relationship between the training and the profits. They tolerated the training activities, without great conviction, up to the time when the company laid off a lot of people during a recession. Then they closed their expensive training center, and my friend lost his job. When the decision was made, there just was not any understanding or support for his activities among the top executive group.

There is a brighter sequel to the story. My friend did a lot of soul-searching during the period between jobs, and when he finally got another, also in a scientifically oriented organization, he completely reformed his strategy. Initially, he did not make a move without making the rounds of his client managers to discover whether they had a need for it. He saved his creativity for solving their problems and meeting their needs. He asked lots of questions before he developed anything. When he finally had a training product to offer, he needed to do very little selling since he was producing to the order of his customers. From running one of the most isolated and achievement-oriented training operations I have seen, he came to run one of the most connected and responsive support-oriented ones I have worked with. His training probably was not as creative and groundbreaking as it had been before, but it was many times more appreciated.

The support orientation to service comes ultimately from the heart, in contrast to the achievement orientation, which flows from the mind and from the will.

It springs from our empathy and sympathy with the needs, problems, and dilemmas of other human beings and from the wish to respond and to help. Where the achievement orientation is clever, creative, and determined, the support orientation is compassionate and caring.

Examples of Role-Oriented Service: The American Way

We Americans are not greatly inclined toward the support orientation to service. We tend instead toward the role orientation. I am particularly struck with the contrast on those occasions when I fly an American airline to Europe and then go on a European airline to a further destination, particularly if my onward travel is on Aer Lingus, the Irish airline. American cabin attendants at their best are efficient, attractive, and friendly. Irish cabin attendants radiate warmth. In my experience, transactions with them have a personal quality that is indefinable but unmistakable. It is a blend of being present for the weary traveller and being genuinely interested in him or her as a person.

I do not believe the difference is a matter of training with these airlines so much as it is the style of a national culture. That is not to say that organization cultures cannot be led or shaped or changed, but if they are left to themselves, they will take the shape and the style which their employees bring with them when they come to work in the morning. If you want to change the style, you have to start there and work with what you have.

Another example of the difference was brought home to my partner and me when we emigrated to the United States from England some years ago. I had been away for eight years; my wife was born in Britain. We were both struck by the difference in service that we encountered around getting various household services: rug cleaning, appliance repair, plumbing, department store deliveries, opening bank accounts, and the like.

The American organizations we dealt with tended to be large and well organized compared to their British counterparts. They had precision systems for delivering service and, by and large, the systems worked. However, if your need was not provided for by the system, you were up against a blank, uncomprehending wall. There was often, literally, no one you could talk with about your problem.

An Example of Support-Oriented Service

The contrast is illustrated by an incident I remember in a London restaurant after a late dinner. The hostess called a taxi to take us to a midnight sleeper for the North. The minutes went by, and no taxi came. It began to look as though we would miss our train and my meeting with clients the next day. Seeing our distress, the hostess volunteered that her boyfriend was picking her up after work. Although it was well out of their way, they happily took us round to the station. We caught our train, and we carried the glow of their generous act with us on our journey.

The incident proves nothing by itself, but it has been repeated in less dramatic ways many times. In Britain, systems for service delivery are not so highly evolved as in the United States, and they often do not work very well. When they do not, there is usually a human being on the other end of the telephone with whom you can talk about your problem. Often you can evoke the sympathy of that person for your plight, and when that happens, acts of individual kindness occur. The rule is bent, or you are put a bit ahead of your rightful place in the queue, or someone goes out of his or her way to help.

The Role Orientation Constricts the Heart

In the United States, we emphasize the system, and often the system does not permit the individual to respond from the heart. The rule is not flexible, or as is the case for service representatives who work over the telephone, transactions are monitored by supervisors for brevity. Taking the time to listen and help is discouraged.

Tight, efficient systems do not permit people to respond from the heart. People who work in them become frustrated and irritated by their lack of freedom to respond, and they close down emotionally. They check their compassion and their empathy at the door, because to experience warm feelings for people they are prevented from helping would create painful internal conflict.

I believe customers are coming increasingly to place a higher value on the warmth of the support orientation in their search for service. They are looking for service transactions where they are treated as worthwhile individuals; where their opinions about what they want and need are respected; where they are assisted by people they can relate to on a level of equality; and where caring and kindness characterize the human interactions.

This is the trend I see over the recent past, and I am not sure why. Perhaps it is the growing realization that we are all going to have to do with the same or a lower standard of material living as time goes on. If we do not look forward with the same confidence to moving ahead, we may want to enjoy where we are a bit more. Perhaps it is the feeling that too many of our transactions are with systems, too few with people. We want those fewer interactions we have with people to be of a higher quality. Perhaps it is the "high tech, high touch" trend John Naisbitt (1982) talks about. Perhaps, living in a competitive, abrasive, and insecure world where relationships are often transitory and easily fractured, we are developing a "hidden hunger" to be loved a little bit more.

Whatever the reason, customers and the organizations which serve them are growing more sensitive to service quality. When organizations become concerned about improving service, they tend to see it in terms of their own cultural biases. It is that tendency which this discussion is intended to counterbalance. Increasingly, when customers talk about wanting better service, they mean the style of service that is typical of the support culture. That does not mean customers do not want efficient systems or excellent, innovative approaches to meeting their needs. They want these and more. Organizations which do not learn how to listen to customers from the perspective of the support framework will not understand what they are hearing. They may put effort into improving service in ways which customers are happy enough to have but which do not meet their deeper priorities, their hidden hungers.

Love and Service

A lot of people want to give warmer service than they are permitted to. In my experience, people who give service are more often frustrated by the circumstances, systems, and procedures under which they must operate than they are by the people they serve. And when I talk to leaders and managers about balancing achievement with support in their organizations, there are far more wistful looks in the audience than there are antagonistic ones. Many people are urged by their hearts to be kinder, more responsive, more supportive in their business interactions. In the support orientation to service, people's needs to be cared for and to be treated as individuals come together with the unmet need most of us have to be more nurturing and responsive in our business lives.

We are often blocked by the driving, competitive climates of our organizations and by the rigidity of systems set up to assure that customers have uniform service at a price. Most organizations are too far out of balance to be able to integrate caring service with efficient systems and the drive for bottom-line results. They recognize the need for change, but they cling to what they know best, unable to let go of its security in order to reach for something which seems riskier at the same time as it offers improvement.

It is a genuine risk. The relaxation of controls can permit sloppy, uncaring performance as well as service from the heart. Responsible managers will not let go of control unless they can have some trust and confidence in the improvements in service to be expected.

In this respect, service is like quality. So long as mistrust is behind the inspection of people's work, they will not assume personal responsibility for it, and quality will be a persistent nagging unsolved problem, beset with adversarial relationships. When people are given and accept responsibility for their own quality, that situation improves, sometimes dramatically. I believe that service will prove amenable to the same approach that has worked with quality: top management commitment combined with systems designed to give the management of service over to the people who deliver it.

Support-oriented service cannot be faked. It will only work if the process is managed from the heart, not done just because it is good business but because it feels right. It is not enough for business leaders to believe in service as a support-oriented activity; they have to "walk their talk" as well, serving the service providers from their hearts, whether the providers are internal staff or work with customers.

That is very simple, and also very hard. It is hard because most organization cultures do not support development of the heart. It is simple because there are certain behaviors which, practiced faithfully, will open the heart of the one who practices and will warm the hearts of those affected. When the leaders I work with ask me what I mean by practicing love in business, here is how I suggest they treat other people and the organization.

- Give credit for people's ideas and build on their contributions.
- Listen to people's concerns, hopes, fears, pain: be there for them when they need an empathetic ear.
- Treat people's feelings as important.
- Be generous with your trust. Give others the benefit of the doubt.
- See others as valuable and unique in themselves and not simply for their contribution to the task.
- Respond actively to others' needs and concerns; give help and assistance when it is not your job.
- Look for the good and the positive in others, and acknowledge it when you find it.
- Nurture others' growth: teach, support, encourage, smooth the path.
- Take care of the organization. Be responsive and responsible to its needs as a living system.

These are the signs and signals of love in business, and they are the behaviors of a support orientation to service. For many of us, they also define a discipline that can lead us in the direction of greater personal satisfaction and continued growth—across the frontier of our own hearts.

CHAPTER THIRTEEN

CULTURE AND LEVELS OF CONSCIOUSNESS IN ORGANIZATIONS

In 1990, I began to study Eastern spirituality, influenced by my travels in India. "Culture and Levels of Consciousness in Organizations" is the first of my papers to derive directly from those studies. I had never been completely satisfied with my culture model, although it has nearly always satisfied others. Although the model, and the questionnaire based on it (Harrison and Stokes, 1986 [1992]), adequately differentiated organization cultures as to style, it did not discriminate the higher, finer variants of a particular culture from the lower, darker examples. I have always had a strong interest in and commitment to humankind's striving toward the light, and I was convinced that each of the four cultures I had described manifests itself in organizations in both higher and lower forms.

For example, the power culture, which in my and Stokes's questionnaire is presented in a somewhat unfavorable light, can be seen in some organizations in a higher form. In its higher form, those with power show a strong concern for the welfare, education, growth, and development of those in their care. Benevolent paternalism may be nearly dead in the United States, and perhaps we need not lament it deeply. However, it has a long tradition and is still alive and viable in much of the world. I wanted my model to reflect the differences between light and dark in each of the four organization cultures I had identified.

I thought I could create from the culture model a more comprehensive theory of organization dynamics, which could then serve as a guide to differential diagnosis and intervention into organizations. I had long observed that different organiza-

Source: Originally published as a monograph (Clinton, Wash.: Harrison Associates, 1990). Reprinted here, with revisions, with permission of Roger Harrison.

tional cultures seemed to call for different kinds of interventions. For example, team building was often my intervention of choice in what I was calling the achievement culture, whereas I got better results working one on one with individual leaders in power cultures. I wanted to create a model that would explain these differences and permit me and others to plan change strategies which would be more effective and less painful for all concerned.

I also wanted my model to account for differences in *enlightenment* or *levels of consciousness* between examples of a particular form of organization culture. I had been working since 1987 on a model of levels of consciousness in organizations, and I found support for my thinking in the *gunas* in Hindu spiritual thought. The idea contained in the gunas is of a progression from lower levels, which are heavy, dull, and self-oriented, to higher levels, which have more energy, more light, and less attachment to sense gratification.

I could see similar differences in organization cultures. For example, the power culture can be expressed in oppression and exploitation of underlings, or it can be seen in a benevolent idea of the responsibilities of the powerful for those in their care. The latter and higher form of the power culture includes ideas of stewardship, protection, loving support, and responsibility that are missing in the former and lower form. The idea of the gunas was also helpful in pointing to possible organization cultures that are different from those we observe, cultures we do not see because the right conditions for their flowering do not currently exist in our society.

I presented the first version of my new culture model in the spring of 1990, at a meeting on the future of organizations

convened by the Association of Teachers of Management at Stratford-upon-Avon. The model, though ragged, was well received. I was asked by the conference organizers to write a longer piece for inclusion in a book on organizational futures. The request was a real gift because it provided me with the impetus to think through the details of my emerging model. However, the editors had difficulties finding a publisher, and by the time the book was finally published in 1994, I felt my new work on organizational learning (Harrison and Dawes, 1994 [Chapter Twenty-Four]) was more appropriate to the book's audience. Therefore, although it has been much circulated in draft form, "Culture and Levels of Consciousness in Organizations" has not yet been published.

My earlier model of four organization cultures is fully described in the paper in the preceding chapter, "Organization Culture and Quality of Service." Since writing "Organization Culture and Quality of Service" in 1987, I have worked over the model several times, and my new work has found its way into a book on the planning and management of change, *Humanizing Change: Matching Interventions to Organizational Realities* (Harrison, Cooper, and Dawes, 1991). I now have two models I am happy with, one "big" and one "little." The more elaborate and complex model satisfies my need for completeness and elegance, and it stimulates the interests of more theoretically inclined colleagues. The briefer one is useful for presentations to more general or pragmatically inclined audiences. I am satisfied with each, and the work feels complete in that I am ready to move on. The "big" model is presented in this chapter, the "little" model in Chapter Fourteen.

One of the beliefs and principles underlying my work as a consultant is that organizations differ in their *levels of consciousness,* just as all living organisms do. By a *higher level of consciousness,* I mean a greater awareness than was previously manifest, an ability to take in from the environment a wider range of information, and also more complex information, organize it, and *respond to it* in a way which enhances the survivability and the quality of life of the organism.

The "good" organization has this higher level of consciousness, which permits it to deal more effectively with internal and external change and stress, play its part in taking care of the environment, and provide a healthy and satisfying place to work for its members. For an organization, higher consciousness leads to greater success, not only as measured by limited financial criteria but also when judged against the same sorts of criteria we might apply to evaluating a person's life: contribution to society, morality and godliness, quality of relationships with others, and so on. Table 13.1 contains my definitions of higher and lower consciousness in organizations.

For those who cannot accept the idea of an organization having a consciousness, or indeed, being more than a collection of people, all I ask here is that you join with me in exploring how organizations act *as if* they were living systems. Think of it as a metaphor or construct, no more real but perhaps as useful as the idea of a "national character."

Current Issues of Consciousness in Business Organizations

The importance of shifting from lower to higher levels of consciousness in organizations has surfaced recently in management writing and thinking. Although others do not usually use my terms, my model resembles others in the genre of transformational thinking about management. From Peters and Waterman's "excellent companies" study (1982) through Peters and Austin's *A Passion for Excellence* (1985), Peters's *Thriving on Chaos* (1987), and Pascale and Athos's *The Art of Japanese Management* (1992) and *Managing on the Edge* (1990), there runs a theme relating organizational effectiveness to such qualities as those I have identified as typical of higher states of organizational consciousness: integrity; high purpose; ability to manage diversity, tension, and contention; integration of the spiritual and the mundane; and an emphasis on serving the organization's stakeholders. These qualities are in the air today. The idea of levels of organizational consciousness seems to me a useful way of talking about these qualities and planning how to develop them.

Consciousness and the Management of Diversity

In his interesting and useful book *Managing on the Edge* (1990), Richard Pascale and makes a strong case for the skill of "contention management" as a central factor

TABLE 13.1. CHARACTERISTICS OF HIGHER AND LOWER CONSCIOUSNESS IN ORGANIZATIONS.

Lower Consciousness in Organizations	*Higher Consciousness in Organizations*
Fear is an important element in controlling and directing behavior.	Internal commitment is the important element in controlling and directing behavior.
Links between organizational parts are few; information flow is typically one way and rigidly constrained.	There are many links between parts; communication is typically two way and unconstrained.
The organization tends to react without reflection or consideration of alternate responses. Short-range considerations usually prevail. The organization's behavior is "caused" by outside forces and events.	The organization reflects on its alternatives before acting. Long-range considerations often prevail. The organization's behavior is "caused" internally by the conscious desires and decisions of its members.
The organization has a narrow and stereotyped repertoire of responses to situations. It deals poorly with diversity and change.	There are a wide range and variety in responses. The organization deals well with change and diversity.
The organization learns by trial and error rather than by design. Time and energy are directed into action, not learning.	The organization invests significant time and energy in learning about its environment and in studying and improving its performance.
The organization is closed to information from outside that disconfirms its self-image; internal questioning is discouraged.	The organization actively seeks feedback from outside and engages regularly in self-questioning.
The organization is fragmented. The parts are isolated from one another. They act to maximize their own performance without considering the effects of their actions upon the whole.	The organization is integrated. Parts understand the needs of the whole. They consider the effects of their actions on the whole and act to maximize the overall results.
The organization is motivated primarily by the hope of material gain.	The organization is motivated by a sense of high purpose and a wish to serve.
The organization is untrusting and exploitative in its stakeholder relationships (with customers, suppliers, employees, the community).	The organization tends to trust other entities and it follows high principles of "right action" (integrity and fairness) in its stakeholder relationships.
Conflict between parts of the organization is personalized and is resolved by who is strongest or can muster the most allies.	Conflict is about what is the "best way," what is "right," or what is the "caring thing to do." Conflict is resolved by reference to reason, principles, and love.
There is a split between the sacred and the secular. The organization's life is almost entirely materialistic. Higher values are seen as inappropriate criteria for decisions.	There is a merging of the secular and the spritual. Work becomes to some degree spiritualized, and nonmaterialistic values are invoked as criteria for practice.

that differentiates consistently successful organizations from their competitors. Organizations that are good at contention management do not choke off controversy and debate through the use of power or the avoidance of conflict. They seem to be able to tolerate more or less continuous disagreement, even on rather fundamental issues of strategy, structure, and policy, without becoming overly anxious or disorganized and chaotic. This ability to tolerate diversity of views is certainly typical of higher levels of consciousness, in organizations as in individuals.

Consciousness and Spirituality

Pascale also notes that in the West, work and spirituality have been radically separated, and he gives some credit for the greater energy and commitment in Japanese business organizations to the ability of those organizations to integrate the secular and the sacred. He points out the role of science in splitting our minds from our souls and our doing from our feeling, and he asserts that our current task is to heal those splits. After all, people in our society experience most of their social contact at work and often also socialize outside of work with people they meet at work. Our organizations tend to split people into their personal and productive parts, denying themselves access to people's higher, finer part. Thus, it is small wonder that business, in the United States at least, focuses so exclusively on such material values as profit and market share, neglecting the care of the soul, and the care of the whole society. Higher levels of organization culture lead to more integration of the whole person into work. They permit the business to broaden as well, taking on the function of making meaning as well as making money, and giving employees an opportunity to contribute to making a better life for others (Pascale, 1990).

Motivation and Consciousness

Abraham Maslow popularized the idea that a satisfied need is not a motivator. Human needs exist in a hierarchy, and as soon as one is satisfied, the next higher one emerges (Maslow, 1954). Maslow's theory of the hierarchy of needs is now known by almost every manager who has ever attended a behaviorally oriented course. My understanding of Maslow's model is outlined in Figure 13.1.

A New Theory of the Hierarchy of Needs

When I was teaching organizational behavior at Yale in the sixties, I asked my students to conduct some informal research on Maslow's model by interviewing their friends. Most of their respondents reported that their ego needs were rather well satisfied but they felt deprived in their social needs. I pondered these results, which

FIGURE 13.1. MASLOW'S MOTIVATION MODEL.

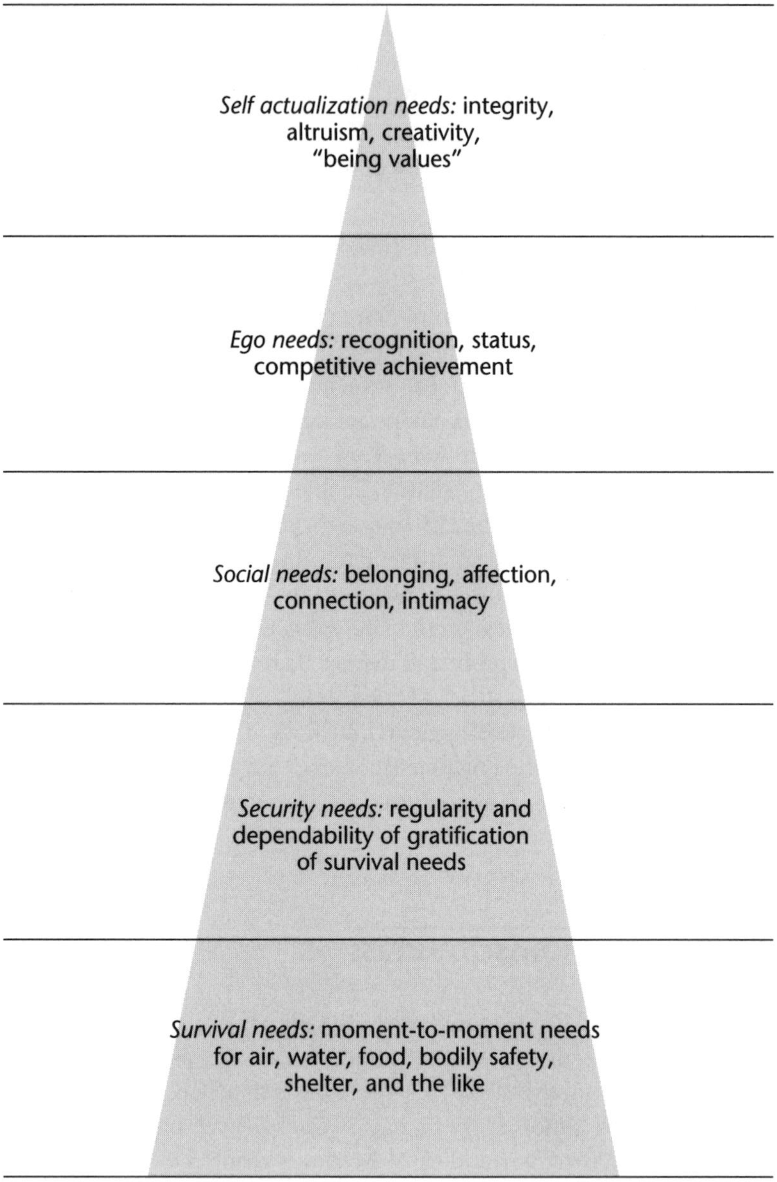

Self actualization needs: integrity,
altruism, creativity,
"being values"

Ego needs: recognition, status,
competitive achievement

Social needs: belonging, affection,
connection, intimacy

Security needs: regularity and
dependability of gratification
of survival needs

Survival needs: moment-to-moment needs
for air, water, food, bodily safety,
shelter, and the like

seemed to me to cast some doubt on Maslow's model, and I looked at another model of human needs, McClelland's tripartite model of motivation. McClelland identified *power, achievement,* and *affiliation* as the basic human motives (McClelland, 1953). Eventually, I hit on the idea of a new model in which Maslow's idea of a hierarchy was combined with McClelland's idea of the three basic motives.

I believe that Maslow mixed up motives with what I call levels of consciousness. A better map of the territory of human needs would define the survival, social, and ego needs as basic and universal. As each of these three basic needs is met at a lower level of consciousness, the individual moves up the ladder and begins to operate at the next higher level in meeting his or her needs in that same area, or *motivational domain.*

Maslow's survival need seems to me a basic human motive for seeking physical sustenance and protection from harm. I see it as the root need behind the drive for power, one of McClelland's basic motives. However, we experience and meet this need at more than one level of consciousness. We begin by depending on others for everything we need, and then we reach out into the world to exert more and more control and self-determination over the sources of gratification (food, shelter, clothing, and the sources of sensory pain and pleasure and also of money, the means to procure and secure these things). We compete with others for material goods and sensory pleasures, but we may also become altruistic, taking pleasure out of giving these to others.

Maslow's social needs refer to the basic human need for love and nurturance. McClelland has called this domain the need for affiliation. We know that this need, too, is fundamental and present in all humans, from studies which show that infants do very poorly when not held, stroked, and the like. Again, there are different levels at which we meet this need. As infants, we first respond to loving from others, then develop means and skills for drawing it to ourselves. Later we may discover as much joy in giving love as in receiving it.

Maslow's ego needs seem to me to refer to basic needs for competence, mastery of skills and knowledge, and learning. McClelland labels them the need for achievement. Because they are higher up on Maslow's pyramid, they are described in his model in terms that suggest a higher level of consciousness than does his description of survival and social needs. As I see it, from the lowest to higher levels, the ego needs begin with the infant needing help in learning how to do things and how the world works. Very early, though, children begin to explore and experiment on their own. They begin to learn from their own experiences, and they practice their skills. They are still sensitive, however, to evaluation of their competence by others, whether adults or peers, and thus their self-esteem is dependent upon others. Later, the individual competes with others to demonstrate skills, learning, and creativity. At higher levels of competence, the individual may become quite immune to criticism and praise. She or he develops internal standards of achievement and competence that are used to reward the self for good work. At the highest level, competence is exercised for the sheer joy of the art and for the intrinsic satisfaction of learning new skills and knowledge.

For my derivative model, I have chosen to call my three *motivational domains* by the same names that McClelland used in his careful research to classify human needs and motives (McClelland, 1953). Thus, in Figure 13.2 I use the terms *power, achievement,* and *affiliation* to refer to three basic domains, each of which can exist

FIGURE 13.2. INTEGRATION OF MASLOW'S HIERARCHY WITH MCCLELLAND'S THREE MOTIVES.

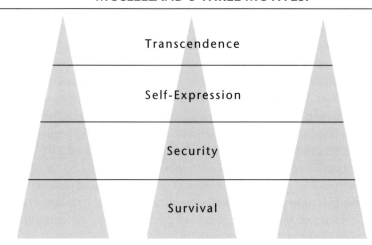

at one of four levels, *survival, security, self-expression* (Maslow's ego gratification), and *transcendence* (Maslow's self-actualization).

The four levels are, of course, different levels of consciousness, each pointing to different means or processes for gratifying our needs. At the survival level, we go for immediate gratification in the moment, without much thought for the future. At the security level, we are dependent upon others for gratification of our needs, and we endeavor to find and maintain stable relationships with others in which they will meet our needs.

At the level of self-expression, our interest is in taking charge of the means of gratifying our needs. As adolescents and into adulthood, we rebel against those who seek to control us or keep us in the dependence of the security level. We compete with others to be the strongest or wealthiest (power), the cleverest or most skilled (achievement), or the most attractive (affiliation). We take satisfaction from recognition of our qualities in these areas, from seeing ourselves as exemplifying high levels of personal development. We seek to increase our skills, our artistry, our creativity, and our level of functioning in whichever of the domains we are operating.

At the level of transcendence, we take pleasure in giving, creating, and behaving according to the highest values of a given domain. We obtain intrinsic satisfactions from "right action," regardless of the fruits of the action. We operate from a state of consciousness that is seen in the world's great ethical and spiritual systems as a very high level of being and doing in the world. For example, in the domain of power, a person might take satisfaction in securing justice for others, in protecting the weak from exploitation and harm, and in exercising power for the highest good of the whole (stewardship). In the domain of achievement, a person obtains intrinsic satisfaction from learning, from craftsmanship, and from creating, regardless of whether anyone else sees or values the achievement. In the domain of affiliation, one enjoys giving love and nurturing others, whether or not the affection is returned.

Consciousness Differences Within Individuals

An individual may be at different levels on each of the three pyramids shown in Figure 13.2 because the circumstances of life offer varied opportunities for challenge and fulfillment in the different domains. Thus, the Yale students whose interviews provoked my original venture into theory building had lots of opportunities to internalize self-concepts of competence and achievement—just to be selected to attend Yale was a recognition of scholastic attainment. They came from families that valued and rewarded achievement. But their personal affiliation histories were probably more mixed. For many, love and affection were problematic needs, uncertain of gratification.

I worked on my integrated model for a number of years before I thought I had it right. I was interested in the way individual growth seems to cycle between polar opposites, in this case between separation and connection. At the lowest level, survival, the individual is isolated and alienated. Then he or she connects to others in a dependent mode, security. As the egoistic self-expression needs emerge, the individual differentiates, perhaps rebels, and separates emotionally from those on whom he or she is dependent. Once having freed themselves, people are able to establish connections and relationships on a more equal, mutual basis.

Adapting the Consciousness Model to Organizations as a Culture Model

I first published my consciousness model some years after I did the original work (Harrison, 1979). When I began to think about levels of organization culture, I reviewed the earlier work and decided the model would serve my needs well. It seemed to me that organizations I was working with were going through the change from security to self-expression, and in those that had made that shift, I could feel longings emerging for renewed connection and cooperation. When I shared my emerging model of levels of organizational consciousness with colleagues and clients, the feedback confirmed my impressions. Here is a description of the model as applied to organizations.

I think of organizations as providing "fields" for their members' growth and development, whether or not they have been designed to do so. The qualities of each organization's culture determine which of the domains of human motivation will be open to members for obtaining satisfactions and evolving through the levels of consciousness. Similarly, the qualities of our society's culture channel our energy into certain domains, allowing us to find satisfactions and growth in those

FIGURE 13.3. FIVE LEVELS OF ORGANIZATIONAL CONSCIOUSNESS IN FOUR DOMAINS OF ORGANIZATION CULTURE.

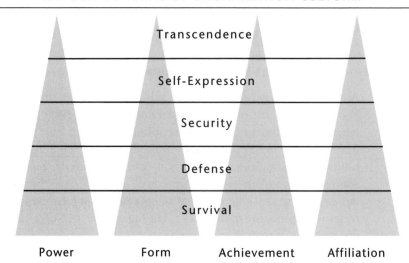

Transcendence

Self-Expression

Security

Defense

Survival

Power   Form   Achievement   Affiliation

domains but putting barriers in the way of our growing in other domains. Therefore, in building a model of organizational consciousness, I have kept McClelland's three domains of power, achievement, and affiliation as fields of organizational activity and concern. Because these domains are associated with basic human emotions, they attract our energy and provide issues and dilemmas to be resolved in our organizational lives. Every organization has to provide for the satisfaction of human needs in each of the domains, or for the control and suppression of the motive which a domain represents.

In adapting the motivation model to organizational levels of consciousness, however, I have added the fourth domain of *form*, because that is another field in which organizations show their levels of consciousness and channel human energy. No theory of organizational consciousness could be complete without dealing with form as it manifests in organizational structures, systems, procedures, and rules and regulations. How these are designed and how they are experienced by organization members are important aspects of the qualities and styles of an organization's culture. When form is narrowly controlling and constraining, it constricts the human spirit, and it limits growth in consciousness. When form is created in service to the task *and* the organization members, then it supports evolution into higher levels of consciousness.

In contrast to the four levels of individual consciousness, I have identified five levels of organizational consciousness: survival, defense, security, self-expression, and transcendence. (Defense is discussed later in this section.) The model of five levels in relation to the four domains is shown in Figure 13.3.

Figure 13.4. gives an expanded overview of the five levels of organizational consciousness.

An organization's culture alternates between the poles of separation, or alienation, and connection as it evolves through the levels, first differentiating then integrating into greater wholes what has been differentiated. The overview in Figure 13.4 shows how the isolation and fragmentation of the lowest level of inte-

FIGURE 13.4. OVERVIEW OF FIVE LEVELS OF ORGANIZATIONAL CONSCIOUSNESS.

Transcendence

A culture of meaning, purpose, and love. People join to give rather than to get. Work, contribution, and relationships are enjoyed for their own sake, not for rewards. Thus, people are not easily managed by the application of incentives or punishments. They value diversity. They operate according to high principles and ethical standards because it feels right to do so. They see the organization as part of a larger whole and manage it for the benefit of all stakeholders.

Self-Expression

The culture is irreverent, self-reliant, and individualistic. Structures are fluid and open. There are few sanctions for violating rules. There are few supports for individuals. It is "sink or swim." Members compete strongly. Loyalty, common purpose, responsibility, and mutual support are devalued or given lip service. Autonomy, energy, confusion, conflict, and constant change are characteristic. Often there is more learning and creativity than productivity.

Security

The culture is stable and exerts strong control over members. Rewards provided by the organization are reliably available to conforming members. Norms, rules, and standards are consistent, known to all, and conformed to by most. Sanctions are applied to bring deviants into line. Energy of members is devoted to maintaining the system and doing the work. People act and are treated as though the organization is more important than they are.

Defense

The culture is out of balance and not working. The demands made on members are not compensated by matching satisfactions. Organization members feel deprived or in deficit, as more energy is required for fewer results. In denial of failure, and in the attempt to prop up the system, leaders exhort or coerce people to do more of what is not working. Although almost all may recognize the need for change, people are too busy keeping their heads above water to find time and energy for learning new ways.

Survival

The organization struggles to survive and grow, moving from crisis to crisis. Motivation is from hope of success and fear of failure. People accept strong control from the top and will sacrifice for the organization's survival. There are few systems, little planning, many short-term quick fixes. Learning is by trial and error; "organizational memory" is lacking. Typical situations include turnarounds and new plant and business startups.

gration, survival, and of the related level of defense give way to the ordered, hierarchical patterns of the security level. These ordered but constraining and rigid cultures make way, in turn, for openness, personal freedom, and expansion of the human spirit at the next higher level, self-expression. Then, at the level of transcendence, cooperative connections are reestablished but without the rigid hierarchical and patriarchal forms of security cultures. I struggled a bit with the name for that higher level. Some of the candidates were actualization, mutuality, integration, and alignment. I finally settled on transcendence as having the fewest misleading connotations!

The Special Case of Defense

The level of consciousness I call *defense* is not a step upward on the path of progression to higher levels but describes the holding-on reaction that can often be seen when an organization finds that its adaptive patterns at the security level no longer work well. The culture of defense reflects a struggle to prevent a descent to the level of survival. At the same time, it is indicative of an unwillingness to move into the looseness and disorder that characterize learning how to thrive at the level of self-expression. An organization at the level of defense is stuck between evolution and devolution, and both of those alternatives look much the same to its leaders and members. Many organizations operating at the security level experience strong internal and external stresses from rapid changes in markets, competition, technology, workforce characteristics, and the environment. The security culture does not deal effectively with rapid change because of the barriers to communication and cooperative problem solving that are built into rigid bureaucratic systems. Nor does the security culture get the best out of its people's skill, will, and spirit, because it tends to honor these qualities only in people at higher levels of the organization.

With vision and wisdom, the leaders of a security organization under stress may prepare it to move to the level of self-expression, loosening controls, empowering individuals, flattening organizational structures, and so on. It often happens, however, that the leaders, and indeed all the organization members, deal with stress in the time-honored way of denial and defense: doing harder, faster, and with great determination the things that are not working. That quality of redoubling the effort to hold onto outmoded forms, systems, and values defines the level of consciousness I have named defense.

In the following section, I describe how each of the five levels manifests in each of the four domains.

Levels of Consciousness in the Domain of Power

Figure 13.5 is an overview of the ways power is used and experienced at each of the levels of organizational consciousness.

FIGURE 13.5. FIVE LEVELS OF POWER.

Transcendence

Stewardship
Justice and principled action are the norm. Leaders are servants and stewards, chosen for wisdom and state craft. They influence through respect and loyalty, exercising power for the good of the whole. They are mentors to subordinates, giving responsibility commensurate with readiness.

Self-Expression

Political
Political sophistication is needed to get ahead. Leaders are self-oriented careerists. People enjoy power, playing power games for fun. They are adept at wheeling and dealing, forming and maintaining alliances, and empire building.

Security

Authoritarian
There is a stable hierarchy and pecking order. People serve the leaders in return for rewards, favors, and protection. Leaders are directive, demanding compliance and punishing errors and failures. They are generous and indulgent with loyal followers.

Defense

Tyrannical
Domineering, threatening leaders exploit weakness, influence through fear, and manipulate information to maintain power. Power is exercised for personal gain, arbitrarily and capriciously. Political infighting is ruthless and to the death.

Survival

Organizational Jungle
Power is fragmented. There is constant jockeying for position. Each is out for himself or herself, and the devil take the hindmost. Alliances are shifting and unstable, built on immediate advantage.

At this time, many organizations are moving from the security/authoritarian uses of power to the self-expression/political configuration. In organizations where power is an important domain, this transition means that one can no longer count on pleasing the boss for safety and steady advancement. Those eager to get ahead must learn to form coalitions, trade favors and information, and become sensitive to the political consequences of what they say and do. Not all organizations operating at the level of self-expression are highly political, however. In some, much of their energy is invested in the achievement domain, and the relevant behaviors are very different, having to do with being recognized for creativity and competence (see Figure 13.7).

Levels of Consciousness in the Domain of Form

The domain of form has to do with structures, systems, and other impersonal means of channeling human energy and controlling behavior. The ways in which the levels of consciousness manifest in the domain of form are shown in Figure 13.6. There are hopeful signs in some organizations of a movement toward the responsive level of form. An example is the empowerment of operators through information technology, which is being used to give them finer control over their work, instead of using the technology to exert tighter control over the operators. Sociotechnical systems redesign, in which operators work with engineers and managers to improve production systems, is another development that moves form into this higher level. The same is true of programs in which operators are educated and empowered to identify and solve quality problems. Unfortunately, many quality programs are little more than training in quality methods, and there is little or no change in level of consciousness. The provision of information alone is unlikely to effect much of a shift in level.

Other organizations, faced with competition and the need for increased productivity and quality, go in the other direction, moving into defense. The leaders assume that what is wrong with quality and productivity is insufficient control of worker behavior, so they institute systems that provide closer surveillance and tighter control, or they replace workers with computers and machinery. While there may be some short-term improvement, their assumptions about the causes are often wrong. Most people in our society are at a level of personal development where autonomy and respect are quite important. Distrust and tight controls are demotivating. When this is the case, the management action results in having more of what is not working in the first place, and the eventual results can be disappointing. We see this in organizations where repeated reductions in the workforce have created a climate of mistrust and anger and a sense of betrayal that sucks energy away from the work and into negative channels.

FIGURE 13.6. FIVE LEVELS OF FORM.

Transcendence

Responsive
Form serves function. Technology and systems empower workers to manage own operations. People have whole jobs; know how their work fits the whole. Systems and procedures are designed and modified by workers in consultation with specialists. Workers are responsible for quality and often set production targets.

Self-Expression

Iconoclastic
High energy, creative, often chaotic. People bend rules, cut red tape, ignore rules and formal channels. Self-managing individuals do what they think needs doing. Free form, open communication. People admired for testing limits, using the system to beat the system.

Security

Bureaucratic
Form dominates function. Control by rules, systems, technology. Managers overloaded with detail. Procedures, many and detailed, are designed by specialists. Management responsible for quality and productivity. Workers responsible for showing up, following directives.

Defense

Frozen
Problems addressed by creating more rules, inspections, and controls, by limiting discretion and rigidly enforcing rules. Operations are mired in red tape. People avoid risk, responsibility, exposure. Leaders, swamped with detail, have no time for strategy.

Survival

Adhocracy
Expediency replaces planning. Unsystematic , chaotic work processes. Unclear roles and authority cause conflict and overlap, or tasks fall between the cracks. Problem solutions forgotten as soon as learned.

Levels of Consciousness in the Domain of Achievement

The domain of achievement is about work, productivity, quality, and creativity. It relates to the domain of form in that form provides the structures and the context for work. We can think of the domain of form as *social architecture*. When we design systems and organizational structures, we are creating the walls, rooms, and corridors that channel activity, information, and energy. The domain of achievement has to do with how people work, lead, and manage in those structures, and the spirit which they infuse into their work.

Figure 13.7 shows how the five levels of consciousness manifest in the domain of achievement. Expediency, the lowest level, is typical of startups, some new product introductions, business turnarounds, and other rapidly changing situations. In my work with high-technology companies and R&D organizations, I have found a number of rapidly changing organizations that remain in a chronic state of expediency, kept there by their inability to progress beyond the level of adhocracy in the domain of form. Without systems and structures that work, it is hard to move beyond this lower level of achievement.

To my eye, the organizations characterized by such writers as Tom Peters as having "a passion for excellence" (Peters and Austin, 1985) often have cultures that are a mixture of enthusiastic compliance and fanaticism (the levels of security and defense). There is often a strong addictive quality to such organizations, which has been well described by Schaef and Fassel in *The Addictive Organization* (1988). They are places where people can find in overwork and continual crises some solace for loneliness, unsatisfactory relationships, and spiritual emptiness. These states are characteristic of the darker side of life at the level of self-expression. Unfortunately, members of such organizations spend so much of their time and energy in work that it is often impossible for them to address the sources of their dispiritedness directly and effectively. Their addiction to work sets up a circular process from which there seems to be no escape, and the organization supports and rewards their workaholism.

I do not believe that we in the profession of organization development have yet found anything approaching an effective way of addressing addiction in organizations, partly because we are almost never asked to address it. On the contrary, our more addicted clients go to considerable trouble to throw us off the scent. I wish I could propose something helpful in regard to this issue. Probably an organizational version of the twelve-step program developed by Alcoholics Anonymous is a way to begin, but how to get an organization to enter and stay in treatment currently has me stumped!

Self-expression manifests in the domain of achievement as the pluralistic or collegial organization. Readers will recognize many technical, scientific, and professional organizations in this description, including medical and legal practices, universities, and some quite large research and development organizations.

I have experienced one or two organizations at the highest level in this

FIGURE 13.7. FIVE LEVELS OF ACHIEVEMENT.

Transcendence

Integrative/Visionary
Vision and purpose are high minded and responsive to stakeholders' needs. Means are of high integrity. Vision is tested against results and stakeholder feedback. The entire team shares credit for achievements. People work with joy in consciousness of "right action" and "right livelihood." Balance is maintained between work and private lives.

Self-Expression

Pluralism
Organization is collegial, loosely structured, with many autonomous units. Diverse local visions are pursued with passion, energy, creativity. Autonomy and individual achievement are valued more than teamwork. Coordination, common vision, commitment to the whole are difficult to achieve. Administrators are devalued.

Security

Enthusiastic Compliance
Contribution and competence are rewarded by status and recognition. People contribute willingly, subordinating personal lives to work. They cooperate inside, compete outside. The organization's values are articles of faith; the mission is unquestioned. Competing values are dismissed, ignored. People are elitist in jargon, dress, and attitudes to competitors, customers, and the public.

Defense

Fanaticism
Noble ends justify ignoble means. Narrow goals are pursued regardless of cost to outside stakeholders. Sacred cows and articles of faith must not be questioned. Warped vision is maintained by isolation from the environment and suppression of criticism. Work addiction forces long hours, whether or not required by tasks.

Survival

Expediency
Seat-of-pants navigation and inspiration take the place of planning. Chaos, continual change, trial-and-error learning characterize operations. Commitment is to immediate success. Poor communication leads to frequent reinvention of the wheel. Watchword is "whatever works."

domain, the one I call integrative/visionary. One was the Procter & Gamble plant at Lima, Ohio, which I visited in the mid eighties. It had a culture that seemed to me to operate at a very high level of consciousness in all the domains. It is hard to maintain high consciousness in one domain and be at a much lower level in the others. Consequently, the domains blend together quite a lot in organizations that are operating at the level of transcendence, and that was the case in this plant. There was an almost palpable feeling of love in the plant, and at the same time, there was very high energy for quality and productivity. People in teams competed for production and quality records, but they were very supportive and caring as well. Shop-floor workers had designed and implemented major innovations in the systems and the equipment they used, resulting in such great savings to the company that the innovations were closely guarded secrets. The teams managed themselves, and the plant manager saw himself as a facilitator, a coordinator, sometimes a mediator, and often a liaison person and advocate with higher staff and management in Cincinnati. There were humorous stories told about how managers transferred in from other parts of Procter & Gamble would sometimes try to overuse their power to direct and control. The point of the stories was that they were always foiled and either learned to work in a more collaborative way with workers or had to transfer to another plant.

Levels of Consciousness in the Domain of Affiliation

Figure 13.8 shows how the levels of consciousness manifest in the domain of affiliation, which deals with the qualities of relationships. As before, the survival level, alienation, refers to a culture of separation in which people are blocked from relationships or are unclear how to meet their relationship needs. For example, in new or chaotic organizations, the lack of accepted social norms, stable groups, and networks may be a barrier to connecting and belonging.

The level of security is called comfortable because it represents a stable social system in which issues of membership, inclusion and exclusion, and affection are well defined and understood and in which most of the members are able to meet their needs by conforming to social norms.

Again, when something disturbs or breaks up the established patterns of relationship, the culture can evolve to the self-expression level or devolve into the defense, or dysfunctional, level. When a culture defends its established patterns in the affiliation domain, people put a lot of energy into maintaining their threatened patterns rather than learning new ways of meeting their needs. Their defense usually takes the form of tighter social groupings, tougher sanctions against nonconforming members, and stronger barriers against entry by outsiders. The groups dig in and hunker down.

The individualistic and separated relationship culture described as narcissistic is what one would expect from a group of self-oriented egoists, people who have

FIGURE 13.8. FIVE LEVELS OF AFFILIATION.

Transcendence

Mutuality
Affection is given freely (not given to get); diversity, inclusivity, and cooperation are appreciated. Interdependence and part/whole relationships are understood; inner/outer connections are nurtured. Process sophistication and climate of support permit working through of sensitive issues (for example, performance, value differences).

Self-Expression

Narcissistic
Image is valued above substance. Diversity and flouting of social norms are admired and emulated. Transient, competitive, manipulative relationships are common. Enhanced ego is major relationship goal. Pairs and in-groups isolate themselves from the whole, in mutual admiration societies.

Security

Comfortable
Conformity to group norms is price of belonging. Conflict is avoided to preserve relationships. Harmony may interfere with task performance. People are treated equally when their competence is unequal. The organization is often run by an old boy network, or its mixed-gender equivalent.

Defense

Dysfunctional
Gossip and covert backbiting are prevalent beneath surface harmony. People are preoccupied with relationships and process to the neglect of tasks. Cozy groups and cliques isolate and scapegoat nonconforming members. Outsiders are experienced as an intrusion. Socializing with colleagues is often a condition for acceptance.

Survival

Alienation
Everyone is a needy taker; there are no givers. Deception and manipulation are used to obtain acceptance, belonging, and affection. Relationships are therefore shallow, short term, and exploitative.

been released from the constraints and the dependency of security. They take charge of their own social lives and rely upon their own attractiveness and social skills to meet relationship needs. They tend to compete with people with whom they are in relationship, which makes for high levels of intensity. They have high expectations for relationships, and when they do not find what they want, they look elsewhere. In California's Silicon Valley, where I live and work, this pattern is fairly common in organization cultures that have strong self-expression orientations. It is also prevalent in organizations of talented individual contributors and successful professionals. Observe in the area of consulting, for example, the national conferences of organizations like the Organization Development Network or the Association for Training and Development.

In those few organization cultures that fit the criteria for the transcendence level, people are connected, but relationships tend to be both cooperative and free of compulsion. Not only is there a tolerance for diversity and difference, as at the narcissistic level, but there is also a deeper attempt to understand and appreciate people for who they really are and to find ways of using differences for mutual learning. Relationships are more about giving than receiving, and the affiliation culture fosters a higher level of emotional maturity on the part of its members here than it does at the lower levels. Again, I have seen only one or two organizations that seemed to me to meet the criteria for this level. One was a group I worked with in the Peace Corps and that inspired an early paper (Harrison and Hopkins, 1967 [Chapter Nineteen]). Another was the Procter & Gamble plant at Lima, Ohio, referred to earlier. These organizations combined high task performance with close ties of affection, giving me cause to believe that achievement and affiliation can be compatible and mutually supportive. The more common view in business organizations is that the energy that goes into relationships is taken from the task. My observation is that loving, as distinct from seeking love, is energizing. When people can meet their relationship needs in organizations in healthy ways, they have more energy to give to the task, not less. Although we are far from knowing everything there is to know about the social architecture for facilitating the development of transcendence, what we do know from experiments such as the Lima plant is mostly ignored and violated.

Differences in Energy, Activity, and Level of Consciousness Among Domains

In understanding any organization's culture, it is important to identify not only at what levels of consciousness it operates but also which of the domains carry the most energy, excitement, and activity. It is also true that organizations, like people, may operate at different levels in different domains. For example, most business organizations operate at a lower level of consciousness in affiliation than they do in achievement. Since achievement is more highly valued and nurtured in our Western societies than affiliation, there is less energy put into affiliation and less opportunity for satisfying one's affiliation needs at work. There is therefore less opportunity for the organization to move up the levels of consciousness in the affiliation domain than there is in the achievement domain,

Having asked for a good deal of patience from readers while I laid out the results of my model building, I now want to show how we can use the model, as consultants and change managers, to diagnose and intervene effectively in real-life organizations.

Progression Between Levels of Consciousness

A useful feature of this model of levels of consciousness is that it shows us where an organization is heading in its evolution. In my experience, there is a "natural" progression in individuals from lower to higher levels of consciousness. Unless blocked, the internal forces of growth will move the individual along the path to higher levels. I see the same tendencies in organizations. However, in both organizations and individuals, there is nothing inevitable about such a progression. Most of us are cases of arrested development in one or more domains and so are most organizations. What is important to know about ourselves, and about our organizations, is that the inherent forces toward growth are there, awaiting release, and it is seldom too late to grow.

Some individuals seem to be born with higher levels of consciousness "wired in," so that they evolve to higher levels more quickly and easily than the rest of us. Some organizations too are born at higher levels of consciousness, because their founders have the wisdom, vision, and values to start them at the higher levels. Others never leave the lowest level, often because of the stamp placed upon their cultures by a founder's consciousness and will.

Following Gurdjieff (Ouspensky, 1957), who in turn followed more ancient traditions, I think of an organism as existing at a given state of consciousness until there is some external shock to the system. The shock is an event or series of events that renders the organism's current way of being and doing untenable or inadequate. Beliefs and value systems are brought into question by the shock; the world becomes unacceptably unpredictable and senseless. The organism's ability to survive and/or thrive is threatened, and its thought and behavior become disorganized and chaotic.

If the external shock is light enough or of brief duration, the organism, whether individual, group, or organization, will intensify its efforts to forcibly fit the new reality to its old values and beliefs, and it may succeed in doing so. If the shock is too great, the organism may not survive as a viable system. Individuals become ill or go mad; organizations too sicken and die. If an organization is well resourced with talented people and strong finances, it may take a long time to die, living on its stored energy and growing weaker over time.

If the shock is optimum, the organism will go through a process of disorganization followed by reorganization at a higher level of consciousness (for example, with a greater ability to process complex information). As the "new science" has discovered, both inorganic and organic systems undergo these processes (Wheatley, 1993). Like so much of the wisdom of the ancients, that idea is no longer esoteric but is becoming generally accepted at the leading edge of scientific thought as "the way things work."

What Can We Do to Help?

If we know that it is "natural" for organizations to move to higher levels of consciousness, and we know the qualities of the next level, then it becomes easier to help the transition along. We identify those forces that are moving in the direction of the natural progression. We work to strengthen them and to remove barriers in their path. We do not always have to invent forms and solutions. Rather, we can trust the self-organizing properties of the organism to find forms, systems, and processes appropriate to the new demands placed upon the organism.

What this self-generated process of healing (moving toward wholeness) most needs in order to progress is a loosening of constraints to communication and action. We can aid the communication by bringing the parts of an organization together in a atmosphere that is supportive of open communication about what people are seeing, feeling, and doing. In the same vein, self-organization is blocked and hindered by anything that restricts the free flow of information and energy in the organization, keeping the parts isolated and ignorant of what is happening in the whole.

The Normal Path of Evolution

Organizations tend to progress through the levels in this order: survival, security, self-expression, transcendence. In the normal progression, the survival stage separates the strong from the weak. The strong become the leaders if the organization survives, and they set the norms and the cultural tone of the organization as it moves into the more stable and, for most, more satisfying security phase. In the security phase, the organization develops and maintains a cultural system in which people are inducted into their parts when they enter the organization. Their relationships are *given* to them by the organization, and the focus is on the *parts* the individuals play, not on the individuals themselves.

Normally, an organization will be propelled into moving from the survival into the security mode by the successful problem-solving activities of organization members and by growth in size. As organizations grow, they must learn to process information more efficiently, create forms of organizational memory, and coordinate efforts between people who may never see one another face to face. The shocks that propel survival organizations into movement often have to do with the breakdown of the organizations' inadequate structures and systems under the pressures of rapid growth. To make the shift from hands-on control by a strong leader or dominant coalition requires that those leaders give up personal control in favor of more efficient and impersonal systems and procedures and a structure of delegated authority.

The Current Movement from Security

In many organizations today, there are strong internal and external pressures to move out of the level of security because of the mediocre results in quality, productivity, and innovation that are characteristic of traditional organization cultures. Under the pressures to evolve, organizations are leaving the comfortable and well-known level of security, but as I have pointed out above, they are not all moving to higher levels of consciousness. Some of them develop cultures of defense in the attempt to hold on to stability and security.

In organizations making the upward shift, there is a loosening of coercive controls, an increase in empowerment of the individual, and greater levels of autonomy and personal responsibility. In organizations that are subject to the same pressures but that are resisting or unable to make the shift, there are signs of defense: tighter controls; closer supervision; and pressures to conform to ever more demanding organizational norms regarding level of effort, hours at work, adherence to standards, and the like.

The Potential Movement from Self-Expression

At the level of self-expression, the focus is once more on the individual and not so strongly on the collective. The organization provides opportunities for personal success, learning, and growth, but the risks of personal failure are much higher than at the level of security. The organization is looser, more fragmented. There is more space for individuals to "do their own thing," and also more opportunity for people to fall through the cracks, to become isolated and alone.

One challenge of the self-expression organization is to evolve ways to coordinate and cooperate that serve both individuals and the work, rather than disempowering individuals and inappropriately constraining their use of their skills, intelligence, and creativity. Another challenge is to overcome the isolation, burnout, and addiction to work that seem to be endemic to self-expression organizations. Both these challenges require reconnecting people in forms and systems that are more collegial and cooperative than the bureaucratic and controlling structures of the security level. Task forces, project teams, and matrix organizations are all ways that have been used to meet these challenges. Organization development interventions such as Dialogue and Future Search (Weisbord and others, 1993) also serve the need to create cooperative and noncoercive connections among peers. The connections so created not only improve information processing and planning in the organization; they also nurture the development of bonds of caring and support. Thus, they favor movement toward transcendence in an organization's culture, both in the domain of achievement and in that of affiliation.

I have not studied examples of transition from self-expression to transcendence. It is clear to me, however, that many organizations that have stable self-expression cultures are struggling with issues of coordination and alienation, and that some are experimenting in directions that should lead them toward the constellation of qualities I have called transcendence.

Using the Model in Planning Change Strategy

The levels of consciousness model can be used for differential diagnosis and intervention in organizational change. A thorough treatment of change strategy is the subject of *Humanizing Change* (Harrison, Cooper, and Dawes, 1991) and will not be attempted here. However, some signposts can be erected to illustrate the utility of the model in planning and managing change.

Let us begin by being clear that organizations do not usually enter into change processes primarily in order to change their cultures. If they do, they are making a mistake because their target of change is the most elusive, least concrete, and most difficult to manipulate of an organization's attributes. Calling a change effort a "culture change program" invites people to spend a lot of time sitting around talking about how they are going to change the culture when they could be figuring out how to do their work better or smarter. It plays into the hands of those people who want to believe they are changing without really doing anything.

Organizations generally undertake conscious change because someone wants them to perform better. Then, when people begin to identify the things the organization will have to do to improve its performance, culture appears as a barrier to doing them. To take one simple example, improving product quality seems to require a high degree of employee participation. In power-oriented cultures, people are reluctant to speak up to the boss and take initiatives to change the way things are done. Their willingness to withhold their participation is often greater than the boss's commitment to the quality program. This becomes a serious cultural limit to the success of the program.

My approach to using the culture model in a change program has two aspects: organization diagnosis and intervention strategy and tactics. The first strategic issue to be addressed is the definition of the desired changes in as concrete terms as possible. What are the variances (areas where results are not acceptable) and weaknesses that are to be overcome? What competencies must the organization acquire (what must it *learn, know,* and *be able to do*) in order to eliminate the variances? Many organizations have instituted change in order to solve some problem only to find that the solution weakened the organization in unanticipated ways. Therefore, it is as important to specify the strengths to be preserved as it is to identify the weaknesses.

The next task is to identify the nature and extent of culture change that are required in order to support the acquisition of the required competencies. In doing this, it is helpful to think of the organization as a living organism and to remember that the more you ask it to change, the less energy it will have available for daily work. It behooves us to intervene no more than is required to obtain the desired competencies. By the same token, when we intervene strongly in an organization, the organization members not only have to deal with their work problems, they also have to deal with the intervention. If the intervention has been imposed on them, it will usually be experienced as an alien force rather than the aid and improvement it is supposed to be. We can best aid transition to a higher level of consciousness when we empower and support organization members to become aware of how what they are doing affects the whole. Then we can help them to diagnose and solve their own problems rather than our imposing a solution to a problem they may not experience themselves as having. Of course, that homily has been given over and over again since the earliest days of our profession. It bears repeating because it is true. It needs continual repeating because it is so much harder to facilitate people's planning and problem solving than it is to plan and solve problems for them!

Strengthening the Current Organization Culture

Long ago, I wrote about the importance of intervening no more deeply in an organization than is required to achieve the desired results (Harrison, 1970 [Chapter Two]). What I wrote then is especially applicable to making decisions about culture change. By *depth of intervention*, I mean the degree to which the change impacts deeply held attitudes and preferences of organization members about who they are, the values they hold, and the ways they prefer to relate to one another. For example, groups to whom I expose my model often express a need to move from a power or form culture toward achievement or from the level of security or defense toward self-expression. These interventions demand substantial changes in organizational and personal identity and in operating values. They not only require a shift of level of consciousness, but they also change the amount of energy and activity invested in each domain (power, form, achievement, and affiliation). Such changes are difficult to achieve, requiring long periods of time and creating considerable turmoil and stress within an organization. When people talk about culture change, they usually mean a shift of this magnitude, one which requires people to give up deeply imbedded beliefs, values, and behaviors.

However, some ways of working with organization cultures require less thoroughgoing change and are thus easier on the organization and its members. One way is to strengthen the current culture, raising it to the highest level of functioning that is possible within its most cherished values and beliefs. Most organizations that are looking to change are not at the highest level of functioning that can be obtained within their current basic cultural assumptions. For example, the leaders may use power in ways that serve their own personal needs and wishes but weaken the organization. Or the systems, procedures, and structures may be poorly designed, so that they hinder rather than serve the task. Strengthening a culture means bringing it to the top of its capability without changing its fundamental values and beliefs.

Usually when people get excited about culture change, they want to overturn some established values and beliefs that are cherished in powerful parts of the organization. I would be the last to say that the values and beliefs of most business organizations are ideal as they are. However, I am greatly opposed to our undertaking adventures with deeply held values and beliefs which we cannot bring home with success. Often the organizations that are targeted for culture change prove the most resistant to change, having put off needed changes for too long already. If we work *with* their energy and *within* their belief systems at first, then they will experience the change process positively, and they will be ready for bigger leaps later on.

We shall, of course, use our intuition and judgment to determine what kinds of changes will best make use of the ways the energy of the organization is currently invested. The levels of consciousness model tells us where to look. We shall want to move the level of consciousness higher within those domains in which the organization is highly invested, rather than shifting between domains. Most difficult is a double shift, moving up a level and across domains at the same time, yet that is just what some business leaders are asking for from their consultants and their organizations.

Strengthening a Power-Oriented Organization

My observation is that when organizations have most of their energy invested in the domain of power, they are more comfortable with changes in the way power is used than they are in moving to a major focus on another domain altogether. People can discriminate good power from bad, and they can tell the difference between power used for self-oriented purposes and power exercised in service to the organization. The first step in moving a power-oriented organization to a higher level of consciousness, then, is to shift its use of power. We do not try to shift its focus to the domain of affiliation or achievement, though we might try to get some work going to transfer energy from the processes of personal control to control by systems and structures.

In a power-oriented organization, strengthening the culture means moving from the leaders' capricious and arbitrary use of power toward a management style in which leaders' expectations are clearly stated and people know the consequences of complying or not. The ideal power-oriented leader at the security level is firm but fair, and generous toward loyal subordinates. However, even predictable injustice and harshness are more stabilizing to a culture than random rewards and punishments. As long as people know what they can and cannot get away with, they can achieve some degree of security.

Power-oriented leaders can also strengthen their cultures by decisiveness and by setting a clear direction when others are fearful and confused. They can use their authority to focus the energy and resources of the organization in those areas that are critical to success, provided the leaders have the competence and wisdom to know what these areas are.

To further perfect a power-oriented culture requires true wisdom, statecraft, and integrity on the part of the leaders. They set an example of fairness, compassion, and personal responsibility. They use their power to insist on the organization's doing what is right. In their personal conduct, they are above reproach. Their judgments are tempered with mercy. They act for the good of the organization and not for their own personal gain. They are mentors to their subordinates, fostering their growth with a judicious combination of challenge, discipline, and love.

To me, it is more than a little sad how old-fashioned these qualities seem as one reads them. They remind me of stories about George Washington and Abraham Lincoln that were told to me in school and stories of some of the great business leaders of the late nineteenth and early twentieth centuries. The virtual disappearance of these ideas, at least in the United States, seems to me to have left business leadership with too low a moral ceiling for the health of our businesses.

Strengthening a Form-Oriented Organization

In a form-oriented organization, strengthening the culture means having well-designed and clearly articulated systems direct and channel members' energies into efficient task performance. It means having rules and procedures that relieve members from having to make the same decisions over and over. It means tracking what works and what does not work and making sure that the organization learns from its experiences.

It means, also, that policies affecting the welfare of organization members are clearly set forth and consistently applied. Again, it is ideal if the policies are fair and just, but it is a step up if there *is* a policy and everyone knows what it is and can count on its being applied.

Complexity and endless elaboration of rules, procedures, and policies are hallmarks of an organization in defense. The best systems are comprehensive but simple and elegant: people know how to find out what they do not know and the required approval processes are direct and uncomplicated.

Further evolution within the domain of form means subordinating the systems and structures to the needs of the task and the organization members. Participation and empowerment at the working level are the keys to making the transition. We invent information systems that allow people to track their own results in real time rather than sending the results to a manager who then controls the workers. We create structures in which influence and information travel laterally and diagonally, rather than ones in which information goes up and directives come down. We involve people in creating their own rules, methods, and procedures. We design jobs so that people can control the outcomes for which they are held accountable.

Whereas at the level of security, the individual gives up autonomy and submits to control by a system that he or she cannot readily change, at the level of transcendence, the systems empower the people doing the work, and the people are empowered to change the systems when they do not work. The Procter & Gamble plant referred to earlier is typical of this orientation in which the systems serve the workers rather than the workers' serving the machine.

Culture Change: Biting the Bullet

Sometimes organizations have already squeezed all the competitive advantage they can out of their cultural orientation and are bumping up against the true limits of their current culture. An example comes from two consultants who attended one of my Humanizing Change workshops. They were from a tobacco company that had a long tradition of enlightened paternalism. Most of the people in their plant were from families in which multiple generations had worked for the company. There was a strong family feeling in the organization; people were "good soldiers," doing what they were told with commitment.

In the domain of form, the equipment was the latest and best, and it was designed to take possibilities for human error out of the production process. The systems were likewise machinelike, and their quality matched the quality of the equipment. Both were the best that could be bought. Production managers in the company had reluctantly come to the conclusion that a major culture shift was the only way they could accomplish further significant changes in quality and productivity. After listening to the two consultants tell their story, I could only agree. Although I do not know what eventually became of this change effort, it did meet some of my criteria for undertaking culture change, so I had modest hope for the consultants in their project.

Criteria for Success

There are four criteria for success in culture change projects, and they all make a difference in any attempt to make a major shift in culture (Harrison, Cooper, and Dawes, 1991). I state them strictly, and that is intentional. The lack of any one of them can render our efforts ineffectual or extend the resource drain on the organization intolerably.

1. *Leadership able and committed to operate in the mode of the new culture.* The leaders have the values and modes of perception typical of the culture to which the organization is supposed to move, and they are able to walk their talk—to demonstrate by practice and example what the new culture will look and feel like.

2. *A critical mass of members with latent needs to operate at the higher level.* Organization members are ready and able to become more responsible, self-managing, and empowered. They are not basically dependent or authoritarian in their personal makeup. They live personal lives outside work that use the skills and ways of behaving and perceiving that are typical of the new culture. It is not required that all the organization's members, or even a majority of them, meet these requirements. It is enough that there be a significant minority who do and that the change be managed in such a way as to link these members and give them visibility, status, and influence.

3. *Organization slack: resources that may be invested in learning.* Making a change in organization culture requires that almost everyone in the organization learn to behave, think, and feel in new ways. While people are learning, they will not perform at the same level as they have in the past. I counsel clients that if they are serious about making a culture shift, they must be prepared to suffer a decrement in organizational performance for a time or to provide additional resources to achieve the same level of performance. Change may be paid for in the currencies of money, time, people, and acceptance of substandard work or, more likely, all four. There is some choice of mode of payment, but the payment must be made. Needless to say, clients do not want to hear this.

4. *Optimum pain: enough to make it uncomfortable to stay where the organization is, but not enough to paralyze people's problem-solving capacities.* Optimum pain for change exists when people recognize that significant aspects of the way the organization operates are not working; they believe that if they knew a better way to operate they could adopt it successfully; and the organization is able to invest the resources of time, money, and personnel in making improvements while continuing to meet current operating demands.

Organizations that are fat and happy do not feel the need to change in transformative ways. They are content to make incremental changes that do not threaten established ways of thinking and behaving. The level of pain is suboptimal for change when people generally feel things are working well enough. They perceive the costs of change to outweigh the gains.

When the organization is in continual crisis and is using all its resources just to meet current operating demands, it is probably in too much pain to undertake substantial change. Since change requires learning, nearly every significant change results in an initial decrement in organizational performance while people are on the learning curve. In such cases, diversion of resources to manage the change process may well reduce the organization's current performance below the level required for survival. The organization can only afford to adopt quick-fix improvements that require little basic change. It can't win for losing.

Loosening Organization Cultures: The Essence of Moving from Security to Self-Expression

Although *planned* culture change efforts do not yet have a great track record, I believe many if not most business organizations are going to *evolve* toward higher levels of consciousness. They will do this because they need to cope with rapid change and because global competition requires them to evoke a much greater proportion of their members' will, skills, and creativity. There definitely are things we can do to help them make that shift, and these things have to do with the process of loosening rigid cultures.

Much writing in the management literature today is about the need for looser structures and systems: greater local autonomy, fewer rules and regulations, more open communication, and the like. These changes give the essential flavor of what it is like to change a culture from security to self-expression.

When we move from security to self-expression, we loosen the culture's control over its members in whatever domain the shift occurs, making room for greater variability in individual behavior and in the different parts of the organization, and allowing greater flexibility. Such shifts also result in more chaos and confusion, especially at first. Later, the design of more flexible and supportive systems can support both the task and the people.

Anything That Reduces Fear Helps the Shift Along. Many if not most people in the workforce today are able and motivated to operate at the self-expression level, and they want the satisfactions that such organizations can give. Only the coercion and fear used to control behavior at the security level prevent people's moving to a higher level. Thus, anything that reduces fear and coercion in a security-level organization will tend to propel its level of consciousness upward: supportive and participative management, employee involvement programs, loosening the rules and approval processes, giving more local autonomy and budgetary control, and so on.

Of course, we all know, to our sorrow, that it is not quite that simple. In the first place, power- and form-oriented managers in security-level organizations generally have strong personal motives for keeping the controls in place, and even when they are convinced to experiment with looser management, they do so gingerly, in a tentative way that sends mixed messages to the organization members.

The recipients of those messages have their own reasons for keeping the status quo. In order to take advantage of the looser controls, they have to take personal risks. They have been so long accustomed to narrow boundaries and to coercion, control, and mistrust that they are fearful of stepping into the hitherto forbidden territories of autonomy and freedom. They act a bit like the concentration camp inmates after World War II who, when the gates were opened, still huddled inside the camp. The machine-gun turrets were deserted, but the fire zones around the camp were still active in their minds. They could not will themselves to step into their fear. They were so terrified of the consequences of acting autonomously that they had forgotten that it had once been satisfying.

I once worked with a young, idealistic engineering manager who took over plant maintenance after his dictatorial predecessor retired. He had been on a management course, and he was looking forward to introducing participative management to his maintenance supervisors. When the time for the next scheduled maintenance shutdown approached, he called his supervisors together and asked them to write down their ideas on improving the process and to present them at the next meeting. At the next weekly meeting, he called for their contributions but got only bowed heads and shuffling feet in response. This went on until, with the shutdown fast approaching, he took over and planned it himself. In a later interview, he said to me, "My predecessor told me these guys weren't too bright; I guess he was right." In interviews with the supervisors, I heard, "We knew he didn't mean it." Everyone said he wanted the change. No one was willing to pay the cost in risk and fear of failure. I decided the score was Security Culture: 1, Organization Members: 0.

Often the only way trust and confidence in the leaders' intentions to open the culture can be established is for courageous managers to create a power vacuum by pushing authority and responsibility downward. Then they have to hang out there, with all of the responsibility and not much control, until their subordinates move in and take hold. It does work if the leaders can stay the course, accepting the inevitable betrayal of their confidence and trust as part of the price. Most cannot stand the anxiety and stress, and who can blame them? The good news is that it is getting easier, as more young people come into the workforce prepared to take autonomy and personal responsibility.

Programmatic Culture Change. What makes programmatic culture change efforts such as employee involvement and Total Quality Management so attractive is that they endeavor to create *structures* that support participation. By giving training in participative techniques (working in groups, collaborative problem solving, and so forth), they build confidence and reduce the risk for lower-level people in taking more initiative and responsibility. They certainly seem to have been successful in improving quality and productivity, and the quality of working life.

It seems to me, however, that the organizations where such methods have been tried often resemble security more than self-expression cultures. Management stays firmly in charge, running the quality and involvement programs. The organization exchanges a system that does not work well for one that works better, but the gains in energy and creativity are incremental, not revolutionary. It seems trite to repeat the aphorism, "No pain, no gain," but it may be accurate; in my experience, people do not obtain their freedom and learn to use it responsibly without at least going through an inner struggle and usually an outer one as well.

Environment Is a Stimulus to Change. Loosening tight cultures at the level of security is uphill work because the prevailing culture resists and both the leaders and the people consciously or unconsciously cooperate with the culture. There is, however, a countervailing force, which presses some organizations inexorably to at least try to loosen the culture and shift to a higher level. It is that traditional power- and form-oriented organizations at the level of security do not work very well in fast-moving highly competitive environments. They take too long to change direction, and they underuse the intelligence and creativity of workers. So we shall continue to see organizations making the commitment to change and taking the attendant risks because that is their most viable competitive alternative. For example, see the recent cultural changes at Ford Motor Company described by Richard Pascale in *Managing on the Edge* (1990).

Choosing a Style of Intervention to Fit the Culture

The culture model can help us choose an appropriate style of intervention and leadership for a given level of consciousness or pattern of dominant cultural values. Organizations at the level of survival or defense need structure and firm but fair leadership. They need to get out of chaos and into a stable state in order to devote their members' energy to solving long-term organizational problems rather than crises. Consultants can provide helpful systems and structures. It is not uncommon for successful consultants to an organizational turnaround to be asked to take on management positions.

A corollary of this principle is that survival and defense organizations do not respond well to interventions in which issues are aired but not resolved. Issues that cannot be dealt with quickly are best handled in less public ways. The organization already has more problems than it can handle; people, whether leaders or consultants, who surface more issues than solutions will quickly come to be seen as part of the problem Harrison (1981b [Chapter Five]).

Survival and defense organizations respond well to consultants and leaders who are doers and problem solvers and who can provide quick fixes for sticky organizational problems. Conversely, those whose contributions are primarily conceptual, or whose orientation is to facilitate the organization in solving its own problems, tend to make members of such organizations feel anxious and helpless or impatient to the point where the helper's own survival in the system will soon be in question!

Security organizations require that consultants and managers earn their stripes by meeting organizational norms. Such issues as manners and dress can count for a lot at the outset of the relationship (especially in form cultures), as can the ability to pick up and use the language and metaphors of the organization (useful in achievement cultures). This is not to say that competence will not be recognized and appreciated in the end, only that consultants can set up needless barriers for themselves by failure to pay attention to such "superficial" norms.

Much of the work consultants do in security organizations lies in helping the culture to work better rather than in changing it. As an example, many form-oriented organizations run ineffective, time-wasting meetings, and their strategic planning is often more an extension of past trends into the future than it is real planning. Interventions that offer more efficient ways of holding meetings and planning can provide a real service, but in order to be effective, these new methods must eventually be installed as standard operating policies. Mere demonstrations of a better method will usually not stick.

In working with organizations at the security level, a consultant can and usually must use the strengths of the culture to influence the culture. This means that in power-oriented organizations one works through the boss. In achievement-oriented organizations, one uses task forces and off-site problem-solving meetings. As a consultant, one can get away with interventions that are unfamiliar in the culture, but this tactic means that organization members use a lot of their energy in learning how to play the consultant's games. One cannot easily introduce interventions that violate strongly held organizational norms or beliefs about what is proper and what works.

Consultants' Difficulties in Working with Security and Defense Cultures

It is common for organization development consultants to be firmly committed to a particular process of change, usually one compatible with the control processes of achievement and support organizations. In my experience, we need help from the control processes that are accepted and effective in the dominant culture of the organization. Most organizations are mixtures of power and form cultures and rely heavily on personal control and the use of systems and rules. I find that when I honor the dominant culture and obtain support for my work through it, I can be more successful later on in introducing interventions that violate the norms and ask members to go outside their accustomed patterns. It is as though we have to bow to the old gods of tradition before we can introduce the new gods of change.

The principle is just common sense, but it bears mentioning. It is another way I use the culture model to sensitize myself to what has to be attended to in the change process. For example, if I am planning an off-site meeting for diagnosing organizational problems in a traditional organization, I know that before I can successfully implement any changes in response to the problems surfaced in the meeting, I have to find the appropriate power holders, whether individuals or functional units, to sponsor the follow-on work. It is not enough to "turn people on" and develop lots of enthusiasm for the possibilities for change. I have to hook the change process back into the organization in such a way that it is energized and managed when the great ideas that people had during the off-site have to compete with the daily task of getting the wash out.

Sustained Effort at the Level of Self-Expression

In organizations at the level of self-expression, resistance to change is not the problem that it is at the security level. People are looser, more autonomous, more ready to experiment with new methods and ideas. Such organizations are often high energy places where people are very committed to their work and have little patience with anything that interferes with it. The problem is to get people's attention in the first place, to get them to set time aside to look at organizational issues. Then, once something has been tried and found successful, it is difficult to get any sustained cooperative effort going to implement change beyond the local area in which it is first tried.

Organizations at the security level resist change, but there is such an emphasis on control that once a change proves successful in one part of the organization, the tendency is to apply it across the board (whether that makes sense or not). Organizations at the level of self-expression are much more open to change, but there is so much local autonomy that dissenting members can easily agree to disagree about the value of the change. This organizational looseness means that one usually has to work the same issues over and over again as one works through the different parts of the organization. Consultants working in such organizations easily come to feel frustrated and undervalued. It helps me when I can understand the problem as systemic rather than as an indication of personal inadequacy.

I know that in working with a self-expression organization I shall have a lot of little successes but the big ones will elude me. For example, I once worked for three or four years with the top management group of a very successful national research and development laboratory, trying to get the group to agree on common policies for such things as career paths, budgets and overhead charges, and the way the matrix organization should work. This very achievement-oriented organization was receptive to organization development and frequently used consultants to facilitate team-building and problem-solving meetings at lower levels. The top group, however, successfully resisted all my efforts. Privately, individuals would agree that some of the things I was endeavoring to get their agreement on were desirable; as a group, they were unwilling to force consensus on dissident members.

Such cultures are *metastable*. That is, they can tolerate a lot of changes without changing their fundamental culture much. Universities and colleges are excellent examples of this metastability. They tolerate a great deal of individual variation in their members, and they have successfully resisted fundamental systemic change for centuries.

Centrality of Values in Transcendence Organizations

Organizations at the transcendence level are much more likely to make decisions on the basis of fundamental values than are those at lower levels. While they are interested in doing things better, their first commitment is to *doing the right thing,* particularly where people are concerned. They are able to manage the tension associated with inaction while they explore alternatives and build consensus, even when it seems to an outsider that action is imperative. I worked once with a Zen church that operated several businesses and was going through a serious leadership and financial crisis that had the organization deeply split into factions. It was a situation that would have torn most organizations asunder. I marvelled at the capacity of the leadership group to hold their painful feelings and their anxieties, patiently exploring the alternatives and carefully sounding people out on their opinions, trusting that wisdom and right action would eventually emerge from sober discussion and meditation. It was such a contrast to the ready, fire, aim approach that is typical in the high-tech organizations with which I frequently work. I marvelled, too, at the success of this approach over time, as the organization slowly coalesced around new leaders and pruned its businesses back to what it could manage, staff, and sustain financially.

The culture model helps me to make sense of all my very different experiences with organizations. It helps me, too, to size up an organization much more quickly than I could without it, to tailor my approach to the culture, and to understand and correct for the inevitable surprises and reverses that I encounter in helping clients manage their change processes.

CHAPTER FOURTEEN

ORGANIZATION CULTURE AND THE FUTURE OF PLANET EARTH

"Organization Culture and the Future of Planet Earth" was originally published in 1993, so it is a current statement of my perspective and my passion. Here I continue to develop the organization culture model, in the attempt to arrive at a statement of it that preserves the idea of different levels without the complexity that was introduced by laying five *levels* on top of four separate *domains* of organizational culture. My underlying concept of domains and levels of culture remains the same, but I have been able to get back to a model with four categories, at the expense of some conceptual precision. I have found that this simpler model works well for presentations to nonprofessional audiences, and I have also developed a new questionnaire (see Harrison, Cooper, and Dawes, 1991) to assess an organization's culture using the model described in this paper.

We live in a time of great change: I believe it is a time of *renaissance*, or rebirth. As in the historical period we refer to as *the* Renaissance, it is a time of the breaking of boundaries and constraints, and we are now, as then, experiencing what Freud called "the return of the repressed." We see great violence, cruelty, and callousness side by side with a revival of the best that is in us: spirituality, selfless service, and creativity in thought, science, and the arts. Our inner demons and

Note: Originally published in *Vision/Action* (the journal of the Bay Area Organization Development Network), 1993, *12*(3), 23–27. Reprinted here, with revisions, with permission of Roger Harrison.

angels alike have been released from the fetters of orderly tradition, and we are much bewildered by the rich but constantly changing mixture of light and darkness in which we find ourselves.

Our time is given special poignancy by the threats under which we live. We have been "gifted" with the capacity to destroy ourselves, and no sooner have we gained some relief from the threat of nuclear war than we realize that we are drifting—or galloping—toward levels of pollution that pose grave risks of poisoning the capacity of this planet to continue to nurture our life and that of the many species who share this globe with us.

I am convinced that the system we have can do no other than continue to despoil the planet, and within the small sphere that I occupy, I have thought long and as deeply as I can about the systemic qualities that may be viable in the time to come. The various models of organization culture I have put out over the years define the stages of my thought about organizational and societal evolution—where we have been, where we are now, where we are going. (My models of organization culture are a bit like Monet's famous series of paintings of a field of haystacks. Each painting captures the subject in a slightly different perspective or light, but it is the same subject in each painting.) I believe the latest of these models maps the changes in organizations yesterday and today, and it tells me what to look for and work for in my consulting. (The following description of the model is condensed from *Humanizing Change,* Harrison, Cooper, and Dawes, 1991.)

Model of Organization Culture

I have identified four archetypal organization cultures: *transactional, self-expression, alignment,* and *mutuality.*

Gratification-Driven Cultures: Transactional and Self-Expression

The transactional culture is typical of traditional business organizations, operating on fear and hope of reward and exercising control through personal power or through impersonal bureaucratic roles, structures, and procedures. Another word for the transactional archetype is *patriarchy.* It has been the dominant societal and organizational form in the Western world for centuries, if not for millennia. McGregor's Theory X (1960) is a statement of the basic assumptions of the transactional culture. Most companies have operated on this model in the past, and many still do.

In the transactional organization, OD is strongly countercultural. Transactional clients are oriented to structural and procedural changes, replacement of personnel, quick fixes, and manipulation of reward systems. Many practitioners have recently found themselves redefining OD to include these things, which is fine with me. However, I have little heart for such activities.

The transactional form has been challenged during the recent past by a set of values and social arrangements based on individuality and autonomy that I call the self-expression culture. This culture's basic assumption is similar to McGregor's Theory Y (1960): people have an internal motivation to produce and create and they work best when they are given meaningful and intrinsically satisfying work and are trusted to manage themselves. The self-expression culture is often found in small high-technology firms, some R&D and consulting organizations, and many associations of individual professionals such as doctors and lawyers. Steve Jobs and the Macintosh group in the early days of Apple Computer provide an example of the self-expression orientation (mixed with strong elements of the alignment culture that I describe later).

There has been a great increase in the number of organizations with strong self-expression elements in the last decade or two because individuality and the celebration of self are developing strength in the larger culture. People want and are coming to expect to have challenging and meaningful work through which they can learn and grow, and they want to be given responsibility and autonomy in the doing of it. In the seventies, when I first put forward the idea of what I then called the *person culture* (Harrison, 1972b [Chapter Ten]), I could identify only a few organizations that exemplified that thrust. Now strong self-expression influences can be found in many if not most organizations that depend on individual creativity for their success, as well as some that do not. Organization development in self-expression organizations often centers on the development of teams and of individual influencing skills because of the difficulty of achieving common effort in self-expression systems (see Chapter Thirteen). This OD work can be satisfying, but it has to be done over and over again because self-expression organizations suffer from short-term memory loss.

Value-Driven Cultures: Alignment and Mutuality

I call the remaining two cultures of alignment and mutuality *value driven*, as opposed to *gratification driven*, because the motive power in these cultures lies beyond the satisfaction of some need or lack. It may be altruistic, at least in part, and the motivation is always more than material. These cultures are either directed to the pursuit of some ideal, principle, or goal that is intrinsically valued, or they have a strong caring or service orientation. Aligned organizations appeal to the intellect and the will; mutuality organizations are of the heart, evoking the love and compassion of their members. Figure 14.1 shows how the four cultures relate to one another in a roughly hierarchical fashion.

In our society, the more common of the value-driven organizations is the aligned, or vision-oriented, organization, one in which common effort is achieved by voluntary commitment to an overarching purpose. Like self-expression, alignment appeals to people who are working on the development of their autonomy. Unwilling to be ruled by positional authority and disrespectful of formal systems,

FIGURE 14.1. FOUR ORGANIZATION CULTURES.

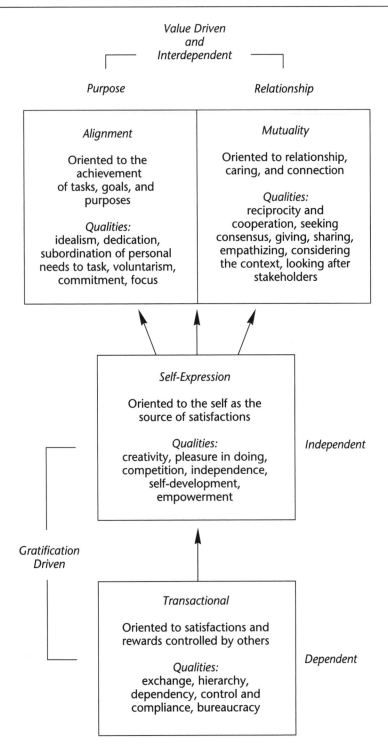

Value Driven
and
Interdependent

Purpose   Relationship

Alignment   *Mutuality*

Oriented to the   Oriented to relationship,
achievement   caring, and connection
of tasks, goals, and
purposes   *Qualities:*
                                   reciprocity and
Qualities: cooperation, seeking
idealism, dedication,   consensus, giving, sharing,
subordination of personal   empathizing, considering
needs to task, voluntarism,   the context, looking after
commitment, focus   stakeholders

Self-Expression

Oriented to the self as the
source of satisfactions

Qualities: Independent
creativity, pleasure in doing,
competition, independence,
self-development,
empowerment

Gratification
Driven

Transactional

Oriented to satisfactions and
rewards controlled by others

Qualities: Dependent
exchange, hierarchy,
dependency, control and
compliance, bureaucracy

they will yet willingly surrender some part of their newly won freedom to a vision, ideal, or purpose that gives meaning and value to their work. They can, indeed, experience a sense of enhanced self-worth and empowerment from being part of a group pursuing valued ends.

The basic assumption of alignment is that one finds meaning and personal worth in sacrifice to something bigger than and outside of oneself, whether that something be a leader, a nation, a principle, a cause, or simply a challenging task to which one has become committed. The alignment culture is typical of nations engaged in wars of national survival and can inspire great heroism and self-sacrifice. Both sides in World Wars I and II typified the idealism of the alignment culture, as did international communism in the thirties and forties. More recently, the Peace Corps and the civil rights, antinuclear, right-to-life, and pro-choice movements have each given us examples of alignment. So have terrorist organizations, religious cults, and Islamic and Christian fundamentalism. In workaday organizations, people who have participated in such situations and settings as new business and new plant startups, nuclear test shots, and intensive care units report that these aligned cultures can provide deep personal satisfactions and evoke personal commitment of a high order. As we see from these diverse examples, an organization does not have to be good or noble to be aligned. A team planning and implementing a safecracking or the Great Train Robbery can have many qualities of alignment.

The popularity of such activities as vision and mission development workshops and training in visionary leadership attests to recent interest in creating aligned organizations, as does much of the work called *organization transformation* (OT). Such OD work can be useful and satisfying when it is supported by a willingness on the part of top management to place themselves in service to the vision (Harrison, 1987a [Chapter Nine]). But when transactional leaders create a vision and then endeavor to enroll their organization in it without undergoing a transformation in their own team culture, the effort becomes an exercise in Machiavellian manipulation, self-deception, or both.

In mutuality cultures, people find meaning in *relationships*. These cultures exemplify the values of connection, cooperation, appreciation, respect for diversity, caring and looking out for one another, and community. The driving force in such cultures is human love in its larger sense of friendship, brotherhood and sisterhood, empathy, and compassion rather than romantic or erotic feelings. Mutuality cultures operate through networks of mutual caring and reciprocal responsibilities rather than through power hierarchies or formal structures, rules, and procedures.

The mutuality ethic is one of responsibility and caring rather than rights and justice. It derives from the feminine side of people's nature rather than from patriarchal archetypes. Its basic assumption is systems oriented and participative: we are not independent but exist as parts of the ever larger systems that nurture and sustain us. Every action we take affects everything else in the system; thus, we need to appreciate our connections in order to act responsibly.

My idea of the mutuality culture has much in common with Riane Eisler's feminist *partnership model* (1987; Eisler and Loye, 1990). My transactional culture sounds much like her *dominator model*. We differ, however, in my including the less polarized cultures of self-expression and alignment. Both of these cultures are nonhierarchical ways of managing relationships in which both the masculine and the feminine may be expressed. I believe it is important to identify and name mixed models and transitional forms. Otherwise, our choices are too stark, and our creativity tends to be overwhelmed by anxiety.

Examples of the mutuality culture are hard to find in business organizations except in their informal and unofficial aspects, such as the "grapevine." I have seen mutuality working in balance with alignment in production plants organized around self-managing teams. Such diverse OD work as training in managing diversity, systems thinking, and work on whole systems (for example, Future Search conferences, Weisbord and others, 1993) shares the basic assumptions of the mutuality archetype. Also, the sociotechnical systems approaches that have been such an important part of the movement to redesign work are based on learnings from the mutuality cultures at the coalface in the British mining industry (Trist and Bamforth, 1951). Unfortunately, in much recent work (for example, work on "reengineering" the production process) the "socio" part of "sociotechnical" systems has been missed.

Where We Are in the Cultural Development of Organizations

Today many organizations have strong elements of the self-expression culture and are looking for the common effort and singleness of purpose typical of aligned organizations. Mutuality has attracted little interest on the part of business leaders. There is a hunger for community within organizations, as well as within society generally, but we do not know how to get there from our egoistic, individualistic orientations.

Progression in the Evolution of Cultures

There is a natural progression in the cultural development of organizations: from transactional to self-expression, then on to alignment, and (sometimes) thence to mutuality. This is not to say that other transformations are not possible, only that we can see organizations moving from transactional to self-expression all around us. There is some evidence about how the further transformation to alignment works, and I believe that strong environmental pressures are developing that will influence organizations to move toward mutuality in due course. More of my ideas about the evolution of organization cultures are to be found in "Culture and Levels of Consciousness in Organizations" (Harrison, 1990a [Chapter Thirteen]). Here, I describe my reasons for believing that the mutuality orientation offers answers to the following fundamental issues with which organizations currently are struggling:

- Dealing with complexity and chaos through organizational learning
- Improving quality and service through appreciation
- Healing the trauma of rapid change
- Working with diversity

For me, bringing mutuality into organizations defines the cutting edge of OD, the area in which we consultants can make a real difference through our insights and actions. I should like to influence my colleagues in OD to focus their hearts and energies on this challenge during the nineties and beyond. Already there are promising initiatives involving two of these organizational issues: *organizational learning* and *appreciation*.

Dealing with Complexity and Chaos Through Organizational Learning.

I have said elsewhere (Harrison, 1992; Harrison and Dawes, 1994 [Chapter Twenty-Four]) that the greatest enemies to organizational learning are fear, competition, and a narrow focus on problem solving that leads people to take actions that further perturb the system.

Learning is restricted by competitive feelings and attitudes. In most organizations, the level of competition is unhealthy and inimical to both individual and corporate learning. Not only does information become a scarce resource in the battle of all against all, but the experimentation and risk taking that are essential to high-order learning are avoided for fear of falling behind others in the endless footrace toward success. In mutuality cultures, competition is balanced by cooperation, and individuals and groups hold themselves jointly responsible for results. Information is shared more willingly and communication is the norm rather than the exception.

People in transactional, self-expression, and alignment organizations are motivated by fear and/or task urgency to decide quickly and move ahead, but uncertainty, anxiety, and fear of failure lead them to spend large amounts of time in inconclusive meetings and other unproductive busyness. To men and women of action, reflection and deep investigation are often seen as wasting time. They would rather act now and then take their next steps based on the result. Such trial-and-error problem solving leads to a permanent fix only if the true causes of the problems are close in time and space to the symptoms. If the causes are hidden in the complexities of a larger system, then trial-and-error problem solving inevitably creates new problems, contributing to the endless cycle of *problem-fix-new problem* in which most organizations find themselves.

Initially, deep reflection leads to individuals' experiencing situations as more complex than they first appeared and thus to increased anxiety and frustration. Reflective learning activities that might lead to greater clarity about the consequences of action are avoided because in the short term they increase pain. It requires courage and will to break the cycle by taking the time to continue examining situations in greater depth and complexity. The mutuality culture supports this more reflective, inclusive approach because members habitually take into account a complex web of relationships and responsibilities in determining what is to be done. Because they are less centered on self and mission, they are more open to system and context.

In mutuality organizations, demands for change and ever higher performance are balanced by compassion for human frailty—for the doubts, fears, reluctance, and resentment that most of us experience when we are required to change and grow. In such organizations, we do not always have to project an image of competence and confidence. We can share our uncertainties and frustrations and, in sharing, lighten our individual loads.

Currently, the most promising approaches I have seen consultants use to facilitate organizational learning have strong mutuality aspects. There is a growing recognition within our profession, if not yet among many of our clients, that no group within an organization, least of all a power elite, can see either the organization or its environment *as a whole* and that the best way to deal with complexity is to look at it *all at once* rather than break it down into parts. This realization is leading us to find or invent methods to bring together all the stakeholders—managers, employees, customers, suppliers, investors, and so forth—to work on the whole organization. Two such methods are Future Search (Weisbord and others, 1993) and the technologies of participation of the Institute for Cultural Affairs (Spencer, 1989). I have been impressed and heartened by recent reports of successful large-group problem-solving and strategy planning sessions involving from 50 or 100 people up to as many as 2,500 people in a room at the same time, building a common understanding of the context for strategy and then finding ways to move forward together.

Such approaches create mutuality through both cognitive and emotional processes. Cognitively, they build a shared understanding of the web of interdependencies that connects all the stakeholders and binds them to a common fate. This balances the individualistic fantasy that says we can live our lives independently of others and that we can profit at the expense of others in other than the short term. Cognitively, these approaches tend to sweep away our private local maps of reality, replacing them first with "blooming, buzzing confusion" (James, 1982), and then with a shared but rather fuzzy and intuitive common map of the *whole territory.* Emotionally, these large-group approaches foster *unity within diversity,* by letting groups of stakeholders who may be in conflict appreciate one another's common humanity. These approaches give everyone a chance to be heard. They develop shared ownership in the decisions and initiatives that are the outcomes of the large-group processes. By dwelling on what is in common rather than on what is in conflict, they change people's perceptions of their relationships with one another in ways that foster a sense of oneness and predispose people to cooperate rather than compete.

Improving Quality and Service Through Appreciation

I have previously discussed the relationships between organization culture and quality of service (Harrison, 1987b [Chapter Twelve]). To recapitulate, service to internal or external customers is a reflection of how people experience relationships within their own organization. *As within, so without*—as we treat one another within the organization, so we treat our external stakeholders. People in mutuality organizations are treated as *participants.* They have a voice in decisions affecting them, and they reciprocate by considering their stakeholders in making decisions. They go well beyond focusing on what will benefit their own task or mission and advance their own goals. They take into consideration the needs of their colleagues, other internal groups, and such external stakeholders as customers, suppliers, the community, and the environment. The faculty of learning about and responding to how others think and feel is what I call *appreciation,* after David Cooperrider's (1990) work, and Bill Smith's insights (1993). It is a deep understanding, held with compassion. Appreciation is fostered by ways of working that bring people together in dialogue and in cooperative activities. They meet not only to solve problems and make decisions but also to share and understand what is happening in different parts of the organization, to learn what others are thinking and feeling about those events and how they are valuing the events, and to give and receive help.

Healing the Trauma of Rapid Change

Currently, people in many organizations are experiencing the darker side of the self-expression modality in the breaking of the dependency contract that used to exist between employees and large bureaucratic companies. If we look back about twenty-five years, it was the people, not the companies, who began to break that contract in the sixties and seventies. Formerly, security was the benefit offered for conformity and compliance. Then people began testing the boundaries and pushing for more autonomy. They withdrew their loyalty from the organization in favor of looking after themselves (see, for example, Maccoby, 1976). Now organizations are reciprocating by treating employees as independent contractors who can be dispensed with when convenient or expedient. The ties of loyalty and dependency typical of the patriarchy are giving way to an impersonal instrumentalism in which employees think of the organization as a playing field in which the game is for everyone to win as much as he or she can. Leaders reciprocate by treating both employees and environmental quality as expendable pawns in larger games between organizations in which planet Earth is the playing field.

Employees are finding themselves less empowered and less autonomous than they thought they were. As available resources shrink, games in which it once seemed as though everyone could win become bitter struggles for survival. Employees are wounded and traumatized by what is going on, and many are having to do the work of those who have been made redundant in addition to their own work. They are angry, resentful, anxious, stressed, and overworked. They and their organizations are in urgent need of healing (Noer, 1993). At the same time, companies are endeavoring to install such approaches as Total Quality Management, which require strong commitment and a high degree of alignment between employees' goals and those of the organization. It is a bit like asking a surgical patient in the recovery room to get up and run laps.

About eighteen months ago, I began to think about reframing the concept of our work in OD, from what I have always thought of as the rather grandiose "change agentry" to "organizational healing." I talked about this with other consultants, and eventually I invited some to attend what I hoped would be the first meeting of an Organizational Healing Network. To my pleasure and surprise, thirty people turned up for the first meeting. We sat in a circle, and each person spoke of what brought him or her to the meeting, how he or she was experiencing the need for healing in organizations, and how he or she was dealing with that need. It was very moving to me, and I know to others as well, to sit in a group of OD consultants, most of whom have fair-sized egos, and hear no one try to score points by talking about his or her innovative interventions or successes achieved in healing organizations. Instead, people spoke from the heart about the pain and grief in organizations, their sadness and frustration at not being able to help more, and their wish to find ways to help. People spoke also about their own need for healing and the difficulty of trying to help others when one is in pain or grief oneself.

I believe organizational healing is currently the most appropriate way we can express, to the benefit of clients, our own longings for a climate of love and nurturance. Merely framing our work as "healing," as distinct from "changing," shifts our perspective enough that we can begin to see needs and opportunities to serve that we could not see before. My colleague Sandra Florstedt and I have recently completed our first project designated as organization healing. We found it an inspiring and heartwarming process. I have now conducted workshops on organizational healing for human resource professionals both in the United States and the U.K. In these workshops, I found a great sense of compassion and heartfelt concern for the pain being experienced by organization members, and the same wish to help that I had found in the consultants I convened in the Bay Area. Out of these workshops came ideas about what we can do to heal organizations, along with some intriguing questions.

I have used a model called The Castle and the Battlefield (Harrison, 1963 [Chapter Eighteen]) to understand the healing process in organizations undergoing painful change. The castle represents safety, security, reliable gratification of one's needs, and confirmation from others of who one thinks one is. It is "the way things were" or "the way we expect things to be." The battlefield represents the arena of change. It is characterized by threats, challenges, wounds, and opportunities. The threats and wounds are experienced in present time; the challenges and opportunities point to uncertain and contingent possibilities of future gain. Clearly, if one had to balance the satisfactions of the castle with those of the battlefield as described so far, most people would choose to stay in the castle (and, indeed, many people do so choose when they can).

There is another factor present in the battlefield, the need to learn and grow, risk and stretch oneself. When this need is active in members of an organization, they will forsake safe, gratifying situations in favor of changes, challenges, and the pursuit of dreams. It is the opportunity to fulfill this need in alignment organizations (and also in self-expression organizations) that makes them exciting places in which to work.

People adapt best to change when they experience a balance between castle and battlefield. In practice, this means that during times of painful change they require "safe havens" to which they can retire where they are affirmed in their values and beliefs, supported in their self-image and self-esteem, and protected from stress. Such safe havens are usually found in the informal social system of an organization, in relationships with co-workers. Organizations in which people work mostly in teams provide more "castle time" than those in which people are more isolated.

In times of change, and in self-expression cultures at any time, the informal social structure is often inadequate to provide the amount of support needed, and it becomes important to create castle settings, structures, and processes such as special project teams, feedback and sensing meetings, support groups, counseling sessions, and the like.

Today, when many organization members are experiencing loss of status, professional identity, job security, and remuneration, the organization often takes on the qualities of the battlefield. When the organization culture values masculine virtues, such as strength, toughness, and suppression of softer feelings, leaders are usually unable to sense needs for support, compassion, and relief from stress and are unwilling to provide for them. When resistance to change inevitably arises and effort falls off, these leaders try to drive the organization to greater levels of effort.

However, organizations are not machines; they are organisms with a life of their own, and the natural patterns of energy and adaptation to change in organisms are cyclical and periodic, as shown in Figure 14.2. We can help our clients to see those patterns and to work with them, planning "push" initiatives for high activity periods and castle time for periods when the organization needs rest and recovery. People in mutuality cultures are sensitive to flows of energy and feeling, both within and without the organization. They respond more readily to needs for support, nurturance, and maintenance of relationships. They naturally provide castle settings and castle time. During these times of turbulent change, that sensitivity to process can provide a true competitive edge for the organizations that have it.

The Organizational Healing Workshop sessions I have conducted have raised for me an intriguing and important question about cycle times for people adapt-

FIGURE 14.2. CYCLICAL MODEL OF ADAPTATION TO CHANGE.

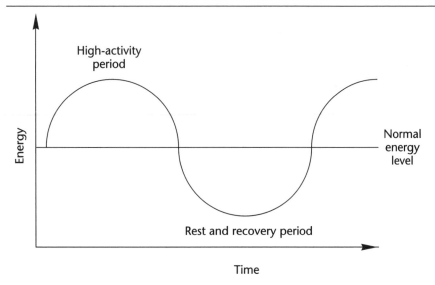

ing to traumatic change. The Kübler-Ross model of adaptation to trauma has a lot of face validity (Kübler-Ross, 1969); most of us know from personal experience what it is like to go through the stages of shock, denial, rationalization, anger, depression, and adaptation. It takes most people and most organizations a long time to pass through those stages, a lot longer than the timeframe around which most of our clients are willing or able to wrap their minds. Rather than undertake directly to heal their organizations, most leaders and some consultants just push the organizations harder to perform, interpreting the healing process as resistance. Are there ways to help organizations heal more rapidly, or are we stuck with a natural process that cannot be hurried? Is there a way to "surf" on change, or must we swim laboriously through waves of grief?

Most of us have seen individuals and groups who have adapted rather quickly to difficult and challenging changes, seemingly bypassing the stages of the Kübler-Ross model or at least truncating them significantly. What distinguishes these people from others, and can we create conditions that will help other individuals and organizations do likewise? I do not know the answers to these questions, but I think I know where to look.

The work of Victor Frankl (1959) on the qualities that made for survival in Nazi death camps comes to mind. Frankl found that a *sense of meaning* distinguished those who survived. We all know that people willingly endure great loss and hardship in shared service to a valued goal or purpose. The goal provides *meaning*, and directing the will toward achieving it provides *alignment*. Both the organization cultures of alignment and of mutuality can be healing. Being in a culture of alignment takes us out of ourselves and gives meaning and value to sacrifices we are called to make. Mutuality provides support and compassion and permits us to move through our grief.

However, the current wave of downsizing does not often foster either alignment or mutuality because the sacrifices are not experienced as being *shared,* and they are often undertaken to ensure higher profits for investors. It is hard to convince a person who has been pushed out of the lifeboat that his or her sacrifice was necessary in order to keep the boat afloat when those on the upper decks of the organization appear to be untouched. In contrast, organizations that truly opt for integrity and shared sacrifice are able to frame changes in ways that provide meaning and a sense of purpose to the losses that members are required to endure.

Another place I would look to discover how to move more quickly through the trauma of change and loss is in the teachings of the world's great spiritual masters, East and West. Spiritual practice has much to teach us of nonattachment, of letting go, and of surrender. These qualities are not highly prized in our competitive and egoistic culture, but they offer another key to grace in the face of change. When I am working on the development of an organizational vision with a group that I believe to be in grief and pain, I provide time and support for group members to grieve, asking them to move on only when they are ready to turn their faces to the future. I invite them first to face and move together into their pain, and I find that that permission leads to their letting go of their attachments to the past. When people adopt the *intention* to let go and move on, they can do so, although they may indeed have to rework that process a number of times before it is complete.

Mutuality brings love and compassion to heal our wounds, and it aids in our letting go of past hopes and expectations. We create a culture of mutuality when we help organization members grieve for their losses together. Harrison Owen tells an inspiring story of how he created rituals of grieving for the personnel of a plant that was going to close and how the people then pulled together and performed miracles right up until the last day. The group he describes has strong elements of the mutuality culture (Owen, 1990).

When we can create organization cultures that have a blend of alignment and mutuality, we shall have conditions that make for rapid adaptation to change and loss. However, in singing the virtues of mutuality I do not want to imply that there is no darker side. Among other failings (Harrison, Cooper, and Dawes, 1991), mutuality organizations can be prone to an unhealthy preoccupation with process at the expense of the task, and they can become so bogged down in reflection and the search for ever deeper meanings and understandings that they are unable to act. In my work on organization culture, I have argued for *balance,* so that the dark side of one cultural archetype is balanced by the strengths of another. Currently, the weight that human will and intellect cast in the organizational scales is heavy, and it is insufficiently balanced by heart and intuition. It is that balance I would like to see us redress.

When I look to the future, then, I see the development of the mutuality orientation in organizations as a challenge worth accepting, not only for the well-being of all who work within organizations but also for their stakeholders: customers, suppliers, communities, and the Earth. Especially for the Earth, because we shall never learn to care for and protect the environment that nurtures us until we commit to nurturing one another.

The task of balancing the power of our wills and intellects with the power of our hearts looks formidable at this period when most organizations are preoccupied with struggles to compete, to overcome, and to survive. I am sustained in my hope by the belief that the things business leaders say they want *cannot* be achieved without a shift toward mutuality in organizations. I refer especially to the acknowledged need for organizations and all their members to commit to quality and to focus on customer needs and interests.

We are endeavoring now to achieve a commitment to quality and customer focus through effort, through the design of better systems, and through the rewards and punishments of the transactional organization. But true commitment is freely given from free hearts and minds, and it is only that kind of commitment that leads to permanent improvements in quality and customer orientation. Many organizations are continuing to work through the old patterns, putting more time and energy into approaches that do not work very well, trying to fit Cinderella's shoe on her sister's foot. When the universe wants to encourage us to learn something new, it puts extraordinary barriers in the way of our following the old ways. The reason for us to try using love, support, and intuitive learning to transform our organizations is not that these are better than will and rational analysis—it is that we have applied a great deal of the latter and they are not working.

We must not be naïve in this endeavor. Love is not enough to lead us out of the woods in which we are lost. We shall require intelligence and purpose in the form of directed will to chart our path and pursue it. But our first task must be to stop, listen, and attune to one another and to our environment. When we do, we shall find understanding and assistance we did not know were there.

How to start? Some years ago, I first put forward the idea that it might be important to release the power of love in organizations (Harrison, 1984 [Chapter Eleven]). I wrote some discussion questions that consultants and clients could consider together in order to deepen their understanding of what I have since come to call the mutuality culture and to enhance their appreciation of the *connections* that exist between their organizations and the organizational environment. Those questions still seem relevant, and for many organizations, they will be new. I give a version of them here in the hope of stimulating thoughtful dialogue on issues raised in this paper.

- Where do we see love at work in our organization? What stops us from seeing and talking about it? How does what we see or not see shape our understanding and actions?

- Of what large purposive systems is our organization a part? How, if at all, does our organization's purpose become attuned to the larger system's purposes? If the planet had a purpose, how would our organization relate to it? How would we know?
- Does a focus on goal achievement block learning in our organization? How, and how well, does our organization learn?
- What messages do we receive from different parts of our environment? Are there some parts whose messages we consistently ignore? What would happen if we listened to these parts?
- With respect to goals, are we for the most part *pushed* by events or *pulled* by our vision of a desirable future outcome? Does it make a difference in the stress we experience in work?
- What is the relationship between our stated strategy and what we do? If our strategy does not determine our actions, what does?
- What losses do we fear in the future? How do we deal with that fear? How do we react to people who have different fears? How can we help each other with our fears?

May dialogues such as this help us find our way home before dark!

PART THREE

ON COMMUNITY DYNAMICS

For years, I have been interested in community living and in the organizational dynamics of communities. I have been especially interested in communities with a spiritual base, and for a long time the idea of living in such a community appealed to me. During the eighties, I found ways of working with intentional communities that permitted me to observe from the outside. I worked with the leadership group of a Zen community while it went through a difficult transition. I participated in the "organization diagnosis" of the New Age Findhorn Community in Scotland. I served on the board of directors of a Findhorn-inspired retreat center in California. I participated in a long-term study group on community living, which birthed a fine book on the subject, *Creating Community Anywhere* (Shaffer and Anundsen, 1993). In 1990, I joined the Ananda Community, a spiritual community established by J. Donald Walters. As a community member, I have deepened my experience and

thought about community in a new and more personal way.

This section consists of three short essays written at different times in my work with communities. Each essay addresses some aspect of integrating the divine into community life and spiritualizing the work we do with the physical and the mundane. The first essay, "A Model of Community Culture," describes my experience of being "gifted" with an organizational model for community that has proven widely applicable and helpful in understanding some of the differences in values and energy flow that arise over time in communities. In it, I show how I believe a focus on *spirit* can harmonize and bring into balance competing needs and forces, which may otherwise pull people's energies in different directions.

The second essay, "Looking on the Dark Side of a Center of Light," was written when I was on the board of the retreat center, at a time when the community was facing deep financial difficulties. I felt our New Age faith and trust in the power of our vision to manifest what we needed was getting in the way of our dealing effectively with reality. The paper presents my view of the appropriate relationship between focus on vision and focus on physical reality as we work to birth our dreams.

The third, longer paper, "Building Attunement in Community Through Social Architecture," speaks of organizational design in community. It introduces the concept of social architecture and applies it to the task of building and strengthening the spiritual center in community life.

The large Zen community was my first community client, and I learned much from community members about ways of learning, doing, and deciding that were different from anything I had come across in business. At the time, I was working with and writing about the concept of *attunement* (Harrison, 1984 [Chapter Eleven]), a word I originally learned from François Duquesne, a leader in the Findhorn Community. Attunement is a word I use frequently in speaking about how to bring the power and wisdom of the divine into our work in the world. In its larger sense, attunement refers to a way of thinking and acting (doing business) that continually attunes to *the whole,* meaning all the connections among the parts of one's organization or system and all that organization's connections with the wider environment. Other words for this way of thinking and acting are *appreciation* and *holistic thinking.*

I especially like the word attunement because of its connotation of music and harmony. An enterprise conducted according to the principles of attunement seeks to be in harmony, both internally and with its many stakeholders: suppliers, customers, community, and the ecosystem that it affects and from which it draws energy and resources. The Zen leadership gave me my first practical experience of attunement in action. The experience demonstrated to me that attunement as a way of making decisions works.

I now use attunement to refer to a process whereby members of a group "tune in" to their sense of the highest good and open themselves to receiving intuitive guidance from that source. When such guidance is received, it is shared with others. If consensus is not achieved at once, the process is reiterated, with each member continuing to seek guidance in the light of what has been said so far. The method seems to be practically identical to decision-making processes traditionally used by the Society of Friends (Quakers). The Zen leadership group with which I worked sought to do its business in this way. Its deliberations were slow, even ponderous, with many silences and frequent references to the needs and opinions of other groups and individuals whose interests needed to be held in consideration. The group was *inclusive,* wanting to keep everyone connected, involved, and feeling as though their interests were being served. Working with the group was inspiring for me because it was then one of the few times I had seen attunement working in the world, contributing to an organization's being productive and taking care of business. Attunement is a powerful and practical way of bringing *spirit* to bear on community and organizational issues. I refer to it often in the three papers that follow.

CHAPTER FIFTEEN

A MODEL OF COMMUNITY CULTURE

This paper contains its own introduction, but some readers may not know much about the Findhorn Community, in which the story told in this paper is set. Findhorn is a New Age "center of light" in Scotland. It offers experiential education in such areas as living in community and cooperating with and receiving help from nature spirits in gardening and other earthly endeavors. It provides a home for artists and craftspeople, and it hosts conferences, like the one I discuss in this paper, designed to bring out the spiritual dimensions of modern-day issues. Findhorn is unusual in its endeavor to govern through attunement to a higher good and purpose. It has trained many leading New Age thinkers and has inspired similar attempts to build community in several nations. Its early history and dominant ideas are described in Dorothy MacLean's *To Hear the Angels Sing* (1983).

In 1987, Celest Powell and I were invited to present a paper at the conference From Organization to Organism, which was being held at the Findhorn Community, in Scotland. We were also invited to stay after the conference to conduct an organization diagnosis of the Findhorn Community, and to present our findings to the whole community. Following my work with the Zen community, the Findhorn experience was my next window into the organizational world of

Note: Originally published as a monograph (Clinton, Wash.: Harrison Associates, 1987). Reprinted here, with revisions, with permission of Roger Harrison.

intentional communities. In conducting our diagnosis, Celest and I interviewed representative members of almost all of the groups involved in Findhorn: long- and short-term members and guests; those in current or past leadership roles, including Eileen Caddy, one of the founders; and so on. We took voluminous notes on what our informants told us and then went off to integrate them into a coherent presentation to the community.

During the conference, we had presented our initial version of the organization culture model given in Chapter Thirteen. We expected we would be able to fit our Findhorn data to that model, but the data stubbornly refused to cooperate. I felt, as I have felt at other times, that we were trying to fit Cinderella's slipper to the foot of one of her sisters—there was always some important part of what we had learned that was left over.

We were due to present to the community after dinner, and at four o'clock in the afternoon, we still did not have a coherent model to give them. What to do in the short time remaining? We could force-fit our data to the model we had, which was incongruent with my sense of professional artistry though it might have satisfied our audience. Or, we could continue to search for an alternate model, but performance anxiety was beginning to impair our creativity.

Findhorn is a place full of New Age mystique, in which communion with angels and nature spirits (*devas*) is commonplace. Although I did not at that time see myself as a person who could participate in such communication, I was desperate for help, and I suggested we go over to the meditation sanctuary to see if any guidance was to be found. Once there, I lay on the floor under the center of the dome and invited the Angel of Findhorn to give me a model that would illuminate our data for the benefit of the community. Within a few minutes, a new model that fit our data came into my mind. We hurried off and spent the dinner hour putting our presentation onto charts and were ready just in time for the meeting.

The presentation itself was a little anticlimactic. Our audience was polite and interested, and they confirmed that in our model we had caught the conflicting forces within their community. There was a brief discussion following our presentation, and that was that.

The Model

Nevertheless, the model has served me well since then in working with other intentional communities. I wrote it up originally in 1988, and I have now modified it slightly (see Figure 15.1), adding *power* to the issues of *individualism, alignment,* and *relationship* that are included within the model and changing the definitions of the elements slightly. The communities I work with recognize themselves within the model, and it initiates frank and open discussions about community issues and dynamics.

The four forces of power, individualism, alignment, and relationship that surround the center of the diagram exist in any organization. Each tends to be *cen-*

FIGURE 15.1. MODEL OF COMMUNITY CULTURE.

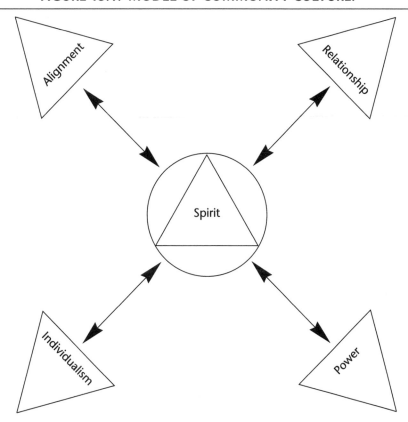

trifugal in that it pulls in a different direction. The forces are thus divisive in their effect on the organization or group. I define each force as follows:

Alignment refers to the workings of *purpose* in the group. A group is aligned when there is a strong sense of mission and when there are common goals and values to which the members are committed. An aligned group asks a lot of its members, and the members respond by giving freely of their time and energy because they believe in the work the group is doing. They work long hours, sacrifice personal and social needs, and identify so strongly with the group that their work does not feel like a sacrifice. Aligned groups tend to be workaholic, high energy, and cooperative on the inside. They tend to be competitive on the outside, tolerant of disagreement about means but intolerant of dissent about ends.

Relationship refers to the workings of *love* or *heart* in the group. A group is in relationship when the members have strong feelings of caring and connection with one another, when members' being together is just as important or more important than the task or work they do. Members of attuned groups enjoy being together. They willingly spend time and energy making sure that people are included and comfortable. They like to find consensus. They work to heal hurt feelings and damaged relationships. They spend a lot of time together, whether working or playing, and they are always ready to celebrate. Members of relationship-oriented groups tend to be caring, close, and open with their feelings. They are more than ordinarily aware of their *connections*, internally and often with the wider environment as well. They may have difficulty surfacing conflict, and they are so committed to everyone's feeling all right about decisions that they may have difficulty getting on with work.

Individualism refers to the workings of *self* or *ego* in the group. A group is individualistic when its members focus primarily on their own growth and on meeting their own needs. Members of individualistic groups are devoted to personal development as a dominant value. Members will support one another in "doing their own things," but they tend to compete for the resources the group has to offer: time, attention, love, and influence. Individualism-oriented groups tend to be exciting and creative, with a lot of energy, but members' energy may go off in all directions, and members may have frequent conflicts over goals. People get along well when everyone is learning and growing and working on his or her own development, but members find it hard to get dull, boring tasks done. Everyone wants to join in the party, but no one wants to do the dishes or take out the garbage afterward.

Power refers to the workings of *influence* and access to *resources* in the group. The power orientation in a community is often expressed in competition for status and the right to make decisions for others about what to do and how to do it. Hierarchies, role differentiation, and decision-making rules are ways groups deal with the power needs of their members. They are also ways groups organize to get things done. Power may be exercised in the service of getting the work done, or it may be sought to meet personal needs. Disentangling personal and group power issues is one of the knotty problems in the management of the community's life. Issues of power and individualism are often intertwined as some seek to control others while some seek space and autonomy to do their own thing.

How the Four Forces Create Community Culture

These four forces are present in differing degrees in every group, and the balance among them creates much of the emotional climate, or *culture*, of the group. When a group is in transition, the balance among these forces is disturbed, and people take sides around the values of each orientation. These conflicts are divisive, and many groups fall apart in trying to resolve them. Every community must find a balance among the forces and find a way to hold itself together in the face of the tension. In business or government, the tension is managed by the application of power and structure: the control of monetary resources and the power to make and enforce policies and procedures. In intentional communities and voluntary organizations, there has to be something more intangible that holds the whole together. Sometimes it is a common purpose, a passion for doing particular work in the world. Sometimes it is what I call *spirit*, the fifth force in the diagram.

Spirit is that sense of unity or oneness that is beyond individual purposes and emotional entanglements between people and even beyond the passion for doing good. In a community like Findhorn, spirit is experienced through members' meditating together and through their *attuning* to higher guidance. When people join together in asking to know what is for the highest good and they open themselves to receiving that knowledge, they are invoking spirit. The guidance, when and if it comes, arrives as intuitive knowing, free from the influence of egoistic hopes and fears. Spirit, in a group which knows how to access it, can be a powerful unifying force against the opposing pull of the other four forces. I put it in the center of the diagram because, unlike the others, it is never divisive but integrating and healing.

Using the Culture Model

This model is an explanation for trials and difficulties, but it does not immediately offer a cure. As long as we are human, have differing needs and values, and are not constrained by power from pursuing our differing visions, we shall have to struggle for whatever measure of harmony and community of purpose we achieve. Models such as this one are useful because they tell us the likely limitations and constraints on growth and development in groups and organizations. This particular model is useful in emphasizing the centrality of *spirit* and attunement to the highest goal as a unifying force that overcomes the divisiveness of all the others.

Of course, any one of the other forces can assume the center. We can find relationship-oriented communities that are organized around friendship, putting harmony and good feeling above all else. We can find others where power is the dominant force, where everything is subservient to the will of the dominant individual or coalition, who alone determines the priorities and the balance among competing needs. Or alignment in the form of a common purpose may be the organizing principle, and all else—individual needs, relationships, and formal hierarchies—bends to the power of the mission and vision of the group. And of course, some individualistic groups are always on the verge of falling apart because their dominant principle is for everyone to do as he or she pleases.

Seeking Integration Through Attuning to Spirit

When dominant, each of the forces suppresses important needs of individuals or the organization as a whole. In my view, the virtue of the concept of spirit as the unifying force is that it embraces all the others and holds them in balance for the good of the *whole,* meaning not only the whole organization but the whole of everything, the highest good. When a community seeks to attune itself to the highest and to hold in its consciousness the good of the whole, then all the other forces and agendas at the group, interpersonal, and individual levels are brought into relationship in service to the whole. They are not suppressed; they are balanced.

Of course, this ideal of balance is difficult to attain in practice. It is unstable, and even when it has been attained, it must be worked at continuously. It is not a "soft" or easy ideal—it leads to frequent or even continual conflict over what is the highest and what constitutes the good of the whole. Even groups that have a central religious commitment may find a barrier to the realization of spirit if their religion also enshrines one of the competing processes, such as power or alignment. Then religion may discourage continuous attunement to guidance. We long for certainty and stability, and having found our version of Truth, we resist looking further. But spirit, in the sense in which I hold it, being continuously in flux and change, is impatient of final truth. And spirit speaks to us from all of nature, not from any single authority. Guidance and truth are thus open to all, and the sources from which they may spring are as varied as the universe in which we live. A tree, a rock, a river, a bird, a flower—all may be messengers of spirit. So also may be the lowliest, the craziest, the newest, and the most naïve members of our community, as well as the most sophisticated and experienced, and those the furthest along whatever path we have chosen to follow as our spiritual or religious discipline.

Then how shall we know the true voices from among all the others that clamor to be heard, from inner as well as outer sources? Perhaps by becoming as still as we are able and quieting the voices of ego and desire, acquired knowledge and experience, and our mental models. Perhaps by listening with respect and compassion to the voices of our fellows, even, or especially, when they seem ignorant, foolish, or out of touch with reality. Perhaps by holding our bias for action in check long enough to hear one another out in dialogue and reflection, and to inquire further into the deeper mental structures that underlie our differences. Perhaps by prayer, asking for guidance in the faith that it will be given, with a willingness to follow it into the unknown.

Obviously, I do not have any complete answer for how communities can achieve a consensual understanding of what the voice of spirit is telling members in any particular situation. What I do know from experience is that the fruits of the willingness to listen deeply, to let go of our own ideas, and to follow guidance wherever it leads are cumulative. I do not venture to hope that practice will make us perfect, but I know that it will make us continuously more whole.

CHAPTER SIXTEEN

LOOKING ON THE DARK SIDE OF A CENTER OF LIGHT

ooking on the Dark Side of a Center of Light" was written during a difficult period when I was on the board of directors of a New Age retreat center in financial difficulties. Often, intentional communities present a mirror image of business, being strong on faith and vision but ungrounded in their relationship to the world of money. This paper is concerned with maintaining a balance between one's vision and the current mundane reality. It will be of use to anyone endeavoring to lead or manage an organization founded on vision and values, whether a business or a community.

"Looking on the Dark Side of a Center of Light" was originally written as a letter to my colleagues on the board, and I have preserved that form of personal address in the version that follows.

During our current discussions about the financial future, I have been impressed with a shared reluctance in our community to look failure and disaster in the face. I am concerned that we may cloak an unwillingness to deal forthrightly with reality in the guise of a faith in miracles and a commitment to manifesting our visions through positive thinking. In this letter, I want to say why I believe that taking a hard look at the dangers and the risks we face is essential if we are eventually to bring our vision into reality.

Note: Originally published as a monograph (Clinton, Wash.: Harrison Associates, 1989). Reprinted here, with revisions, with permission of Roger Harrison.

Some of you have said to me that dwelling thus on the dangers that beset our community is "negative thinking," inconsistent with faith in our vision and belief in miracles. There is room for us to differ about such things. I do have faith in the power of the vision. However, I believe the vision is most empowering when we place it in tension with current reality.

The Relationship Between Vision and Current Reality

Manifesting a vision begins when we specify a state which does not now exist and which we devoutly desire to bring into being. We create a vision of the highest good. That vision exists *in tension* with current reality in that the two are not yet congruent. If they were, we would not have or need a vision. Our vision would be the same as our statement about what current reality is.

It has been shown by Robert Fritz (1989) and later elaborated upon by Charles Kiefer and Peter Senge (Senge, 1990), that whether we act in organizations or as individuals we are most likely to succeed in manifesting our visions when both of the following conditions apply:

- We elaborate the vision in great detail, and together, we frequently rededicate ourselves to it: for example, through repeated affirmations.
- We describe current reality in great detail, particularly where it deviates from our vision, and we explicitly acknowledge the distance between the vision and reality. We do this with the same rigor with which we affirm our vision.

Rubber Band Metaphor

When we hold the vision and, at the same time, allow ourselves to be fully aware of current reality, we set up and maintain a continuous tension between the two. It is as though there were a rubber band connecting the vision and reality, as in Figure 16.1 (this rubber band theory is part of Charles Kiefer and Peter Senge's Leadership and Mastery course). The distance between the two stretches the rubber band. By holding firm to the vision, we fix it as an anchor. It seems that neither the human mind nor the universe likes an unresolved tension. The anchored vision exerts an attraction on reality, and reality begins to move toward the vision, reducing the tension.

Most of us have had the experience of having our intention firmly fixed on a vision. When we are also painfully aware of how far we are from its realization, this awareness programs us to observe and take advantage of every event that impacts our project. We begin to see opportunities where before we saw barriers. Our creativity is enhanced, and we receive inspiration. Heaven begins to move in mysterious ways, and large and small miracles occur.

FIGURE 16.1. THE TENSION BETWEEN VISION
AND CURRENT REALITY.

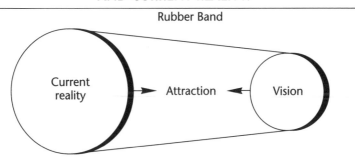

Source: Fritz, R. *The Path of Least Resistance.* Walpole, N.H.: Ballentine Books, 1989, p. 114. Used with permission.

How We Degrade Our Visions

However, since we really do not enjoy living in tension, we tend to find ways to reduce the discomfort of being aware of the differences between reality and our vision. There are at least three ways we can reduce the tension, and all of them weaken the process of manifestation.

• The first way we degrade our vision is to bring it closer to current reality. We may say to ourselves, "That's unrealistic. Let's set our sights a little lower, so we can have the satisfaction of achieving our goals." When we do this, the tension is relieved, and there is then less pressure on current reality to move in the direction of the vision.

• The second way we weaken the process of manifestation is to ignore or to deny current reality. We may focus exclusively on the vision, saying, "We need to think positively. We don't want to get stuck in negativity and fear by dwelling on our troubles." Or we may keep ourselves unclear and fuzzy about the threats and dangers in the environment by never allowing ourselves to dwell on them or be specific about them. When we focus exclusively on the vision, we tend not to take personal responsibility for the changes we want. We leave it to a higher power, hoping for miracles.

• The third way we weaken the process by which the vision attracts reality is through collusion between leaders and followers. It often begins with leaders not trusting that followers will hold their faith and commitment in the face of the stark reality of limitations, strategic errors, dangers, and failures. The leaders then minimize threats and withhold bad news. The followers, for their part, are content to believe that the leaders "wouldn't be there if they didn't know what they were doing." They do not question the leaders' image of invulnerability, and they do not seek to know the difficulties and dangers. They place their trust in their leaders rather than in their own efforts and the power of the vision.

The Ingredients of Manifestation

I believe that manifesting a vision takes place through a combination of perceptual focus, directed effort, and divine intervention. The first two flow directly from maintaining the tension between vision and reality. The awareness of that tension directs our attention to events and entities in our environment that are relevant to our task. We become highly sensitized to what will help or hinder our success, and we move quickly to apply our effort where it will make a difference. Divine intervention seems to depend on our doing this. When we are excruciatingly aware of how each event and process we observe affects our project, and when we devote ourselves body and soul to doing the best we can to achieve our vision, the universe seems to move to help us. As was said in another generation, "The Lord helps those who help themselves." I prefer to think of it as God saying, "Do the best you can, and I'll help you out." I call this "tough visioning." We do not use our vision and faith to spare ourselves the discomfort of knowing we are not where we want to be but rather to mold ourselves into a cohesive group and to spur us to our best efforts. Both business entrepreneurs like Steve Jobs and New Age pioneers like Peter Caddy know this and do it. They believe in their visions, and they take personal responsibility for manifesting them.

Soft Visioning: The Dark Side of New Age Faith

Until now, I have seen our group engage in much "soft visioning." Soft visioning denies or ignores environmental threats. We use faith in the vision to soothe ourselves against what might otherwise become immobilizing anxiety. This is the dark side of New Age faith, where we turn our faces toward heaven because we cannot stand the unpleasantness of looking at the real world. And while we look hopefully toward heaven, dark reality is sneaking up on us from behind and may shortly engulf this enterprise.

I know we can overcome our difficulties and eventually see our dreams come true. I am equally sure that to succeed in this enterprise, we must be as willing to look at the dark side as we are to see the light.

It is heartwarming to be able to relate that this group did, after much stormy debate, come to grips with its very difficult and perilous current reality. Once it faced up to its financial situation, it began to work with its investors and customers creatively and with integrity. A new plan for financing was developed to replace the one that was not working, and at this writing, the organization is solvent and growing, both in the mundane realm and in spirit. Another perspective on the story of this group is given in Chapter Thirteen of *Creating Community Anywhere* (Shaffer and Anundsen, 1993).

CHAPTER SEVENTEEN

BUILDING ATTUNEMENT IN COMMUNITY THROUGH SOCIAL ARCHITECTURE

I wrote "Building Attunement in Community Through Social Architecture" together with Celest Powell. Like the paper in Chapter Sixteen, it was an epistle to the board of directors of a New Age retreat center. Celest and I were both members of the board, and the letter contained our thoughts on the importance of bringing a greater spiritual focus into all the members' life and work. The idea of attunement put forward in this piece is active and energetic. It gives another perspective on the concept of attunement described in the first section of Chapter Fifteen, "A Model of Community Culture."

I n a lecture he gave at Findhorn in the early 1970s, David Spangler said:

> In a centre such as this one we do not come together to learn techniques of attunement. What we do come together for is that in and through our love, our respect for each other, the help that we give each other, the openness and trust that we offer to each other, we can discover our home, a state and place of consciousness where we are no longer propelled into search, into longing, into loneliness, but where we know that we are one, one with ourselves, one with each other, one with life, one with God. . . . Attunement is the simplest thing in

Note: Originally published as a monograph coauthored by Celest Powell (Mountain View, Calif.: Harrison Associates, 1989). Reprinted here, with revisions, with permission of Roger Harrison.

the world; because, in the mind of God which is essentially our mind, there is no separation. There is only closeness. So attunement becomes a process of changing our image of travel and distance, and aligning it with the Divine image of Oneness, and non-separation. It is as simple as one heart beat following another; one breath following another. . . . There is no space that separates us from that for which we long. But the secret of arriving there is completely a secret of giving. Attunement is a manifestation of the out-breath, . . . the giving forth of the being, to whatever surrounds it in its environment and to itself. But we think of attunement in exactly the opposite fashion. We think of it as a receiving, as a sitting in silence and awaiting a voice or a Presence to communicate itself to us. . . . That puts us into a very passive state; puts us into a non-creative state. And it puts us into a state of a form [sic] of spiritual selfishness where we await for the Divine Voice to come to us.

Creating Community Through Living the Qualities We Desire

Spangler's words are a commentary on giving and receiving, a call to live our ideals, to walk our talk, and to become that very love for which we long. The search for human community animates us, and we can translate Spangler's remarks into the context of that search. He seems to be saying we shall find community when *we live those qualities* which we look to find in community. We do not need a place or an organization; rather, we must live with others as though we were already in community. That would seem to mean sharing freely with all others the love, the helpfulness, the compassion, and the giving that we imagine we would find if we were living in the caring community we desire to inhabit. We shall experience those qualities as we put them out to others, and our nurturing of others shall nurture and uplift us.

As we think about our search for community, we realize that, like many others, we are looking to receive that which is missing in our lives. We imagine that when we become part of a group of people who care, we shall become more loving; when we are with others who cooperate, we shall lose our competitiveness; when we receive nurturance, we shall be more giving. Spangler's observations are a potent reminder that in the spiritual as in the mundane world there is no free lunch: if we are to be fulfilled, we must be both cook and customer, both priest and parishioner, both lover and beloved.

What then of the search for community and of the effort in which we are jointly involved, to build here a social system which manifests our ideals and our longings for a life of work and love that celebrates the human and divine spirit, replenishes the planet, and raises consciousness in ourselves and those whose lives we touch? Is the attempt to grow a more perfect and nourishing social organism an effort to project our needs onto an outside structure, an effort doomed to failure because we are all looking to receive more than we are able to give?

Possibly it is. But we (Celest and Roger) believe that every effort we make to realize our highest needs, no matter how misguided, brings us along the path toward the kind of truth David Spangler articulates. Each effort at community is a classroom in which we can learn to give, to take personal responsibility for creating the kingdom of God, and to see ourselves and others both clearly and compassionately. The question to be addressed in creating real communities is not just whether they will meet our needs, but whether they can be better designed as supportive contexts for our learning to give, to work, to love, and to find the God within. That is the question addressed in the remainder of this essay.

Social Architecture and the Design of Our Community

Social architecture is the body of knowledge about creating organizational structures, roles, systems, and procedures that will best fulfill the purpose of the organization and, at the same time, meet the personal needs of the organization's members. If we take as given David Spangler's idea that to achieve attunement requires learning to give, to manifest that which we long to be given, then the task of social architecture in building an attuned community is to create an organization that fosters, teaches, and supports all its members in manifesting love, in finding the divine spirit within themselves and others, and in giving service to mankind and to the planet.

Energy Channeled Through Time and Space

Social architecture, like its physical analogue, is the art of creating spaces that support activities desired in the organization and that discourage others that are not desired. A well-designed building channels the flow of human activity and energy: for example, open-plan offices encourage direct interaction and sharing of information; separate offices discourage it. In neither office plan do we need to make rules about how much people communicate with one another. The design constrains and channels the flow of energy and makes it easier or harder to communicate.

Similarly, by the way we design work processes, roles and responsibilities, authority relationships, reward systems, and the like, we encourage certain kinds of behaviors, attitudes, and learning processes, and we discourage others. If we are clear about what processes and behaviors we want to encourage in order to facilitate attunement, we can design our organization to facilitate them. If we do not design our organization consciously to facilitate the attitudes and behaviors we want, some of our organizational arrangements will almost certainly channel energy and attention in ways which are contrary to our purposes. This is as true in the spiritual life of the community as it is in its social and economic aspects.

Joys and Sorrows of Individualism

Because we are very individualistic people, our approaches to spiritual growth emphasize the values of freedom of choice, self-development, and personal initiative. We have strong egos; we are action-oriented; we value novelty and become bored easily; we assert our needs for autonomy. We tend to mistrust authority, whether in the form of texts or gurus; we want to find our own paths to enlightenment rather than take a guided tour. In our spiritual practice, we chafe against requirements and discipline.

We have the longings that go with our predilections. Feeling alienated, we search for intimacy and dream of community. Competing, we wish for cooperation and teamwork. Going it alone and doing our own thing, we are lonely; we hope to find companions traveling the same paths. It is this longing for wholeness that leads people like us to alternative institutions such as this community, where we look for the gentler ways that we do not easily create for ourselves at the same time as we are alert to resist authority, discipline, and constraint. We believe that the people who are attracted to this community have within themselves the need to give love, to cooperate, to contribute their effort, and to respond to the divine in one another. The challenge to us is to design settings in which they will be led gently to experience these qualities in themselves, without strongly provoking their fears of control and authority.

Design Principles

What are the principles for designing such settings? One is *maximum feasible choice*, meaning that we give as much freedom and autonomy as people are ready to exercise responsibly. When people make their own choices as to how and what to learn or how to perform their work, the learning or the work is more highly motivated and more in tune with their unique needs and capabilities. The difficult part is to decide what constitutes responsible choice, and what level of responsibility people are ready for.

We can approach this by being clear in advance about the *boundary conditions*— what are the minimum requirements for learning or work that we are willing to accept. For example, in the area of spiritual development, we might decide that the boundary condition was for everyone in our community to commit to regular spiritual practice. A tighter boundary might specify the amount of time each day we wanted people to spend in their practice. A still tighter one would prescribe that the time was to be spent in meditation. Even tighter would be to fix the type of meditation in which we would engage.

When people are at an early stage of development, whether in regard to their emotions or to their skills and abilities, boundaries need to be more prescriptive. As people develop, the boundaries widen.

Whether boundaries are tight or loose, a key principle in this approach to design is *accountability at the boundary*. It is at the boundary that our commitments are tested and our contracts are fulfilled. This principle implies monitoring or assessment to keep the process conscious. In formal learning settings, accountability may be to an instructor or to a group of fellow learners. In a community, accountability is usually to one's peers.

We often confuse freedom with no accountability. In the model proposed here, accountability begins where freedom ends. The two are complementary and define one another, just as the rim of a cup defines that vessel. There can be no freedom without a boundary just as there can be no cup without a rim. Freedom is total within the boundary. Within that time and space, one is responsible only to oneself (or one's peers in an autonomous group) for what one does and how one does it. The boundary is where one becomes accountable to someone else for having met one's commitment or delivered on one's promises. In this model, the question is never whether or not we are accountable. The question is when and to whom we are accountable and how specifically the requirements for our performance are defined.

Thus, the design question for building attunement in community becomes how to specify the boundaries at which we are accountable to one another for our learning, our growth, and our performance in manifesting the qualities of attunement about which David Spangler speaks: loving, giving, showing compassion, and appreciating the divine spirit in ourselves and others. Within those boundaries, we are free to spend time and energy as we will; at the boundary, we are responsible to the community for the results we achieve.

Principles for Living Together

If these theoretical concepts are useful, we should be able to use them to make some design decisions about how we structure and manage our community. In illustrating how we might do this, this essay will make some statements about the kinds of behaviors and attitudes the members of our community could manifest. Please take these as personal views of the authors and as illustrative only, since our community has yet to create consensus on its desired principles.

- Community members share a sense of vision and high purpose that is sufficiently well articulated that it serves as a guide to the individual for his or her day-to-day actions.
- The primary question posed to prospective members of this community is, "What can I contribute?" rather than, "What will I receive?" Members are attracted by the opportunity to serve the vision.
- Following Kahlil Gibran, members believe that work is "love made visible." Each task is ennobled thereby and given heart. Members take satisfaction in doing work well. Members think in terms of "our job," rather than "my job" and "your job," helping out wherever they see a need.

- Members love one another and take care of one another. It is considered as important to build and maintain loving relationships as it is to get the work done.

Who Are Community Members?

In order to create arrangements and agreements that will foster these principles, we need first to decide who are members of the community. Again, this essay suggests only a provisional answer to that question: people become members of our community when they make a commitment to its vision and purpose or when they participate in programs here in which community living is a significant aspect of the design. According to this definition, people who come as individual guests would, during their stay, be members. People who attend programs offered by workshop leaders who use our retreat center simply as a source of board and lodging would not.

Toward Implementation

It would be presumptuous to do more in this essay than sketch the outlines of how we might implement our principles in daily practice. The authors have given the matter some thought, however, and offer some examples here of how implementation might be approached.

Developing a Sense of Vision and High Purpose

Our community needs a well-articulated purpose and sense of mission on which there is true consensus. People need to feel that there is something here that is bigger than their individual wants and needs, something worth giving their energy and love to, even making sacrifices for. We need to state our vision of what we are doing in the world in a way that makes people feel good to be associated with it.

A clear vision permits us to set forth the principles by which we mean to operate. When we can agree on those principles, we need fewer rules and regulations. We can operate within wider boundaries and be accountable for the *effects* of our actions rather than focusing on the actions themselves.

Our vision includes the priorities we set on tasks and people. Our community produces goods and services that attract others' energy in the form of money. That task is vital to the survival of the community, and we place ourselves in service to it. At the same time, the community only exists because we ourselves have need for it. The structures and systems of the community are in service to its members and should operate in such a way as to empower everyone.

If a statement of vision and purpose is to serve as a guide for individual action, it must be "bought into" by those who are now members, perhaps by means of a "vision workshop" in which members join together to create their statement of purpose and of the mission of our community in the world. This statement should be as specific as possible regarding the principles and practices we expect members to follow in order to manifest the vision.

For "temporary" members (those who come and participate in the community's life for brief periods of time), the vision and mission statement would be part of their orientation, along with an explanation of the principles and practices we follow in order to manifest the vision.

Experiencing Membership as an Opportunity to Contribute

We offer association with our community as a chance to serve rather than to be served. We do not make distinctions between those who contribute money and those who contribute time and energy. But we encourage people to think of supporting the community with both time and money rather than being passive investors. We do not focus only on the big investments or gifts but go for a broader base of support, with many small contributions.

Michael Phillips (1974) tells a story in *The Seven Laws of Money* that is relevant here:

> Not too long ago a group came to me and wanted to buy a gigantic piece of land. It was a group oriented around an Eastern religion and they naturally wanted to raise *money* for the gigantic piece of land. I said "You don't want money, you want supporters. You can go out and look for supporters and in the process ask for money, but don't forget what you're really after. Supporters." They did this. They contacted countless people, always asking for a small amount of money but in the process realizing that the commitment of a small amount of money was a commitment of support. And, of course, it was the support that built the institution and helped it grow. The institution is still growing. If this religious group had gotten a grant in the beginning it probably would have blown their whole future. Where would their supporters and friends and energy have come from, especially when the grants and funds began to run out in two or three years? [p. 148]

Experiencing Work as Love Made Visible

In our working lives, we manage by the vision. We articulate a set of principles that bring the vision and purpose of the community down to the level of everyday decision guidelines. Each of us is accountable to everyone else for adhering to these principles in carrying out his or her work, no matter what his or her role or leadership status. While we must have well thought out systems and procedures for efficiency and economy, the rules are subordinate to the principles by which we live and work. Our systems are simple, readily modifiable, and understood by all. We work together to improve them.

We bring love into our work by doing it well, even the parts that do not show. We care for our physical environment, picking up, cleaning up, painting, and decorating, so that the place manifests the love we have put into it. We serve guests and one another with simplicity, harmony, and elegance. We care for our community in the way we conserve and maintain its resources, looking after tools and equipment, husbanding resources, reducing waste. We manifest our love of the land by following nonpolluting practices, by recycling, and by reducing our use of nonrenewable resources.

Experiencing Distributed Leadership

Organizations that empower the membership tend to be flat, with few levels of hierarchy. Leadership is distributed rather than concentrated in a few hands. Leaders see themselves as in service to the community. People have the opportunity to become competent generalists. Jobs are shared or rotated, and people have continuing opportunities to learn one another's skills.

Rotation of leader and member roles, role-sharing, and cross-training foster each person's knowing and caring for the whole. When people become competent at several roles, we have a more flexible organization. Conflict between people doing different jobs is easier to resolve as they come to appreciate one another's difficulties and needs from having done one another's work.

We are accountable to one another for performance of our tasks. We design and use a peer review process to assess our performance of tasks against the agreed standards for the tasks and for cooperative teamwork.

Loving and Taking Care of One Another

We spend the time to get to know one another personally, to develop ourselves as a cohesive and mutually supportive group. We regularly conduct "clearings," where conflicts and bad feelings can be processed, and we take time out to deal with individual disturbances as they come up. We agree on a set of norms such as the following for how we want to treat one another:

- *Appreciating.* We give credit for ideas and contributions. We build on others' ideas. We acknowledge one another's abilities and qualities.
- *Nurturing.* We teach, mentor, support, and encourage one another. We take satisfaction in one another's successes.
- *Valuing.* We see each person as worthwhile in himself or herself. We value one another as sacred vessels of the soul rather than only for the contributions we make.
- *Trusting.* We give each other the benefit of the doubt. We each look for, evoke, and respond to goodness in the other.

- *Listening.* We empathize with one another's concerns, hopes, fears. We take time to hear each other's feelings and to respond from the heart to them.
- *Giving.* We give generously of our time, energy, and resources in service to one another's needs. We give more than expected, more than a quid pro quo.
- *Harmonizing.* We initiate problem solving and peace making, and search for win-win solutions to conflicts. We avoid judgments and provocations by avoiding "you" statements in favor of "I" statements. We look for the positive intent in others' behavior. We forgive.

Balancing Growth on Four Levels

The work and social life of the community are arranged so as to foster the health, growth, and development of each member in all four areas of life: physical, emotional, mental, and spiritual. Members are expected to grow in each of these areas and to contribute to one another's growth.

We are each accountable to one another for our physical, emotional, mental, and spiritual development. Together, we set mutual expectations and develop broad-based agreements on developmental goals and how we will know that these goals have been achieved. Following the principle of accountability at the boundary, individuals choose and carry out their own ways of meeting the goals. The community institutionalizes and supports the individual's self-development by setting aside times and places each day in which people can work on their own development. People may choose to work in groups in order to make use of peer support.

Evaluating Performance

We design a peer-review process in which people account for their self-development activities. In early meetings, they set personal goals and commit to them. In future meetings, they restate their goals and describe their activities in pursuit of the goals and the successes and difficulties they are experiencing. They receive feedback and help from other members.

Our Message and Our Hope for the Future

The ideas set forth in this essay are not offered as a proposal for reorganizing our community. Rather, they are what we, the authors, came up with when we began to play with David Spangler's insights, combined them with our observations of this and other communities, and began to develop our own ideas on the design of intentional communities. We have applied the ideas of social architecture to the problem of building an attuned community, an organization which fosters, teaches, and supports all its members in manifesting love, in finding the divine spirit within themselves and others, and in giving service to mankind and to the planet.

We believe that if we are clear about what processes and behaviors we want to encourage in order to facilitate attunement, we can design our organization to facilitate them. Whether or not the specific suggestions given here are appropriate to our own community, the concept of social architecture holds promise for designing intentional communities so that their structures, roles, systems, and procedures best fulfill the purpose of the organization and, at the same time, meet the personal needs of the organization's members.

In approaching this task, we have been guided by two principles: *maximum feasible choice* and *accountability at the boundary*. Following these principles enables us to maximize individual freedom in choosing the *means* by which we work toward the goals of community at the same time as we ensure that each is accountable to the others for pursuing community goals and for the results they achieve.

These ideas are offered, then, in the hope that we may dialogue, experiment, and learn together about such issues, for the benefit of our community and of our own growth and development. You are invited to join in this adventure!

My essays on community are a work in progress. The papers in Chapters Fifteen, Sixteen, and Seventeen are at best fragments of what there is to be said about the design and management of intentional communities. More of my thoughts on the subject can be found in the story of my life in community since 1990 and in my reflections on the importance of *surrender* in community and, indeed, in organizational life generally. These musings are contained in my professional autobiography, *Consultant's Journey* (Harrison, 1995). I continue to explore the subject in dialogue and through experience, because I believe that as we learn to build community in our organizations we shall also learn to heal ourselves and our planet.

PART FOUR

ON LEARNING
AND EDUCATION

My energy and attention during my career have been about equally divided between education and consulting. As a consultant, I have always focused on enabling learning for my clients. However, I have never been enormously enamored of the role of teacher, especially when the role is focused on the transfer of information from teacher to student or on the evaluation of student performance by the teacher. I have found these transferring and evaluating activities as distasteful when I have been a teacher as I did when I was a student. I have always loved learning things for myself and finding ways to encourage others to do the same. Thus, this set of papers is largely concerned with creating the conditions under which people will be stimulated to engage in learning for themselves. It is also concerned with minimizing the blocks and barriers to learning. The first paper, "Defenses and the Need to Know," dates from my T-group days in the sixties. It puts forward a model

for balancing confrontation and stress in experiential learning situations. Quite recently, the model has resurfaced in my work, as I concern myself with ways of moderating the trauma and stress produced during the massive organizational changes of the present moment.

While I was at Yale University in the sixties, I struggled long, and ultimately successfully, with the question of how to create an enclave of empowered and active learners in my classroom, finding ways to buffer the influence of the traditional authoritarian milieu in a prestigious mainstream university. In this work, I was led into exploring and inventing some theory and practice of "social architecture." During this period, I also applied what I was learning about the design of experiential education to the training of Peace Corps volunteers for service in Latin America. My paper with Richard Hopkins, "The Design of Cross-Cultural Training: An Alternative to the University Model," was intended both as a guide for designing training relevant to overseas performance and also as a general critique of traditional university educational methods. To my delight, it was received as such by radical students and faculty engaged in university reform during the sixties. When I left Yale in 1966, I abandoned my academic ambitions in favor of a full-time consulting career. As a kind of legacy to others, I wrote "Classroom Innovation: A Design Primer," containing everything I then knew about motivating and empowering students.

I spent the late sixties and early seventies establishing myself as a freelance consultant, and then I returned to my educational interests, prompted by the success of my efforts to design a form of experiential education for European managers that did not depend on small-group processes for its energy. The paper "Developing Autonomy, Initiative, and Risk Taking Through a Laboratory Design" describes my early work in this area, and it was followed by "Self-Directed Learning: A Radical Approach to Educational Design." The latter paper, like "Classroom Innovation," was intended to set forth a coherent theory and practice which could be followed by others so inclined.

"Toward a Strategy for Helping Redundant and Retiring Managers" was published at a time when the first of many waves of layoffs and redundancies was beginning to be felt in Britain. The paper outlines what I knew at the time about the conditions needed for individuals to heal from the stress and trauma of losing their work. It then puts forward a proposal for educating those who have lost jobs, using methods of self-directed learning taken from my autonomy labs (first described in "Developing Autonomy, Initiative, and Risk Taking Through a Laboratory Design").

Finally, "Steps Toward the Learning Organization" is a brief summary of a longer monograph on organizational learning. The latter will eventually find its way into a book, but for the present, the summary allows me to share my thoughts on how to be a learning-oriented organization development consultant and also forms an appropriate conclusion by bringing together the twin strands of consulting and education that have made up my career. The summary also introduces my recent thinking on the blocks and barriers to organizational learning and on the close relationship between healing and learning in organizations.

CHAPTER EIGHTEEN

DEFENSES AND THE NEED TO KNOW

I first published "Defenses and the Need to Know" in 1963, midway through my six years as an assistant professor at Yale University. It was a milestone for me because the writing of it signaled the end of a writing block that plagued me during my early years at Yale. Not coincidentally, it is the first paper I wrote that was neither empirical nor experimental but was about the practice of what we at that time called applied behavioral science. My lack of interest in experimental and quantitative work was the main reason for my deciding not to pursue my original academic ambitions. It took me quite a while to find my voice as a writer, and when I did, it was as a philosophical and reflective practitioner rather than as an academic psychologist.

The paper reflects my heavy involvement at that time in the practice of group dynamics and T-groups. As a T-group trainer, I wanted to create conditions for maximum learning in the group with which I worked, and that sometimes meant that people were confronted quite strongly. At the same time, I had experienced enough psychological pain and anxiety myself that I wanted to keep the groups safe for the participants. This paper presents a way of thinking about that dilemma that I found helpful in keeping balance and safety in my groups.

I believe the paper is relevant on a larger scale today, when so many organizations are undergoing radical change and subjecting their members to trauma and loss. I have recently revisited the castle and battlefield model put forward in this paper, incorporating it into new work on organizational learning and healing

Note: Originally published in *Human Relations Training News,* 1963, *6*(4), 1–3. Published next in P. R. Lawrence, J. A. Seiler, and others (eds.), *Organizational Behavior and Administration* (Homewood, Ill.: Irwin, 1965). Reprinted here with permission of NTL Institute.

(Harrison, 1984 [Chapter Eleven]; Harrison, 1992; Harrison, Cooper, and Dawes, 1991). The model is quite serviceable in understanding any situation that involves threat, pressure, and stress along with the simultaneous need to learn new behaviors and ways of thinking. In the sense of having high demands for learning and change, the world of business has now become one great T-group!

The purpose of this piece is to discuss the ways we have of protecting our views of ourselves and others. Specifically, it is intended to rescue the concept of *defensive behavior* from the ostracism in which it is usually held, restoring it to its rightful place as a major tool of humankind in adapting to a changing world. I also consider how defenses may help and hinder us in really profiting from a learning situation.

Let us consider how we understand the world we live in, and particularly those parts of it concerning ourselves and our relations with other people. First of all, we organize the world according to concepts, or categories. We say that things are warm or cold, good or bad, simple or complex. Each of these concepts may be considered a dimension along which we can place events in the world, some closer to one end of the dimension, some closer to the other.

Actually, we cannot really think without using these categories or dimensions to organize our thoughts. Any time we consider the qualities of ourselves, other persons, or events in the inanimate world, we have to use categories to do it. We are dependent for our understanding of the world on the concepts and categories we have for organizing our experiences. If we lack a concept for something which occurs in the world, either we have to invent one or we cannot respond to the event in an organized fashion. How, for example, would a person explain his or her own and others' behavior without the concept of love and hate? Think how much behavior would simply puzzle or confuse him or her or, perhaps, just go on by without really being perceived at all, for lack of this one dimension.

Concepts do not exist in isolation; they are connected to one another by a network of relationships. Taken all together, the concepts we use to understand a situation plus the relationships among the concepts are a *conceptual system*. For example, we may say, "People who are warm and friendly are usually trusting, and hence, they are often deceived by others." Here we have a conceptual system linking the concepts friendly warmth, trust in others, and ease of deception. Because concepts are linked one to another, the location of an event on one concept usually implies something about where the event is located on each of a whole network of concepts. It is thus almost impossible to take in a small bit of information about a characteristic of a person or event without its having a whole host of implications about other characteristics.

Images and stereotypes operate this way: when we discover that a person is black or white, is a PTA president, a social scientist, a wife, or a husband, the category to which the person belongs evokes in each of us a complex set of associated qualities, characteristics, stereotypes, prejudices, and memories. We have beliefs, attitudes, and expectations about the person's behavior, which are in part conscious, in part below the surface of our attention. Most of the time, we then operate on the basis of that mental network, or conceptual system, without thinking too much about it

The study of defenses, like the study of stereotypes, is the study of the processes which protect the organization of conceptual systems in the face of information and experiences which, if accurately perceived, would tend to disconfirm, break down, or change the relationships among concepts in the system.

Why should conceptual systems be resistant to change? Actually, if they were simply intellectual exercises, they probably would not. In real life, conceptual systems come to have value attached to them. The values seem to be of two kinds: one kind I will call competence value. By the *competence value* of a conceptual system, I mean its value for helping us to be effective in the world. After all, the conceptual systems we have were developed because we needed some way of making sense of the world, of predicting what kinds of results would follow from what kinds of causes, of planning what kinds of actions we needed to take in order to accomplish some desired result.

People have the conceptual systems they have because in some important situations the systems proved adaptive for them; by seeing the world in just this way, they were able to get along better, to be more effective, to prepare better for what was coming next, or just to feel better about themselves or others. For human beings, conceptual systems are, in a very real sense, very nearly the most important survival equipment we have. Animals have instinctual patterns of response, complex systems of behavior that are set off without thinking in response to fairly fixed patterns of stimulation. Humans have to do it the hard way, by developing systems of concepts that make sense of the world and then using these systems to make decisions as to what to do in each situation. Those conceptual systems that pay off over and over again tend to become parts of our permanent equipment for understanding the world and for deciding what to do in it. If we were to lose these systems, we would become like ships without rudders; we would have lost our control systems and, with them, our chances of acting in an organized, intelligent fashion to meet our needs. This is what I mean by the competence value of conceptual systems.

Unfortunately, no conceptual system fits the world perfectly. In the interests of economy, we simplify and leave things out as being unimportant: for example, we act as though relationships that are statistical (they are only true most of the time) are necessary and hence hold true all of the time. On the rare occasions when the relationships do not hold, we tend to overlook the inconsistency, rather than trying to understand why things did not go as expected. We may, for example, conceptualize the qualities of warmth, lovingness, and femininity as incompatible with a ready ability to express anger. This conceptual system may not change even in the face of strong anger on the part of a woman about whose warmth and femininity we have ample evidence in the past. We simply pass it off as, "She's not herself," or, "She's not really that mad," or even, "Deep down inside, she isn't as warm and feminine as she appears to be." We go through a lot of mental gymnastics to avoid seriously questioning a conceptual system which has proven useful in the past. So, frequently, the last alternative explanation we consider is, "It is perfectly possible for a woman to express deep anger readily and still be warm, loving, and feminine." Such an alternative would mean the significant alteration of a conceptual system.

The trouble is, you cannot just alter one little conceptual system at will and let it go at that. The links between concepts are too complex and too tight to change one or two relationships in isolation. One change leads to another, and pretty soon, a major reorganization is going on. It may be, of course, that the reorganization may lead to substantial improvement in our understanding and effectiveness in the world, but in the meantime, because our new ways of seeing the world have yet to be adequately tested and confirmed, there may be considerable turmoil and confusion when we question relationships that once seemed solidly established.

Of course, the more important the particular conceptual system in question is in making it possible for us to meet our needs, the more strain and upset are involved in changing it. For example, one might believe that heavy objects fall more rapidly than light ones. The disconfirmation that would follow upon learning that all objects fall at the same rate would perhaps be uncomfortable but only moderately so. Consider, however, the anxiety and stress that could be produced by the discovery that complying with another's demands does not always make the other like you and may, indeed, have the opposite effect. For a person who has relied in his or her interpersonal relations on the techniques associated with such a conceptual system, its disconfirmation may have the dimensions of a major crisis in life.

So, much of the time we hang on to our not-so-accurate conceptual systems because they work for us most of the time and to give them up would plunge us into mild or severe confusion without any real promise of eventually attaining a more accurate, effective reorganization. The picture does not look so good for personal improvement, and before I finish, it will look even bleaker.

There is another kind of valuing that goes on when we place events into conceptual systems, and I will call it *evaluation*. This is the well-known process of believing that some states of affairs are better and some are worse. In most conceptual systems, there is an element of evaluation: most concepts have a good end and a bad end, and we would rather see events come out on the good ends than the bad.

Again, it is less important to see events come out well in some areas than in others. When we consider the conceptual system "Red sky at night, sailors' delight./Red sky in the morning, sailor take warning," we may indeed prefer that the weather come out on the red "at night . . . delight" end rather than on the red "morning . . . warning" side, but if on a given occasion, it does not, we do not ordinarily get too upset, nor do we feel responsible for our failure to predict the weather.

The closer we get to conceptual systems that are concerned with our self-perceptions and our important relationships with others, the more important evaluation becomes and the more uncomfortably responsible we feel when events do not fall on the valued ends of the concepts. Thus, if we value love as against hate and intelligence against stupidity, it becomes important to protect conceptual systems that organize events so we can see ourselves as brilliant and loving. When maintaining the valued perception becomes too important, people may desperately protect quite maladaptive, ineffective conceptual systems in order to maintain a favorable perception of self or others.

Sometimes, competence value and evaluation compete for influence on the conceptual system. For example, some persons have led such difficult childhoods that it is only by seeing themselves as bad, worthless people that they can seem to make sense out of the awful things that people they trusted have done to them; at the same time, they have needs for self-esteem and for seeing themselves at the valued ends of concepts. These people may experience considerable conflict between these two motivational influences on their conceptual systems.

These, then, are the *defenses*. They serve to keep us from becoming confused, upset, and rudderless every time something happens contrary to our expectations. Frequently they protect our liking for ourselves and others when we and they fail to live up to our ideals. Defenses give life as it is experienced more stability and continuity than could ever be justified by reference to the contingency and complexity of real events alone. Defenses keep our relations with others more pleasant and satisfying than they might otherwise be, protecting us from our own and others' anger, and helping us to go on loving people who are usually less than perfect and sometimes less than human.

At the same time, these same defenses block our learning, often dooming us to make the same mistakes over and over again. They make us blind to faults of our own we could correct as well as those we can do nothing about. Sometimes they make us turn the other cheek when a good clout on the nose would clear the air and establish a new and firmer footing for an honest relationship. They can, in extreme cases, make so many kinds of information dangerous to our conceptual systems that we narrow and constrict our experiences, our feelings, and our thoughts, becoming virtual prisoners of our own protection.

I believe there is in each of us a kind of counterforce that operates in the service of learning. Let us call it a need to know, or a drive toward competence. We are used to thinking about physiological needs, and we recognize there are probably social needs, such as needs for love; but we often overlook the need for competence and knowledge. Yet it is in operation all around us. We see it in the baby who begins to explore as soon as he or she can crawl; we see it again in the "battle of the spoon," where the child actually gives up the certainty of getting the food in his or her mouth for the less effective but exciting experiment of "doing it myself." We see this need again as the adolescent struggles to carve out a life that is uniquely his or her own; and we see it reflected in our continuing efforts to understand and master the world as adults. People who read history for pleasure, who have creative hobbies, or who attend personal growth experiences are all manifesting this drive to competence and knowledge.

The need to know is the enemy of comfort, stability, and a placid existence. For its sake, we may risk the discomfort of examining and revising our assumptions about groups and people; we may expose ourselves to the anxiety-provoking experience of "personal feedback," in which we often learn others do not see us quite as we see ourselves; we may place ourselves in groups where we know in advance we will be confused, challenged, and occasionally scared. Some of us expose ourselves to such situations more than once; to me, there could be no more convincing proof that the need to know is frequently stronger than the desire to maintain the comfort and stability of accustomed conceptual systems.

The sensitivity training laboratory thus frequently becomes a battleground for the struggle between our desires to increase our competence and understanding and our defenses. In this battle, we tend to take the side of the need to know, and like partisans everywhere, we malign, attack, and propagandize against the other side. Sometimes we forget that both sides are parts of a person and that if either side destroys the other the person loses a valuable part of him or herself. This is particularly true in the case of defenses. We know from clinical practice and, I think, from personal experience and logic, that when our first line of defense becomes untenable, we drop back to another one, a sort of "second-string" defense. Unfortunately, since we usually put our best and most adaptive defenses out in front, the second string is apt to be even less effective and reality oriented than the first. To put it strongly, the destruction of defenses does not serve learning; instead, it increases our anxiety that we will lose the more or less effective conceptual systems with which we understand and relate to the world, and we then drop back to an even more desperate and perhaps unrealistic defense than the one destroyed. Though it may seem paradoxical, we cannot increase learning by destroying the defenses which block it.

What we can do is create situations where people will not need to stay behind their defenses all the time. We can make it safe for them to sally forth from behind the moat, so to speak, secure in the knowledge that while they are exploring the countryside no one will sneak in and burn the castle.

People need their defenses most when they are most under threat and pressure. To make a mistake or become confused or admit to ourselves that the world, ourselves, and others are not quite what we thought they were means that while we are revising or building new conceptual systems we will not be able to cope as well as before with the "slings and arrows" of difficult situations. If we need every bit of competence we possess, we simply cannot afford to give up conceptual systems that are tried but not perfect in favor of exciting new ways of looking at things that are untested.

It is for this reason that I do not believe we can really begin to learn deeply from one another in a sensitivity training group until we create relationships of mutual support, respect, and trust. When we know that others will not place us in situations where we need every bit of our competence to cope with what is going on; when we know they will respect our own personal rate of growth and learning; when we know we have friends to help if we get into difficulties exploring new relationships, understandings, and behavior; then we can begin to look hard at the inadequacies in our ways of making sense of the world. We can examine those "exceptions to the rule" that we have always half-expected might prove the rule inadequate; we can afford to really explore why ways of behaving that used to work fine are for some reason not producing satisfactions for us the way they used to, or why they seem to work with some people but not others; and we can really listen to the things people say that indicate they do not see us quite the way we see ourselves.

Out of this kind of exploration can come new and more effective conceptual systems, new ways of behaving that go along with them, and the excitement and pride that accompany increases in competence and knowledge. And when the excitement is over and the new ways have been tested and integrated and have become habitual ways of seeing and behaving, I hope we will not be surprised to find that under conditions of stress we defend them against new learning just as strongly as we did the old. For these two partners go hand in hand: the need to explore and learn and the defenses against disconfirmation and confusion. We need them both; the challenge is to know how we can create conditions under which we can suspend one to enhance the other.

CHAPTER NINETEEN

THE DESIGN OF CROSS-CULTURAL TRAINING: AN ALTERNATIVE TO THE UNIVERSITY MODEL

The Design of Cross-Cultural Training: An Alternative to the University Model" was the winner of the 1967 Douglas McGregor Memorial Award. I published it jointly with Richard Hopkins, the client with whom I did the development work that led to it.

During my years at Yale University, from 1960 to 1966, I struggled to create in my own classroom the freedom, excitement, and felt relevance of the T-group. At first, I failed utterly because I did not know how to bridge the gap between my vision and my students' expectations. I did not give up, however, and I was continually designing, experimenting, and redesigning my classroom based on my ongoing experience. The early years were unrewarding, both for me and for my students, and I was sustained in my vision only by positive experiences with experiential learning I was having with students in other settings. One of those settings was the College Leadership Laboratory, variations on which were given for student leaders and their advisors by the National Training Laboratories (NTL), at Bethel, Maine, and at campuses all over the United States. I was very active in the NTL program for college students, and

Note: Coauthored by R. L. Hopkins and originally published in *Journal of Applied Behavioral Science,* 1967, *3*, 431–460. Reprinted here with permission of Journal of NTL Institute.

my experiences in these labs of the vitality, excitement, and camaraderie between students and staff sustained me in my conviction that higher education could be transformed if only we experimented enough with our methods.

The other setting in which the new methods worked was the training of Peace Corps volunteers for overseas work. From 1963 on, I took part in a series of innovative training programs for the Latin American division of the Peace Corps, programs in which I had the chance to try out and to validate my ideas about education for application and for living. These experiments were not always successful, but each one increased the knowledge and experience I needed to forge a radically new way of teaching and learning and apply it to the challenging task of preparing young people to live and work independently overseas. "The Design of Cross-Cultural Training" presents the results of a spectacularly successful educational and organizational intervention carried out in the Peace Corps Training Center in Puerto Rico, an experience that convinced me that my colleagues and I were on the right track, not only in training for cross-cultural performance but in our approach to higher education generally.

I viewed myself at that time as one of a small (and scattered) band of educators, mostly NTL trained, who were working from the inside for the radical reform of higher education in North America. As such, I intended this paper not only to report the success of an educational experiment in the Peace Corps but also to sound the call for the broader reforms that were so close to my heart. I wanted to encourage others who were working for change in colleges and universities, both faculty and radical students, and I wanted to propose a philosophy and program for the redesign of the classroom. I wanted this paper to say to colleagues and students, "We did it in the Peace Corps; you can do it in your classrooms."

I was moderately successful in my aim. The paper was picked up, copied, circulated, and fairly widely read in the circles I desired to reach. At a conference of reform-minded faculty and students at Dartmouth College in the late sixties, I was greatly warmed by the appreciation I received, particularly from the radical students present. It seemed we were in the vanguard of a wave of change that could revitalize higher education and make it truly relevant to life and work.

In a little while, however, our hopes were overtaken by events. The movement for university reform was co-opted by the antiwar movement. Its energy became politicized, and it went out of the classroom and into the streets. The forces of tradition reestablished their hegemony, and the university system proved once again that it, along with the Roman Catholic Church, is one of the most stable and resistant to change of all our institutions. I soon turned to business and industry as the focus for my activities, believing that the next advances in teaching and learning would occur there, where the relevance of education was subject to practical evaluation and cost-benefit analysis, rather than in higher education. In retrospect, I feel I made a wise choice, but as an educator, I feel my heart has always been where I undertook my first innovative attempts, in the college classroom.

The inapplicability of traditional university-based training has become a chronic complaint in organizations that must prepare large numbers of persons for service overseas. In the Peace Corps, for example, which in almost seven years now has trained more persons for overseas work than any other civilian government agency, complaints about the irrelevance of traditional classroom training have been growing steadily since the first volunteers entered training. (The Peace Corps continues to train most of its volunteers at universities, for a variety of reasons not having to do with the quality of training, but a vigorous effort is made to influence the training institutions to design programs that differ sharply from the standard curriculum design.)

The complaints are not directed toward the content of the traditional academic disciplines that bear on overseas work. The content can be relevant to performance in an alien culture; moreover, the acknowledged experts in the subject matter fields appropriate to overseas work are found in universities and colleges for the most part. The dissatisfaction is with the ways in which such subject matter is taught.

When returned Peace Corps volunteers talk about their training, they do not complain about incompetent professors; they complain about the sense in which their experiences in training, however interesting or well presented they may have been, simply did not prepare them for the total life they had to lead overseas. Despite the overall success of the Peace Corps, it has not been uncommon for even a "good" volunteer to take five or six months, or one-fourth of his tour overseas, to become fully operational in an overseas environment.

Now, prospective Peace Corps volunteers are highly motivated students, keenly aware that their success in a strange and alien environment will depend in large measure on their ability to deal with the dynamics of the culture in which they will be working. Above average in commitment to their work, energetic, imaginative, and intelligent, they exhibit a happy blend of attitudes and motives. Yet, primed for a really stirring training experience as they are, many of those who have completed their two years abroad seem unusually dissatisfied with the training that preceded their overseas tour. Somehow, training had little more bearing on what actually happened to them overseas than the rest of their middle-class life experiences, including their experiences in college prior to the Peace Corps.

The purpose of this paper is to examine the basis for such discontent by dissecting the relationships between the ends and means of training for cross-cultural performance. The conclusion to which the analysis leads is that the traditional methods of higher education simply will not get the job done. Nor are they well suited to training for any application situation that requires the ability to adapt to or to act in unfamiliar and ambiguous social situations. (Included in this category would be all types of community development or community action work, at home or abroad, especially when such work is with the disadvantaged, as well as work in institutional subcultures that differ basically from the "outside world.")

Further objectives of this paper are to present a conception of some learning processes that can lead to the ability to cope with ambiguity and to take action under stress, to present some design principles for such training, and to specify the kinds of skills and competence needed to design and operate effective cross-cultural training programs. Finally, the paper details a Peace Corps training program in which some of these design principles were tested.

The Problem of Education for Overseas Work

With few exceptions, formal systems of higher education in the United States provide training in the manipulation of symbols rather than of things; reliance on thinking rather than on feeling and intuition; and commitment to understanding rather than to action. These systems were designed originally for the training of scholars, researchers, and professionals, for whom rationality, abstract knowledge, emotional detachment, and verbal skills are primary values. These systems, however, are applied across the board to almost all students, regardless of individual occupational goals. The criteria of performance used to evaluate the effectiveness of the traditional educational experience are familiar to all of us. They consist of tests, papers, reports, and the evaluation of performance on laboratory problems. With few exceptions, these methods of evaluation are verbal and intellectual.

There are attempts to provide action-oriented and experience-based learning models in many institutions of higher learning, but these less intellectually and more emotionally involving learning settings tend to be peripheral and ancillary to the main work of the college or university. Student governments and student organizations, for example, have an ambiguous, unintegrated relationship to the faculty and the classroom. The status of deans of students and directors of student activities is cloudy, when it is not second-class. The classroom remains a stronghold of rationality.

How the Traditional University Model Fails

When colleges or universities are approached to design or conduct training for work overseas, the resources made available to work on the problem are often those of the traditional part of the organization. Training design is usually based upon the university model.

Until quite recently, for example, the typical Peace Corps university training program was chopped up into components which conformed, by and large, to university departmental lines, and time was assigned to each component on an hourly bloc basis: so much to language, so much to technical studies, so much to area studies, and so on. Such a program was more than likely conducted in an environment that differed little from the one the trainee had just escaped, with all or most of its *in loco parentis* rules and regulations, its classrooms and blackboards, its textbooks and reading lists, its blue-book examinations, its air-conditioned dormitories and student-union atmosphere.

In many of these programs, the environment was restrictive and authoritarian, a kind of exhausting endurance contest, which the trainee survived by a sort of game-playing designed to get him through the Peace Corps selection process as painlessly as possible. Recognizing that *something* ought to be different in a Peace Corps program, university project directors typically designed programs that ran from dawn to dark—and beyond—up to as much as sixty-five or seventy hours a week of intensive instruction for eleven to fifteen weeks. Thus, although one of the prime objectives of training was to convince the prospective volunteer that he was no longer a college student, he was placed in a training environment where he was treated as one.

In any case, the goals and methods of this model focus upon the development of the student's intellectual capacity and on a certain kind of gamesmanship that enables him to *cope* with the training program. There is no manifest concern with his feelings, with an ideal behavior model, or with the interpersonal aspects of the work he may be doing. Students in a typical university setting spend most of their time reading and writing, more time talking about ideas than acting on them, and their professors are much more interested in students' ideas than in their feelings. To be emotional as opposed to rational and objective, at least in the classroom, is to transgress the bounds of appropriate student or professorial behavior.

Universities and colleges do succeed in influencing students to move toward the traditional goals. Students do become more rational, more critical, more detached, and more adept at the manipulation of words, symbols, and abstractions. In terms of the desired outcome of training for cross-cultural work, the university model can provide an *intellectual* understanding of cultural diversity, of values and assumptions that differ from students' own.

The Missing Interpersonal Links

Nothing in this paper should be construed as suggesting that this kind of understanding is of no value or that it is totally irrelevant to overseas work. It does not, however, provide a trainee with all he needs overseas. Its weakness is that in those aspects of overseas performance having to do with interpersonal effectiveness the traditional model offers little help. This is a serious weakness. The experiences of all our overseas agencies—private, governmental, religious—have demonstrated that the human elements of overseas work are at least as important as the technical ones in the success of a job or mission, and that overseas personnel are much more likely to be deficient in these human aspects of work performance than in technical skills. The gravest problems of Peace Corps volunteers, said David Riesman in a recent seminar on the Peace Corps as an educative experience, are "emotional and interpersonal."

By *interpersonal effectiveness* the authors mean such functions as establishing and maintaining trust and communication, motivating and influencing, consulting and advising—all that complex of activities designed to inculcate change. In overseas jobs, the performance of these relationship activities must take place across differences in values, in ways of perceiving and thinking, and in cultural norms and expectations.

Divergent Goals Detailed

The requirements just described suggest a very different set of goals from those of the university model. To sharpen the contrast, Table 19.1 lists some important and divergent goals of the two educational enterprises.

Even though the goals on the left-hand side of Table 19.1 are not universally honored in North American colleges and universities, they do represent a spirit or ideal of academic excellence. They have a pervasive influence on the values and behavior of educators. They are important goals that have contributed much to our civilization. The transfer of these goals from generation to generation is not the least important function of higher education. The trouble is that they are often not relevant in an action situation.

The goals on the right-hand side of the table are typical of the aims of Americans working closely with counterparts in overseas situations. They are not universal, but they represent the reach and thrust of many persons who are concerned and active in the improvement of overseas effectiveness. These goals are also operative in a number of domestic programs, especially in community development activities.

Contrasting Learning Styles or Meta-Goals

University education and cross-cultural training are sharply different, too, in what Schein and Bennis (1965) have called the "meta-goals" of training. Meta-goals are approaches to learning and personal development which the learner acquires in the *process* of being educated in a particular system. In other words, meta-goals represent what the learner learns, in addition to the *content* of instruction, about how to approach and solve subsequent problems outside the classroom.

Meta-goals represent the problem-solving processes, the learning styles, which the trainee or student becomes committed to in the course of his educational experience. Meta-goals have to do with learning how to learn. In some learning settings, for example, an authoritative person acts as the source of solutions to problems, while in others, the learner must look to peers or to himself for information and suggestions. Such differences can be critical in overseas work.

Table 19.2 lists some meta-goals of university education, contrasted with meta-goals that seem appropriate for the cross-cultural training situation.

TABLE 19.1. CONTRASTING EDUCATIONAL GOALS OF UNIVERSITY AND OVERSEAS EDUCATION.

Some Major Goals of University Education	Some Major Goals of Overseas Education
Communication. To communicate fluently via the written word and, to a lesser extent, to speak well. To master the languages of abstraction and generalization, for example, mathematics and science. To understand readily the reasoning, the ideas, and the knowledge of other persons through verbal exchange.	*Communication.* To understand and communicate directly and often nonverbally through movement, facial expression, and person-to-person actions. To listen with sensitivity to the hidden concerns, values, and motives of the other. To be at home in the exchange of feelings, attitudes, desires, and fears. To have a sympathetic, empathic understanding of the feelings of the other.
Decision making. To develop critical judgment, the ability to test assertions, assumptions, and opinions against the hard facts and the criteria of logic. To reduce susceptibility to specious argument and to be skeptical of intuition and emotion. To search for the best, most rational, most economical, and most elegant solution.	*Decision making.* To develop the ability to come to conclusions and take action on inadequate, unreliable, and conflicting information. To be able to trust feelings, attitudes, and beliefs as well as facts. To search for the *possible* course, the viable alternative, the durable though inelegant solution.
Commitment. Commitment is to the truth. It requires an ability to stand back from ongoing events in order to understand and analyze them and to maintain objectivity in the face of emotionally involving situations. Difficult situations are handled by explanations, theories, and reports.	*Commitment.* Commitment is to people and to relationships. It requires an ability to become involved, to give and inspire trust and confidence, to care and to take action in accordance with one's concern. Difficult situations are dealt with by staying in emotional contact with them and by trying to take constructive action.
Ideals. To value the great principles and ideals of Western society: social justice, economic progress, and scientific truth. To value the sacrifice of present rewards and satisfactions for future advancement of these ideals and to find self-esteem and satisfaction from one's contribution toward distant social goals.	*Ideals.* To value causes and objectives embedded in the here-and-now and embodied in the groups and persons in the immediate social environment. To find satisfaction, enjoyment, and self-esteem from the impact one has directly on the lives of others. To be able to empathize with others who live mostly in the present and to work with them toward the limited, concrete goals which are important to them.
Problem solving. A problem is solved when the true, correct, and reasonable answer has been discovered and verified. Problem solving is a search for knowledge and truth. It is a largely rational process, involving intelligence, creativity, insight, and a respect for facts.	*Problem solving.* A problem is solved when decisions are made and carried out which effectively apply people's energies to overcoming some barrier to a common goal. Problem solving is a social process involving communication, interpersonal influence, consensus, and commitment.

At the level of meta-goals, university education and cross-cultural training diverge significantly. The sources, settings, and approaches of the former tend to be formal, bookish, rational, dependent on authority, and lacking in opportunities to gain competence in learning through interpersonal contact.

TABLE 19.2. CONTRASTING META-GOALS OF UNIVERSITY CLASSROOMS AND CROSS-CULTURAL TRAINING.

Traditional Meta-Goals of College and University Classrooms	Appropriate Meta-Goals for Cross-Cultural Training
Source of information. Information comes from experts and authoritative sources through the media of books, lectures, and audiovisual presentations. "If you have a question, look it up."	*Source of information.* Information sources must be developed by the learner from the social environment. Information-gathering methods include observation and questioning of associates, other learners, and chance acquaintances.
Learning settings. Learning takes place in settings designated for the purpose, for example, classrooms and libraries.	*Learning settings.* The entire social environment is the setting for learning. Every human encounter provides relevant information.
Problem-solving approaches. Problems are defined and posed to the learner by experts and authorities. The correct problem-solving methods are specified, and the student's work is checked for application of the proper method and for accuracy, or at least for reasonableness of results. The emphasis is on solutions to known problems.	*Problem-solving approaches.* The learner is on his own to define problems, generate hypotheses, and collect information from the social environment. The emphasis is on discovering problems and developing problem-solving approaches on the spot.
Role of emotions and values. Problems are largely dealt with at an ideational level. Questions of reason and of fact are paramount. Feelings and values may be discussed but are rarely acted upon.	*Role of emotions and values.* Problems are usually value- and emotion-laden. Facts are often less relevant than the perceptions and attitudes which people hold. Values and feelings have action consequences, and action must be taken.
Criteria of successful learning. Favorable evaluation by experts and authorities of the quality of the individual's intellectual productions, primarily written work.	*Criteria of successful learning.* The establishment and maintenance of effective and satisfying relationships with others in the work setting. This includes the ability to communicate with and influence others. Often there are no criteria available other than the attitudes of the parties involved in the relationship.

Need for Freedom to Learn Independently

The meta-goals also differ profoundly along the dimension of freedom. It is here that the inappropriateness of traditional educational systems for overseas work is most evident. The high degree of control and dependence upon authority common in the college classroom does not lead to the development of a learning style facilitative of success in an overseas environment. This is not just because freedom is a good thing and everyone ought to have a lot of it. It is because so much external control implies a dependency on experts and authorities for direction, information, and validation. When the learner is deprived of these sources of support, as he is almost certain to be in the overseas environment, he is in an uncomfortable and sometimes emotionally crippling situation. He not only must solve new problems in a new setting, but he must develop a new learning style, quite on his own. This experience—not knowing how to learn without traditional supports—may be productive of a good deal of the anxiety and depression grouped under the rubric, "culture shock." It is certainly responsible for much individual failure, even when it does not lead to chronic depression and anomie.

Education for cross-cultural applications should train the individual in a system of learning operations that is independent of settings, persons, and other information sources not found in the overseas environment. If the trainee can be educated to be an effective and independent learner, he need not be filled with all the information he can contain before going into his new job. He will have the capacity to generate his own learning as needed. Indeed, he will have to generate his own learning in any case, whether he is trained to do this or not, for the simple reason that no training agency can train for every exotic contingency, for every aspect of life and work in another culture.

Risks of Emotional Encounter

The other dimension on which the two learning models described here differ is that of encounter—the extent to which the emotions, values, and deeper aspects of the self are actively involved, touched, and changed in the learning process. The intellectuality and the formality, the emphasis on ideas and on the written word, the appeals to logic and reason implicit in university education, all combine to encourage an emotional distance from the learning material and a relativism about values.

But it is not possible to maintain such emotional distance from the sights, the smells, the sounds, and the customs of an alien culture. (And for one who is attempting to effect change or to act as an adviser in another culture, it is certainly not desirable, either.) Those aspects of life that in one's own culture are familiar and that would be supportive if they were present overseas (eating habits, standards of hygiene and cleanliness, language, social systems, subliminally perceived signals of all kinds) are *not* present, and their absence is emotionally disruptive. One's assumptions and values are called into question again and again by the most trivial kinds of events. The interpersonal competencies that work well in one's own culture suddenly do not work anymore. The cues are different. One can avoid the encounter only by retreating into some kind of physical or emotional enclave, into the kinds of American compounds that wall off "Yankees" from "natives" all over the world.

Education in the classroom teaches one to deal with emotionally loaded questions of value and attitude by analyzing and talking about them in an atmosphere of emotional detachment. Such a scholarly, scientific attitude is appropriate to the task of *understanding;* but by sidestepping direct, feeling-level involvement with issues and persons, one fails to develop the "emotional muscle" needed to handle effectively a high degree of emotional impact and stress. Lacking emotional muscle, the individual under stress tends to withdraw as much as possible from exposure of his self-esteem, or at the other extreme, he impulsively risks too much in an effort to get the anxiety and suspense over with. Either of these reactions to stress can, and often does, lead to failure overseas. Thus an important objective in training for overseas work should be the development in the trainee of the ability and willingness to take moderate emotional risks in situations where his sense of self-esteem is involved.

The concept of moderate risk taking can be illustrated by examining the alternatives one faces when a friend or colleague has become noticeably unapproachable, cold, and unresponsive. The alternative actions one may take can be classified as low, moderate, or high risk, according to which emotional impact to one's self-esteem is likely to result. Low-risk alternatives might include withdrawal from the relationship or resort to written rather than oral communication. High-risk alternatives might include retaliation with some kind of personal attack on the colleague, reproaches for his unfriendliness, or demands to his face that he change his behavior. The low- and high-risk approaches allow the causes of the situation to remain unknown and not dealt with. They are designed more to ease the tension and uncertainty than to solve the problem.

In contrast, the moderate-risk approach is characterized by a willingness to increase tension somewhat in order to obtain information about the difficulty. Such an approach might take the form of asking the other person if there is anything the matter; indicating that one is puzzled about the behavior of the other; trying to arrange increased interaction in nonwork settings to see whether a relationship can be built on some more personal foundation; and so on. The important thing is not that these attempts be successful in resolving the problem but that they develop more information about it with moderate risk of further damage to the relationship. They also all involve some increase in tension for the subject, since failure might be painful. Moderate-risk approaches require more ability to stand emotional tension over a period of time than do the others.

The ability to deal directly with a high degree of emotional impact is not likely to be developed in the university classroom. The kinds of problems dealt with in the classroom neither require nor reward attempts to turn the learning situation into an opportunity for interpersonal encounter.

In summary, then, the classroom approach is poorly adapted to training persons to operate in settings, overseas or anywhere else, where they must define and attack problems without the aid of authoritative or expert assistance (freedom), and where the degree of emotional, attitudinal, and value involvement is so high as to require dealing directly and continually with emotionally laden issues (encounter).

An Alternative Model for Cross-Cultural Training

Design principles for cross-cultural training differ from those of the university classroom. The purposes of cross-cultural training are to (1) develop in the student more independence of external sources of decision, information, problem definition, and motivation; (2) develop in the student the emotional muscle he needs to deal constructively with the strong feelings which are created by conflict and confrontation of values and attitudes; (3) enable the student to make choices and commitments to action in situations of stress and uncertainty; and (4) encourage the student to use his own and others' feelings, attitudes, and values as *information* in defining and solving human problems.

The design principles that proceed directly from these aims and goals include the following:

Require Here-and-Now Problem Solving

The individual should be continually exposed to situations that require him to diagnose what is going on, define a problem to solve, devise a solution, and take action upon it. Because information and theory not used in the problem-solving process will not be readily available to the learner when he must solve problems under stress, *information is not presented which is irrelevant to the solution of real problems that the learner will be asked to solve in the here and now.*

Require Trainees to Work with Immediate Data

Immediate data are data gathered by observation of the physical environment and experience with persons involved in some problem, as distinguished from second-hand and abstract information obtained from experts and authorities. Learning to use immediate data, particularly from the social environment, frees the learner from dependence on authoritative sources of information. In cross-cultural training designs, problems should be constructed so that their definition and solution require the problem solver to develop information from the persons who are present with him in the problem situation.

Require Choices Among Competing Values

Almost any action a person takes in a culture other than his own involves a confrontation between his values and those of the host country. In the marketplace, in work situations, in businesses, in social relations of all kinds, the visitor abroad must confront and cope with unfamiliar values and customs. Thus the problems which the learner deals with in training should also require a confrontation with opposing values. Furthermore, it is not enough that the learner examine these value conflicts with interest and detachment. In the cross-cultural application situation, he will not be able to escape choices among conflicting values. The choices he makes will have important consequences. Therefore, in the training situation the learner should be confronted with problem-solving situations that force him to *make choices among competing values, choices that have consequences for his relationships with others in the training situation.*

Require Trainees to Put Learning into Action

A basic problem in cross-cultural training design may be stated inelegantly as "connecting head and guts." This means that training designs which lead only to understanding are never good enough. Training problems must require that the person *experience* the emotional impact of the phenomena with which he is dealing, as well as understand them. He must be able to translate ideas and values into direct action, with all its attendant risks and difficulties. This requires that the learner influence others to action.

The principle, then, is that training situations should require that discussion and analysis lead to decision and action on the part of the trainee. This would imply, for example, that even the best-led discussion group is only half a training situation because it does not lead to action.

Use Authority to Support Trainees in Active Learning

On the one hand, the authority of the educator or trainer should not be used to diagnose situations, define problems, provide information, or select alternative courses of action for the learner. If these functions are performed for the learner, he learns through dependency on expert or authoritative help.

On the other hand, plunges into anarchy and laissez-faire may so traumatize the learner that he must spend most of his energy in defending himself emotionally from the learning situation. If he is allowed to, he may defend himself by sidestepping confrontation with problems and the hard work on their definition and solution that is the heart of the learning process as prescribed here. A delicate and unusual use of authority is thus called for.

It is clear that authority must not be used to deprive the learner of the opportunity to have his own experience. In general, he is not provided with information, but encouraged to seek it; he is not given solutions, but asked to come to conclusions on his own; he is not told what action to take or how to take it, only that action is expected of him.

Authority is used to support the learner in his first steps in an unfamiliar learning environment. He is not left completely without sources of help. He is encouraged to experiment, to try and fail and try again, to take risks, to express himself and his values in words and action. He is rewarded by those in authority, not for succeeding or getting the right answer or expressing the right opinion, but for engaging actively and wholeheartedly in the learning process.

The restrictive side of this use of authority is that the learner *is* to some extent "fenced in" to keep him in contact with the problems he is expected to solve. Sanctions or punishments are applied, not for goofing up but for goofing off; not for making mistakes but for failing to act; not for taking an illogical or unreasonable position but for failure to take a stand.

Apply Trainers' Expertise to Creating the Design and Supporting the Learning Process

A premise of this model is that a person does not learn to exist effectively in another culture simply by being provided with information about that culture. Although we can predict to some extent the general types of difficulties the learner will have to face in the cross-cultural situation, we cannot predict with any certainty the exact information which he will need to solve the particular difficulties challenging him.

We can, however, specify the conceptual framework which the learner needs to make sense of an alien and ambiguous social situation and to take action in that situation. The learner's need for expert help is less to provide information about the *content* of the other culture than to teach the problem-solving *processes* and to develop the feeling-thinking linkages that are primary goals of these proposed training designs.

The expert interacts with the learner first through designing situations constructed so that, as the learner follows his own natural adaptive styles, he will be confronted with the processes and problems which it is desired that he assimilate. These are "free movement" situations in that the learner's specific actions and activities are only loosely prescribed: he is free to solve the problem in almost any way he chooses.

Further, the educator should help the learner reflect about his experience. The process of linking thought and feeling is as difficult when one begins with a concrete problem and moves toward conceptualization of the experience as it is when one starts with ideas and facts and tries to move toward action based upon an intellectual analysis. The educator does not simply construct problems and then sit back while the learner runs through a maze like a rat. At the very least, the educator should ask the learner what meaning the experience had for him and what, if any, connections and generalizations he can make between this particular experience and what he knows about himself, his goals in the cross-cultural situation, and his own culture and the alien culture. The educator's role is that of any teacher working intuitively to ask the right questions at the right time. Without this kind of guidance, it is just as possible for a person to have an experience-packed and emotionally laden but conceptually meaningless learning experience in cross-cultural training as it is for him to have an intellectualized and detached but emotionally bland one in the traditional classroom.

It is not unusual, for example, for returned Peace Corps volunteers working as staff in a Peace Corps training program to see their overseas career as a kind of kaleidoscope of impactful, difficult, rewarding, but essentially unconnected experiences. The returned volunteer often does not have a clear conception of the processes which he used to adapt himself to the culture, to develop sources of information, or to formulate and test hypotheses about problems. When he communicates to trainees he often communicates at the level of "war stories." These anecdotes usually have as their implied message: "It's no use to prepare for much of anything, because whatever you expect, it is not going to come out as you anticipated."

Many of these veterans of the real world seem not to have been able to turn their own experience into real learning or to make it available as training for others. They have been through an experience-based learning situation in their overseas assignment without learning anything that they see as clearly transferable to other social situations. They have not been able to conceptualize their experiences, partly because they were not taught how to do so during their training period. But of course, learning has occurred; it is latent, waiting for some structured conceptual framework into which it may be fitted in a coherent way.

The purpose of experience-based cross-cultural training is to inculcate somehow in the learner the ability to see and know what he is learning and has learned, so that he can articulate it afterward and act on his learning consciously. The role prescribed for the teacher, the educator, in such a learning system is one of aiding in an inductive rather than the traditional deductive learning process. He helps the learner to verbalize his feelings, perceptions, and experiences and to draw conclusions and generalizations from them. If the teacher succeeds, the trainee will not only be more successful in the field situation; the entire experience will become a richer and more rewarding one for him. He will, in one degree or another, have learned something about how to learn.

Application: A Case Study

The principles of training enunciated here have been applied in an actual training situation. During the summer and fall of 1965, the authors collaborated—one as project director, the other as consultant—in the design and implementation of two community development training programs at the Peace Corps Training Center in Puerto Rico. The two programs will be referred to as one program: they were planned together, operated under the same design, and ran concurrently, although the training that is described took place at only one camp.

The Peace Corps Training Center consists of two camps located in a semi–rain forest area of central Puerto Rico about fifteen miles from the coastal city of Arecibo. Each camp has a capacity of about 110 trainees. Trainees live in simple wooden cabins. There is no indoor plumbing or hot water. Nature is kind (despite 140 inches of rain a year), but life is primitive.

The camps were utilized until the fall of 1964 as so-called Outward Bound camps, where trainees were received before or after university training for three or four weeks of rigorous, graduated physical activities designed to confront trainees with challenges which stretched their capacity to deal with stress. In September 1964, however, after a small pilot project, the camps were converted into a full-scale training center for Latin America. Since that time, only full-length (ten to twelve weeks' duration) training programs have been conducted there.

In the summer of 1965, the staff of the training center consisted of a director, five assistant directors, four psychologists responsible for trainee assessment, an administrative officer, an associate administrative officer and thirty maintenance workers and cooks, two nurses, about fifteen native-speaking language informants, and finally, approximately thirty former Peace Corps volunteers (PCVs) from Latin America (average age twenty-five), who constituted the core instructional and coordinating staff. The resident staff was supplemented in each cycle by twelve to twenty academicians and technicians who came to the training center for stays of three to ten days each.

The remainder of this paper will draw heavily on the training program. But it should be understood that the program was not conducted under rigorous laboratory conditions. No systematic effort was made to collect objective data while it was going on. Two projects were involved:

The Ecuador RCA/Colonization Project included forty trainees—two recently graduated engineers, eight nurses, and thirty so-called B.A. generalists. They were to work in newly colonized areas of the Oriente region of Ecuador as elementary teachers or technicians and, what is more important, as community development workers.

The Latin American Regional Arts and Crafts Project included forty-two trainees, all artisans (weavers, potters, metal workers, painters, and so on), several of them graduates of art schools or technical institutes. They were to be divided among three countries—Ecuador, Chile, and Bolivia—where they would work with native artisans in developing exportable handicraft items through the organization and administration of producer cooperatives.

As in all Peace Corps training programs, these trainees were subject to the Peace Corps selection process. Eighty-two trainees reported for training; fifty-seven were sent overseas. Twenty-five trainees, in other words, either resigned or were, as the Peace Corps euphemism goes, "selected out."

In previous programs at the Puerto Rico center, the director's authority role had been that of a traditional academic administrator. He designed the curriculum, scheduled all training activities, and left the subject matter to the faculty. For the most part, material was presented in the standard way: the instructors talked; the trainees listened, took notes, and asked questions. In this case, though, the young staff was offered autonomy and the chance to design and conduct its own program. The director and consultant would be on hand to participate as they were wanted; they would advise and make comments, but they would not run things. Responsibility lay within the staff itself.

Ultimately only about one-third of the staff members accepted this offer of active participation. The others went along with the resulting design, or in some cases, resisted it. Staff members planned the experimental program over a period of about six weeks, meeting for several hours daily seven days a week. At the end, they were ready to take the risks involved in a model that differed significantly from the training they had received before their Peace Corps tours and that also differed from the training previously conducted at the training center.

General Characteristics

The training program, as it was designed, was to have these general characteristics:

- From their arrival, the trainees would be encouraged to participate actively in the planning of their program. In fact, in a sense, there would be no program unless they planned it by determining what kind of training program was needed in order to reach the objectives they had formulated.
- Formal classroom lectures would be played down; small-group interaction would be played up, as would informal interaction of all kinds.
- Except for Spanish (four hours a day) and weekly evaluation sessions (to be discussed later), attendance at the "happenings" of the program would not be compulsory.
- An effort would be made to do away with component labels and thus to "integrate" the elements of the program.
- The program would be "experience-based." There would be ample opportunities furnished for "doing things," such as organizing and operating "academic" subjects through research projects, and so on.
- Trainees with needed skills would be urged to teach them to others, formally or informally. The emphasis, in short, was to be on trainee activity, not passivity.
- Emphasis would be placed throughout on awareness of the environment of the training program: of what was going on and how the trainees were reacting to it (and to one another). This was to be achieved through weekly small-group "evaluation sessions." The personnel of these core groups, including the leaders, would remain fairly constant throughout the program.

The actual program did not turn out so neatly as its blueprint, of course. Some trainees took to this kind of design; some did not. Several staff members demonstrated anxieties under the inevitable pressures of the program. Although there were many pressures to revert to the standard model, somehow this never happened. Trainee morale was extraordinarily high; the trainees did in large measure take responsibility for their own training, and especially for defining the goals of training. Four major elements seem to have combined to make this a unique educational experiment.

Notable Elements of Successful Experienced-Based Training

Staff Preparation. The first notable element of the training was the degree and intensity of planning that occurred before the trainees arrived. The kind of design advocated here cannot be conducted by an unprepared staff or by a staff that has not confronted, grappled with, and in some measure dealt beforehand with most of the issues such training raises. When using traditional classroom models, one can assume that the other educators are using roughly similar designs. Much more communication among the training staff members is needed to develop commitment to a new model, to test whether proposed training designs do in fact exemplify the model, and to resolve inconsistencies among different parts of the program.

It is not necessary to build a seamless united front in the planning phase; but in a program designed to shift the orientation of the trainees away from a dependence on authority to reliance on their own abilities to diagnose, gather data, and develop independent solutions, it is important that all the learning activities work toward this meta-goal. While there is room for the application of a number of personal teaching styles by staff members in such a program, it is important that there be basic consensus on the importance of giving trainees as much responsibility as they can manage, on the desirability of trainee activity-initiative as opposed to passivity-receptivity in all learning settings, and on the responsibility of staff members continually to help trainees build connections and bridges between their training experiences and the situations for which they are preparing in the field.

It is easy to provide trainees with experiences and problems to solve. It is more difficult to think through the learning and adaptation processes that must take place in these experiences, to help trainees devise ways of collecting data on them, and to aid trainees in conceptualizing the processes so that they may be applied in overseas situations, which on the surface may seem to be radically different from the projects assigned during training. This form of elaboration requires the trainee to take account of the training experience, to dig into it to formulate hypotheses and questions, rather than float on its surface. Without such elaboration, experiences are not converted into learning. Trainees should receive assistance in conceptualizing and generalizing their experience. It is impossible to reproduce or simulate or even to know precisely what conditions will be faced by trainees in an overseas situation. Crude simulations may be the best available. The *processes* of diagnosing and taking action on a problem are similar in the training and application situations, but the content of the problems is different. Unless the trainee has help in abstracting the process from the particular events he experiences, he will face difficulty in translating what he has learned into usable form.

He will not receive this help from staff members who have not been deeply involved in planning the program and who do not manifest the commitment that can result only from involvement. Involvement of this depth and intensity cannot be developed in a traditional administrative situation. The teacher must write his own job description through interaction with his colleagues. The planning phase must constitute a training phase for the staff.

It is important, too, that much of the planning bear on process issues—that is, the interpersonal and behavioral patterns that can be expected to develop in the course of training. There is a very real sense in which the planning phase can be a kind of mock-up of the training program that is to come, with the staff members experiencing similar conflicts and anxieties, which they must work through before they are ready for the innumerable interpersonal transactions that will make up the actual training program. In planning for this program, much of the focus of the work of the consultant was on staff process issues and their relevance to training. By the time the participants arrived, staff members could empathize with the confusion, hostility, and anxiety which this program would create for the trainees, simply because the staff had experienced and examined similar feelings as they sought to relinquish the security of traditional classroom models and plan a venture into the ambiguous and unstable world of experience-based training.

Since small-group activities were a critical design characteristic in this model, the staff needed well-developed skills in managing group discussions. The need for skill was especially acute where trainees were being asked to reflect on their own performance and experiences in the more stressful parts of the program. Trainees understandably resisted connecting their behavior in the training situation with how they were likely to function in the overseas situation. When trainees sought to withdraw from the ambiguity and stress of being responsible for their own learning, they had to be confronted with this avoidance pattern. All of these problems in learning require sensitivity, skill, and compassion on the part of the staff. The consultant spent considerable time with the staff members working on these skills of discussion leadership. This involved both theory and practice during the planning phase and observation and consultation with individual staff members after the program was under way.

Use of Authority. The nontraditional use of authority was of first importance in this program. A studied effort was made throughout the program and in the basic design to wean the trainees (and the staff) away from a traditional reliance on authority in learning settings. In addition, the staff members sincerely tried not to use authority arbitrarily and especially not to use it in defining the goals of the training program for the trainees or in playing any kind of role *in loco parentis.* The trainees were treated like responsible people, capable of making their own decisions about the vital issues of training. Throughout the training program, the staff members attempted to "level" with the trainees, to keep them informed, and to avoid manipulation of trainee behavior by explicit or implied reference to the threat of deselection. As a result, the trainees tended to trust staff members, despite occasional difficulties.

The earliest manifestation of the nontraditional use of authority in the program came with the orientation, which was a prelude to the subsequent activities of the program. The trainees arrived in Puerto Rico with expectations of receiving more or less traditional classroom training, with perhaps a dash of exposure to Puerto Rican life thrown in for seasoning. The orientation was the first opportunity to break this set and to begin the staff-trainee dialogue which would, hopefully, lead to new attitudes and assumptions about the learning process. The trainees were told (although they did not fully understand at the outset) how the staff would and would not use its authority; what kinds of information, direction, and help the staff would provide; and against what criteria their performance would be evaluated.

The staff made it clear that the trainees were responsible not only for the maintenance of the training camp but also for the organization of their own governing bodies, the parceling out of work, disciplinary action against slackers, and the formulation of camp rules and regulations. The freedom to create social structures was so different from what college administrators offer to students (most of these trainees were just a few weeks out of college) that it set trainees back on their heels.

They were further shocked to learn that the training program was unplanned, at least in the conventional sense, and that attendance at most activities was not compulsory. Instead, they were given written information about the countries and work situations into which they would go in some four months and were asked to meet in small groups with staff members to discuss what kind of training experience this information implied would be useful.

Thus the orientation began to build a conceptual framework for the training. It illustrated how authority would be applied in the program, and it began activities in support of this framework. In a design of this sort, authority is not absent. It is used differently and with less intensity than is customary, but it *is* used. It must be. Trainees must understand that there are people around who know what they are doing. Many of the trainees need support in beginning to use their own resources for learning. They are well adapted, most of them, to the passive-receptive learning role. They do not abandon it easily. Why should they, when it has worked for them in the past? They profit from authoritative encouragement, even when authority is used to prescribe the use of resources rather than to assure continued dependence.

As it happened, in the Puerto Rico programs there were wide variations in the ability of the staff members to work with trainees in helping them to get the most out of their experiences. Those who were least committed to the experience-based model vacillated between excessive and inadequate control over trainee activities. On the one hand, they were concerned lest the trainees "get out of hand" and the staff members lose control over the community. On the other, they tended to see the alternative to rigid control as being no staff influence at all over trainees. It seemed to be particularly difficult for them to conceptualize and practice the supportive authority discussed earlier, possibly because they had never been on the receiving end of it. This was a continuing concern throughout the training and was the subject of much discussion among both trainees and staff members. It was also another major focus of the consultant's work with the staff.

Emphasis on Process. The third distinctive element in the program was the emphasis placed on process issues and on developing awareness of the total emotional, interpersonal, and organizational environment in which trainees and staff were living and working.

Throughout the training period, trainees were urged to consider the camp and the training program as a community to be charted, researched, understood, and if need be, changed.

In the weekly evaluation sessions, trainees were urged to review the organizational climate of the program and their relations with one another, and to comment on such phenomena as the power structure in the training center and the formation of trainee subgroups. The first group of trainees to arrive at the center was encouraged to consider and deal with its feelings of intergroup competition arising from arrival of a second group a week later, and vice versa. When crises occurred, those affected by them were urged to analyze what had really happened and why the principals had acted as they did.

The Project Approach. The training program consisted of large and small problem-solving projects, planned for the most part by the trainees themselves, who related to the staff through a complex of formal and informal interpersonal and intergroup transactions. The term *project* is used here to describe an activity requiring a learner to:

- Obtain information from the social environment (communication).
- Formulate and test hypotheses about forces and processes present in the environment (diagnosis).
- Select and describe some part of the situation that is to be changed or altered (problem definition).
- Plan action to solve the problem (commitment, risk taking).
- Carry out the action, enlisting the help and cooperation of others (influencing and organizing).
- Verbalize attitudes, perceptions, and tentative learnings from the experience (cognition and generalization).

Projects should be the heart of an experience-based training program. They may take almost any form: they may be short or long; they may overlap with other training activities; they may involve activity inside or outside the training location. In the programs described here, trainees established cooperatives, they planted gardens and raised chickens and pigs, and they organized mutual teaching-learning activities for the sharing of specialized skills such as accounting, welding, and arts and crafts. They participated in such staff-designed projects as rock climbing, trekking, survival experiences, construction tasks, and field training in Puerto Rican villages. The emphasis on trainee-developed projects reinforced the staff's initial message regarding autonomy, responsibility, and initiative. The more aggressive trainees responded eagerly to the message; the less independent trainees tended to substitute the leadership of other trainees for the authority they found missing in the staff. Often, not being required to do anything specific, they did nothing. Some trainees were capable of accepting autonomy with regard to both the ends of a project and the means; the less creative, the less able, the less independent, the less trusting required the specification of ends before they could proceed to devise the means of getting there. In no case, however, were both the ends and the means specified. Tasks were designed to require trainees to diagnose a situation, develop a variety of possible approaches, and select one, and to take initiative to produce the end result desired.

In the training-center-as-a-community project, trainees set goals as homely as influencing the dining room to serve a wider variety of food and bringing other trainees to a higher level of sanitation and neatness in their living quarters. A principal activity was the trainees' persistent efforts to influence the staff to provide learning resources in the form of reading, lectures, and discussions. This hunger for learning was in sharp contrast to the avoidance games many of the trainees had shared with their college classmates only a few weeks earlier.

The critical factor in a project-focused program is the manner in which staff members support and assist the trainees in elaborating their projects. At one extreme, a project may be presented to a group of trainees to solve as best they can, with the learning falling where it may. No special effort is made to organize comparisons between experiences, to examine value issues or conflicts, or to encourage conceptualization of the influence styles and interaction patterns used by different individuals in planning and executing the action.

At the other extreme, an effort may be made to force learning from each part of the experience. Trainees may be convened in small groups and urged to formulate the problems of diagnosis, conflict, influence, and organization implicit in their project. Staff members participate in work and planning sessions as process consultants whose role is to help participants to observe and become aware of the social forces with which they are dealing in the here and now.

It is the elaboration of an experience-based training design which requires a high order of staff skills. It is much easier to provide trainees with problems to solve than it is to think through the social and individual processes which will be going on, devise means of bringing them to light, and aid trainees in conceptualizing the experience so that their learning may be applied in later overseas situations that are on the surface quite different. It is here that the discussion leadership skills of the staff become critical, for they must be used to draw out of the trainee the principles and generalizations which are latent in the experience. If this does not occur, much of the potential learning will be lost.

Most of the staff members worked hard at performing this function, although they found it among the most difficult of the responsibilities they had accepted in designing an experience-based program. Many of the trainees were adept at avoiding examination of the implications of their experience, particularly when the experience was stressful and anxiety provoking. The staff members were understandably reluctant to push such confrontation. Considerable learning was undoubtedly lost through caution and lack of skill, but during the course of the program the staff members' effectiveness as inductive teachers increased steadily with practice.

Field Training. The trainees in this program spent a total of almost a month in small Puerto Rican villages where they faced problems of adaptation similar to those they would confront in Latin America. Here, too, efforts were made to assist the trainees in designing projects around their field living and to convert the projects into real learning afterward.

Puerto Rico, of course, offers an almost ideal transitional environment for trainees bound for Latin America. But if adequate help in conceptualizing and generalizing is available, almost any alien situation can become a meaningful field-training assignment in preparation for cross-cultural work. For urban dwellers, rural living may be alien; for members of the middle class, experience with the poor, the angry, and the disadvantaged provides real confrontation. It is *desirable* to conduct field training in a culture similar to that for which a trainee is being prepared, but this is by no means essential. The important thing is to create as much cultural distance as possible from the life the trainee has been living, so that the values and attitudes that have worked for him before are no longer adequate. The cultural content may differ from that of the area for which the trainee is bound, but the process problems that grow out of confrontation are similar.

Integration of Content and Process. A persistent problem was how to make fact, theory, and opinion about the cultures to which the trainees were going and the jobs they were to do relevant to the problem-solving environment of the training program. On the one hand, lectures and books seemed to provide an escape from involvement and confrontation for those trainees who needed to defend themselves against the personal exposure of the program. On the other hand, for those trainees who did become heavily involved in projects, the lectures and readings often seemed dry, abstract, and unreal. Trainees were given responsibility for organizing the use of visiting lecturers, which may have increased their feeling of responsibility, but it did little to connect the content to problem-solving processes.

Martin Tarcher has recently described a feasible approach to the integration of content and process (1966). In a program for community leaders, he created project teams as the central learning units. The teams were responsible for using data from an exhaustive community survey to diagnose and plan action for development of the community. Outside lecturers were asked to familiarize themselves with the same data and to introduce only material directly relevant to the solution of the problems revealed in the data. Thus content input was directly tied to the problem-solving process. There is strong reason to believe that only content which can be used and practiced in the training situation is usefully learned in an experience-based training program. Tarcher's design meets this criterion.

Behind the Design: The Teacher

Even those who are attracted to the approaches to learning described here may well ask where the teachers will come from to carry them out. Clearly, the desired skill mix is sharply divergent from the blend of intellectual competence and verbal facility found in good classroom teachers.

The teacher in an experience-based program is involved with people, not books; with real situations, not abstractions. He must collaborate closely with his colleagues. In his work with students, he will do little presenting and much listening. Instead of organizing content material, he will seek patterns, principles, and generalizations in the reactions of trainees. Subject matter competence is useful, of course, but it will not get the job done without true competence in the facilitation of learning through focus on process. The traditional systems in which most of us were formed do not value the subtle and sophisticated teaching skills described here.

There are, however, incompletely exploited sources of the competence which is needed. Industry, government, and the military all have had to develop methods of education that will pay off in immediately transferable skills. Educational innovation and change have been much more rapid in these applied settings than in colleges and universities. Industrial trainers in particular must be open to innovation and experimentation, or they do not survive.

For the overseas agencies, such as the Peace Corps and the Agency for International Development, a ready source of *potential* educators exists in those returning from the field. The Peace Corps program discussed here was conducted largely by former volunteers, few of whom had previous teaching experience. As our strictures about staff planning and preparation imply, though, it cannot be assumed that persons with practical experience are necessarily qualified to teach and communicate it. This is a particularly unjustified assumption when the proposed training is highly inductive. The "practical" man has at his disposal a fund of war stories, which purport to illustrate how to handle various concrete and specific situations abroad. But concrete and often-undigested experiences such as these are of limited value. The practical man, if he is to become an effective trainer, must learn to conceptualize the cross-cultural learning experience in terms applicable to experience-based learning. For example, if a practical community developer can come to see working with trainees as another kind of community development, then he is well on his way to translating his cross-cultural experience into training design. He will have begun to understand the learning process in which he participated overseas and to consider how such experiences might be simulated for trainees, in process if not in content.

Many cross-cultural workers, however, are so practical and concrete in their thinking that they learn only those aspects of a culture which they directly encounter. They find it difficult to generalize beyond their own experiences. They may have learned, but they have *not* learned *how* they learned.

Then there are those who have taken part in cross-cultural experiences who *have* learned how to learn, and who can, with further training, build experiences which will transmit what they know to others. To do this requires a clear understanding of such principles of learning as those described in this paper. The conceptual framework for experience-based training is not implicit in our educational background. We operate comfortably within a traditional learning system both as pupils or teachers, but this does not mean that we *understand* the conditions which facilitate learning and the transfer of learning to an application situation.

When, therefore, an individual is asked to participate in the design and conduct of training radically different in form from traditional models, he needs a basic education himself in the teaching and learning process. He needs supervised and assisted experience in designing training, conducting it, and evaluating the results. He needs to work with others who are also struggling with the tasks of putting together and operating experience-based training designs.

The Climate for Innovation

The plans proposed in this paper have no fail-safe ingredients to protect them from failure. The launching of educational innovation requires more than a blueprint for success.

Fortunately, there are some resources and forces toward innovation of the kind proposed here. Our culture is highly pragmatic. Americans are receptive to ideas that work. Supporting this pragmatism are the experiences of those who have lived in the cross-cultural situation, who have been open to their experience, and who have been able to generalize from it.

In addition, there is a small body of experience-based pedagogy which provides crude models of what this training may look like and accomplish. Practitioners of sensitivity training have been using experience-based pedagogy for some time. There are experimental schools, and even a college here and there, and a growing number of practical training settings where efforts are being made to develop and refine experience-based education. The models are available, but they must be refined and adapted to the purposes at hand.

Lastly, the climate for educational innovation has never been better than it is now. For the first time in recent years, students (and some of their professors) in institutions of higher education are beginning to question the goals and procedures of their education. There is a hunger for educational experiences which involve the whole person, which get to the heart of the matter, which seem to have a more direct connection with life as it is lived in our relativist, kinetic, peripatetic, crisis-ridden society. Perhaps this questioning is the prelude to changes in our diverse but tradition-bound institutions of higher learning. In the hope of influencing that change, this paper has been written. For we cannot escape the conclusion that the design principles enunciated here might have validity in preparing people for the ambiguities of life at home as well as for life abroad.

CHAPTER TWENTY

CLASSROOM INNOVATION: A DESIGN PRIMER

I began my professional career at Procter & Gamble Company in 1956, working as an internal consultant and researcher. My intention was always to move on to university teaching, however, and in 1960, I was recruited to teach at Yale by Chris Argyris. I spent the summer between leaving Procter & Gamble and beginning at Yale with the National Training Laboratories, learning to facilitate T-groups under the tutelage of Warren Bennis.

So it was that when I arrived at Yale, I was thoroughly steeped in the principles and practice of experience-based education, and I wanted to structure my classroom as much like a T-group as possible. By that I mean that I wanted my students to take responsibility for setting their own goals and for managing their learning, while I served in the capacity of facilitator, coach, and counselor.

My first attempts at putting this naïve scheme into practice failed. Most of my students saw me as incompetent rather than permissive, and they resented what they saw as my unwillingness to do my job. I had no support for my experiments from senior colleagues either, who advised me to direct my creativity into my research, where it would do my career some good. However, I persisted. I had never much liked school myself, from the day I began kindergarten right through graduate school, although I did well in my studies. I only discovered the real excitement of learning when I went to Procter & Gamble and was given a free hand by a very permissive boss who asked only that I find ways to make myself useful as a psychologist. My experiences in T-groups opened further vistas of self-managed learning to me, and I was passionately

Note: Originally published in P. Runkel, R. Harrison, and M. Runkel (eds.), *The Changing College Classroom* (San Francisco: Jossey-Bass, 1969). Reprinted here with permission of Jossey-Bass Publishers.

committed to a new vision of empowerment in learning.

I had help from Howard Perlmutter,
who came to Yale as a visiting professor in
my second year there. He shared his concept of *social architecture,* in which one designs social structures so as to channel the
flow of energy and facilitate the connections and interactions that will aid the
goals of the designers. At first, I had
wanted to neutralize my own authority
and minimize the influence of grades in
my classroom. Freed from coercion in my
classroom, students had withdrawn their
energy in order to devote more time and
attention to teachers who demanded
more. Now I saw that I could use my authority to set learning goals and standards
to keep students' energies in my classroom, at the same time as I gave the students a lot of freedom to explore and
experiment within that setting. I began to
experiment with using the social needs of
students, their wish to create and maintain
good relationships with one another, to
motivate excellent work in my courses. I
not only had students working in groups,
but I gave them the power to influence
one another's grades. Year by year, as I
learned to use social architecture more
creatively, the performance *and* satisfaction of my students rose. At the end of my
last semester at Yale, I received the kind of
reward I most appreciated—a rave review

in the Yale students' own guide to courses
and teachers.

"Classroom Innovation: A Design
Primer" grew out of a long-distance
relationship with a fellow worker in the
experience-based classroom, Philip Runkel
at the University of Oregon. We corre-
sponded for a time, and then decided to
collaborate in editing a book that would
bring together the innovations of colleagues who were exploring similar issues
on campuses across the United States. I
had by this time left Yale and was working
overseas. I regarded the paper as my
legacy to those who would come after me
as teachers, since I did not expect to work
again in academia. As it turned out, the
principles I put forward in the paper were
directly applicable to my future work in
designing education and training for business and industry (as will be seen in Chapters Twenty-One and Twenty-Two).
Reviewing the paper now, I see in it not
only a set of guidelines for the design of
learning experiences, but also the rudi-
ments of a philosophy of design for organizations of all kinds: communities,
businesses, and so on. The more recent
paper in Chapter Seventeen ("Building Attunement in Community Through Social
Architecture") shows how I believe my
way of thinking can be applied to the design of intentional communities.

My purpose in this chapter is to draw some guidelines from behavioral science that will enable the university teacher to design innovative courses and
classroom situations that will work. A classroom that works is one where the learning processes and outcomes occur as intended, and where the qualities of social
interaction between students and teacher and among students support the in-

tended learning. This paper is not intended as a treatise on learning theory; it is an attempt to extract from learning theory some practical implications for the conduct of teaching in the university classroom. Principles and concepts are presented that have relevance for the decisions teachers have to make when they depart from the well-trodden paths of tradition and strike out into the wilds of educational experimentation. I have called this paper a primer because that is all I know how to write. The applied art has not advanced to the point where we can write advanced works on social engineering and design. The most I aspire to is to transmute some of my own experience into concepts that indicate the choices that have to be made in designing educational systems for higher learning and to explain why I believe some choices are better than others.

Before going ahead, I should like to be clear about the value position from which I am writing. This is not a paper about how to design learning situations for any learning goal whatsoever; it deals rather with the problems of maximizing values I believe are important. The values are the same as those Richard Hopkins and I put forward in a previous paper on the design of cross-cultural training (Harrison and Hopkins, 1967 [Chapter Nineteen]). I believe there are close parallels between the problems of transition from one's own culture to another and the problems of living and learning in a society in flux such as ours. Our culture requires people to become increasingly adaptive and responsive to change. This fact implies a number of changes in the appropriate goals of university education, and these changed goals underlie the design principles of this paper. Instead of educating to prepare students for one career, we need to educate for multiple and sequential roles, even while we do not know what the demands of the roles will be. We need to build education as a lifelong process taking place both inside and outside formal institutions. We need to convert students from institutionally directed education to self-directed education. We need to move students from reliance on authoritative sources of information toward developing and evaluating their own sources. We need to move from a focus on the content of learning to an equal or greater concern with the process of learning. Students in our classrooms need to learn how to continue to learn, and not merely to learn the facts, principles, and theories we present to them there. We need to change educational systems in which the learner is primarily a passive recipient of learning, by designing systems in which students actively create their own learning. We need to move from a criterion of learning that stops with achievement measured in the classroom toward a focus on application in the real world.

The rapid pace of change requires the student to "own" his learning. He should be prepared for active, self-directed exploration and inquiry throughout life. A major design objective is thus to maximize freedom of the learner.

I further believe that there is a relevance gap between the focus of much university education and the situations in which that education is to be applied. The gap is not so pronounced where the aim of education is instrumental—the acquisition of specific knowledge and tools for producing goods and services. It becomes large when questions of values, goals, and emotionally charged choices are involved in the application of learning. We are better at training people how to do things than we are at helping them learn to make choices; we teach students what they need to know to serve the needs of a profession or organization, but we give them little help in deciding whether the goals of that profession or organization are worthy of commitment.

I believe that our higher education usually makes it easy for our students to split their values from their behavior—a splitting that is central to the alienation endemic in our culture. The separation of facts and theories from values and emotions that we foster in the name of rationality and objectivity continues into organizational and professional life, where it contributes to performance without commitment and action without responsibility.

Since this paper is primarily a design primer rather than a critique of university education, I shall not belabor the connection between rationalism in the classroom and alienation in society. I do want it to be clear that I believe classroom design should lead wherever possible to significant encounter for the student with the values, choices, and dilemmas embedded in subject matter, and that the encounter should be as real, involving, and emotionally significant as possible. This does not mean anti-intellectualism. Rather, it is a bias in favor of involving the student in a real way with meaningful and important issues requiring choice, commitment, and consequences.

All classrooms are complex social systems. However, university classrooms have had a ritualized, stereotyped character that makes it possible for both students and teachers to perform their respective roles with very little understanding of the forces and processes involved in the system. Everyone knows it is the role of the professor to lecture, make reading assignments, give examinations, evaluate assigned work, and assign grades reflecting the student's achievement in a course. Everyone knows it is the student's role to attend lectures, to identify and take notes on those contents the teacher regards as important, and to do the same with assigned reading. The whole is to be held ready for production on demand: in class, in papers, and in examinations.

We are introduced into this ritual around age six, and we stay with it until we are in our early twenties—longer if we become graduate students and teachers. Graduate students learn the ritual so well that usually it is not necessary to train them to be university teachers; they have played opposite the teacher so long that they know the role—they have, in effect, understudied it. Although it is a nervous, scary experience to face one's first class as a university teacher, this is usually because we do not know if we will be able to live up to the demands of the role, not because we do not know what those demands are. Most of us quickly learn to perform adequately if not brilliantly, moving with little stress from the audience to the stage.

When our rituals fail to produce the expected results, we face a sudden increase in our need for knowledge and concepts that will help us separate what is efficacious in our teaching and learning from what is merely ritual; we need concepts that will furnish better guidelines to what is wrong and what to do to correct it than a system of blind trial and error. Since most of us are trained more in the ritual of the classroom than in its art and science, we resort to trial and error for improving our classrooms. We begin by trying to improve our practice of the ritual: better lectures, assignments, tests, and so on. We experiment with smaller classes, with ungraded assignments, and with group grades for group assignments.

As we tinker, we encounter and learn the dynamics of the classroom social system in a way we could not when we merely played our parts within the ritual. We find the system resists some changes, accepts others. Some changes have intended effects; others go badly awry. Some roles we prescribe for students and for ourselves require skills, abilities, and attitudes that they or we do not have. We encounter apparent contradictions: an innovation works in one classroom and not in another, and we begin to search for the reasons.

My own curiosity about the social psychology of learning systems began when I tried to apply, in the classroom, some of the practices I had learned in the conduct of sensitivity training and consulting in industry. To my surprise, it seemed that giving students freedom to direct their own learning was more likely to produce apathy than involvement. To add to my confusion, I found that my *group-centered* techniques were eminently successful when I conducted weekend training in leadership for student leaders at other colleges and universities, but when I tried similar things in my own classroom, students were confused and suspicious.

I began to discover that if I wanted to change my classroom I had to learn to use or to neutralize the forces already existing in the system: rewards and punishments and students' reactions to them; values and standards about the appropriate behavior for students and faculty; needs and wants present in students but unmet by the university environment. I began to understand how the students' personal development prepared some of them to welcome and use freedom in the learning situation, but caused others to shrink back from freedom, or abuse it, appearing either too irresponsible or too dependent to use it effectively. I began to see how the pressures from other parts of the university organization and culture limited the measures I could take in my classroom; for example, I found that when I reduced the pressure of grades on my students they often used the extra time to work on courses of other teachers who were not so lenient.

As my understanding of the forces became more detailed and systematic, I found that my experiments and innovations worked better. Students were more highly motivated, and they produced better work. The outcomes of my educational experiments became more predictable. I gained greater skill in diagnosing what was going wrong and in intervening to save a failing experiment. Out of these experiences has grown a rough framework of concepts and principles that serves as a guide in deciding what is important to provide for in designing successful classroom experiences.

The overall aim of this paper is to help the innovative teacher to understand what changes in values, attitudes, skills, and behaviors are implied by his design, both for his students and for himself. He should be able to identify probable sources of resistance to change and be ready to work with them, counting the resistance as part of the job of innovation. The design of a learning system, like politics, is the art of the possible. The ideal classroom will not exist in any university we shall see within our lifetimes. We hope to be able to push much closer to the ideal as our knowledge becomes more systematic, detailed, and accurate.

Three Types of Learning: Conceptual, Instrumental, and Rote

If we are to train students to own their learning, we must choose among alternative learning processes in the classroom. In this section, I shall discuss three types of learning: conceptual, instrumental, and rote. Ultimately, we want to promote learning that not only results in the mastery of the content of a discipline, but also trains the student how to learn. Traditionally, we have been more concerned with learning content than with learning how to learn. If we are to produce active, self-directed, lifelong learners, however, the latter becomes as important as the former—perhaps even more important. Specific content may eventually become obsolete or irrelevant to the learner; what he learns about how to explore the world, to gather and evaluate information, to make and test hypotheses will never be out of date.

The processes of conceptualization and theory building are central to the task of learning how to learn. Practically, the learning activities of discovery and application are the realization of these processes. By discovery, I mean that we expose the learner to a variety of experiences, events, facts, and phenomena, expecting that he will uncover relationships, categories, and concepts that order and explain his experience. The teacher provides the experiences, and the student actively makes sense out of them, finding the meaning in the events. The teacher has provided the conditions for learning, but the learning process remains the property of the learner. In the case of discovery, the learner goes from the concrete experience to the abstract theory or concept; hence the learning process is inductive.

Application or hypothesis testing is the deductive obverse of discovery. The concepts and theories are given, and the learner's work consists in applying them to the solution of particular problems or to the understanding of experience. The teacher provides the organizing concepts, and the learner uses them as tools to manipulate events or to understand them.

Both the inductive and deductive learning processes are active and contribute to learning how to learn. In each case, the learner has to do something with what is given him: build theory or test it. Both can provide an experience of encounter. The experiences of which the learner is asked to make sense inductively can be designed to evoke values and have emotional impact as well as to be intellectually stimulating. The application of concepts and theory to action may have value implications and dilemmas of choice.

Two examples from my own teaching illustrate the processes. In one course in the psychology of administration, I wanted students to learn and test Maslow's (1954) theory of motivation deductively. I presented the theory, using lectures and reading assignments. Then I asked my students to conduct interviews among first-year students at the university, in which they were to elicit as much information as possible about the motives and needs of the first-year students and test whether the theory was adequate to account for what they found. Where their results deviated from the theory, I encouraged students to modify the latter, thus beginning the inductive process that should always follow the failure of a concept or hypothesis (see also Chapter Thirteen).

In a different course on group behavior, I asked students to keep a diary of significant events that occurred during the biweekly unstructured meetings of the course. At the end of the semester, they were to derive concepts and theories of group behavior from these records of experience. In this example, the students moved inductively from experience to the discovery of concepts.

In both these examples, I was concerned not only that the students learn about psychology, but also that they learn about how to use theory and how to learn from experience. I was concerned about the students' learning how to learn as well as about their learning of content. I believe that rote learning is greatly overused in the university classroom, with the result that students commit to memory a great deal of material that never gets related to anything more significant than the next examination. The problem is not that the material that is learned by rote is unimportant, but that we often assume that, once it is learned by that method, the teaching and learning job is done.

Since rote learning will probably be with us for the foreseeable future, we need to find some way of counteracting its tendency to make students passive and uninvolved in learning. For example, the effective methods for teaching modern languages reduce the rote learning of vocabulary to a minimum and never allow it to interfere with active use of a language in conversation. When we move toward an emphasis on active use of each bit of information to accomplish some result, we are going away from rote learning and toward instrumental learning. The terms of the learning equation shift from "X goes with Y" to "to accomplish X, do Y." This is obviously a more active process of learning and is more consistent with our values.

Some of the innovative courses described in *The Changing College Classroom* have large components of instrumental learning of techniques, those of Runkel (1969) and Seiler (1969), for example; and the one by Horn (1969), especially, is built around instrumental learning principles. We should, however, be aware that our choosing to provide students with tools always involves consequences for learning how to learn. The student who works out his own methods of approach most owns his learning. The student who has a wide and free choice of methods and techniques that can be applied to his own goals also has ownership, especially if he is required to make the choice on his own. Obviously, one cannot always make the ideal choice, especially when there is much content and method to be learned. However, the consequences of overcontrolling the instrumental learning of students may be severe. This is illustrated by an example from industrial experience. A large American chemical company extensively recruited research chemists in Europe for a time during the 1950s, to compensate for a shortage of chemists trained in the United States. After several years' experience, however, the company decided that the Continent was not a good source of research personnel. The company discovered that young chemists trained there found it hard to take individual responsibility and to carry projects forward. As one manager put it, "They are so used to having the professor tell them what to do, that if you give them a project, they wait around for someone to tell them how to do it. They have no confidence in their own ability to conduct research." These chemists had learned a general method for doing research (to ask the professor), which did not work when they were left on their own. They had also acquired an image of themselves as low in the ability to generate their own approaches to problems. Though they were well trained in their basic discipline, their instrumental learning about how to solve problems required a relationship to authority that was not available in the U.S. organization.

To summarize my point of view regarding the selection of learning processes in the design of classroom experiences: I favor giving a high weight to learning how to learn. Conceptual learning processes give the learner most freedom and ownership of the learning process and can best prepare him to be self-directed and independent in his future learning. Both inductive and deductive processes are advantageous: the former being the generalization of concepts and theory from experience, the latter being the testing of theory and its application to the solution of problems.

The lower learning processes have less desirable consequences. Rote learning tends to develop a passive and dependent orientation to learning, and instrumental learning is often tightly controlled by the teacher's selection of goals and means to the goals. However, instrumental learning can in part be given back to the learner when the teacher encourages exploration and experimentation in the choice and practice of means to goals.

Motives, Needs, and Goals

An understanding of the motivational aspects of classroom design is badly needed in American universities. A theory of motivation can help the classroom designer make intelligent choices about the needs and incentives upon which he will base his designs. Man is a wanting animal. When one need is satisfied, others arise and become motive forces. While it is possible to satisfy a particular need, it is not possible to satisfy all the needs of a person. Although we tend to think of human needs as fixed and static, they are changing and dynamic, first one and then another emerging, becoming potent, achieving satisfaction, and then fading into the background. Give a man bread and he wants respect; give him respect and he wants love.

Universities, like other social systems, control the behavior of their members through the application of incentives (rewards and punishments). For the incentives to be effective, they must meet important and currently active needs of the members. Otherwise the incentives will not control behavior, and the system will begin to break down. When our assumptions about the people's needs turn out to be inaccurate, things can go wrong very fast. The behavior of others in the system becomes unpredictable and uncontrollable. Now [1969] this is happening on university campuses all over the world, where many students are becoming inexplicably unresponsive to the incentives applied to control their behavior. It is a reasonable hypothesis that the students' needs have changed while the incentive systems have not.

My model of motivation postulates three basic human needs actually or potentially active in everyone. The model is a modification of an original concept by Maslow (1954). *Physio-economic needs* are those for very broadly defined creature comforts: anything from the most basic essentials of existence like food, water, shelter, and clothing to such unessential but comfort-producing incentives as automobiles, dishwashers, and shorter working hours. Social systems for the production and distribution of goods and services originally take much of their motive force from physio-economic needs. *Social needs* are those for love, acceptance, belongingness, and closeness to others. This need includes all wants and desires pertaining to loving and hating, being close and intimate, and spending time by oneself or with others. *Ego needs* are those for competence, knowledge, status, and respect. Wants and desires relating to self-esteem, self-confidence, achievement, reputation, and recognition are all included among the ego needs. A given kind of behavior can be controlled by incentives in any one of the three need areas. For example, a student may enroll in a particular course because it is on the path to a degree and an economically secure life (physio-economic need), because his friends are also enrolling in it (social need), or because he is oriented toward the mastery of the subject matter of the course (ego need). We never know exactly what the active needs are that students bring with them to our classrooms, but we can be sure that they are not identical. The most viable and effective classrooms are those in which behavior that is desirable from the point of view of the system (work or learning) can lead to a variety of rewards. In other words, they are classrooms in which people with varied needs can all be rewarded for contributing to goals the teacher also values.

In universities, I have been impressed with the narrow range of rewards (those limited to the ego area) offered in most classrooms for effective performance. We offer recognition for knowledge and competence through grades, academic honors, and the personal respect of teacher and classmates. Some teachers and courses, by no means most, offer exciting opportunities for intrinsic satisfactions to be gained from the growth and development of one's understanding and intellectual capacities. Very rarely do the formal learning systems of the university provide much in the way of social satisfactions, and those that have been available informally are being badly eroded by the size and bureaucracy of the universities. Affection and liking between students and teachers become impossible when they spend little time in face-to-face contact. The same is true for students in their relations with one another when work assignments are individual and when living arrangements are not communal.

In the survey that some of my students made of first-year students, the needs found to be the least well satisfied were social needs; my upper-class students have confirmed, in diaries I asked them to keep, that this deprivation is only partially made up after two or three years in the system. The social needs of students are relevant to the designer of classroom processes in two important ways. First, the goals of classroom design, as I have outlined them above, emphasize encounter as a significant educational goal. Learning that is low on encounter is not experienced by students as relevant and will not easily be applied to choices and actions in the real world. Educational systems fail significantly to approach the goal of encounter when students' relationships with teachers and one another are impersonal, lacking in emotional impact, and without important consequences for the individuals' social needs. Second, such educational systems fail to motivate significant numbers of students whose social needs are more active and potent than their needs for the ego rewards traditionally offered in the classroom. Social needs of students must be attended to if only to revitalize the classroom and stimulate learning. This means that systems of rewards in classrooms should be designed so that the learning process will either be intrinsically socially rewarding or will lead to social rewards for the effective and highly motivated learner.

I have been treating needs as though they were to be met directly by rewards or, in reverse, by punishments or the withholding of rewards. However, goal-seeking operations vary not only in the three basic need areas but also in the social processes that satisfy the needs. These processes will be assessed according to their levels of influence. Teaching, after all, is a process of influence.

Compliance

At a rather low level of need satisfaction, the individual is prepared to enter into what Kelman has called *compliance* transactions with the environment (1958, 1961). The individual is deprived enough and hungry enough to be concerned mainly with getting the next satisfier and avoiding the next punishment or deprivation. The distinguishing characteristic of compliance is that the person being influenced is oriented to external sources of reward and punishment, and behavior is consequently controlled by the outside agent who administers rewards and punishments. If external sources of satisfaction fail the individual, he has few resources of his own on which to fall back. He is often confused and lost. In the area in which his need is high, he is likely to have underdeveloped values and standards of ethical behavior and to take what he can get when and how he can get it. He is relatively unresisting to exploitation by others, and he will exploit them in turn when opportunity offers. He is oriented to the present and near future and finds it difficult to put off present wants for future advantage.

In the classroom, we find dependent students responding to rewards and punishments in both social and ego need areas. Some students work hard for grades, fear failure, go to great lengths to impress the teacher with their willingness to work and their mastery of what he has assigned, and seldom take any risks that might result in punishments, such as disagreeing with opinions of the teacher. They are employing compliance processes in the ego area. Other students exert themselves to be pleasing and likable. They may amuse other students and the professor; they avoid conflict and controversy for fear of offending others; they may spend a great deal of time in socializing to the detriment of their work; their effectiveness as students may be at the mercy of whether the girlfriend or boyfriend or the roommates are at the moment accepting or rejecting them. They are functioning at the compliance level in the social area.

From the point of view of the learner, compliance management is most effective when the need is strong and when the individual has few resources of his own to use in achieving satisfaction independently of external sources of reward and punishment. It is least effective when the need is weak or currently well satisfied, and when the individual has readily available alternate sources of satisfaction. From the point of view of the classroom designer, compliance systems are most useful when the response desired from the learner can be closely specified and compliance observed. The effective administration of rewards and punishments depends on one's being able to specify, in advance, the response which one requires from the learner, and then to observe whether the response has been produced, and to reward or not accordingly. Compliance management lends itself to rote and instrumental learning. It does not work as well where discovery and hypothesis testing, or invention and application, are the major learning processes, because in these cases, it is precisely the external control of behavior from which we are trying to shake the learner loose. Nor does it work well when the teacher does not control rewards that will satisfy the active needs of his students. Most influence in schools and universities is compliance based, with the teacher as formal authority.

The progression from one level of need satisfaction to another seems to be a developmental process in which stages have to be gone through in a regular order. There are two processes relevant to this moving up and out from dependency and passivity. One is a moving away from others; the other a new kind of moving toward others. The moving away involves a counterdependent orientation in which the individual struggles to free himself from control by others. He shows a new willingness to endure deprivation to avoid domination, secure in his feeling that the deprivation is temporary and, at least to some extent, under his own control. He separates himself from the ideas, attitudes, and standards of others; after having been conforming, he becomes iconoclastic. In the ego area, we now find students rebelling against domination and dependency. Sometimes they avoid schoolwork for extracurricular activities where they can attain recognition, respect, and a feeling of growing competence without submitting to the control of assignments, examinations, and grades. Sometimes they seem to go on a kind of private strike, in which their productivity and their grades take a sudden nosedive. Sometimes they become argumentative and contentious, challenging the authority and competence of the teacher. In the social area, we find people who are emerging from dependency developing an increased willingness to take risks with love and friendship. They become more likely to fight with their friends and to violate the standards of acceptable behavior. They may exploit the exploiters by trying to see how many people they can have in love with them at the same time or by using friendship to manipulate others.

Identification

It is possible to become fixated, or stuck, at any stage of development. Dependent and counterdependent orientations can become life-styles for individuals or for whole groups and societies. If development continues naturally, however, the moving away of counterdependency is followed by the moving toward of *identification*. With identification, influence takes place through the influenced person's wanting to be like or to learn from a model. The influenced person seeks the influence, out of his own needs for self-definition, rather than complying in return for rewards or in fear of punishment or deprivation. Another aspect of identification is the establishment of relationships in which the person finds identity and self-definition through the way others act toward him. If I am a member of a group that treats me as likable and worthy of friendship and trust, I will be willing to meet its standards and requirements to maintain the identity the group confirms. If I belong to a group or organization holding an elite status in my profession, I will be willing to accept its influence in order to continue to see myself as elite. Any relationship contributing to a person's own sense of success, competence, or worthiness of love can be a source of influence through the person's desire to maintain that support for his identity. Identification processes are significant sources of influence in the classroom. In Cytrynbaum and Mann's typology (1969), they are found in the teacher as ego ideal and the teacher as person. The popular image of a good teacher is of a person who serves as a model for students, inspires them to the highest ideals, sets them a good example, brings out the best in them. These are ways we have in everyday speech of talking about influence through identification. Identification is also significant in the influences students exert upon one another. Students develop an image of the ideal student that is not at all the same as the faculty's image, which is less likely to embody social attractiveness than is the students'.

Internalization

At a certain stage in the development of the individual, he may develop beyond being greatly dependent on others for the satisfaction of his needs. He may acquire a strong sense of his own identity and a correspondingly clear and strongly held set of values. In the normal course of development, most of us come to operate from internalized values and standards a large part of the time and in a number of areas. We are not honest just because we are afraid of being caught but because we identify ourselves as reasonably honest persons; we do not give love only to receive it in return but because we feel love and we see ourselves as warm, loving persons; we do not achieve just for the acclaim and respect of others but we work for the pleasure and satisfaction we find in a job well done. When we are operating from such values and from our abilities to give, create, and love, we can truly be said to be self-directed and to own our own lives. People who are operating in such an inner-directed mode of need satisfaction tend to be rather unresponsive to coercive influences or to identification processes. If the rewards or the relationships offered to these inner-directed people reinforce their values and sense of self-identity, they respond, but their values take precedence when there is a conflict between inner and outer influences. If such persons can be subjected to massive and unrelieved environmental control, their values and sense of self can often be broken down and they can be made externally directed again. For most of us, this can happen to some degree in times of personal stress or deprivation: when we are without money and hungry, or unloved and alone, or failing and unrecognized in our work. Some of the time, however, most of us operate more from our values than from our interests (the latter being defined as getting the most satisfaction for the least effort).

University students may be more subject to external coercion than are the adults they will become. Certainly, they are more likely to be deeply involved in the processes of identity formation than they will be later. Many of them, however, operate much of the time upon strongly internalized values firmly rooted in a clear sense of identity. Unfortunately, because of the increasing gap between students' values and those embedded in the structure and operation of the university, the attempts at influence made by teachers are often irrelevant or counter to students' values. When this happens, particularly if the coercive pressures are great enough to make them feel really oppressed, students either do not respond or they resist. Even when the values of students and teachers are not conflicting, students do not like to have their self-direction taken away from them; they react as though the coercive pressures were being used to *dedevelop* them. The self-directed student may then avoid direct involvement by playing the game while investing his real concerns and energies elsewhere, perhaps by trying to learn in his own way, while fending off control with whatever means of resistance he can muster; perhaps by trying to change the system by joining university reform movements; or by using the system to further his own needs and values if he can find ways of doing so; or by dropping out of the system. However, he will not fit into the system and be a good, integrated member of it unless it offers him opportunities to direct his own activities according to his own values.

The question for the classroom designer becomes, how does one exercise his responsibility for teaching and at the same time encourage self-direction on the part of students? Some part of the answer may be found in the use of the influence process which Kelman calls *internalization* (1958, 1961). It has also been called *expert power* (French and Raven, 1959). If we assume the individual's own values as a major driving force, we can still facilitate learning and influence behavior by inducing the individual to see new or different ways to maximize his values. This may be done through giving him information or by introducing new concepts that help account for events and experiences he has not previously been able to integrate into his problem solving. We do not directly offer the individual rewards and punishments as inducements to learning. We aid him in discovering ways in which he can increase his own satisfactions, assuming his own needs will provide the stimulus for learning. We do not seek to inspire the student with a vision of what he can become. Instead, we assume that he knows what he wants to become and wants to learn whatever will bring him closer to his own ideals of being and doing.

Different characteristics of the teacher become important in influence through internalization. What is important is the credibility of the teacher and his ability to develop the student's trust in his own competence and motives. This is so because, if the teacher is successful in his influence attempt, the student will personally experience success or failure as his own responsibility. Influence through internalization never takes the responsibility away from the influenced person.

In the process of internalization, the encounter between the student's values and the consequences of his actions is maximized. The teacher is responsible for his own competence and for his own honesty, but he stops short of making choices for the student about what the latter should learn or how he should learn it. He serves as an aid to the student's own learning, not an instigator of it. Influence through internalization facilitates conceptual learning by discovery and hypothesis testing. The teacher facilitates learning of concepts not only through his personal relationship to the student but also through his designs for learning. Given the increasingly large classes and depersonalizing of relationships between students and teachers, the most effective way to influence by internalization is by classroom design. This means that we design the classroom so that the student can act upon his own values and goals in the process of learning. Sometimes this means that he selects his own learning tasks, sometimes that he determines his own approach to some task which the teacher sets. The more freedom of choice and action the student has, the more opportunity there is to involve his own goals and values and to own his learning experience.

Creating Classroom Designs Based on Identification and Internalization

Much of the remainder of this paper explores the problems and difficulties we face when trying to move from the traditional compliance-based influence systems in the classroom to designs that maximize internalization. The discussions are based on the hierarchical model of learning, needs, and influence processes set forth earlier and summarized in Table 20.1. "Lower," more concrete externally directed processes lead by stages of development to "higher," more abstract internally directed processes. Processes at a given level go together, fit with one another and reinforce each other. Learning process, influence process, and the level of need development at which the student is operating are interdependent.

Compliance tends to result in rote learning and in instrumental learning. Simpler, mechanistic learning processes are favored by deprivation and high levels of need on the part of the students. High need levels make students accept the dependency that accompanies influence through compliance. Appropriate teaching styles and classroom design for the effective use of compliance include clear specification of expectations and reliable rewards for performance, frequent assessment of performance, and a firm but fair style on the part of the teacher.

Identification presupposes a higher level of independence and an active search for identity and values on the part of the student. It leads to learning that is value relevant and likely to become integrated with the individual's values and goals. Identification depends upon the teacher's knowledge and skill in design, and on his personal qualities as a role model.

Internalization presupposes a degree of value development on the part of the learner, to the point that he is willing and able to endure deprivation and postponement of immediate gratification in the service of learning and of his values and standards. This ability to operate independently of external rewards and punishments permits self-directed exploration and manipulation of the environment. Internalization lends itself to conceptual learning by the methods of discovery and hypothesis testing.

A great deal of design ingenuity is required to create a classroom process based on internalization, particularly when there are fixed principles, concepts, or skills which it is decided in advance are to be taught. The teaching style that facilitates internalization is one of competence, trustworthiness, and honesty. The teacher avoids judging the performance of the learner except against the latter's own standards. Instead, he provides accurate, objective, but nonevaluative feedback in which he simply describes what the effects of the student's behavior are without praising or blaming. He provides information, ideas, and help in formulating concepts, rather than being a source of reward, punishment, and external control.

Traditional Classrooms: Mixtures of Needs and Motives

Classrooms contain students at a mixture of need development levels. These students do not respond to influence in the same ways, but the teacher cannot usually choose his students; he must try to educate them all, or he must work with some and let the others get along as best they can. The vast majority of students

TABLE 20.1. HIERARCHICAL MODEL OF CLASSROOM PROCESSES.

Influence Processes	Ideal Teaching Style	Design Principles	Major Learning Processes	Level of Student Need Development Required
Compliance ("lower")	Firm but fair; clear and consistent about what he expects and what the consequences are of compliance and noncompliance.	Clearly specify desired behavior and learning; accurately and frequently assess success and failure; make rewards reliably forthcoming for success, withheld for failure. Source of reward may be teacher or other students, but in either case, standards of performance are made clear in advance.	Rote learning, including the mechanistic learning of concepts and theories without integration with the individual's values and goals. Instrumental learning through rewarding of correct behavior.	Subsistence: the student has strong needs for rewards offered within the classroom, with little opportunity or ability to obtain alternate satisfiers of the same needs elsewhere—a level of need and lack of resources leading to willingness to endure a high degree of dependency.
Identification	When modeling: exciting, inspiring and admirable. Persuasive and charismatic. When engaged in self-defining relationships with students: empathic and accepting. Treating the student as though he is what he would like to become: for example, responding to the student's competence and likeability.	Maximum contact and interaction between student and identification models (teacher or students): thus, an emphasis on groups and collaborative learning tasks. Find and train persons with whom students can readily identify (other students, graduate students). Know and work within the values of the student culture.	Instrumental learning through modeling effective behavior. Conceptual learning through adoption of the ideas, values, and theories of valued and attractive others.	The student has some confidence in own ability to satisfy own needs. The student is engaged in the building of a sense of identity and self-worth within the need area and receptive to identification models and to adopting the ideas and standards of valued others or of others who value him.

have learned to get along somehow in learning situations where there is much influence by compliance in the ego area. Behavior is manipulated through grades; students are encouraged to compete; competence consists not only in meeting some standard, but in being better than one's fellows. Cooperation between students in their work is usually defined as cheating, either actual or borderline. Along

Influence Processes	Ideal Teaching Style	Design Principles	Major Learning Processes	Level of Student Need Development Required
Internal-ization ("higher")	Competent, trust-worthy. Providing reliable informa-tion and useful ways of under-standing experi-ence. Providing nonevaluative feedback about the student's be-havior, abilities, and accomplish-ments. Judging only against the student's own val-ues and standards.	Involve and acti-vate students' own goals and val-ues. Allow maxi-mum opportunity to set own goals and make choices as to approaches to problems. Pre-pare designs in which the student can experience the consequences of thought and action for achiev-ing or failing to achieve his or her own goals.	Conceptual learn-ing through dis-covery and hypothesis testing. High integration of learning with values and goals of the student.	The student has considerable con-fidence in ability to satisfy own needs, willingness to endure depriva-tion for periods of time in the service of own values and standards, strong sense of own iden-tity and well-developed values and standards, an ability to give as well as a need to receive need satisfactions.

with this basic compliance pattern is a less formal system of influence through identification. Teachers model the behavior they expect from students and do their best to inspire and draw out commitment to academic values. There are few op-portunities for self-direction and influence through internalization. Those which exist are usually reserved for specially selected students who enter honors programs or independent study.

Side by side with the classroom learning system is the student culture, which is based largely on social needs and motives. The two cultures often conflict, es-pecially where the competitive reward structure of the classroom interferes with the development of friendly, cooperative relationships among students. The style of adaptation to this "normal" classroom culture varies with the strengths of the ego and social needs in the individual student. The student culture has more in-fluence over those with stronger social needs.

Students who have strong needs for the rewards offered by the formal com-pliance system will tend to be controlled in the way the system is designed to con-trol them. They will attend classes, take notes on lectures, complete assignments on time, study hard, and write examinations that reflect what they think the teacher wants. They will try to obtain the maximum rewards for the minimum work and may not show a great deal of concern as to the intrinsic value of academic activities.

Students whose level of development is above that of the most dependent re-lationship are usually in a state of at least partial conflict and defense against the compliance relationships in the classroom. They may try to manipulate or outfox the system, sabotage or rebel against it, or withdraw from it. If there are acceptable identification models available in the persons of the teacher or effective students, this conflict may be reduced. This occurs when the student is able to identify with the values associated with being a good student.

Most of the time, I think, most of our students are rather peripherally committed to formal academic activities and defend themselves against too much influence from the teacher or his classroom design. They respond to the occasional inspiring teacher, but they do not see the classroom as a place where their own values and goals can be pursued. They do not devote more energy and time to work than is necessary to get the rewards they need from the system. They comply, but they do not commit themselves. Instead, they keep their commitment to academic work low, so they can devote themselves to activities that promise more opportunity for growth and identity development. Most students have learned to write the classroom off because it does not satisfy their needs very well.

The teaching experiences reported in *The Changing College Classroom* suggest that the normal classroom situation is not wholly favorable for the introduction of classroom designs relying on ego needs satisfied through internalization. Some few students quickly grasp the opportunity for self-directed learning and use it. Many others respond initially with some combination of anxiety, confusion, mistrust, resentment, or apathy. One major cause lies in the discrepancy between the social needs of students and the ego-based reward structure of the traditional classroom.

Having high levels of ego need, teachers tend to design their classrooms as though social needs do not exist or will not be aroused in the classroom. However, social needs are aroused as soon as students are in the presence of other students or the teacher. Classroom designs often go awry when we fail to take this into account. For example, in *The Changing College Classroom*, it has been suggested that small work groups of students spend a fair amount of time unproductively (Runkel, Harrison, and Runkel, 1969). The students themselves report that they feel guilty about the wasted time. I suspect that much of the time seen as wasted is spent in satisfying social needs. Because the satisfaction of these needs is not designed into the task, activities directed toward meeting them are tangential to work and are evaluated negatively. Another common example has to do with classroom participation. Students who are too active in demonstrating their knowledge in class often irritate others because they make the others look stupid or lazy by comparison. Students know they may be disliked or avoided by others if they appear too bright in class, and for many whose social needs are strong, this inhibits their performance.

If social needs are not designed into the classroom, they will operate anyway, perhaps in a disruptive way. Furthermore, students' relationships with their peers are a significant part of their life experience, their concerns, values, and goals. The classroom can hardly be said to be high on *encounter* for the student if we continue to act as though the only important human relationship in the classroom is that between student and teacher. The classroom becomes at least partially irrelevant to the student's values and goals unless his relationships with other students can become a contribution to and a vehicle for the learning process.

Using the Social Needs to Foster Learning

If the social needs of students are to become significant in the learning process, students must work together. In practice, this means that we shall want to use groups as learning settings. Undeniably, groups have some disadvantages. To begin with, the opportunity to interact with others affords occasions for social punishments and deprivations (rejection, dislike, boredom, and so on) as well as for satisfactions. Also, people in groups can be happy and satisfied without these feelings being connected in any way with learning. The task of the designer is to connect effective learning with the attainment of social satisfactions by the learner. Several times, I have had the experience of designing a course around a term-long group project that counted for most or all of the grade in the course. If the group worked well and was satisfying to its members, all was well. However, if the members of the group had interpersonal difficulties (disliked one another, struggled for power, and so on), members became discouraged partway through the course and began to withdraw from the group activity. This is always a danger when students are required to work collaboratively. Most have had little experience working in groups, since the traditional classroom emphasizes individual activity. They do not know how to work out the appropriate division of labor or deal with competition, over- and underparticipation, and unwillingness to work on the part of individuals.

I can make some practical suggestions for increasing the likelihood that learning groups will be productive and satisfying to their members and that an occasional failure will not be disastrous for the unlucky individuals in the failing group.

Try to compose groups so that competence is evenly distributed among them. This can be done by grade point average, by grades on previous tests or projects in the current course, and so on. In this way, each group will have some very good resources as well as some members who have to be helped or carried by the other members. The less effective students will be exposed to more effective ones who may serve as identification models for them. Most students will have had little contact with one another's work habits; working closely with effective students has been shown to have a good effect on the work of underachieving ones. Cahn (1969) gives a good example of the process of student modeling.

Try to compose groups so that there is as little interpersonal conflict as possible. Energy that has to be spent in dealing with conflict, competition, and disagreement is subtracted from that available for the learning task. A good deal of work has been done to study the effects of grouping members who have different personal characteristics, and I have reviewed some of this work in a theoretical paper (Harrison, 1965a). Of particular interest is FIRO-B, the instrument described by Schutz, which measures individual preferences for different kinds of interpersonal relationships (Schutz, 1958). I have experimented successfully with groups composed on FIRO-B scores to try to reduce conflict and maximize cohesiveness and satisfaction of group members (Harrison, 1965c). For example, I distributed evenly among the groups people with low inclusion scores, so that no group would have too many members who did not really like being in groups. I identified highly dominant people and placed them with others who were more willing to accept influence. I gave each group some members who were not at the extreme on any of the scales.

Another way of composing compatible groups is to allow members to select their own groups, preferably after they have had some experience with one another. Before deciding, they might discuss, in rotation, the qualities they would look for in a work group member. People tend to be more committed to making a decision work if they have participated in it, and group members who have chosen their own group will not give up as quickly as they would if the choice were the teacher's. This method conflicts with the suggestion made above that groups be composed to have an even distribution of talent. One has to make a choice.

Let the group decide differences in individual rewards. Sometimes students have complained to me that group projects are unfair because everyone receives the same grade, even though some students are unable or unwilling to do their share of the work. The project work is completed at the last minute by one or two highly motivated group members, often working alone. Because it is against the informal standards of students to put pressure on one another to work harder, it is difficult for students to deal unaided with members' underproductivity. The same problem is reported by Culbert (1969), South (1969), Torbert and Hackman (1969).

I have successfully dealt with the problem by having the students distribute rewards (grades) within the group on the basis of individual contribution. Students worked together on a task in four- or five-person groups, producing a report to which I assigned a grade. Each student then ranked the others according to their individual contributions to the group product. The average of the group members' rankings was fixed by the grade I had assigned to the group's product. Individual members' grades were adjusted higher or lower than this average according to the average rank they received from the other members rating their contributions. The students with whom I used this method accepted it as fair, and the group products were among the best I have received.

Legitimize leadership in the group. Students are encouraged, by the traditional reward structure of higher education, to compete with one another for grades, academic recognition, and entrance into graduate schools and the professions. They become unwilling to accept influence from other students; to preserve some friendliness and collaboration in the system, the peer culture develops strong norms in favor of leaving one another alone where scholastic matters are concerned. However, group work requires considerable mutual influence for its success. Since students do not readily develop arrangements for directing and coordinating the activity of group members by themselves, I usually give a push by prescribing or suggesting an authority structure in the group. I often ask a new group to spend some of its early meeting time discussing what leadership functions need to be performed, and how the group would like them performed. Since most students prefer to operate under a chairman, I may ask them to discuss the characteristics they would like in a leader and then to select one of their number for the post. After such a discussion, group members are more likely to select a leader who can be a model they can identify with.

I have also successfully channeled the distribution of grades to individuals through group leaders chosen by students. Again, a group grade, assigned by me to a project, set the average of individual grades, and the leader assigned higher and lower grades to reflect individual contribution. The leader's grade was set by the teacher. The purpose of channeling rewards through the group and legitimizing leadership is to make the compliance influences in the classroom support the effective functioning of the group. Otherwise, some students may correctly view the group as irrelevant to the goal of obtaining high individual grades.

Reduce the threatening aspects of group work. Students may accurately assess their effectiveness as group members to be low. The norms of the traditional classroom legitimize individual treatment of the student by the teacher. I have found that, to legitimize my group design, it helps to explain exactly why I feel the design is appropriate to the learning task and what benefits I expect students to derive from it. I solicit suggestions from students about the design, especially about the grading features, and modify it where there are strong objections. I give students as much participation in the decision about adopting the design as I can so that they will be committed to making it work.

In addition, it is possible to provide options that reduce the fear of failure. Students can be given a choice whether to do a given task individually or in a group. Group projects can be limited in duration and scope. I now usually use several projects, never longer than two to three weeks. Groups can be re-sorted for each new project, so that individuals have a fresh start each time. Runkel (1969) uses a different procedure for reducing threat and pressure: he gives term-long projects, but permits them to be continued into the following term; the lack of a deadline decreases anxiety and stress.

I do not view the use of learning groups as a panacea for the defects of the traditional classroom. However, groups still offer the best vehicle for students to meet social needs through productive learning activity. Carefully designed and managed, learning groups can increase involvement of students in the classroom, and provide them with opportunities to pursue their personal values and goals in the learning situation.

Using Compliance to Foster Learning

If it were possible to make pure *internalization* classrooms productive, this would be an ideal development. Unfortunately, it is usually beyond our reach. In such a classroom, there are no grades, no assigned projects, papers, or examinations. The teacher provides learning resources (readings, lectures, laboratory equipment, for example) but does not prescribe their use. Without rewards and punishments applied in the classroom, students who are highly oriented to external satisfiers of their ego needs tend to withdraw. They use their energy and time to obtain satisfaction in other coursework, where the traditional pattern continues. In present-day universities, where most students have to work hard to get good grades and to graduate, nearly everyone is somewhat responsive to coercive pressures. Attendance and effort drop off in noncoercive classrooms, except on the part of those few students who are genuinely self-directed or who are motivated at the level of identification. From a practical point of view, the noncoercive classroom seems nearly unworkable unless students can be selected for it or strong identification relationships can be established early. It is as though students' time and energy are attracted to the area of greatest coercion.

For this reason, I take the apparently contradictory position that in classrooms where internalization is heavily relied upon, there must also be some coercive features. I usually assign grades on the basis of some assigned work, but as far as the actual conduct of the work is concerned, the students are given quite a lot of freedom to choose projects, approaches, and learning resources. The power to reward and punish is used to *fence in* the students so that they will stay in contact with the learning situation and to *fence out* the competition and demands of other activities, both curricular and extracurricular. Students are given great freedom as to what they will do in the course, but the traditional rewards of grades are contingent on students' applying themselves vigorously to the task of learning.

Such designs, using mixtures of compliance-oriented and internalization-oriented influence, create difficulties for many students. For the student who is quite dependent, who values grades but has little confidence in his ability to obtain them, these designs produce a great deal of confusion and anxiety because they violate the principles for effective compliance-based learning. The student does not have a clear specification of the behavior desired. He knows he is expected to produce something that will be graded, but often he is not told what to produce, how to produce it, or against what criteria the work will be judged. His attempts to get clarification from the teacher may well be rebuffed. The dependent student may give up, feeling that his chances of getting a good grade are very low.

The mixture of compliance and internalization also creates difficulties for the majority of students whose development in the ego area is high enough for them to take some responsibility and self-direction. These students are often engaged in a defensive rebellion against the coercive pressures of the classroom. To the extent that they need the rewards of the compliance system, they will play the game, trying to manipulate the system so as to get maximum rewards from minimum effort. To do this, they need the same kind of information that the dependent student requires: an exact specification of the way the rewards and punishments will be administered. Then they can meet the minimum requirements with little wasted time and effort. Often such students do not value and enjoy learning for its own sake, nor do they have well-developed skills for self-directed learning. They are not confident that, if they put themselves wholeheartedly into the process of self-directed learning, the result will be intrinsically satisfying or will be highly valued by the teacher. Such students often mistrust the motives and trustworthiness of the teacher. They ask themselves why a teacher suddenly takes an interest in the growth and freedom of students. They may not believe that the choice of project or approach is really free. They may feel that the teacher who offers them choices is keeping back a clear notion about what he will reward in order to make them work harder.

I have had the experience of getting students to make a provisional commitment to self-directed learning only to lose their involvement midway through the course. It is discouraging. Once it occurred because I set students a group task that was beyond their ability. When the reports were turned in, I graded them on the quality of the products, which was not high. The students had actually put in considerably more time and effort than the reports showed. They felt cheated and punished. They had committed themselves to do a difficult, ambiguous task, had done their best to develop approaches to it, and were now being punished because the projects did not come up to my standard. The feeling of excitement and discovery that had existed at the beginning of the course was replaced by an apathetic despair that was never completely overcome.

Using Identification to Foster Learning

Identification processes are midway between compliance and internalization and tend to be compatible with both. Identification offers a key to the transition between the two extreme and antagonistic processes. Unfortunately, our ability to serve as identification models for students is often quite limited.

One of the significant changes that has taken place in higher education during the years since World War II is the progressive weakening of the influence of the teacher through identification. Part of this is caused by increasing class loads and the consequent depersonalizing of the relationship between teacher and student. With increased distance, the establishment of influence through identification depends on the teacher's ability to perform as an inspiring, charismatic lecturer. Skills in establishing self-defining relationships in face-to-face relationships become less relevant because fewer and fewer students spend significant amounts of time in direct interaction with teachers.

Part of this change can probably be traced to the increasing specialization and "technicalization" of the disciplines. The academic is increasingly restricted to being an ego-oriented model of the competent, knowledgeable professional, rather than inspiring identification with himself as a person with warmth, understanding, concern, and wisdom. A further consequence of technicalization is that more and more of the academic's time is spent in becoming and remaining competent in his discipline, and he is less and less oriented toward establishing and maintaining personal and mutually self-defining relationships with students.

In addition, the teacher is losing his potency as an identification model for students, along with other members of his generation (parents, professionals, leaders in industry and government, and so forth). The orientations of students who are coming to universities are changing from economic achievement and intellectual goals toward more emphasis on the quality of life and experience. The teacher may well have sacrificed his own social satisfactions in the pursuit of academic excellence. He is often ill equipped by background and personal values to model the kind of person students want to become.

All these factors seem to conspire to reduce the effectiveness of identification with the teacher as an influence for learning in the classroom. The result is that students turn to other students for their models, developing a peer culture increasingly divergent and out of touch with the values and attitudes of the faculty, and teachers fall back on compliance models of classroom management for lack of effective alternatives.

The remedies for these difficulties lie in the domains of reform of the university organization, redefinition of the role of teacher, and redesign of the training of academics. The question is, what can the innovative teacher do with the resources available to him: himself, his students, and the authority and prestige of his role in the university?

The Choices Available to Us as Teachers

The teacher has choices in two domains: the design of the course and his own style. In choosing to lead students and himself toward higher learning processes, the teacher must avail himself of all the sources of empowerment that are available to him. It is not enough to have a good design. The structure of the course only provides static conditions that permit or inhibit growth. The teacher must choose his behavior as well. He can choose to lead students toward internalization models or to keep them back in a compliance mode. The behavior of the teacher himself is at the center of the dynamics of what actually happens.

Given the fact that most of us are not, in our persons, overly inspiring models for students, I believe we still have a good deal of choice as to the impact of our behavior on the transition to internalization models. In Table 20.2, I compare and contrast compliance-oriented and internalization-oriented behaviors that

TABLE 20.2. BEHAVIORS INFLUENCING SELF-DIRECTION
AND RISK TAKING BY STUDENTS.

Compliance-Oriented Behaviors	Internalization-Oriented Behaviors
Making all the decisions about how the course is to be run. Ignoring or turning down attempts by students to change rules, assignments, deadlines, formats, or subjects. Adhering closely to rules and standards and showing neither fear nor favor in administering them. Avoiding or ignoring feedback from students about their reactions to and evaluations of the course and the teaching and about their needs and desires for change.	Finding ways to place alternatives and choices before students and to modify the content or conduct of the course in response to student influence. Being approachable and understanding in management of the classroom. Using rules and deadlines as ways of helping students manage their time and direct their effort. Being willing to revise or suspend rules when students come up with a better way or when to do so would encourage students to push ahead and take moderate risks. Soliciting and using student feedback during the course, as well as after.
Presenting ideas, facts, and opinion as though they are immutable, demonstrated truth. Winning discussions and arguments with students through superior logic or academic authority. Being careful not to make mistakes or be wrong, and not to expose or publicize one's own errors when they occur.	Questioning and speculating about one's own dogma and discipline. Being impressed or convinced by student thought, criticism, and argument. Showing students when they have made a point or changed one's thinking. Taking risks with ideas, admitting the possibility of being wrong. Exposing one's own mistakes, errors, and inadequacies of knowledge and competence without shame.
Presenting only neat, cleaned-up end results of thinking and research: positive conclusions, findings, facts. Focusing on what is known or authoritatively thought. Dealing with the content of the subject and excluding the processes of search, controversy, and speculation by which knowledge is generated, destroyed, and reconstituted.	Presenting the processes of thinking and learning in all their untidiness, contingency, and deviation from rule. Discussing controversy and search in the past and present, stressing the shifting, temporary nature of our conceptions of truth. Discussing one's own thinking and research, not only in terms of results and certainties, but also in terms of the personal processes of search, choice, evaluation of ideas and findings, and deviation from formally accepted rules of scientific procedure.
Showing mistrust of students' abilities as self-directed learners. Providing instructions which prevent students' having to make choices under conditions of uncertainty. Providing guidelines, information, and answers for any problems which students will face in completing assignments.	Showing confidence in students' abilities as self-directed learners: by leaving many choices open, providing guidelines and instructions that are incomplete and must be filled in by students, raising questions for which answers are not provided. At the same time, standing ready to provide more support and structure when uncertainty and ambiguity threaten to immobilize students' abilities to act.

affect students' freedom and risk taking. In Table 20.3, I make the same kind of comparison for behaviors affecting the depth of encounter with students' goals and values. Each teacher and graduate assistant can apply at least some of the facilitative behaviors without appearing awkward or phony.

Some facilitative behaviors are possible for each of us, but no teacher can demonstrate them all. Sometimes other students are better sources of the behavior than we are. There are several ways, varying greatly in formality, to use graduate and undergraduate students as learning models. At the informal extreme, several experiments indicate that placing effective and ineffective learners together in work groups, discussion sections, or living arrangements results in the less effective students identifying with and adopting the behavior of the more effective ones. Students who are effective learners are, in general, more liked and esteemed by other students than those who are not.

Graduate students used as teaching assistants vary greatly in their effectiveness as role models for students because they are sometimes too strongly identified with the values of the academic world they are trying to enter. Instead of using

TABLE 20.3. BEHAVIORS AFFECTING ENCOUNTER: THE INVOLVEMENT OF STUDENTS' VALUES AND GOALS.

Compliance-Oriented Behaviors	*Internalization-Oriented Behaviors*
"Sanitizing" the subject matter by avoiding value issues, personal goals, and human relevance. Attempting a value-free, objective, and detached presentation of issues. Avoiding the action consequences of knowledge and opinion. Limiting students to talking and thinking, short of action.	Emphasizing the values, goals, and personal choices that are involved in or relevant to the subject matter. Being open about one's own attitudes and values regarding the subject matter. Comparing and contrasting one's own values with those of students, others in one's own field, and society as a whole, and encouraging students to do the same.
Presenting one's own values, opinions, and goals as facts. Investing one's point of view with the weight of academic or personal authority. Using one's persuasiveness and ability in argument and controversy to make students feel inadequate in their own positions or to make them reluctant to expose their values and opinions openly.	Owning up to one's own values but without coercing students to adopt them. Being persuasive without being domineering. Reinforcing students when they question values and choices of the teacher and when they offer alternatives. Being sensitive to the level of persuasion that will stimulate students without shutting them off.
Ignoring or rejecting the values, attitudes, and points of view of the student culture. Alienating the subject matter and oneself from the problems, aspirations, and goals of students. Dealing with intergenerational conflicts as temporary differences between superior, wiser adults and less competent, immature youth. Arrogating special privileges and rights to the older generation.	Learning the values, issues, and points of view of the student culture. Relating these issues to course content wherever possible. Dealing with intergenerational conflict as a controversy between equals, with different goals, interests, and lifestyles, but with equal access to the truth and equal right to be served.

the closeness of the graduate to the student culture, we usually try to strip it away. In doing so, we make it likely that they will have the same difficulties we have in relating with students. If we can avoid this natural desire to perpetuate ourselves, we can train graduate students to take the role of a mature student rather than that of an immature professor in their teaching assignments. We can work through trained graduate or undergraduate assistants by establishing close relationships with them and having them, in turn, work closely with smaller groups of students. Graduate assistants can be most effective if we try to select student-like graduates, and then help them be sensitive, effective members of their own generation rather than stiff, awkward members of ours.

Our innovation in these matters has not, perhaps, progressed very far. I believe that the development of techniques and designs for using students to teach students is the most promising area for experiment in higher education. This is true partly because the shortage of teachers and our increasing preoccupation with the generation and application of new knowledge make us less effective identification models for our students. There is also an increasing generation gap in values and needs between us and our students. Students are going to take one another for role models anyway; therefore we can and should shape this inevitable process in the service of learning. In this connection, the reports of Runkel (1969) and Cahn (1969) are of particular interest. They show quite clearly how effective students can be in helping one another to learn while at the same time maintaining their own position as students.

A Design Issue

I want to look next at a design issue that influences the level of learning process at which students will be able to operate. It has to do with balancing freedom and risk against the anxiety and fear of failure that many students will experience when exposed to free form (ambiguous) learning designs.

Freedom and the opportunity to take risks reduce the certainty of reward and increase the possibility of failure. Students whose development toward internalization has not progressed far will experience anxiety and fear of failure when uncertainty and freedom are increased. Moderate anxiety stimulates effort and problem-solving activity; higher levels tend to immobilize students, make them withdraw from involvement, or make them defensive and antagonistic. Defensive reactions interfere with learning and with the development of effective student-teacher relationships. Some ways of controlling anxiety and fear of failure through classroom design and teacher behavior are suggested here.

Although a high tolerance for ambiguity is a desirable personal characteristic for the innovative teacher, the production of extreme ambiguity for students is not. Most students need to feel that there is someone in the classroom who knows what he is doing. For example, I spend considerable time during the early days of an innovative course explaining the overall course design, the teaching goals I am working toward, what each project or exercise is supposed to accomplish, and what will be expected of students. Student assistants who have previously taken the course can also reduce anxiety (see Runkel, 1969). Just the fact that the student assistants have volunteered to come back and help out is probably a powerfully reassuring message to the newcomers.

In the area of grades, students often need to know that there is some form of insurance against risk. One way of doing this is to set a floor under grades, a minimum level of reward that can be obtained for compliance with basic course requirements. Usually it takes the form of giving a middle grade for minimum performance, for example, for meeting all assignments. The teacher takes a risk that some students will be undermotivated to perform because of the low level of pressure. He hopes to make this up by the involving and intrinsically motivating characteristics of his design.

To reduce the likelihood of early failure, I give an early project that is fairly easy to do well, and grade it liberally. I indicate clearly where I think students could have been more effective on the task, but I do not give really low grades unless there is evidence that inadequate time and effort were expended.

Students tend to have time at the beginning of a term for interesting projects, before the coercive pressures of exams and papers in other courses catch up with them. I use the early part of the term for projects that require a lot of outside work and, as exam time approaches, I reduce the workload. I thereby reduce the likelihood of high stress, anxiety, and failure.

I have found that it is easier for students to apply and test concepts and theories than it is for them to build their own conceptual framework to explain experiences. At the beginning of a course, I usually present students with some concepts and assign to them the task of applying the concepts to data they gather. The project for which the class was asked to interview other students to test Maslow's theory of motivation is a case in point. If I want students to build their own theory inductively from experience, I usually hold that task until later in the course.

The concept of choosing one's own level of risk can be generalized to a design principle. Where possible, students should be able to choose among different degrees of structure, direction, and risk in dealing with the same subject matter. Some students might want to build theory; others will be ready only to apply or test concepts; still others will prefer to take an examination on the material. Of course, following this principle can multiply the teacher's work enormously. It is most likely to be needed where there are wide differences in readiness.

Students are more willing to commit themselves to self-direction and risk if they have some influence over the choice. When I am about to introduce a task that will make students anxious or violate their norms of the student culture, I usually submit it to debate in class. I explain what it is I want them to undertake, and why. I invite them to suggest objections and modifications, and I accept these if I can. On one occasion, I abandoned a project because of student objections.

The need for students to have influence does not stop when the decision is made. When things go wrong, it is important to me to receive rapid feedback. For example, I encourage students to let me know, well in advance, if they are going to have trouble meeting deadlines, so that the problem can be discussed in class and the deadline changed if it is unrealistic.

A Content Issue: When Less Is More

If one is committed to the development of self-direction and the students' ownership of their learning, difficult choices have to be made about content. Unfortunately, it is possible to process a great deal more information in a mechanical and routine way than when the information is to be made relevant to the learner's experience. I have never found it possible to cover as much material in a design maximizing self-direction and involvement as my colleagues can by using more traditional designs. If a student is out interviewing, or observing, or messing about in the laboratory, he cannot be reading or memorizing at the same time.

This has posed no conflict of goals in my classroom. I was not preparing people to be psychologists; I was training them to think psychologically. I did not feel that it was important that they be able to conduct rigorous research investigations nor that they have a firm grounding in the basic facts and findings of my discipline. Where there is a good deal of material to be covered, teachers will be in conflict over the desire to train students to become active, involved learners and the pressure to get on with the job. This is particularly distressing when one's course is a prerequisite for others and there has been an organizational decision about what students should master at each level. Even if the teacher subscribes to the belief (as I do) that the deeper exploration of a limited number of concepts is generally preferable to the more mechanical learning of a large number of facts and relationships, he may not have a wholly free choice.

I have only limited help to offer in this dilemma. I believe that programmed and instrumental techniques increase the efficiency of rote and instrumental learning and save time for higher educational processes. Students can go through texts and programs on their own.

Programmed units can be alternated with projects designed for more active learning. Perhaps passing tests on the informational content of a course could serve as the entrance requirement for more involving activities. In the latter, the focus would shift from the superficial acquisition of a lot of learning to the exploration in depth of a few ideas and concepts. Horn (1969) has shown how programmed instruction itself can be made involving and self-directed. However, his approach would also run afoul of a departmental decision to cover a fixed syllabus, since it permits the breadth or depth of focus to be determined by the individual learner.

I believe it is important to separate routine, compliance-based learning activities from self-directed projects so as to preserve the integrity of the latter. Students who are under pressure to work on routine mechanical material to be tested and graded will find it difficult to commit themselves at the same time to more ambiguously defined and self-directed tasks. External pressures should always be reduced when self-directed activities are called for. In this way, some measure of internalization can be preserved, even in classrooms where there is pressure to cover a lot of ground.

Summary

I have begun by setting goals for the university classroom: that it maximize freedom, encounter, and learning how to learn. Following on from those goals, I have examined the processes by which learning may take place. The goals can best be met by conceptual learning, through discovery and through the testing of concepts and theories. Rote learning and the simpler forms of instrumental learning tend to constrict the student's freedom. Material so learned is often isolated from the values and goals of the individual. I have discussed the levels of development, from dependency on external rewards through the search for values and a stable identity to the full expression of one's potential based on internalized values and standards.

At each level, students respond to different kinds of influence processes. Dependent students respond to influence by compliance: the giving and withholding of relatively tangible rewards. As students free themselves from dependency, they become responsive to influence through identification with the behavior and values of the teacher or other students. As the identity, values, and standards of students become more stable, they become less easily influenced by external rewards, and students have less need for identification models. Influence through internalization processes then becomes effective; the teacher becomes more a consultant to the student's learning activities and less a director or inspirer of learning.

The university classroom contains a mixture of students: a highly dependent minority, a majority seeking values and identity, and another minority that is independent and self-directing. This mixture is usually managed by compliance, with supplementary reliance on identification. The minority of dependent students is effectively influenced through this system, while the majority responds with a mixture of defense and compliance. The learning processes stimulated by the traditional system fall far short of the ideal of high freedom, high encounter, and learning how to learn.

It appears that identification, as a transitional process, can alleviate the strains of the mixture of compliance and internalization in the ordinary classroom.

Unfortunately, acceptability of teachers as identification models has been reduced by social trends and organizational developments in the modern university. However, it is still possible for teachers to use their own behavior to facilitate movement toward higher learning processes. We can also design classrooms where graduate and undergraduate students can serve as identification models for others. The social needs of students can be used to facilitate learning through identification. A natural vehicle is the learning group. I have presented some ways of designing and managing such groups.

Classroom innovation can benefit from a conceptual framework and from some practical guidelines. In the end, however, the innovative teacher is engaged in a self-directed learning experience of his own. Though he can share important parts of the journey with colleagues and students, the most difficult stages will be the loneliest ones. I hope this paper suggests some ways less hard and long. That is all any guide can do. The choices and their consequences belong to the traveler.

CHAPTER TWENTY-ONE

DEVELOPING AUTONOMY, INITIATIVE, AND RISK TAKING THROUGH A LABORATORY DESIGN

I originally undertook the development of the Laboratory in Initiative, Autonomy, and Risk Taking, or autonomy lab, as a kind of challenge to my own creativity, something that seemed worth doing for the intellectual excitement of exploring uncharted territory. I had been living and working in Europe for a couple of years and was given several opportunities to conduct T-groups there. I found the groups low in energy and participant involvement, and I was curious to test my ideas about the causes and to test alternatives that I thought might work better. When I conducted the first autonomy lab, together with Jacques Mareschal of IBM, it gave me a great thrill to see the impact it had on participants. Shortly thereafter, I decided to devote most of my time and energy to the further development of the method.

That felt risky. I had practiced in Britain for several years and had succeeded in establishing a thriving practice as an organization development consultant. It would be a major transition in my professional life to recast my work as that of management educator. However, I was a little dissatisfied with the impact I was able to have on the very large, bureaucratic organizations with which I was then working. I hoped that by changing my focus to the exploitation of this powerful new tool, I might be able to do more good in the world. I conducted the first autonomy lab in the summer of 1971, and after a year's experience with the method, I was ready to make the shift. By 1973, after I published "Developing Autonomy, Initiative, and Risk Taking Through a Laboratory Design," I was well launched in my new career. In the early

Note: Originally published in *European Training*, 1972, 2, 100–116. Reprinted here with permission of *European Training.*

seventies, I designed and promoted a host of variations on the method in all sorts of management education settings, and I took it as far afield as southern Africa. I used the method in business schools, under the auspices of Charles Handy at the London Business School and Hans van Beinum at the Stichting Bedruifskunde in Rotterdam. I designed a self-managed learning approach for training organization development consultants, applying it with Fritz Steele in the Program for Specialists in Organization Development offered by the National Training Laboratories Institute. Then in the United Kingdom, Ian Mangham and I created a three-month program in the manage-

ment of change using a self-directed approach.

Eventually, my use of these methods led me, together with David Berlew, into the development of the Positive Power & Influence Program (described in Chapter Twenty-Two) and the creation of a management training business that involved me until 1981, when I once again turned my attention toward organization development. Although I have done little training in recent years, I have never lost my enthusiasm for the principles described in the following paper, which I have found to provide a strong and flexible foundation for the empowerment of the learner in whatever setting they are applied.

The scene is a fifteenth-century castle converted into a hotel, standing in the midst of rolling countryside somewhere in Northern Europe. The characters are twenty middle managers, about half line and half staff, and two behavioral scientists. The time is a Sunday evening, the opening session of one of the early Laboratories in Initiative, Autonomy, and Risk Taking. The first behavioral scientist is speaking.

> Most of us, most of the time, are so bombarded with expectations, demands, and influence attempts of others that it often becomes very difficult to hear messages from *inside* about what *we* would like to do, how *we* think the job ought to be done, what experience *we* think would be interesting, exciting, and good for our own growth. In most management development courses, it's the same: we're exposed to a lot of pressure to be more sensitive to people or more rational in our approaches to planning, to be more receptive or more proactive, and in general, to follow out someone else's formula for managerial success. Everyone seems to have a slogan, a package, or a formula he wants to use to change our behavior, our values, our styles.
>
> In contrast, this laboratory is an exercise in finding your own interests, strengths, and paths to growth and development. We don't believe there is one right way to do any job as complex as the ones you hold, not least because you all have different strengths, motivations, backgrounds. We believe neither that managers are born nor that they are made; on the contrary, we think that in

large part they create themselves. This laboratory will provide, we hope, a week of open time and a wide variety of resources for you to do just that. We hope that by Friday you may have a clearer idea as to some of the ways in which you would like to grow and develop and that you will have learned quite a lot about how to explore and use the environment actively to further your own growth.

In order to facilitate your listening to yourself, we will place as few restrictions on you as we possibly can. In fact, the only required activity in this laboratory is a two-hour meeting from four to six each afternoon, for which you will be divided into two groups of ten, each meeting with one of us. These meetings are obligatory, and in them, you will be expected to share with others what you have been doing. The meetings are a chance for the staff to keep in touch with everyone in the lab, and we hope that they will also be an opportunity for you to learn from one another's experiences, to help each other to make best use of the learning resources here, and to deal with any of the issues that arise between you and the staff.

There are no times which are arbitrarily assigned to work or to free time. The time is all free for you to use in your own best interests: to work, to play, to contemplate, to be responsible or irresponsible. Unfortunately, the hotel management is not as flexible as we are: the hours between which various meals can be taken are posted over there on a flip chart. So far as we are concerned, the only requirement that you be anywhere or do anything in particular is the two-hour daily meeting.

Before our meeting began, those of you who were wandering about will have noticed that this main conference room is stocked with a large variety of learning resources. In selecting them, we have tried to offer as many options as possible about learning processes. What they all have in common, however, is that they have been selected to enrich your thinking, experiencing, and understanding of yourself as a person, in relationship to other people, and in your role as a manager. On the table over there, are various diagnostic instruments which you can use to assess your own management style, your blocks or difficulties in creative problem solving, your preference for one or another learning process, your dominant motives, and so on. Across the room, there is a collection of books and articles. We have included writings about behavioral sciences in management, humorous and serious observations on organizational life, messages on how to achieve fulfillment and personal growth, and even some fairly subversive writings about how to change organizations from the inside. The library doesn't necessarily reflect our views about what is true, good, or right; it does, however, represent our choice as to what is interesting, significant, or worth thinking about.

You will have noticed that we have also provided a variety of games and exercises. Some of these are standard management training and group dynamics exercises, where we have run off all the materials you need to conduct the exercise. Others are handbooks or manuals of exercises which you may want to thumb through and try out. We have also selected a variety of psychological games which we think you may find interesting, and we have on hand some tape-recorded instructions which allow you to conduct group and interpersonal learning activities without staff assistance. Lastly, we have provided a set of exercises called the Blocks to Creativity which permit you to explore in a self-directed way fourteen different barriers to personal productivity and creativity and, we hope, to overcome these to some extent.

This array of materials is far more than enough for anyone to cover during the week, and we hope you will be as selective as we have been wide ranging in choosing it. In order to give you a good start in exploring these materials, we have made four lists of activities that we believe to be interesting and useful. These are posted on the walls. We suggest that between now and the beginning of the meeting at four tomorrow afternoon you complete at least one exercise from each of the four lists. There is one list of diagnostic exercises, things you can do to assess your styles or skills or to uncover some difficulties you may have. There is one list of exercises that can be done alone, another for two-person exercises, and a third consisting of learning activities that require a small group. It is part of your training in initiative that once having decided on a two-person or small-group exercise, you are responsible for recruiting from amongst the participants the other people required to carry out the learning activity. If you get really stuck, you will usually find that one of the staff will be glad to join in.

In exploring the resources of the laboratory, you will find it important not to overlook those of the other participants and of the staff: that is, the human resources which are here. In any collection such as ours, there is a vast array of experience and talent which can be of use to all of us in our own learning and problem solving. The problem is to find out what is there through taking initiatives to get to know the others and interact with them in various settings. As staff, we will take some responsibility for making our resources available. We will try to respond to any request for help, information, or even advice, and we will initiate conversations with you about your activities and learning experiences when that seems to be appropriate. We do not intend to be passive observers of the scene but rather active participants in it. We expect initiatives from ourselves as well as from you, but if our work is to be of most use to you, it had best be shaped by the actions you take toward us.

That's about all we have to say for now. We will be glad to answer questions from those of you who feel the need for clarification; for those who don't, I suggest you get started with one or another of the suggested learning activities on the four lists.

The group breaks up. Some wander a bit aimlessly about the room looking at the materials, others study the lists of suggested activities, and some ask questions of the staff about them. Gradually, most of the participants find something to do: Some go off toward their rooms purposefully clutching stacks of material; others drift off to the bar to discuss this new experience.

Half Past Ten Monday Morning

One participant is deep in conversation with a staff member who had observed that he looked a bit lost and had asked him how things were going. The problem, a common one, is that the participant has been unable to articulate any learning needs that he could see as related to any of the materials offered. The staff member is questioning him deeply about his work and career aspirations and will end by making several concrete suggestions about diagnostic instruments or learning activities in which he might engage.

Several participants are sitting about the room working on the Personal Inventory, which is the diagnostic instrument for the Blocks to Creativity. These are learning materials developed by Sonia and Ed Nevis of the Cleveland Gestalt Institute.* The participants will identify three or four blocks, such as fear of failure, reluctance to let go, frustration avoidance, impoverished fantasy life, or reluctance to exert influence. They will then take a workbook for each of the blocks they have decided they would like to work on.

Each workbook contains about a dozen exercises designed to increase awareness of the block and provide practice in overcoming it. The exercises use a variety of media and materials. Some can be done alone, while others require a pair or a small group of people.

Other participants are not in evidence at the moment and may be in their rooms, walking in the grounds of the castle, or on some errand into the village. For the most part, it appears that people are working alone. There are a couple of pairs, but they seem to be composed of people who have known each other previously. A few initiatives have been taken toward the staff to ask for information about materials, but the participants have so far treated each other rather gingerly.

Four O'Clock Monday Afternoon

In the small-group meetings, the staff members issue a questionnaire asking participants to rate the level of their own risk taking so far, write down the number of initiatives they have taken toward others, and estimate the proportion of time they have been truly autonomous (that is, doing what *they* really wanted to do, rather than simply following custom or the influence of staff and other participants, or doing what they felt their home organization would expect them to do in this kind of learning situation). Each participant is also asked to rate his in-

Author's note: These materials are no longer available in any form since 1994.

volvement in the laboratory at this moment, as well as the degree of positive or negative feelings he has about it.

These results are then tabulated and posted and discussed by the groups at some length. One group is rather divided in its ratings. Some members are highly involved and see themselves as exercising a fair degree of autonomy and beginning to take some initiatives (though not so many as they would like to). Others are completely "turned off." They complain variously that they do not see the relevance of this kind of education to their work; that the materials seem disorganized and difficult to use; that when they try exercises in the Blocks to Creativity they "don't feel anything"; that even if they do learn to exercise autonomy and initiative in the laboratory, they will have little opportunity to do so in their jobs back home; and so on. The most aggressively outspoken and articulate of the "dissidents" is a former military officer, now operations manager for a large international trucking firm. The main burden of his message is that the staff should clarify the precise objectives to be achieved in the course and should set up and conduct those activities required to reach those objectives. He is strongly supported by other members of the group and equally strongly attacked by several others who claim that he has missed the whole point of the laboratory and wishes not only to give up his own freedom but to regiment everyone else into the bargain. The issues are hotly debated but are no closer to resolution at the end of the meeting than they were at the beginning.

During the meeting of this particular group, the staff member leading it remarks that most of the learning activity that he has seen going on was individual or in pairs and asks the group members to explore some of the inhibitions and barriers that prevent them from approaching others and initiating activities with them. There is some fairly open sharing around this issue. The staff member also points out that the staff is willing to suggest, and if necessary conduct, as highly structured learning activities as the participants desire, and that if those who are experiencing a lack of direction and purpose will come along for a chat, he will be glad to make some specific suggestions for learning activities. One or two of the participants visibly brighten at that, but the operations manager is not mollified. What *he* thinks the organizers should do is to establish a clear set of objectives for the course and conduct learning activities that are clearly related to these objectives. That is their job, not that of the participants.

Wednesday Afternoon

The scene has changed considerably. The main conference room where the materials are kept has a disheveled, used look with books, articles, and test papers scattered about where participants have left them. A group of four are gathered round the table playing a game of Executive Decision, a management game that emphasizes judgment and risk taking in buying and selling. Another group are in a corner rolling dice. They are playing a new game invented by one of the staff members on the inspiration of Rhinehart's *The Dice Man* (1971). It is an anti–decision-making game, in which players experiment with how it feels to give up control of their behavior to blind chance for an hour or two. Each of the players has listed several activities that he thinks he ought to or might like to engage in during the afternoon, and the players are rolling dice to see which ones they will actually carry out. The game is designed particularly for people who underuse or inhibit their own playful and creative impulses by an overemphasis on efficiency, planning, and "making every minute count." At the conclusion of the dice rolling, one member goes off to get the hotel's vacuum cleaner and begins to clean and straighten up the main conference room; another goes out to the back of the castle to make a sketch of an erotic bas-relief set into the wall there; a third takes a book and goes to his room to read; and the fourth goes off to arrange a talk with one of the laboratory participants with whom he has spoken very little because his initial impressions of him were rather unfavorable.

Another group is having an encounter session in one of the smaller rooms. The participants are using a tape-recorded set of instructions to guide their activities. They have had one session already, have become very enthusiastic about this (to them) new way of learning and getting closer to others, and they are developing a certain elitist and cliquish attitude toward themselves.

There remain some who are working as individuals or in pairs. Two or three have developed rather well-articulated self-development plans using the Blocks to Creativity. The operations manager is still aggressively skeptical, and although he does not resist attempts to involve him in the activities of others, he initiates none himself and professes himself to be unaffected by those in which he does participate. Another, sadder case is presented by a middle-aged bureaucrat who is simply bewildered by the proceedings. On inquiry by the staff member who has been working with him, it has developed that when he was offered a chance to attend the laboratory by his personnel officer he agreed without questioning what kind of a training course it was to be. Asked why, he replied that "if the company asked me to go to the seashore to dig holes in the sand for a week with all expenses paid, I'd go along just for the holiday." With no objectives of his own and no daily routine to march to from morning rising to bedtime at night, he seems a rather pathetic figure. He reads a bit, walks occasionally in the countryside, but only really comes to life in the late evening in the bar. Other participants are gentle with him and invite him to join in their activities, but occasionally a little contempt shows through.

Friday

The last day presents some marked contrasts. The high tide of group activity having been passed on Wednesday and Thursday, many of the participants are back to individual and pair activities. There is a renewed interest in the Blocks to Creativity and in some of the diagnostic tests. Those who are still working in groups are mostly engaged in some kind of life- and career-planning exercise that is intended as a bridge between the laboratory and the back-home situation. Some few are using a closed-circuit videotape recorder, which was brought in on Thursday so they could "see themselves as others see them" in face-to-face situations. Others are taking inventory of the library materials with an eye to acquiring copies for their own use.

The closing session of one of the ten-person groups proves a serious, hardworking learning experience rather than the expected round of farewells and testimonials. The group works intensively on exploring the difficulty they have had in using the resources of the staff members during the laboratory. Earlier, there had been a confrontation between some group members who asked that the obligatory afternoon sessions be shortened and the staff member who was unwilling to do so; this had occurred on Tuesday afternoon. The staff member had subsequently felt left out and underused, while some of the participants had been determined to "show him" that they were competent to carry out their learning without his help. There now takes place an exploration of the role of authority in learning and some attempts to generalize this back to the organizations from which the participants have come. Participants try to think of ways to help themselves to maintain their newfound autonomy in a situation where authority will at best be neutral to their efforts. Deeply involved as the members are in these issues, the meeting goes overtime and eventually breaks up on a rather thoughtful and serious note.

A New Design for Personal Development

These vignettes from actual training sessions illustrate the core process of a cluster of training designs called *self-directed learning* (SDL). The core process in SDL is autonomous learning. An autonomous learning process can be said to exist in an educational situation when it becomes hard for educators to find participants who need a helping hand in finding something interesting or productive to do. From this point on, the educator's role becomes truly ancillary and peripheral; the participants genuinely manage their own development. Under various titles (motivation laboratory, laboratory in initiative and autonomy, creativity workshops), the basic design has now been used with upwards of 215 participants in some thirteen separate educational events conducted in five different countries (Belgium, England, Ireland, the Netherlands, and the United States). The basic design and philosophy of the laboratories are described above in the opening remarks to the participants by the staff member. The content of the learning materials may vary quite widely, depending on the educational purpose of the event and the background of the participants. The duration of the laboratories has varied from three days to seven, with five or five and a half seeming about the most effective compromise between the ideal and the practical. With one or two exceptions, the laboratories have been exceptionally well received by participants. I generally consider an experience a "success" if the community develops an autonomous learning process, as defined earlier. This usually occurs somewhere in the middle of the laboratory if it is to happen at all. One recognizes that an autonomous learning process has developed in the community when he begins to find it hard to discover participants who need a helping hand in finding something interesting or productive to do. When autonomous learning takes over, the staff member begins to feel a bit useless and out of things and can take a certain melancholy satisfaction in his loneliness in realizing that things are now going well for the most part and are largely out of his hands anyway.

Antecedents of a New Experiential Design

The educational design that is the subject of this paper bears some resemblance and owes considerable debt to the work of others. Particularly notable are Richard Byrd's Creative Risk-Taking Laboratory (Byrd, 1967); The Organization Laboratory, developed by Jerry Harvey, Barry Oshry, and Goodwin Watson (Harvey, personal communication, 1967); and the Laboratory with Flexible Structures created by Max Pagès and his associates in Paris (Pagès, personal communication, 1971).

I came to this radical focus on autonomous learning by stages. During the sixties, I was deeply involved in the sensitivity training movement, working a great deal with the NTL Institute and sharing much of the value and philosophical base that has since developed into "encounter." We learned a lot about how to produce group learning experiences that were deeply moving and impactful for participants. But participants all too often reported massive difficulties in implementing changes in their work relationships, frequently adding that the major impact of the sensitivity experience was on their family lives. It began to be apparent to some of us that the "soft" T-group culture was difficult to apply in "hard" situations where power, authority, and productivity requirements dominate. We began to feel the need for educational designs that would send the participants back into the world tougher and stronger, ready to deal with the pressures they found there.

It also became apparent that the people who came to places like NTL's Bethel, Maine, training facility were increasingly "soft" people. As sensitivity training became better known, participants were selecting themselves on the basis of their values and personal styles, and we began to see an increasingly skewed population of professional helpers, teachers, staff (as opposed to line) personnel, and a growing proportion of participants who either currently were or recently had been in psychotherapy. Such participants found the T-group culture comfortable rather than confronting, and some tended to become dependent on it. Some people became "groupies," who came back again and again to "charge their batteries," unable to create for themselves in the outside world the closeness and openness they so valued in the group. As a social movement, sensitivity training began to feel more and more inbred and encapsulated.

Thus, when I began to live and work in Europe in 1968, I was already beginning to explore ways in which the richness, diversity, and confrontational impact of the group experience could be reclaimed. This impulse to experiment was hastened by my rather unsatisfactory experiences in conducting T-groups with British and European managers. The groups I conducted seldom seemed to develop a great deal of depth or involvement on the part of the participants, and they seemed to require an inordinate amount of energy and skill on the part of the staff in order to make them go at all.

Existential Differences Between European and American Managers

I thought a lot about the possible causes of these difficulties. After discarding the quite plausible hypothesis that I just was not very skillful with such groups, I concluded that possibly the differences I experienced between American and European T-groups had something to do with cultural differences in existential issues. This mouthful of words means that I had decided that the problems or hang-ups that most deeply disturbed European managers were different from the ones that were bothering the Americans I had worked with, and this difference was somehow a cause of the managers' responses to sensitivity training. American managers seemed to me, by contrast with their British and European counterparts, to be rather more lonely and alienated, more disturbed in their family relationships, hungrier for a missing depth and intimacy in interpersonal relationships generally, and more willing to expose themselves and take personal risks to achieve rapid and satisfying connection with others.

The European managers seemed less geographically and socially mobile than the Americans; they were much more likely to have worked with the same company all their professional lives. They frequently lived close to their own and their wives' parents, and they were much less likely to transfer between departments within their firms. They were thus securely embedded in a matrix of organizational, family, and community relationships which appeared to meet their relationship needs much better than was true for most of the Americans. At the same time, the Europeans paid for their stability with a sense of immobilization, entrapment, and a degree of impotence within their organizations. They seemed more often dissatisfied with the amount of authority and responsibility they had, and they were more likely to express themselves in defeatist terms about the possibilities of initiating and carrying out change and innovation. To a person in such an existential situation, a group may not seem to be a source of needed intimacy and acceptance but instead may encapsulate the individual and frustrate his individual growth and development. In my thinking about the problem, I became fascinated with the possibility of designing experience-based training that would make use of the insights gained in sensitivity training but would boldly abandon the forms and technology of the T-group and build afresh something more appropriate to the cultural milieu in which I was then working and living. I set myself the following objectives for the design:

- The learning experience should radically avoid the creation of dependency relationships. In contrast to sensitivity training and encounter experiences, the learning should not depend on the support of a small group, the leadership of charismatic educators, or the use of powerfully coercive educational technology like the T-group (Harrison, 1965a).
- The learning experience should strengthen the learner's initiative and commitment to the pursuit of his or her own learning goals. It should give participants confidence in their ability to manage their own learning, through a toughening experience begun during the formal learning event. For example, participants are encouraged in my training designs to be "self-oriented" in their responses to others who ask them to join with them in group activities. Both forming a learning group and leaving a learning group build autonomy. Passively joining a group and staying in it do not.
- The learning should foster the perception of oneself as a center of energy and decision—an origin of action rather than a pawn of outside forces.

An Experimental Design for Developing Initiative, Autonomy, and Risk Taking

With my like-minded colleague Jacques Mareschal, I developed and conducted the first such laboratory for a group of middle managers in Belgium in June, 1971. It was like the laboratory which is described in the opening paragraphs of this paper. It was called a "motivation laboratory," because we had the idea that it was necessary for a person first to understand his own needs and motives, those most basic wellsprings of energy and activity, before he could take in hand his own personal development and growth. I do not use the original term anymore because it does not communicate very well to the public; but I still agree with this original principle.

The Laboratory in Initiative, Autonomy, and Risk Taking (my current name for the experience) is too new to have been evaluated by research. It has been enthusiastically embraced by most of the participants who have experienced it, but I want to assess it by other criteria. I propose to do this by considering the method as an attempt to put into practice a number of principles or theories about learning, some of which are generally accepted, and others about which there may be more controversy.

The Principle of Internal Motivation

The first principle against which I should like to compare the laboratory is a motivational one.

*Effective training designs make maximum use
of the learner's own internal motives, values,
interests, and felt needs.*

The learner's interests and needs facilitate the channeling of the learner's own motivation into productive learning activities. Minimum energy is required from the teacher or learner in overcoming "resistances."

Thus, a corollary to the first principle deals with the control of behavior during the learning process.

*Needed control of the learner's behavior is accomplished by
providing intrinsically rewarding options, rather than
by telling, selling, or coercion.*

The Laboratory in Initiative, Autonomy, and Risk Taking is designed to be consonant with these motivational principles, and that is one of its greatest assets. It evokes little resistance on the part of participants because of the respect we show to their needs and wishes. The learner is presented with an opportunity to follow his own interests and values wherever they may take him. Much of the design effort is devoted to providing materials which will be experienced by participants as interesting, useful, and rewarding. The message conveyed by staff-participant interactions is well summed up by the phrase, "Try it, you'll like it." Throughout the laboratory experience, participants undertake activities on their own, find them rewarding, and are thereby encouraged to higher levels of independent activity and initiative. By providing a wide variety of materials, the laboratory allows each participant to find some outlet or connection to his felt needs in what has been designed to be a rich and responsive learning environment.

A Coercion-Free Learning Setting. As I experience these laboratories, they are the least coercive of any educational experiences which I have conducted or in which I have taken part as a participant. In this regard, they embody the principle of using *internal motivation,* which I have set forth in two previous papers (Harrison, 1969 [Chapter Twenty], 1970 [Chapter Two]). The entire thrust is for participants to listen to their own needs, wants, and desires, and even gentle persuasion may shift the focus from the self to the person of the educator. Gentle persuasion is sometimes needed (see the following section), but once it has done its work, the staff moves back into a supportive stance.

The Vulnerability of the Learning Process to Participants' Willingness. This lack of coercion is also the Achilles' heel of the method. By contrast with the coercive and norm-setting power of the small group and/or the charismatic leader in other experiential learning methods (T-groups, Synanon sessions, encounter groups, and so on), the Laboratory in Initiative, Autonomy, and Risk Taking applies little or no pressure to keep the learner involved with the learning situation.

It helps a lot when participants make a truly voluntary choice to attend such a laboratory and start out wanting to have a positive experience. In a number of the laboratories, there have been individuals who were sent by their organizations without much respect for their own wishes, who found in the program little to generate enthusiasm, and who opted out of the action for most of the laboratory experience. In the one or two unsuccessful programs I have had, there was a "critical mass" of such people, who absorbed so much of the energy of the others that there was not much left for learning.

Once participants begin working with the materials and with each other and experience the fun and excitement of learning as high play, there is little difficulty in keeping things moving. At first, they are a bit shy and fearful of choice. They seem to be afraid of failure, as though there is some inner shame in making the wrong choice. I provide an annotated card file of the optional exercises, games, and reading materials organized by focus, as follows:

- *Intrapersonal:* useful for exploring personality, skills, attitudes, values, creativity, imagination. Oriented to understanding and experiencing deeper aspects of the self.
- *Interpersonal:* useful for learning about one's styles of interaction with others and for enhancing one's interpersonal skills through practice.
- *Group level:* useful for understanding how groups work and for acquiring skill in working in groups.
- *Organizational level:* useful for exploring and understanding organizational dynamics and the relationship of the individual to the organization.

The Educator as Emergency Road Service Provider. Staff members find it important to watch for people who seem at loose ends and to help them find things to do that meet some inner need. I will interview a participant who seems a little "lost" about what he would like to learn and then suggest to him some activities that might give satisfaction. Many people are not used to being asked or asking themselves, "What would please (stimulate, intrigue, challenge) me right now?" It is hard for them to tune in and listen to their inner voices.

I do not press people to use the learning materials provided. Sometimes I will advise spending time alone, taking a walk, or reading. Most participants respond well to such help. They are like a car with a weak battery. Once the staff can get their motors started, they move along fine on their own. So I work with stalled participants only until they find a direction of inquiry. Then I leave them to get on with it. That and counseling people who want to reflect with an understanding listener on the experiences they are having are pretty much the extent of the staff's professional responsibilities during the free activity period. During the mandatory small-group meetings, staff members facilitate participants in making sense of the laboratory as an innovative learning experience and help them work through whatever feelings come up around their participation.

The Principle of Multiple Learning Tracks

The second principle against which to assess the autonomy lab has to do with the individuation of learning.

The ideal design should permit the individual to spend time and effort upon different learning activities which are appropriate to his degree of background and preparation, his rate and style of learning, and the use which it is projected he will make of the material to be learned.

There are really two lines of reasoning involved in this principle. One is that ideally each individual should have a program of learning tailor-made to his own needs. He should be able to go into great depth on some matters which are new to him or which are likely to be particularly useful in his work or outside life, and he should be able to avoid or deal superficially with other matters in which he may be well prepared or which are irrelevant to his interests and needs.

Choosing and Using One's Preferred Learning Style(s). The individual should be able also to choose and use his strengths as a learner. Some people learn better through concrete experience, others through abstract conceptualization, and so on (Kolb, Rubin, and McIntyre, 1971). While it is desirable that an individual be stretched to strengthen those learning processes which he does not use effectively, I think that people learn most effectively when they are not blocked from using those styles with which they are most comfortable. The totally experiential learning design puts formidable barriers in the way of a person who learns most effectively through abstract conceptualization, just as a formal lecture and reading course is frustrating for a person who learns through active experimentation. Such persons find traditional classroom learning difficult to use and apply in their daily lives. The learning resources gathered together to stock a learning laboratory in initiative and autonomy can easily be designed to offer a wide range of learning *processes* to participants, so that individuals can both use those processes at which they are adept and gain increased skill in those with which they are less comfortable.

A major philosophical theme in this emphasis on individualizing learning is the concept of *equifinality* in learning and problem solving. Basically, the concept means that there are many roads to the same goal, and that each individual will learn best when left to use a road he knows and with which he is comfortable. One of the best examples of the concept is in management by objectives. The idea is that once a goal has been clearly established and accepted, each individual should be free to find his own best means and paths to that goal, using his unique talents and strengths to achieve success. This is in contrast to the explicit philosophy of scientific management that there is one best way to do each job. In management by objectives, a great deal more *trust* is placed in the capacity of the individual to attain goals without explicit programming regarding the precise steps or paths to be taken.

The Meta-Learning Goal of the Autonomy Lab. The autonomy lab makes a similar assumption about the individual as a learner and problem solver, trusting him to find the best combination of activities for achieving his own goals but providing him with opportunities for consultation and access to the resources of others. In carrying out this process, the participant is *learning how to learn:* that is, he is learning how to establish and clarify his own learning goals and to explore the environment for resources useful in attaining the goals. The Laboratory in Initiative, Autonomy, and Risk Taking goes a long way toward actualizing the promise of learning how to learn which was often made but seldom kept by the early proponents of T-groups and sensitivity training. It was difficult for the sensitivity trainers to keep this promise because learning in the T-group depends upon the creation and utilization of a highly specialized learning environment and technology, in which the trainer's skills are very central if not indispensable. This is not the case in the autonomy lab where the individual is encouraged to create his own learning program individually, using materials that are available in the environment and depending upon himself to build those relationships with others that are required to utilize the materials effectively.

The Principle of Optimum Confrontation

The third learning principle by which I like to assess designs has to do with the management of anxiety and stress.

> *The confrontation and resulting amount of anxiety and stress should be maintained for each individual at the level where he is stimulated to explore, experiment, and learn in an active fashion, and it should not be permitted to rise to the point where he becomes immobilized or where his normal ways of coping become so ineffective that he regresses to less effective behavior patterns (Harrison, 1965b [Chapter Eighteen], 1970 [Chapter Two]).*

Groups Seldom Provide Optimum Confrontation for All Their Members. Maintaining the appropriate level of stress and confrontation has been a perennial problem in experiential learning, particularly in sensitivity training and encounter groups. When working with a small group the problem becomes almost impossibly complicated by the obvious fact that the appropriate level for one person is likely to be too much or too little for another. Since groups tend to develop norms about stress (for example, they can be "deep" groups or relatively more cognitive and "talky" in their process), all the members tend to be exposed to the same fairly narrow range of confrontation. This sometimes results in psychological damage to weaker members of the group. Or an entire group may avoid confrontation in order to protect one or two fragile members.

In the autonomy lab, the potentially high stress of a learning experience that is very unstructured in time, space, and direction of activity is balanced by the opportunity for the individual to have free access to learning activities that are very nonconfronting. For example, it is not uncommon to see members who are having difficulty with the lack of structure spending a good deal of time with books and articles until they gain more confidence and are able to use more active exercises. I also find that the more adventurous, emotionally stronger participants are likely to be the first to use such potentially threatening materials as the Group Therapy Game and the encounter tapes. When the safety of this new territory has been explored and established, other members may feel free to join in, but there are always those who never take part in such exercises.

Staff also find that people often choose a cycle of confrontation and withdrawal for themselves that seems to make a rather sensible rhythm of stress and recovery. Of course, groups can be observed to do this as well, but the cycle does not necessarily meet the needs of all the individual members.

Participants Choose Their Level of Confrontation Wisely. It is of course possible that if the individual is left to seek his own level of confrontation he will tend to operate at a level that produces less than the maximum possible learning. In my experience with these laboratories, this seems rarely to be the case where the individual is strongly motivated to learn. What I have been impressed with is the way in which the level of confrontation tends to be maintained by the individual at a level where his learning seems to be *integrable:* that is, most people seem to choose those experiences which take them on from where they are in a series of steps rather than in a great leap forward or "breakthrough."

A program in which the level of stress is self-moderated in this way is not only safer for the individual but probably results in a higher degree of retained and usable learning than more dramatic methods. One of the major advantages of the self-directed learning design is the opportunity it presents for self-control of confrontation and stress. In my experience with this design, I have seldom had cause to be concerned about the effects of psychological stress on individual participants. I could not make a similar statement regarding my experience with sensitivity training.

Evaluating Self-Directed Learning: What Good Is It?

When I get to this point in the exposition of the autonomy lab to colleagues or clients, they are likely to raise a potentially embarrassing question. "It all sounds very good and quite effective," they say, "but of what real use is it likely to be?

How many organizations do you know in the current economic climate who want to train their managers to be autonomous? The whole thing has a very anarchistic ring." Even those who see very readily the utility of this training to organizational improvement usually say that, as far as they can see, the market is far from ready for it.

Constrained as I am to making my living from my consulting and educating activities, I find this kind of feedback rather depressing. However, I do not completely agree with it. It seems to me that, on the contrary, the laboratory design which I have described in this paper, and the many variations upon it which are possible, have substantial prospects for the short-term and an extremely bright future in the longer term.

Where my skeptical friends and clients are right is in suggesting that this particular laboratory design has not much to offer in educating managers to perform roles that are essentially bureaucratic in structure and process.

Toward Learning Organizations

Traditional management training is education for bureaucracy. It teaches the individual to look outside himself for the solutions to problems and for guidelines to action. These are amply provided by the bureaucracy in the form of job definitions, organization charts, procedural specifications, and the like.

However, bureaucracy is under increasing stress from within and without. Donald Schön has very persuasively made the case in *Beyond the Stable State* (Schön, 1971) that the increasing rate of change in society, technology, and the marketplace means that bureaucratic organizations must increasingly give way to organizations which function as learning systems. And learning organizations require managers who can manage their own learning. The days when a highly centralized management could control or even adequately predict its environment are, I think, numbered. Attempts to deal with crisis by recentralization and increasing tight controls from the top will in the long run give way to movements toward building more flexible, internally committed organizations which adapt, innovate, and change themselves more rapidly than could have been thought possible in the old-style bureaucracy. The essential processes in such an active learning system seem to be as follows:

- Goal directedness: an awareness of one's own goals and the mobilization of energy toward them.
- Active exploration of the environment and of one's own resources, leading to an increased awareness of alternative means to goals.
- Action upon the environment.
- The search for feedback, for knowledge of results, and the use of such information to modify action.

In order for organizations to function as learning systems in this way, it is necessary that managers be adept in the use of such processes, and this is indeed what the autonomy lab is all about. No matter what the content of the learning resources that have been provided (and they could run the gamut from human relations to economics and production control), the self-directed learning *process* remains the same.

Managerial Tasks That Need Self-Directed Learning Now

Even now, at a time when economic and social difficulties are being dealt with by an attempt to increase control and direction from the top in most private and public organizations, there are parts of each of these organizations that either are or have a strong need to be nonbureaucratic in their structure and functioning. These are the parts which are in contact with the rapidly shifting, turbulent aspects of the environment, whether these aspects be scientific and technological areas or markets and suppliers or social and governmental forces. Managers who deal with these aspects of the environment have a current and pressing need to become effective and autonomous learners.

There is also a growing category of managers who are given important job responsibilities that are essentially nonbureaucratic or perhaps antibureaucratic in nature. These are jobs which require one to function outside normal channels of communication, to exercise influence without authority, and often to operate in the spaces between more traditional and highly structured subunits of the organization. These managers may find themselves in coordinating and liaison work, in project management, in many kinds of technical staff work, and in organizational change roles. They too have need for a high degree of autonomy, initiative, and risk taking in learning and in working with the individuals and units with which they interact in the organization. These people need today the kinds of education which the autonomy lab design makes possible in a number of content fields, and it is my hope that tomorrow they will be the ones who will help organizations to find ways to change themselves from bureaucracies to learning systems.

Adapting Self-Directed Learning to Other Content

Whether or not one shares my somewhat gloomy prediction regarding the viability of bureaucracy in the medium- to long-term, there is another way of looking at the initiative and autonomy design that I believe is worthy of careful study by those concerned with management education (or, indeed, with higher education generally). I believe that almost any *applied* subject can be adapted with profit to the same basic design that I have used in the laboratories described here.

Managers usually go on courses because they want to learn something related to their work. Typically, the educator makes some guess as to what sort of work situations most of the managers are in and selects from among the things he knows those which he feels it would be good for the managers to learn. The success rate of these guesses does not appear to be very high. I believe the success of such courses in providing real help to managers could be dramatically improved if the resources were presented in a format similar to the design described above.

Initially, the manager entering the course would need to go through some sort of diagnostic procedure, which would have to be carefully designed to relate the content of the course to his own difficulties, problems, opportunities, or responsibilities in his job. The task of preparing such diagnostic material is not familiar to most management educators and would probably be the most difficult phase of the course redesign. Such a task does not, however, seem to me to present any very formidable technical obstacles.

Resources for the course would be made available on a random access basis to the participants. These resources might include materials in a variety of media: books, articles, case studies, audio or video tape-recorded lectures, and the educator himself. The diagnostic exercise would refer participants to particular learning resources according to the type and level of problem the participants presented, and the instructor would also serve as a guide to help match participant needs to learning resources. Participants could, as in the autonomy lab, be formed into mutual help and learning groups which would exchange information about resources and perhaps assist one another in applying learning experiences in the course to individual back-home problems.

Although there are some managers who will find this kind of learning design a bit difficult to get used to and to use effectively, prospective students are more ready for the design than educators are to give it to them. Partly, this is a matter of developing the requisite technical and interpersonal skills to design and carry out such a learning experience, but perhaps more fundamentally, it is a question of the personal needs for control and participation on the part of the educator and of the level of preferred risk taking and trust in the participants. Once a self-directed learning activity is well launched, there may be very little for the educator to do. He or she needs to be available in case his or her expertise is required, but most of the time, the participants are doing all right by themselves, and the educator feels distinctly redundant. Since many educators derive a good deal of satisfaction from students' dependence on them, this can be a rather depriving experience.

The same applies to the control of the learning process. In fact, we do not really control the *learning* process in most management education, but we do control the *activities* and the materials to which participants are exposed. In a self-directed design, however, this control is given up at the outset and cannot be regained without a tremendous loss of confidence on the part of the participants and loss of face on the part of the educator. This means that self-directed education can be a rather risky business. If one gives up the responsibility to participants for determining their own activities and if they are not motivated to take it over, it is possible to have a very uncomfortable situation in which no one has the power to make anything happen. I have experienced this in two autonomy labs, and it was anything but pleasant. Thus the educator must be willing to take more risk than he is normally used to in order to experiment with and perfect a self-directed learning design in his own subject matter area. One is always more highly criticized for an experiment that fails than for carrying on a more traditional process that is boring and ineffective.

The above caveats to the contrary notwithstanding, I have considerable confidence that self-directed learning methods will produce significant increases in the relevance and effectiveness of educational activities, even in subject matter areas outside of the behavioral sciences. I believe my colleagues and I have only begun to learn what we can do. As we explore and experiment, this first report will be followed by others detailing our further learnings.

CHAPTER TWENTY-TWO

SELF-DIRECTED LEARNING: A RADICAL APPROACH TO EDUCATIONAL DESIGN

As a personal development experience, the Laboratory in Initiative, Autonomy, and Risk Taking was a critical success, in that almost everyone liked the experience and learned a lot. The autonomy labs, as they came to be called, appealed to the sorts of people who went to T-groups and encounter groups, and I believe that in Europe the autonomy lab worked much better than these U.S. imports. The labs were a hard sell, though, partly because training managers in large bureaucratic companies were reluctant to send people off to something that offered to return them to work as autonomous, risk-taking initiators of action! Had the labs been invented ten years later, they would probably have been more wel-

come. It was also difficult to specify the outcomes, dependent as they were on choices made by the participants during the program itself.

During the two or three years I worked with the autonomy lab, my colleagues and I designed and conducted programs based on autonomous learning for managers and professionals in ten countries in Europe, Africa, and North America. The methods were modified and extended by educators who attended those programs and went on to run their own. I like to think that I had some modest influence in beginning the vigorous tradition of self-managed management development that has grown up in the U.K. during the last twenty-odd years.

Note: Originally published in *Simulation and Games*, 1977, *8*(1), 73–94. Reprinted here, with revisions, with permission of Situation Management Systems, Inc.

Following my work with the autonomy lab, I was convinced that self-directed learning would empower participants in learning focused content, just as it had empowered their personal expansion in its original free-form process. I experimented successfully with a variety of applications of self-directed learning, all of which were content focused, including programs for training consultants and managers in the management of change, which I designed and conducted with Fritz Steele in the United States and Ian Mangham in Britain. In the early seventies, I collaborated with David Berlew to develop the Positive Power & Influence Program, a program designed to increase the flexibility and effectiveness of participants' interpersonal influence behavior. I spent a decade deeply involved in the design and commercialization of the Positive Power & Influence Program, experiences I describe in some detail in Chapter Five of *Consultant's Journey* (1995). Now solely owned by Situation Systems, Inc., of Hanover, Massachusetts, the program has been very successful and surprisingly durable. Hundreds of training professionals have become qualified to conduct it, and thousands of participants have participated in the program and in its successor, the Positive Negotiation Program. I am told that both programs continue to attract a steady flow of participants.

"Self-Directed Learning: A Radical Approach to Educational Design" was written to bring together in one place the learnings that I and my colleagues garnered about self-directed learning from our experiences with the autonomy labs, from our work in training people for change management roles, and from the application of self-directed learning in the Positive Power & Influence Program. (I have rewritten parts of it to minimize overlap with Chapter Twenty-One, "Developing Autonomy, Initiative, and Risk Taking Through a Laboratory Design." Chapter Five in *Consultant's Journey* describes in some detail the design and commercialization of the Positive Power & Influence Program. Chapter Six, "Personal Power and Influence in Organization Development," in this volume discusses styles of influence.)

I begin this paper with an overview of the design features of the Positive Power & Influence Program. Then I describe a "design template" that underlies this design and its siblings. I continue by elaborating a set of design principles that can be used by others who wish to introduce self-directed learning into their own courses and programs.

In contrast to the looseness and inclusiveness of the Autonomy Labs, David Berlew and I built the Positive Power & Influence Program around a tight model of interpersonal influence styles and skills. Our idea was to begin the program with conventional control by the trainers, and then progressively give more and more choice to participants as they became familiar with the model and were ready to assume responsibility for their own learning. Here are the stages in this process.

Diagnosis and Learning the Model

Before coming to the Positive Power & Influence Program, participants began their learning by filling out the Influencing Styles Questionnaire, and they were also asked to obtain completed questionnaires from four or five colleagues of their choice. Thus they began the program with data for comparing their self-perceptions of their influence styles and skills with the perceptions of others who knew them. We spent the first day of five in structured exercises for learning the model and for diagnosing one's strengths and weaknesses in using the four basic influence styles: Rewards and Punishment, Assertive Persuasion, Participation and Trust, and Common Vision. We used video recording and playback, with detailed observation and recording of the influence behaviors actually used by each participant. Participants thus went away from that first day with coherent and, for the most part, consistent information on which styles and behaviors they used and which they avoided.

Exploring Alternative Influence Styles and Behaviors

On the second day, we gave participants choices among several *tracks* for exploring and experiencing influence styles and skills that they normally underused or avoided. Within each of the tracks, participants chose from a cafeteria of short, structured role-plays. The instructions for these role-plays specified that they were to be carried out using only the behaviors from one of the four influence styles in the model. Thus each track provided a "total immersion" experience of one style. Our intent was not for participants to acquire skill in using the style but for them to get a thorough exposure to the style's "look and feel."

Self-Directed Learning

On the third and fourth days, we moved fully into self-directed learning. We told participants, "Now you have learned the model, and you have discovered which of the styles and skills you use well and which you avoid using. During the tracks, you have explored some styles and behaviors you normally do not use. Now you are ready to make informed choices about your learning goals and to choose your own paths to those goals. You may choose to develop skills in influencing styles you have formerly avoided. You may choose to perfect your use of styles in which you already have quite a lot of skill. The choice is yours."

At that point, we provided participants with an annotated catalogue of learning exercises and activities, and we offered our services to help people choose those activities that would best achieve their learning goals. For two days, they were on their own to manage their own learning, except for mandatory small-group review sessions with a staff member once each day.

Situation Replays

On the fifth day, we once more provided a tighter structure, as participants prepared to apply their learnings in their work situations. Prior to attending, participants had been asked to describe an unresolved influence situation in which they were currently involved and to bring the description with them to the program. During the last day, we had them work in triads to diagnose their influence situations, plan how to resolve the situations, and practice using appropriate influence styles to reach their personal goals. Participants coached each other as they recorded role-plays of their individual application situations and then did them over again until they were satisfied they would be able to carry out their plans under the pressure of the real-life situation.

Experiences with Self-Directed Learning

The Positive Power & Influence Program is only one of the forms in which David Berlew and I, together with our former colleagues in Situation Management Systems, have embedded the basic self-directed learning design template. We have created designs for training trainers in using experiential learning methods; programs in consulting and the management of change; programs for developing entrepreneurial skills and attitudes in engineering and scientific staff; a program for "managing your boss"; and training in the skills of long-cycle selling. All these have been based on the original design template, which consists of the following:

- A clearly articulated conceptual framework
- Initial self-diagnosis, preferably involving participant collection of data from associates and colleagues
- Structured experiences in which participants assess their skills and knowledge
- Some experiential exposure to a wider range of behaviors and situations than the learners are currently skilled in dealing with
- A self-directed skills- and knowledge-building section, using both experiential and more traditional training materials
- Structured application planning

Our experience with these programs supports the following generalizations:

- The format lends itself to a wide variety of program contents.
- The programs develop extremely high participant motivation, involvement, and satisfaction.
- Self-directed learning designs successfully accommodate a wider range of individual differences in level of preparation, readiness for personal risk taking, and learning pace than any other approach we know.
- The programs deal with deeply personal attitude and value issues with less participant stress than do group-based approaches.
- Participants report more concrete and specific examples of work-related application following self-directed learning than they do when the same material

is dealt with by traditional classroom methods or by training designs relying on small-group experiential processes.

The need for self-directed education grows out of the changing environmental conditions in which organizations exist. Organizational environments are increasingly characterized by instability, complexity, and rapid change. Bureaucratic and traditional organizations may manage to insulate their members from some of the impact of these turbulent environments, but such sheltering is effective only in the short- or medium-term. The skill obsolescence of managers and technical personnel illustrates the problem. Technical knowledge and specialized skills are unstable; they have a shorter useful life than that of the person who possesses them. But often, when a person's specific job skills become obsolete or redundant, the person does also, because the capacity to learn and adapt seems to be missing or to have atrophied from lack of use. It is becoming a truism among management development specialists that both organizations and their members need to learn at a rapid rate long past the point at which they were previously thought to reach a stable and mature state and to begin to decline.

With few exceptions, the education available to people in organizations does not focus on the development of this capacity to learn, change, and grow. It tends to be *problem centered*, providing knowledge, skills, or even attitudes that the educator presumes the learner needs. The *learner-centered* orientation that might foster the inner capacity to develop oneself in response to changing demands, difficulties, and problems thrown up by a turbulent environment is missing in most formal education. (This may be one reason why many competent and experienced managers place a low value on formal management education.)

In a rapidly changing environment, the knowledge and skills that are provided the learner in the problem-centered approach tend to become obsolescent rapidly. Thus traditional management education can require that continual work be done on the manager, at considerable expenditure of time, money, and effort. This work could be avoided if the manager were both capable and motivated to develop himself or herself, to devote inner resources to learning, changing, and growing as he or she is stimulated to do so by changing environmental pressures and demands.

This thinking leads to the idea of self-directed learning as a teaching/learning process that involves the manager actively in diagnosing personal learning needs, setting development goals, exploring the environment for educational resources, and carrying out learning activities for himself or herself. This educational process can have both a problem- or content-centered aspect, and a process-centered one: as the participant works on whatever problem he or she brings to the learning situation, he or she is also developing the attitudes and skills required for continuous self-development, for learning how to learn.

In the many spheres of public and private life, complexity is increasing, structures and relationships change ever more rapidly, and acquired knowledge is ever more evanescent and unstable. The need to become both a continuous learner and a self-directed learner presents itself in a multitude of forms to nearly every individual. My thesis is that this need cannot be met by traditional methods of education. Self-directed learning has great promise for releasing *and keeping alive* the creativity and capacity for growth and change that become increasingly dormant in many of us as we age.

To understand why I think self-directed learning is so much more promising than traditional methods for freeing and empowering the adult learner, it is necessary to examine the learning models or principles on which my and my colleagues' learning designs are based.

More Principles of Adult Learning and Educational Design

In my first paper on self-directed learning (Harrison, 1972a [Chapter Twenty-One]), in which I describe the autonomy lab, I articulate three design principles. They are:

- The principle of internal motivation: educators evoke and build on the learner's own felt needs and interests.
- The principle of multiple learning tracks: educators build in opportunities for learners to go their separate ways within the overall program.
- The principle of optimum confrontation: educators provide opportunities for learners to choose their own pace, their own level of emotional stress, and their own rhythms of activity and rest. Educators trust learners to make wise choices in these matters.

After some years of experience with self-directed learning, I can expand on what I said in 1972.

Understanding the Game of Training Design

Every designer of training has to take into account the internal needs, motives, and values of the learner and the external means employed by others to control and influence the learner's behavior during and after the formal learning experience. Most traditional learning methods do not take the learner's internal states into account. When they are considered, assumptions are made about the average or modal learner. The needs, motives, and values of the individual learner are scarcely considered. One reason is that the educator has little or no access to such information when important design decisions are being made.

When one is limited to very general knowledge about the people who are to be influenced, the control and influence processes one chooses tend to be simplistic. The educator does not know the students personally in advance of the program and often does not know the students' application situations either. The educator decides, on the basis of his or her own experience, knowledge, or values, what is to be learned, and then constructs a program to coerce, seduce, or persuade the learner into learning those things. Here are some typical scenarios of the learning games that result.

- *The Classroom Game.* Participants are assigned to training activities as part of their jobs. They understand that they are expected to treat the educator as an authority figure and to take the student role that they have learned in school or university. They listen politely, do assigned reading, take notes on the content, and so on. Sometimes they are required to pass examinations on the content.
- *The Expert Game.* The educator uses prestige or specialized knowledge to convince the learner of the former's superior understanding of the matters under discussion and to encourage the learner to depend on the educator's expertise.
- *The Charisma Game.* By being charismatic, attractive, or sympathetic, the educator presents himself or herself as a model for the learner to identify with. Effective public speakers do this.
- *The Group Process Game.* The educator forms small groups to work on problems or cases. The groups then establish norms of opinion and attitude to which their members conform, at least on the surface. The groups become satisfying to the members and provide comfortable and supportive milieux for learning. The progress of each individual member is facilitated by the group's action. To a large degree, the individuals depend on the group to manage their learning.
- *The Interactive Learning Game.* The educator uses structured tasks, games, or simulations designed so that the desired attitudes and behaviors lead to success. The learner goes through these activities a little like a rat through a maze, rewarded by success for making the right moves, punished by failure for wrong decisions. The immediacy of feedback keeps the learner engaged.

Most trainers and educators use some mix of these learning games in order to influence learners to bring their attention and energy to bear on what is to be learned. These processes applied by the educator interact with the internal attitudes, needs, and interests of the learner. If there is a good "fit" between internal and external forces, they reinforce each other and the experience is felt to be successful by learner and educator. At the other extreme, the external and internal forces may be in opposition, leading to a difficult experience. The educator may have to use all his or her power and skill to overcome learners' tendencies, or if they cannot be overcome, to rediagnose needs and redirect the learning program to meet the demands of the stronger and more active participants.

Education in this vein becomes a competitive game between educators and students: the stronger, more intelligent, and more attractive educators "win" and the weaker, duller, less appealing ones "lose." In traditional education, a good teacher influences the students to achieve predetermined learning goals. The learner has the choice of playing the teacher's game or reacting against it; there are few opportunities for the learner to play his or her own game or develop and operate a personal scoring system. The alternative to dependency and compliance is not independence, but rebellion.

When such education is successful, the student comes away intellectually or emotionally changed but no stronger in the ability to create and manage his or her own learning process. When the learner returns to the work situation, then the changes produced during the educational experience are extremely vulnerable to the environment. If the new learning fits the direction of the immediate external pressures, it tends to be used and retained. If it does not, a new process of coercion, seduction, and persuasion begins, to reeducate the learner to give up or at least suppress his or her newly acquired attitudes, opinions, skills, and knowledge. The final outcome of the educator's efforts is determined during this reentry process, and the educator normally ends up with virtually no control over those events that most determine the ultimate success or failure of the training activities. During the formal training program, tremendous amounts of energy and skill go into control of the temporary learning process, only to be wiped out or undermined by the stronger and more enduring forces of the larger environment.

Most adult educators are aware that much of the time they do not know and cannot significantly control either the needs and motives of the learner or the environmental forces governing application and continued learning. This awareness leads to renewed attempts to win the game through the application of creativity and skill.

Giving Up the Game in the Service of Learning

In self-directed learning, we educators *give up trying to win the game.* We accept that both the learner's own forces and those of the environment are stronger and more enduring than any we control, and we find ways of working selectively with those forces rather than against them. In doing this, we choose to work primarily with the learner's own forces, partly because they are most accessible to us and partly because of our conviction that organizations and the larger society need self-directed learners to cope with rapidly changing environmental forces.

Almost everything my colleagues and I do and achieve in designing and conducting self-directed learning programs stems from this radical decision to serve the participant's growth toward autonomy and responsibility as a learner. I shall describe a number of ways in which we operate to facilitate the individual's identification of his or her own learning needs and goals, and to provide help and support for playing one's own game.

We give participants maximum feasible choice at all points. I have described this concept earlier, and I have shown how Dave Berlew and I designed the Positive Power

& Influence Program to give participants maximum feasible choice. Early on in a learning experience, people may be reluctant to make choices, and they may not know enough to make important or complex choices. So we give them easy, simple choices and work up to the harder ones. Making choices strengthens the learner's ability to choose; so even if it is a matter of choosing one of two nearly identical activities, we give a choice wherever we can.

We balance structure and ambiguity. Because ambiguity and choice produce anxiety and may lead to withdrawal and immobilization on the part of the participant, we carefully work the tension between giving choice and managing stress. Over the life of a program, we reduce our control over the participants' uses of time and space, while providing structure through the learning resources we offer. We provide many structured games, simulations, activities, instruments, and books and articles, and we make available annotated references to all the materials offered. As the program evolves, we give less and less direction as to what activities to do and how to do them.

We provide a clearly articulated conceptual framework and relate all the learning activities and resources to it. We reduce anxiety and dependency by providing clear conceptual maps of the "learning territory." Once participants have learned their way around the territory, the map guides them in diagnosing situations and making choices, and they are less dependent on the knowledge of the educator. Constructing mental models is an important part of our design work. (Note that in some applications of self-directed learning, notably for training consultants, constructing mental models is the work of the learner, not of the educator.)

We try to provide equally valued alternatives. Out of fear and dependency, participants will look to the educators to evaluate choices, alternatives, progress, and participant performance. If we deem a choice worthy of being included in our programs, we give it equal weight with other choices. For example, in the Positive Power & Influence Workshop, we defined and presented each of the four influence styles in a way that favored them equally, differentiating the styles only by describing the results each is likely to achieve. As trainers, we learned to use all four styles flexibly and effectively. We then switched from one to the other frequently, using each with commitment and evident relish.

We use the approaches and methods of traditional education to support the learner up to the point at which he or she can move ahead independently. For example, we use structured exercises in small groups in the early stages of a program to start things moving and support the participants. If we find participants clinging to the same small group in later stages of the program, we encourage them to try working on their own. As described in my earlier paper (Harrison, 1972a [Chapter Twenty-One]), the staff members are quite directive and supportive with those participants who seem to need it, but only to the point at which the participants are able to move ahead on their own.

We articulate and foster social norms that support individual responsibility and indepen-

dence. For example, when we introduce the self-directed portion of the Positive Power & Influence Program, we compare and contrast the norms that foster self-directed learning with the norms of polite social interaction. Here is what we tell participants in the Positive Power & Influence Program, to free them to be self-oriented:

- *It is all right to initiate anything that you believe would be useful for your own learning.* This includes requesting admission to groups already in operation, suggesting that others change what they are doing in order to meet your needs, asking others to reconsider their plans for the use of scarce resources, and the like.
- *It is all right to withdraw or withhold your own energy and resources.* You may opt out of previous commitments when something better comes along. You will want not to join others and will not let others join you when what they are proposing does not meet your needs.
- *The unexamined activity is not worth doing.* Self-directed learning works best when you are conscious of your intentions and goals in undertaking any particular activity. Otherwise, you may tend to join whatever is going on, in order to fill empty time. We encourage you to make video and audio recordings of your activities and review them. We advise you to slow down your activities in order to reflect on what you are learning and to draw out the implications from what you observe.

We help participants become aware of their own learning cycles and use them to guide their activities. The *learning cycle* is our name for the natural process of advance and retreat in learning. I observed in the autonomy labs that individuals would move out and take personal risks (for example, try some activity that was personally threatening) and then would move back to reflect and integrate the experience. During this period, they might be relatively passive (reading books and articles, taking long walks by themselves). The idea of the learning cycle is in contrast to the efforts of many educators, who conduct experiential learning events as if they were dramatic vehicles, building the tension and involvement steadily to a smashing climax. Some of our participants spontaneously manage their own stress by an appropriate cycle of risk and retreat, but others seem to be out of touch with their own learning cycles or seem addicted to emotional stress. These people may have to be guided and counseled in order to connect with natural rhythms.

My colleagues and I believe that the freedom self-directed learning gives to follow this stress-management cycle is a major reason why our programs can deal with highly charged and deeply personal material with a much lower level of stress than is true of programs based on small-group processes. In the latter, all individuals are normally exposed to whatever level of stress exists in the group and are not free either to seek a higher or lower level or to follow their personal rhythms. In self-directed learning, the individual can move in or out of risky learning situations at will. We find that participants do not use this freedom to avoid risk but to manage stress, for the most part responsibly and intelligently.

We design our programs so that the individual is free to move at his or her own pace. I said earlier that self-directed learning designs successfully accommodate a wide range of individual differences in level of preparation, readiness for personal involvement, and pace of learning. One reason is that in self-directed learning, people do not have to keep up with others. We find that participants tend to develop loose, informal groupings around shared readiness for a general pace or risk level. The self-directed format also facilitates individualization of the content of learning, the level of sophistication, and the learning modalities used by participants. For example, for a number of years, I have been involved with programs for training line and staff managers in consulting skills and the management of change (both with the NTL Institute, and in programs offered by me and my colleagues). Historically, such programs have always been plagued by large differences in backgrounds and orientations of the participants. Some would be working on the most basic and general questions (for example, "What is organization development?"), while others would want to hone their skills more deeply in specific areas, such as one-to-one consultation, team development, and organization diagnosis. Some would want to learn didactically and deal with the material at an exclusively intellectual level through lectures and discussions; others would press for experiential activities, skill practice, and a high level of personal exposure and emotional involvement. It seemed to be impossible to achieve better than a poor compromise between these polarized demands. Whatever choices the educators made were sure to disappoint or upset a substantial segment of the participants. The programs always seemed fraught with conflict and stress between participants and staff.

In 1972, Fritz Steele and I developed the first self-directed design for the NTL Institute's Program for Specialists in Organization Development. The usual strife and stress seemed miraculously to disappear. The high emotional level we had learned to associate with participants in these programs was replaced by a sober commitment to work. Some participants arranged for staff participation in lectures and discussions on basic topics; others joined experiential games and activities; still others practiced basic skills using role-playing and videotaped feedback. Some stayed safely within the confines of the spaces provided by the course organizers, while others took the wider community as their learning setting. The energy that had gone into conflict in previous programs over what was to be learned and how it was to be learned was channeled into productive learning.

I have had this experience over and over. Compared to other experiential learning methods, self-directed learning channels more energy into work and less into emotionality. Put another way, if one provides participants with a vehicle that is responsive to their individual learning needs, they do not need to fight to have their needs met.

The Future of Self-Directed Education

Almost any applied subject can be adapted with profit to the basic design template described here. The usefulness of adult education can be dramatically improved if resources are presented in the ways I have described in this paper, so that learners can spend their time on meeting their own needs rather than on responding to the guesses of educators about their needs. There are some adults who find the requirements for self-direction and personal responsibility in learning difficult to adjust to, but my experience is that participants are far more ready for responsibility than educators are to give it to them.

Self-directed education requires that the typical trainer or educator change his or her skill mix. Here is where I have found the most resistance to self-directed learning. Self-directed learning requires a fundamental shift in the locus of control in the classroom, and this shift is difficult for many educators to make. Once participants have gone beyond the diagnostic phase and the self-directed activity is well launched, there is often little for the educator to do. The needs of most educators for authority, visibility, and a sense of personal significance are not well met by the self-directed format.

The amount of detailed design and preparation of learning materials required for self-directed learning goes far beyond that involved in putting together a syllabus and organizing some lecture notes. Some educators do not possess the design expertise required. I expect, therefore, and my experience so far confirms, that self-directed learning methods will be accepted only slowly by educators, in spite of the high degree of acceptance they enjoy with participants. I find most acceptance for self-directed learning among young management trainers who share my dissatisfaction with the rigidity of the traditional games of education. When I supply the detailed design work, they can carry out the training effectively and enthusiastically. Some of my most effective collaborators have been former line managers who are in training positions for a limited time. They recognize intuitively the relevance of self-directed approaches to on-the-job application. Building from the bottom in this way, I expect change to take place slowly. I shall persist, however, because I believe that self-directed learning is the best current approach to management education. It uses the most modern education technology available. At the same time, it is personal and custom-fitted to the individual's needs. In the best sense of the word, it is humanistic in its respect for the individual's capacity to manage his or her own learning and growth.

CHAPTER TWENTY-THREE

TOWARD A STRATEGY FOR HELPING REDUNDANT AND RETIRING MANAGERS

I wrote "Toward a Strategy for Helping Redundant and Retiring Managers" shortly before I returned to the United States in 1976, at a time when British business was undertaking the first of many waves of redundancies and restructurings at middle-management levels. During the time I was living and working in Britain, I observed that economic developments there led those in the United States by a few years, so I predicted that we would eventually see similar phenomena in North America. Of course, I had no idea the process would last so long or cut so deep as it has.

It was clear from the early reports of people who were working with managers who had lost their jobs and were endeavoring to get back on their feet that managers with habits of autonomy and initiative were most likely to weather the transition successfully and create a newly satisfying life. I hoped to persuade some sponsoring agency to support me in applying self-directed learning principles to the reeducation of managers who had lost their jobs. The following article put forward a proposed program for giving help and support that would build initiative and autonomy on the part of participants. I have never had the opportunity to apply the ideas put forward here, yet they continue to seem sound and viable to me.

Note: Originally published as "Towards a Strategy for Helping Redundant and Retiring Managers," *Management Education and Development,* 1973, *4,* 77–85. Reprinted here with permission of *Management Education and Development.*

Duringthe recent recession, redundancies and early retirements of managerial and professional staff have mounted astronomically. Although some of the reductions in staff represent "housecleaning" that the affected organizations have put off for some years, there is every indication that the problem caused by such reductions in staff will become chronic and will remain with us for the foreseeable future. In this paper, I shall present a conceptual framework for planning help for those facing redundancy and retirement and review some concrete approaches which have proven useful elsewhere or which appear promising. I take the point of view that planning to help redundant and retiring managers must adopt a behavioral approach. This by no means implies that economic and administrative aid and the provision of concrete information are not important parts of the helping process. From the point of view of the affected individual, however, redundancy and retirement are events which affect the individual's life patterns extremely deeply. It is not rare for these events to cause traumas and dislocations from which the individual never completely recovers. Help that does not recognize the depth and pervasiveness of the impact of these events must necessarily be superficial and quite possibly misguided.

The Dynamics of a Life Crisis

Personal effectiveness may be considered to be a function of four classes of variables.

- The *situation;* that is, aspects of the environment which impinge upon the individual. In organizations, the situation can be broken down into (1) work systems, (2) social systems, and (3) administrative systems.
- The *skills and knowledge* that the individual possesses and brings to bear in dealing with the situation.
- The *interests, drives, and motivations* that tend to make some activities and outcomes more satisfying and rewarding to the person than others.
- The *goals;* that is, aspects of the situation or of the individual in the situation that the individual is attempting to achieve or maintain.

When an individual retires or becomes redundant, the situational variables undergo a relatively sudden and massive transformation. At a sudden stroke (no matter how long a time he has had to prepare for it), he is deprived of a major life situation in which he is accustomed to exercising his skills and knowledge; finding an outlet for his interests, drive and motivation; and achieving some of his most important life goals. Often, if he has been narrowly and deeply trained in a technical or administrative specialty, he loses the possibility of finding another situation relevant to his skills, knowledge, and interests, which may for all practical purposes have become obsolete. At the same time, the finding or creation of a new situation that will be economically rewarding and/or personally satisfying may require an entirely different set of knowledge and skills in which the individual is either mediocre or deficient. For example, highly technically trained engineers and scientists often find they lack the skills at building relationships with others which are essential to marketing themselves and finding another position in a highly competitive job market.

The sudden deprivation of the work situation thus disrupts the individual's total life processes in a very fundamental way. Such massive disruptions are almost invariably traumatic and far-reaching in their psychological affects. Fink has developed a phase progression model which describes and explains the stages through which individuals pass in their adaptation to highly stressful events. I have been testing this model with managers who have been involved in working with redundancies and early retirement, and there is general agreement on its applicability to the situation. The stages are passed through rapidly or slowly, depending upon the severity of the trauma, but each individual can be expected to spend some time in each phase (Fink, 1967).

The initial phase is that of *shock*. Suddenly deprived of his work situation, the individual experiences a psychological danger that is too great to handle. Many of his problem-solving processes become frozen. He may experience helplessness and extreme anxiety, perhaps to the point of panic. There is disruption of organized thinking and a temporary inability to plan and to carry out purposeful activity. During this phase, redundant managers may be observed for long periods of time sitting at their desks staring ahead and doing nothing, or perhaps wandering aimlessly through hallways or in the streets. They may temporarily be unable to plan even the simplest activity, not knowing, for example, when or how to go home. Others, less immobilized, may be able to go through the motions of their daily routine but may experience so much anxiety that they are unable to think rationally about what to do to improve their situation.

The shock phase is followed by a period of *defensive retreat*. This pattern involves a flight from reality and an attempt to fortify a habitual and familiar reality against the awareness of threatening change. The individual minimizes the impact of the event upon his life. He may state that "things have not really changed" or that "this is just a temporary problem." This kind of wishful thinking is accompanied by a lowering of anxiety and by feelings of relief and sometimes euphoria. It is significant, however, that the improvement in feeling is *not* accompanied by an increase in constructive problem-solving activity. An indicator of a stage of defensive retreat is the person's tendency to reject with indifference or with anger any intrusions of reality from well-meaning associates, friends, or family. Rigid thinking is also characteristic of this phase, and the person is unable to consider the possibility of changes in his life-style, values, or goals.

Except under unusual circumstances, the stage of defensive retreat must eventually come to an end. The individual meets with too many disconfirmations of his fantasy view of reality to maintain it indefinitely. Others refuse to support his unrealistic beliefs, the actions he takes on the basis of those beliefs are unsuccessful, and learning eventually occurs. Thus the individual passes into the phase of *acknowledgment*.

With the loss of the individual's valued image of himself and of the situation, stress increases sharply, and the individual may undergo deep depression and bitterness. The individual finally experiences the negative aspects of reality which he has been defending against, and in the process, he tends to lose sight of positive factors. The rigid cognitive patterns break down, and there is once again some disorganization of thought and problem solving, but this time there is a re-forming of perceptions along more realistic lines. If the reality is perceived as overwhelmingly negative, then the individual may tend toward extreme apathy or even suicide, and the support of others is extremely important during this phase.

As the person rebuilds a view of reality that includes both negative and positive aspects of the situation and of himself, he moves into a phase of *adaptation*. This is the phase in which real planning and action take place. There is a gradual development of a new self-image consistent with the new reality. The person explores his resources, both internal and external, and as he tests them in the real world, he experiences a gradual lessening of anxiety and depression following the success of his efforts. Serious setbacks may throw him back again into a stage of passive acknowledgment, or even into defensive retreat. However, the likelihood of such retrogression is minimized by supportive relationships with others and by a developing life situation in which the individual's effectiveness is on the increase.

Extreme as it may sound, this model is probably at least partially accurate as a description of the adaptation process of most persons as they face up to redundancy and retirement. The significant message of the model is that, in order to be really useful to the individual, outside help and intervention must be very different during the different phases of adaptation to the crisis. The wrong help in a given phase can be damaging as well as useless. For example, strong confrontation during the shock or defensive retreat phases is likely to increase the stress and may also brand the aspiring helper as a person to be avoided. This is not to say that the helper should go in the opposite direction and support the individual in his unrealistic thinking about reality during the phase of defensive retreat. Rather, it appears that the most effective help during this phase is a combination of *consistent* emotional support with an *offering* of reality to the individual, an offering which is not pressed when it raises defenses.

Again, during the acknowledgment phase, a somewhat different style of help is most useful and acceptable. During this phase of depression and bitterness, the individual still needs emotional support but also needs to be generally led to explore positive aspects of his situation and his own resources. Later, during the adaptation phase, the individual needs less emotional support and is increasingly capable of accurate perception of reality. Now he is ready to use information, advice, and training in skills in which he may be lacking.

Toward a Helping Strategy

The previous analysis leads both to a specification of the *elements* that should be present in a program for helping redundant and retiring managers and also to the *priority* and *sequence* in which they ought to be provided.

Minimizing Stress Through Preparation

I understand that recent research on surgical patients has shown that psychological preparation for a trauma can be almost as important as adequate aftercare in helping the individual to survive and to cope effectively. Patients who were adequately briefed as to the unpleasant aftereffects of a surgical operation recovered more rapidly (and more often) than those who were not so prepared. Informal interviews with managers who have dealt with redundancy suggest to me that the same principle holds true in the case of the trauma of separation from the organization. Giving plenty of notice of the impending redundancy seems to be a key to preparing the individual. In particular, there seems to be general agreement that finding another position is not only objectively easier when one has not yet been separated from his old one but that the security of maintaining his old status (no matter how temporarily) is a valuable support for the individual in presenting himself effectively and in maintaining his initiative and drive. Against this must be balanced the discomfort and guilt of others in the organization who must live with an individual who is "under sentence," but the evidence so far suggests this is more a problem for the organization than it is for the redundant individual. Letting things go until the last moment and getting the redundant person off the premises as quickly as possible seems clearly to be a self-serving strategy on the part of the organization rather than a benefit to the individual.

Sometimes it may even be possible to prepare the individual in advance of his being told that he is redundant. For example, George Lehner has devised the What if I Lost My Job? workshop, which consists of one three-hour session for three people at a time, in which individuals are encouraged to begin making some plans in advance of the event (Lehner, 1971). The opposite of this approach is seen in the way retirement is dealt with in most organizations, where the individual and the organization seem to collude in a conspiracy of silence about the serious consequences of the impending separation. The individual is encouraged to act as though he believes that the transition will be pleasant, one which he has been looking forward to all of his working life. This is nowhere more apparent than in the false gaiety of the farewell banquet. This is not of course to imply that retirement is never a happy occasion, but rather to point out that it is not helpful to the individual when we ignore and encourage him to keep silent about the unpleasant aspects.

Strengthening the Support Network

One of the most difficult aspects of redundancy and retirement is that they are transitions into which the individual is impelled at the same time as a major source of social and emotional support is removed. To the extent that the individual's membership in some social networks within the organization is supportive and satisfying to him, he will experience their loss as a deprivation which he must cope with along with all the other difficulties of the transition. In the case of redundancy, and to a lesser extent in retirement, the individual's social relationships with community, friends, and family undergo considerable alteration and stress at the same time. The desperation which this occasions some individuals is attested to by the perennial stories of men who cannot face telling their wives and neighbors about their redundancy and go off each morning dressed for work to wander aimlessly until it is time for them to return in the evening. Such extreme reactions are luckily rare, but for every man who becomes redundant or retires, there is an alteration and usually a loss in the network of social relationships that has supported him. This loss occurs just at the time when, according to Fink's model, the individual most needs support and reassurance as to his basic worth from those around him.

With this process of social deprivation in mind, it seems reasonable to give a high priority to the establishment of an alternate source of social support and confirmation of self-worth. For a variety of reasons, it seems to me most desirable to utilize a small group as the basic helping/learning setting for redundant managers and for those who retire. Such a group should have the following composition and characteristics.

• The group should ideally be an ongoing one, covering the period from when the individual first begins to face his retirement or redundancy until the transition has been effectively adapted to. This is not to say that one-time events cannot have facilitation or learning value, but the trouble is that one cannot predict exactly when each individual will be psychologically ready to confront his problem and utilize the help of others. With an ongoing group, one can work intensively with individuals when they are ready for it and deal with the setbacks and crises as they come up.

• The group should be composed of others facing the same life crisis so that members can develop cohesion and a sense of identification with one another's situations. This is important for reducing the feelings of isolation, self-blame, and worthlessness that are common blocks to successful adaptation.

• It is desirable though perhaps not essential, that a group be led by someone who has experienced a similar life crisis to those which the members are facing. This will facilitate the leader's credibility and reduce the social distance between him and the members.

Developing Initiative Through Helping One Another

The work emphasis in the group discussions should be on self-help and mutual help rather than upon help by the leader or other outside resources. In fact, after some experience, it should be possible to design guidance programs so that the self-help groups need have no leader at all. This has been successfully done in therapy groups, and there is no basic reason why it should not be accomplished with redundancy and retirement groups as well. It is particularly important in the case of the latter, because a major purpose of the small-group activity is for the members to come to see themselves and each other as competent, resourceful individuals, who are capable of giving as well as receiving help.

The activities of the group should be designed to facilitate the development of initiative, autonomy, self-confidence, and feelings of self-worth. To some extent, feelings of confidence and self-worth are generated simply by an individual's being an accepted member of a cohesive group. However, such feelings are rather shallowly based if they depend only on affiliation and not on action and achievement in the real world. Whether one is dependent upon an organization, upon a leader, or upon his peers in a small group, he is still dependent. In the last analysis, the success of the program will depend upon its freeing its participants to make their own paths toward new careers or new involvements in the community. The cohesive small group is thus seen as nurturing the individual through a difficult period of adjustment to the point where he is able to cope on his own. If he then still desires to maintain relationships with members of the group, it will be because these relationships were satisfying in their own right, and not because he is dependent upon them for the strength to cope with the stresses of everyday life.

A Cafeteria of Resources

The key to developing autonomy and initiative in the group is in the way resources are made available to it and the way resources are made available to it and are expected to be utilized. In designing a program such as this, one has the choice of providing a planned sequence of activities that expose participants to resources (people, information, experiences), or of simply making the resources accessible to the participants and allowing them to choose which to use and in what sequence. A key feature of the helping/learning strategy proposed here is that participants would be provided with access to a varied collection of learning aids which could be of use to them in assessing their own resources, exploring the economic and social environment for resources (jobs, business opportunities, skills and knowledge development resources), or improving their functioning as a group (exercises for diagnosing and improving relationship skills and group membership and leadership skills). A great deal of preliminary effort would be devoted to assembling the best possible collection of resources. There would be a list of people who could be contacted to speak to the group on various topics; there would be a library and supplementary bibliography; there would be structured group exercises which could be chosen by the group for its own learning; and there would be a library of films and audio- and videotaped material. It would be up to the group to choose and to use these materials according to the needs of its members. Early in the life of the group, some guidance would be given regarding the choice of materials and activities, but even at this early stage, the group would always be provided with a choice among several alternatives. Subgroups would be encouraged to form to pursue special projects, and as time went on, individuals might develop their own lines of learning activity, but the center of activity would continue to be the small group which plans together as a whole whatever activities are to be carried out. This focus on the group as a whole would be maintained during most of the program in order to enhance the group's value as a source of both emotional support and reality testing for the members.

Learning How to Learn

Learning in the group would take place by critiquing the activities undertaken as well as through the activities themselves. For example, if the group chose to invite a speaker to address it on problems of finance in starting a small business, the members would spend time after the session examining the ways they had used the speaker as a resource and considering how they might improve similar sessions in the future.

A great effort should be made to provide the best possible resources for the use of the groups. This would involve considerable prework by the program staff in interviewing expert resources, arranging for the availability of individual resource people, conducting library research, and sifting through the vast array of film, audio, and video material available. This would moreover be an ongoing task, as the resources would have to be brought up to date continuously. Experience would doubtless show which resources were more useful to which kinds of groups, and this would aid the search as well as facilitate the elimination of some persons or materials from the list.

Summary

The suggested design strategy flows out of the diagnosis of the situation of the manager facing redundancy or retirement. He is at the brink of losing a central source of meaning and self-esteem in his life: his job. Depending upon his investment in work and his involvement in the family and other outside activities, this may represent a moderate to a severe disruption of his life and of his opportunities to meet his needs and achieve his goals. At the very least, it will change radically the social network in which he finds himself and will seriously disrupt, at least temporarily, the daily routine of his existence. In a world in which what a man does is frequently more important to others than who he is, the manager facing redundancy or retirement is about to lose one of the major indicators of his status and worth in the social system: his work and his organizational position.

When subjected to moderate to severe stress of this kind, people go through a fairly predictable phase progression in their adaptive responses. During some of these phases, they are rather inaccessible to help, particularly if the help is of a confronting nature. Throughout the process, there is continuing need for confrontation to be balanced by a high degree of emotional support.

The need for support during a major life transition can most effectively be met by membership in a small group that is composed of persons sharing a common problem and that meets regularly over a period of time during which the stress and adaptation processes can be coped with.

The basic task of such a group would be to help individual members plan and carry out an effective transition to another career or another satisfying life-style. In this, the group would be facilitated by a trained leader (preferably with experience of redundancy or retirement himself) or, after considerable experience with the program, by a program of written instructions for group activities. In either case, the group would be given a great deal of choice in its activities and would move in the direction of greater choice and autonomy with time. The learning process would thus be designed to facilitate the development of initiative and independence on the part of group members. To this end, a rich and varied store of learning resources would be provided by the staff, but groups would have great latitude in choosing which to use. Once chosen, most of the activities would require that the group take further initiative to carry them out.

CHAPTER TWENTY-FOUR

STEPS TOWARD THE LEARNING ORGANIZATION

After Peter Senge's immensely successful book on organizational learning
came out (Senge, 1990), I was not sure
if I had anything to add to the discussion.
However, it was soon evident that it was
not easy to create learning organizations
and that there were, as in anything that
promises to transform organizations for
the better, some dark sides to be explored.
Who better, I asked, than myself, "Squire
of the Dark Side," to explore these matters? I was then working with Charles
Kiefer, Peter's early collaborator, in Innovation Associates, and Peter's book was
bringing in a lot of business to the firm.
Out of the issues and dilemmas posed by
this work, I crafted an internal working
paper for our colleagues, and expanded it
in successive revisions into the monograph

Towards the Learning Organization (Harrison, 1992), too long for inclusion here.
The present paper, originally adapted by
Graham Dawes and published as a contribution to a book on organizational futures
(Harrison and Dawes, 1994), includes
some parts of that longer work. It has
been revised for publication here.

In this paper, I share my vision of the
"look and feel" of a learning organization.
I make a case for distinguishing between
high-order learning and *ordinary learning*.
And I enumerate the criteria I use to identify and promote high-order learning. I define a *learning organization* as one that
does a lot of high-order learning.

I identify barriers to learning that are
endemic in organizations, notably fear and
a bias for unreflective action. I show how

Note: Coauthored by Graham Dawes and originally published as "Barriers to Learning in the Or-
ganization," in R. Boot, J. Lawrence, and J. Morris (eds.), *Managing the Unknown by Creating New Futures*
(London: McGraw-Hill, 1994). Reprinted here, with revisions, with permission of McGraw-Hill Book
Company Europe.

problem-solving activities that are not soundly based on deep reflection into basic causes create ever more problems in a vicious circle. I also identify how some current changes that are going on in many if not most organizations create a need for healing the trauma and stress that block high-order learning.

A section of this paper is also devoted to describing the approach to learning-oriented consulting that I have evolved over the past few years. I call the approach a *learning frame for consulting*. In that section, I bring together my work on self-directed learning and my current approach to consulting. In both of these domains of my professional life, I seek to empower clients to take over many if not most of the tasks of educator and consultant. I give the reader my thoughts on these matters in the form of a set of statements I might make to a prospective client group on how I would (and would not) work with them.

The thrust of this paper is to make the point that the current fad for "learning organizations," like the earlier one for "culture change," is no panacea. To clear away the barriers that make high-order learning difficult in most organizations requires deep commitment and ongoing dialogue among all the stakeholders who are to be part of the learning process. Improving learning, like improving service, is mostly a matter of removing barriers so people can follow their natural bent for learning and serving.

It would have been equally appropriate to put this paper in the earlier section on organization development. I have placed it here because it brings my work as educator *and* as consultant up to the present. I see these work roles as equally important in my life, and thus this particular essay is a fitting conclusion to the accumulated experiences and learnings represented by the papers in this volume.

A s an organization development consultant, I have always concerned myself with people's learning new ways of working and relating together. However, in my practice and in that of others, the focus on learning has often wavered. Sometimes the priority is not so much on learning as it is on fixing immediate problems. There is also confusion between different kinds of learning processes. Training, trial-and-error learning, planned experimentation, work redesign, and strategic planning may all be learning processes, but not all of them build the capacity of individuals to learn, nor do most of them build the systems of cooperation and the shared commitment to learning that foster organization members' learning together on a continuing basis.

It is often unclear exactly what people mean when they talk about the *learning organization*. Here is my attempt to define the elements that are present in most of the minds now pondering the question, "How do we make organizations into learning systems?"

At the Level of the Individual

- Individuals innovate and initiate. They believe that their success in doing so will be rewarded and that failure will be treated as a step in the learning process.
- Individuals develop good learning habits. They ask many questions; they carry out experiments to test their ideas; they freely and openly pool information on what is working and what is not.
- Individuals' thirst for data and firsthand experience exceeds their deference to the opinions of persons in authority.

At the Level of Organization Culture

- The organization is much more egalitarian than most. It treats people as valued contributors. It nurtures and rewards their creativity and initiative.
- People in authority support, expedite, and facilitate the contributions of those who report to them, and they bring a broader organizational perspective to the work of their units. They expect subordinates to be internally motivated and responsive to the needs of their peers rather than motivated by rewards and punishments from above.
- People are expected to try things that do not work the first time, *and* they are expected to learn from their mistakes.
- There is high receptivity to communication up, down, and sideways in the organization. There is an absence of territoriality and "not invented here." It is easy to find a receptive ear for one's ideas.
- Individuals are empowered to contribute in accordance with their ability *and* their developmental needs rather than their position in the organization. Ideas are judged on their merits rather than on the role or status of the person who puts them forward.
- The norms and values of the organization support cooperation and mutual support. People help one another beyond the formal demands of their jobs. People are valued for sharing their knowledge, expertise, and talents rather than devoting these qualities exclusively to individual achievement.
- People celebrate one another's achievements and grieve their losses together. There is a sense of camaraderie, community, and caring.

Readers who are familiar with my work on organization cultures and their associated levels of consciousness (Harrison, 1972b [Chapter Ten], 1987b [Chapter Twelve], 1990a [Chapter Thirteen], 1992; Harrison, Cooper, and Dawes, 1991; Harrison and Stokes, 1992) will recognize in these lists the qualities and characteristics of the cultures I have labeled achievement and support or, in my later work, self-expression and mutuality. Such organization cultures tend to support cooperation, initiative, and personal risk taking. Traditional organizations with strong power- and role-oriented (transactional) cultures tend to block the learning of people at lower levels of the pyramid by relying heavily on rewards and fear to drive performance and by rigid structures, rules, and procedures that block communications and stifle initiative and intergroup cooperation.

At the Level of the Whole System

- People whose roles place them at the edges of the organization are valued for the intelligence they bring about the environment: technological developments, markets, customers, government, and the public. Since everyone in the organization also lives in the environment part of the time, everyone is encouraged to bring in such information. Systems for sorting and distributing environmental information to people who can use it are well developed.
- Everyone is assumed to have a "need to know." A great deal of effort, time, and technology go into developing the *organizational hologram,* in which each part understands, appreciates, and honors its interdependence with the other parts and with the whole.
- The organization develops and uses *participative technologies* for:

    Giving everyone in the organization an understanding and appreciation of the ongoing state of the organization's internal and external functioning and performance and of the environmental demands and opportunities that the organization faces.

    Enabling everyone to contribute to the quality of the organization's strategic thinking and planning.

- The working map of the organization looks like a network rather than a pyramid. It displays task and information interdependencies as well as responsibility and accountability structures.
- Much attention is given to mapping the "nodes" or "ganglia" of the network, those points where all those with significant impact on the success of a task, project, or function come together. The organization develops systems and processes to facilitate mutual learning at these nodes.
- The organization invests heavily in learning. Its time horizon is longer than most, and its strategists are willing, when necessary, to forgo short-term results in favor of longer term positioning.
- Members of the organization have a sense of its purpose and contribution, above and beyond the making of profits. The shared sense of a greater value and meaning to the organization's existence justifies and supports a balance between short- and long-term thinking and between human and economic values.

It is fortunate that an organization need not possess all these qualities and characteristics in order to manifest better than ordinary levels of learning. Many of the qualities and conditions in these lists are rare in today's organizations. However, enough of them are within the reach of organizations I work with to give me confidence that persistence in this developmental effort will bring rewards.

We Must Transform Our Ability to Learn

My confidence stems from my reading of current and future necessity. We all, as individuals and organizations, must *learn how to learn* both continuously and well. The current competitive and exploitative paradigm is rapidly destroying the ability of the planet to support our living—we must transform our ways of thinking, learning, and understanding to higher levels of consciousness that will lead us into harmony with one another and with our greater environment. Individually, organizationally, and as a species, we are in a precarious situation. The things we are doing to cope with our problems are doing about as much harm as good. To thrive, and even to survive, we must take our learning beyond how to do things faster and better within our current frames and concepts—we must learn how to transform ourselves, our organizations, and our institutions.

Perhaps only disaster of a cataclysmic nature will provide enough of a shock to our systems of thought to stimulate the necessary evolution. But the seeds of new thought are forever sown on the edges of the ordinary and the known. I believe that investment in nurturing these seeds of new ways of learning will provide us with patterns for survival in future cataclysmic transitions *and* will pay more mundane dividends in the medium term. Only this belief allows me in good conscience to take on projects for leaders and managers who, no matter how idealistic they are in private, must produce positive results in their imperfect organizations within a reasonable time.

High-Order Learning

To cope with current and future changes, organizations must elevate their learning processes to a higher order. The learning processes in traditional organizations form the contrasting pole, which I do not think of as low-order learning but more as ordinary learning—that is, activities and processes that we typically find in what I have called power- and role-oriented organizations.

Ordinary learning includes training and other learning processes of which the purpose is to transfer to employees knowledge and skills the organization possesses which the employees need to know and be able to do. It includes trial-and-error learning and "learning by doing." It includes problem-solving approaches that attempt to isolate problems and deal with them apart from their context and their systemic connections with other parts of the organization or the environment. It includes the informal and only partly conscious processes by which we learn the culture of the organization: whom we have to pay attention to and whom we can safely ignore; which rules are to be obeyed and which are to be broken with impunity; what the differences are between the espoused values and the values in action; which actions and attitudes lead to reward and recognition and which lead to less pleasant consequences.

Of course, these ordinary learning processes also occur in organizations that manifest high-order learning. For the most part, *high-order learning* is "something more," rather than "instead of." However, ordinary learning processes often act as blocks and barriers to high-order learning. Then we must change our ways if we are to liberate the higher order processes.

Here are some criteria for high-order learning, which will help structure what may otherwise be a rather fuzzy term.

High-order learning requires constant attention to the learning process. Learning is one of the values of the organization's culture. There is a learning as well as a doing component to all of the organization's activities. Taking action includes examining the consequences and results of action, so there *is no action without learning.*

High-order learning is wider and longer in its conceptual scope than ordinary learning. We go beyond the search for immediate causes of symptoms and quick fixes to an attempt to understand the entire system and its relationships with its environment and how those relationships evolve over time. This means that when we address a problem, we will normally formulate it in more complex terms than those in which we originally stated it, in order to understand how it is embedded within the larger system and connected to the system's environment. We will often then discover that the causes are distant in time and place from the effects and symptoms we wish to change.

High-order learning is self-initiated and self-directed. Organization members take responsibility for their own learning rather than relying on authorities and professionals to provide training and development opportunities.

High-order learning is global rather than local in its use of systemic thinking, its focus on the complexity of relationships, and its preoccupation with wholes rather than parts. As the scope of inquiry widens beyond the local, we discover that the solution to a problem in one part of a system usually creates problems for other parts of the system. Thus high-order learning activities are likely to turn the problems that we thought required solutions into dilemmas requiring choice among imperfect alternatives. At the point of decision, we base our actions upon an understanding of the mixed positive and negative consequences that are likely to result.

High-order learning involves articulating and questioning basic assumptions and mental models of reality, rather than limiting inquiry to issues within the current paradigm. High-order learning includes, though it is not limited to, what is commonly referred to by learning-oriented consultants as "second-order learning." It involves questioning the organization's values and norms, particularly those that limit learning through systematically ignoring certain issues, behaviors, and patterns or through defining them as undiscussable.

I call this undiscussable aspect of an organization's culture the *shadow*, because it contains powerful influences on behavior that are unseen and unacknowledged. The influences are not necessarily negative, but they operate outside of our awareness. Bringing the shadow into the light can liberate the creativity and energy of the organization because it increases *choice* dramatically.

High-order learning involves the creation of learning systems. The creating of these *learning systems* is sometimes called *organizational learning.* The organization, operating as an organic learning system, becomes better able to take in and comprehend complex information from the environment and to modify its behavior on the basis of that information. Unless the organization is well developed as a learning system, it will frustrate the attempts of individual members to put their learning into practice, and their knowledge and wisdom will not be fully utilized.

Barriers Against Learning in Organizations

There are formidable barriers to the improvement of learning in organizations. Two of the most important barriers are

- The inhibition of learning by the presence of fear, anxiety, and other strong negative emotions in the organization.
- The bias for action that is embedded in the character of most leaders and managers and in the culture of their organizations.

I shall take up each in turn. I do not have a sure cure to offer for either of them; they are part of the fabric of organizational life. We must take such barriers into account if we hope to create organizations as learning systems, and before leaping to "solutions," we first must be clear about the nature of these and other barriers.

The Barrier of Fear and Anxiety

We know from psychology that a modest level of emotional arousal (anger, fear, excitement) promotes attention and appears to facilitate learning; at higher levels, learning falls off rapidly. What my colleagues and I increasingly see in North America and Europe are organizations in which people are struggling to learn and adapt to ever higher rates of change while they labor under heavy burdens of fear, resentment, and anxiety.

Differences Between Fear and Anxiety. It is important to distinguish between fear and anxiety (angst) in organizations. When I first began my consulting practice,

I could see a fair amount of fear in organizations. People were often afraid of the authority of the boss. Those who had experienced the hardships of the Great Depression were afraid of being without work again. Many people feared to express their personal views of organizational reality, because they feared being "out of step" or being seen as an "oddball." These fears were fairly specific and could be articulated clearly once trust was established with the person.

It is different now. While specific fears of authority, peer rejection, or losing one's job are still active, there are many organizations in which people are considerably empowered and autonomous compared to twenty or thirty years ago. Even in these organizations, however, there seems to be a darker cloud of anxiety that is felt by many if not most people in the organization. It is often very subtle, and much of the time it is nonspecific.

Anxiety does not have an *object* in the way that fear does, and it is often difficult to articulate. It is best known by its effects. These include a general sense of uneasiness or malaise; a tendency to be either scattered or extremely narrow in one's focus; a heightened tendency to engage in addictive behaviors such as substance abuse or workaholism; an inability to concentrate or to reflect deeply about organizational issues; and a preference for short-term thinking. Anxiety can often be more debilitating than fear, because it is so general and pervasive, and because it is so hard to identify and alter the conditions that cause it.

The Prevalence of Fear and Anxiety. Fear has always been present in organizations; however, the trend toward empowerment in many organizations may have diminished fear somewhat. While fear may be decreasing, anxiety may be on the rise. Increasingly, my colleagues report that patterns of anxiety as well as fear are prevalent in the organizations they serve. The patterns are seen in highly successful organizations on a steep growth curve as well as organizations that are struggling to cope with competition. The difference seems to be that in organizations that are doing poorly, there are more specific fears and anger around the possibility of job loss, while in successful organizations people experience more free-floating anxiety.

In addition to feeling economic uncertainty resulting from the waves of downsizing caused by a general restructuring and flattening of business organizations along with hard times and technological displacement, people also feel economically insecure in general. There is a growing sense that our planet cannot sustain the high levels of affluence to which we in the developed nations have become accustomed. While people are not quite ready to believe that the political, ecological, and economic disasters that have befallen the former communist countries will inevitably happen here, we are increasingly aware of complex economic interdependencies that make us ever more vulnerable to one another's troubles.

There is thus a sense of unease and impending doom that hangs over us all, and that is not so much a fear of something specific but the anxiety associated with massive uncertainty about the causes of our difficulties, what the future holds, and what, if anything, we can do to influence the future in a positive way.

Sources of Anger and Resentment. Anger and resentment are also on the rise, as our largest organizations dismantle the implicit contract that has for so long governed the relationship in bureaucracies between the organization and its managerial and white-collar employees. People are increasingly being required to change and to learn new ways of thinking, new attitudes, and new behaviors as a condition of retaining their employment. The choice is ever more frequently between learning and growing or being demoted or unemployed. Even when we are not actively facing such a choice, we know others who are.

What is communicated to organization members is that after years of satisfactory service, they are suddenly not good enough and may be dispensed with if they do not get their acts together. In many organizations, this results in a cloud of negative emotion that hangs over the daily working lives of the members. People in such organizations once felt they had good reason to believe that if they followed the rules and performed adequately they could count on a job for life and a good retirement. Now, ancient understandings, in which security was given by large bureaucratic organizations in exchange for loyalty and conformity on the part of employees, have given way to an attitude of aggressive self-interest on both sides of the employment contract. That implicit contract has been terminated in most organizations in the United States and the U.K., and there is much anxiety, anger, and resentment as a result.

Faced with relentless and repeated reductions in the workforce, many of those who are working today do not know if they will be tomorrow. They feel powerless to protect themselves against impending loss, and they are bitterly resentful toward organizations that increasingly treat them as commodities to be used when convenient and then discharged into the social environment as human waste products of the production process.

Betrayal in Organizations. Much of the anger and resentment that I see in organizations is associated with *betrayal*. One form of betrayal occurs when the more powerful party to an agreement or understanding fails to keep the faith and unilaterally terminates the understanding. People's anger at such a betrayal is not limited to the cause at hand; it is fueled by the many times in the past they have been let down or led astray by someone they trusted on whom they were dependent: parents, older friends and siblings, teachers, lovers.

It is a truism that many if not most organizations are engaged in *transformation,* by which I mean a change in our fundamental ways of perceiving, understanding, and valuing the world about us (sometimes called a *paradigm shift*). Transformations can occur spontaneously, but they are usually set in motion by painful disconfirmation: we find that things are not what they seem, and that they do not work the way they are supposed to. Most transformations involve betrayal in the sense that they involve the unilateral termination of explicit or implicit contracts between the organization and its members.

Betrayal often occurs around reductions in the size of organizations through terminating the employment of people who had reason to believe their jobs were secure so long as they did what they were told and followed the rules. Typically, the pattern involves repeated layoffs; sometimes the sense of betrayal is sharpened by assurances from management that each layoff is the last. Another frequent betrayal involves change in job content or title such that the affected individual loses some aspect of status or identity that the individual feels he or she has earned and has a right to.

The process of change and improvement also contains in it the likelihood of betrayal. People are frequently asked to trust, to risk, and to take initiatives. They are asked to give from a deeper place, going beyond the transactional contracts typical of power- and role-oriented organizations. Instead of simply working for mundane rewards, people are induced to work from purpose and commitment. They are, in effect, invited to work for love, and what is implicitly promised is a kind of new order in which dignity, respect, mutual support, and camaraderie take the place of selfishness, exploitation, and alienation.

When change initiatives lack substance and long-term commitment on the part of leaders, they amount to a seduction of the innocent. Those who "sign on" and "buy in" are those who believe and who trust. When leaders fail to hold the course and deliver the dreams they have created, the sense of betrayal is actually greater than when people lose their jobs through the "normal" operation of markets, technology, and the business cycle.

This is not to point a blaming finger at leaders, who are subject to the same human frailties as the rest of us. It is rather to identify a process that is very costly for organization transformation. We do not readily trust leaders here in North America. When we are induced to overcome our mistrust and give of our deeper selves, any betrayal of our trust builds in deep cynicism, which makes it all that much less likely that future enlightened initiatives can be given credibility. I believe the major reason why it is easier to generate high trust and internally motivated performance in new organizations than it is in older ones is the legacy of old betrayals that exists in most organizations that have any history at all.

Leaders' Underestimation of the Effects of Negative Emotions. The effects of strong negative emotions are consistently underestimated by leaders. People suppress their negativity in interactions with power figures. They are unwilling to be seen as weak, disloyal, or undermotivated, and they may fear the consequences of exposing themselves as such. Thus, in the first place, the expression of negative feelings is self-censored. Fear, anxiety, and anger become undiscussable in organizations.

It is sometimes acceptable to talk openly about others' fear, almost never about one's own. Anger and resentment are a little easier to address, but not much. When strong emotions do surface, the process is seldom experienced as constructive, and thus people's reluctance to deal with the emotions openly is confirmed.

Leaders, for their part, mostly do not want to hear about people's negative feelings. To know that one's subordinates are angry and resentful increases one's own anxiety. To know that they are anxious and fearful leaves many leaders and managers feeling helpless. Most managers are men, and men are frequently ill at ease in dealing with their own distress or that of others. It is difficult for leaders to listen to and acknowledge the existence of emotional problems when they feel ill equipped to deal with them effectively. They feel responsible in part for the well-being of subordinates, and they do not know how to help. So for a variety of reasons, managers and leaders subtly or overtly discourage the expression of negative emotions,

Because they are out of touch with the pain in their organizations, leaders often seek to implement programs that require heavy investments in learning (quality initiatives, reorganizations, service improvement programs, and the like) directly following traumatic organizational events such as major downsizing. In part, they do this because they are themselves under heavy pressure to improve organizational performance, and they are passing that pressure along in the time-honored way of hierarchical organizations. In part, they really do not know how traumatized and stressed the members of the organization are, and when they are aware, they do not know how to heal the wounds.

Learning under such conditions is difficult, and it is usually of a low order. People do what they are told, but they do not take risks and initiatives, do not experiment, and are reluctant to participate. If we wish to approach the transformation of our organizations into high-order learning systems, or if we just want the organization to be a place that supports the learning and growth of individuals and groups, then we must find ways of healing distress and trauma, if only to ameliorate their effects on learning.

The Barrier of a Bias for Action

Organization members often say that they are too heavily loaded with urgent tasks to engage in deep investigation and reflection on the causes of problems. This statement is supported by the amount of time people are putting in on the job. Most of my clients are working harder than at any time in my many years as a consultant; their time is filled not only with managing operations but also with endless meetings concerned with change and solving problems.

Most of my clients see themselves as decisive and action oriented. They say they want the facts required to make a decision and get on with the work of implementing it, and I believe them. I also observe, and they confirm, that in meetings they often fail to arrive at decisions because needed information is unobtainable or the right course of action is not clear or there are serious disadvantages to each of the proposals on the table. Then they are not decisive and action oriented. Rather, they dither and feel frustrated because they seem to be wasting time in endlessly processing the same issues. They often tend to interpret their uncertainty as a failure of the courage to decide; I am more likely to interpret it as the expression of an unacknowledged need for deeper learning.

A Vicious Circle Impedes Learning. People are motivated by task urgency to decide quickly and move ahead, but uncertainty, anxiety, and fear of failure lead them to spend large amounts of time in inconclusive meetings, and in other unproductive busyness.

Most inhabitants of large organizations feel most secure when carrying out the structured, habitual aspects of their jobs in which they know they can be successful. Within this familiar milieu, they are decisive. In the face of the unknown and the ambiguous, they are risk averse and to make a decision feels too risky. Figure 24.1 shows how the aversion to risk under task uncertainty reinforces the bias for action.

Often a decision feels risky because the situation does not lend itself to *solving* the problem at hand; rather, there is a *dilemma* that requires that the participants make and live with the consequences of a choice between alternatives leading to a mixture of desirable and undesirable outcomes.

In addition, the amount of time spent in meetings increases the sense of urgency, and the urgency further reduces readiness to engage in reflective deliberations.

To men and women of action, reflection and deep investigation are often seen as not leading sufficiently quickly to concrete results. They would rather do something now, and then take their next steps based on the results. Thus much of the

FIGURE 24.1. FORCES REINFORCING THE BIAS FOR ACTION.

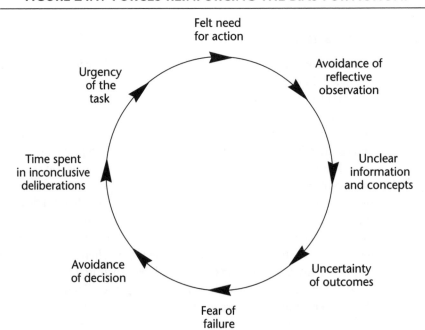

problem solving in organizations takes place through trial and error. Unfortunately, trial-and-error problem solving only leads to a permanent fix if the true causes of the problems are close in time and space to their effects. If they are hidden in the complexities of a larger system, then this method of problem solving usually exacerbates the problems.

Another reason for avoiding deep reflection is that it initially leads to experiencing the situation as more complex than it appears at first, thus increasing people's anxiety and frustration. In this way, learning activities that might eventually lead to a greater sense of clarity about the choices involved and to greater comfort with the outcomes are avoided because in the short-term they increase pain.

It requires courage and will to break the circle by taking the time to examine situations in greater depth and complexity. The encouragement of a consultant helps; the support of a higher authority is more potent. More effective still is a supportive organization culture in which demands for change and ever higher performance are balanced by compassion for human frailty—for the doubts, fears, reluctance, and resentment that most of us experience when we are required to change and grow. In such an organization, we do not always have to project an image of competence and confidence. We can share our uncertainties and frustrations, and in sharing, lighten our individual loads.

Competition Inhibits Learning. Learning is restricted by competitive feelings and attitudes. Partly, these are shared personality characteristics fostered by educational and parenting patterns in our culture. These patterns are intensified and fed by reward systems that foster competition. In many if not most organizations, the level of competition is unhealthy and inimical to both individual and corporate learning. Not only does information become a scarce resource in the battle of all against all, but the experimentation and risk taking that are essential to high-order learning are avoided for fear of falling behind others in the endless footrace toward success.

The patterns of information flow and decision making typical of hierarchical organizations are a serious block to organizational learning. Command (decision taking) is localized at the top of a pyramid, as far as possible from the source of information about problems and difficulties in operations, changes in the environment, and inputs from external stakeholders such as customers, suppliers, community, and so on. Information is supposed to flow upward, and power (decisions, evaluation, and so on) flows downward. Lateral communication is poorly provided for.

Learning occurs most readily when there is a clear and rapid connection between action taken and results. Because of the length of time required for information to move upward in the organization, and because of the serious distortions in the accuracy of feedback brought about by people's responses to power, it is difficult for the decision makers at the top to learn from the consequences of their actions.

Consequences of the Bias for Action. Because these barriers exist, it is easier in organizations to act than it is to learn, and it is easier to act individually than it is to act together with others. The bias for action has been mostly positive in our past history, when what was required to succeed were high energy and the courage to take risks. We are now in a time when the consequences of a bias for action are mostly negative.

In the past, organizations have learned slowly and relatively unconsciously, through their reactions to internal and external changes. They learned by endeavoring to solve problems as they came up, isolating each problem and implementing a solution without much consideration of how the problem was connected systemically to other aspects of the organization's operations. When applying a solution in one place caused another problem somewhere else, that problem was again addressed in isolation. Things did tend to get better, but slowly, and with many fits and starts. However, where the environment of an organization does not change very rapidly, such an approach to organizational learning does work; through trial and error over time, it produces an increasingly good fit between organizational arrangements and such environmental realities as markets, sources of supply, workforce characteristics, and so forth.

The method of learning just described is highly action oriented. It is based on the assumption that there is something we can call "getting it right" and that we can approach it incrementally through closer and closer approximations. Thus, the more quickly we implement each trial solution, the more quickly we approach our goal of excellence. The emphasis is on ferreting out problems and applying solutions with energy and dispatch.

Achievement-oriented organizations are usually highly biased toward action and toward learning through concrete experience and active experimentation, as opposed to observation, reflection, theory-building, and intuition. People tend to embody their learning in action routines, and so are often only semiconscious of what they know. They do not develop their experience to a higher level of generality. There develops a ready, fire, aim mentality that puts organization members always in the thick of the battle, where each action provokes a response that requires another action. The sense of urgency feeds on itself, and people feel themselves unable to take time out to reflect and to understand.

Problem Solving and Action in Complex Organizations. Two factors now militate against the success of such a primitive approach to organizational learning. One is *complexity* in the systems we are endeavoring to optimize; the other is *close coupling* between parts of a system. When a system is complex, there are many parts, each of which has some relationship with all the other parts and is affected by changes in them. Complex organizations have so many parts that we can never know them all nor specify their relationships with one another. In very complex systems, for example, nuclear reactors, the very process of measuring the operations of the system changes its operating characteristics and may make it more difficult to know what is going on.

Closely coupled systems have tight relationships among their parts, such that a change in one part rapidly produces significant change in many other parts. In loosely coupled systems, the changes in one part have less of an impact on the other parts, and the changes take longer to spread through the system. For example, continuous process production systems tend to be tightly coupled, while batch processing systems are more loosely coupled.

Problem Solving: Injurious to Organizational Health? When we intervene in one part of a complex system, we have, in addition to the intended effects on the part of the system we have targeted, many unintended effects in all the other parts of the system. When the system is loosely coupled, these effects have relatively small impact, and their spread is slow. When the system is closely coupled, the unintended effects we produce with our problem solving in one part of the organization are substantial, and they occur quite rapidly.

Thus, in complex and closely coupled systems, local problem solving quickly creates many unintended effects in other parts of the system, some of which will become problems for the people involved in those parts. Those people, in turn, engage in more local problem solving, creating more problems elsewhere. Soon the system begins to churn, and people find themselves working harder and harder in efforts to solve internally generated problems produced by others' problem-solving attempts. Because of the bias for action (as opposed to understanding) that exists in most of our organizations, the pressure created by this second vicious circle leads to more and more frantic activity and less and less thoughtful consideration of what is actually going on and how events are actually related to one another in each problem situation. In these circumstances, it is not too much of an exaggeration to say, paraphrasing the Surgeon General, that "problem solving may be injurious to your organization's health."

The Bias for Action as Addiction. Like the Surgeon General's warning against cigarette smoking, my injunction against problem solving points to a common addiction. It is the addictive quality of action and problem solving that makes them so difficult to change. I think of addiction as any pattern of behavior that is engaged in to reduce pain and fear and that cannot be given up without experiencing the pain and fear that it masks. After years of careful observation, I have become convinced that the frenetic action and local problem solving that go on in organizations today are only partially driven by rational work considerations and are largely part of the addictive syndrome called workaholism. My observations suggest that the pain and fear masked by workaholic norms in organizations are the pain of loneliness and disconnection from others; the fear of failure and inadequacy; and the despair and shame involved in putting one's energy, talent, and creativity into an economic system that each of us intuitively knows is destructive of human health and human values because it is ecologically unsustainable.

The pain of each of those concerns becomes greatest when we take time to be still and quiet. It is eased by activity and especially by activity involving high drama. I believe that in many of the organizations I work with, the sense of drama and urgency masks deep despair and nameless dread, and that our bias for action keeps that despair at bay. Needless to say, this point of view is not popular with clients; it is not even popular with me! Like my clients, I find ease and a sense of meaning in getting involved in their dramas, and my fears of inadequacy are kept at bay by doing my work in ways that are seen as competent, if not always brilliant.

A great deal has been learned about the treatment of addictions in Alcoholics Anonymous and its offshoots. While this is not the place to explore in depth how that work might be applied to organizations, it is worth noting that feeling surrounded by love and support, being challenged to tell the truth about oneself, and having a spiritual life all seem to be important ingredients. Methods that include these components can be used to move toward an understanding of the addictive patterns in our ways of doing and being in organizations and, hence, toward freeing ourselves of dependence upon them. However, having said this, I also have to say that of all the difficult issues we ask clients to confront, constructively addressing a shared addiction (or any shared defense against reality) is the most difficult. Often one has to wait until the organization hits bottom, in the sense of experiencing more pain from the addiction than from the concerns and fears that it masks.

Nothing said here is meant to imply that hard work, high energy, and dedication to the task are in themselves negative or unhealthy, either in organizations or for individuals. It is the meaning and purpose of these patterns that need to be questioned and confronted, not their existence.

For some time, there has been a theme in management writing that deplores the short-term thinking and preoccupation with the bottom line that have become endemic in North American business. That theme points in the same direction as my reasoning. There is a general apprehension that we are not addressing the real problems, that we are not thinking long enough or wide enough. Certainly when our focus shifts from individual businesses to the larger economic system or to the global environment it is clear that continued preoccupation with immediate solutions to local issues is seriously damaging and may destroy those systems upon which we depend for our survival and comfort.

Beyond the Barriers

I have only explored two of the barriers to learning in organizations in this paper. There are others, such as:

- The inability to acknowledge publicly aspects of the organization's doing and being that are contrary to the ways organization leaders and members would like to think about themselves. This produces incongruity and undermines integrity.

- The unmet needs for healing in organizations undergoing major change. Little attention is given to working through the mix of strong emotions produced by high levels of change.

Consultants who are attempting to encourage learning within organizations will have their own candidates for additional barriers. They will also each have their ways to assist managers in going beyond the barriers. In this chapter, I limit myself to identifying factors that are currently operating within organizations and that must be addressed by any viable approach to organizational learning.

As I indicated at the outset, a key tenet of my learning-oriented approach is that when we endeavor to increase the capacity of an organization or group to learn, we must involve clients in the design and creation of their own learning at each and every step along the way. One of my practices as a learning-oriented consultant is to educate clients to carry out activities normally thought to be part of my role as the professional consultant.

I follow a principle I call *maximum feasible choice*. In designing learning experiences, I ask myself at each choice point, "Is there a compelling reason why I should be making this decision or carrying out this learning activity instead of giving the responsibility to the learner or client?" At times, there is such a reason, but by asking the question, I usually find that my clients can do for themselves many of the things I used to do for them, thus enhancing their ability to manage their own learning.

I find that the moment one adopts the principle of maximum feasible choice, it reframes the contract between client and consultant to one that is about *learning together*. It moves me and my client away from conducting events that are set pieces and toward collaboratively designed events that arise organically from the work we do together.

I have developed three criteria for determining what constitutes maximum feasible choice.

- Clients have, or can get, sufficient information to make an informed decision about the issue in question.
- The decision is relevant to their interests; they have a stake in the outcome.
- They are willing to take responsibility for the outcomes of the decision.

Sometimes I do not know until part way through the process whether the criteria are truly met or not. I intentionally tend to err on the side of taking risks on clients' willingness and ability to manage their own learning.

A Learning Frame for Consulting

I approach new clients as a facilitator of their learning. The message I endeavor to communicate through my words and actions includes the following points:

I deeply believe in the capacity of each of my client organizations to learn that which is necessary for the organization to move through its dilemmas and ahead in its development. Your organization has within it the capacity to learn what you need to learn, and very probably there are people here now who have the knowledge and wisdom that are needed to address your situation effectively. Your organization probably does not know that it knows what it needs to address its problems, and that is one of the issues I intend to work on with you. Organizations as a whole usually have access only to the knowledge they are used to using. The knowledge that is now needed exists in individuals and groups that are not currently being called upon to contribute what they know. Almost certainly, there are barriers within the organization against their contributing. In our work together, we shall confront and endeavor to understand those barriers, and work to find ways around or through them. In the process, you will become more adept learners; you will learn how to learn.

You do not need a consultant such as myself unless the learning you have to do requires that you confront and revise more or less deeply held and unexamined assumptions, attitudes, beliefs, and feelings about your work, your organization's culture, and your leadership. You do not need me in order to undertake first-order learning: posing problems and searching for solutions within the matrix of familiar and agreed-upon perceptions, beliefs, and assumptions we call a paradigm. I assume you possess resources and routines for conducting these aspects of your business. I am here to help you go beyond the mental models you currently use to construct reality, and to help you invent new ones that will produce better business results for you. This second-order learning often does require outside help. When we think of our map of reality as reality itself, it does not occur to us to design a better map. My task is to help you identify and describe your mental models, so that you can choose to extend and improve them.

I commit myself to care about your learning and also to care about your comfort and well-being in the learning process. Together, we shall address the task of balancing the wish to learn and grow against the fear of learning and the wish to preserve comfort and security. We shall explore our defenses against learning with respect, and we shall try to move beyond them in ways that are effective but that do not do emotional violence to ourselves.

Habits and Behaviors of a Learning-Oriented Consultant

Here are ways of doing and being that I find useful in bringing a learning orientation to my consulting. Some are habits of thought and language that I believe facilitate high-order learning, while others could be called tools.

- A bias for developing wisdom and understanding, in contrast to a bias for action.

- A penchant for working with wholes, with the whole system: the inner *and* the outer, the manifest *and* the hidden, the light *and* the dark.
- A goal of identifying fear and other strong negative emotions that block learning, and treating them with warmth, love, and support.
- A goal of involving clients in the designing and carrying out of activities that are normally thought to be part of my role as a professional consultant, such as gathering and analyzing organizational data and planning and conducting retreats, team development meetings, and the like.
- A desire to appeal to and evoke the inherent deep caring and sense of integrity of my clients.

Learning-oriented consultancy is not easy to sell. Many prospective clients are looking for training events, and many want something that looks and feels like a quick fix, although they are not comfortable in owning that longing. Even when clients are ready to enter into a relationship such as I have outlined here, the road ahead will be challenging and will require great persistence and faith in their own resources. They may grow fainthearted and give up along the way. They need inspiration and encouragement, and they need to experience a continuing series of small wins.

Design Criteria for Organizational Learning

When generating learning experiences, I have found the following eight design criteria useful. A good organizational learning process:

- Fosters high energy and commitment in the learning process.
- Builds periods of reflection and generalization into the process, to maximize learning from each experience.
- Supports risk taking on the part of the learner and supports the learner in reflecting on and learning from failures.
- Effectively uses the resources of others, both outsiders and colleagues.
- Connects the intellect and the emotions in the learning process.
- Makes the learning process into "real work" useful to the organization and builds accountability for results into the learning process.
- Legitimizes and encourages the use of time and resources for learning as well as for "getting out the wash."
- Turns individual learning into organizational learning through integration of the results into ideas in good currency. These ideas become part of the accepted knowledge and practice of the organization.

Most of these criteria are met poorly if at all by conventional training programs. In the latter, we are typically removed from the work setting into a role-oriented situation, where we learn because it is expected of us, not because we really care about the outcomes. The stakes are small; we are not engaged in real work, and we are not held accountable for the results. Only our heads are involved, not our values, emotions, or operating concerns. When we try to apply our learning back on the job, where real risk and consequences result from success or failure, we find the training has not prepared us to integrate our knowledge with our feelings or to take risks to apply what we have learned. Because in training we are not getting real things done, both we and our supervisors tend to regard learning time as unproductive time. Because others do not see concrete results of what is learned in training, it tends to remain our individual property. It does not find its way into the shared beliefs, ways of thinking, and operating practices that form the ideas in good currency within the larger organization.

Of course, learning does take place on the job in the course of our day-to-day activities. But for a variety of reasons, on-the-job learning tends to be less effective than we would like. We often avoid the discomfort of tackling newer, riskier, less structured tasks in favor of the familiar and the routine. Because there is always another demand to be met, we tend not to pause and reflect on what we have learned before moving on. If we fail, we may be too involved in avoiding the negative consequences of our failure to spend much time trying to learn from it. Because we believe we are expected to be strong and independent, we often miss opportunities to learn from the help and advice of our colleagues or outside resources.

Hope for Organizational Learning

There are, however, rays of hope, some new, some that have been with us for a long time. The scope of this paper does not permit me to enumerate the connections of others' approaches to organizational learning, but I want to honor some that fit the principles I have outlined here. They include Reg Revans's action learning (1980), Ian Cunningham's self-managed learning (1994), David Bohm's dialogue (Briggs and Bohm, 1993), Chris Argyris's double loop learning (1991; Argyris and Schön, 1974), Fred Emery and Merrelyn Emery's search conferences (Weisbord and others, 1993), Scott Peck's approach to building community (1987), and the technologies of participation pioneered by the Institute for Cultural Affairs (Spencer, 1989).

The only thing new about our focus on learning is the focus. Learning has always been there. It has taken the increasing speed of change and the resulting obsolescence of knowledge to make clear that the learning *process* is now more important than the content learned.

That change in focus can have a profound influence on how we experience organizational life. It is only when we speak of learning a specific skill or piece of knowledge that learning becomes static, with a beginning, middle, and end.

When we give learning its central place in the dynamics of our organizational lives, when we nurture it with our best talents, and when we give it the resource of *time*, then we can experience its dynamism.

The difference between dynamic and static ways of thinking about organizations is increasingly significant. For example, we have tended to view change as going from one state of affairs, how things are now, to another, how we want things to be. In that mode of thinking, only the process of going from one static state to another is dynamic. That way of thinking may have sufficed when things were slower moving, but today there is no static state—change is continuous, and we never arrive at an end state. When we apprehend our experience in static terms, we are doomed to continual frustration. Each desired state of affairs that we achieve immediately begins to slide into obsolescence. We find ourselves confused and off-balance as we initiate yet another problem-solving change project to take care of the next set of difficulties.

We need fluid and flexible organizations today as never before, and their appropriate shapes and dominant processes are still unknown. We lack models for how to organize such entities. We do not know how much they will look like the organizations we are familiar with, but I suspect they will be wildly different. The principles of conscious learning will be a major force in determining the new organizations' shapes and ways of functioning. Organizations that embody the principles will continually change—their conscious learning about the tasks they do and about the wider environment in which they operate will direct those change processes.

We set ourselves ends as goals to attain, but it is worth remembering that we never live in those ends, we live in the means. On the individual level, we can discover that learning as a dynamic process is what keeps things alive for us, what makes the world new. For many of us, our experiences of formal learning deny us such personal renewal, and we must recognize that in any learning enterprise, the learning challenge needs to be at a level that is manageable for the learner. Should the challenge be too great, it will serve only to trigger a defensive reaction, and learning will not take place. Conversely, should the challenge, the newness, be too little, it will not be perceived as worthy of our involvement. Operating within acceptable limits of challenge will keep life fresh. The nature of learning is much less relevant than that learning takes place. The stimulus provided, the questioning that occurs, and the enlivening the questioning induces, all justify a *learning orientation*, quite aside from the benefits of the specific content learned.

Such a learning orientation will have positive consequences for the kind of organizations we have. Many of us dream of humane workplaces, where people are able to enlarge themselves, express their creativity, and work within a supportive environment, and we can realize these workplaces only through a learning focus. It will not be easy. When we reflect on the two barriers to learning I have examined here, and consider what we shall have to do to dismantle them, we see that we shall have to make major changes in how we live our organizational lives. We shall have to accept the challenge to acknowledge the powerful negative emotions engendered by much that goes on from day to day in organizations, and to begin exploring ways to deal with them. We shall have to resist flinging ourselves into action to quiet our anxieties and, instead, take the time to reflect before acting. Each of these behaviors will profoundly impact our organizational life experience.

That is the challenge of this essay. Without our addressing the barriers to learning, there will be no effective learning organization. The benefits of addressing the barriers can be great. May this be a case where our pragmatism, driven by our competitive need to learn as individuals and organizations, leads in the direction of our highest dreams for organizations and the highest good for our planet!

REFERENCES

Publications reprinted in this book are indicated by a † and the chapter number in parentheses after the entry.

Albrecht, K., and Zemke, R. *Service America!* Homewood, Ill.: Business One Irwin, 1985.

Argyris, C. *Interpersonal Competence and Organizational Effectiveness.* Homewood, Ill.: Irwin, 1962.

Argyris, C. "Teaching Smart People to Learn." *Harvard Business Review,* May/June 1991, pp. 99–109.

Argyris, C., and Schön D. A. *Theory in Practice: Increasing Professional Effectiveness.* San Francisco: Jossey-Bass, 1974.

Berlew, D. E. "Leadership and Organizational Excitement." *California Management Review,* 1974, *17*(2), 21–30.

Blake, R. R., Mouton, J. R., Barnes, L. B., and Greiner. L. E. "Breakthrough in Organization Development." *Harvard Business Review,* 1964, *42*(6), 133–154.

Blanchard, K., and Johnson, S. *The One Minute Manager.* New York: American Management Association, 1982.

Briggs, J., and Bohm, J. "Dialogue as a Path Toward Wholeness." In M. R. Weisbord and others, *Discovering Common Ground.* San Francisco: Berrett-Koehler, 1993.

Byrd, R. E. "Training in a Non-Group." *Journal of Humanistic Psychology,* 1967, *7*(1), 18–27.

Cahn, M. M. "Teaching Through Student Models." In P. Runkel, R. Harrison, and M. Runkel (eds.), *The Changing College Classroom.* San Francisco: Jossey-Bass, 1969.

Cartwright, D. (ed.), *Studies in Social Power.* Ann Arbor: University of Michigan Institute for Social Research, 1959.

Clark, J. V. "Task Group Therapy." Working paper, Graduate School of Business Administration, University of California, Los Angeles, 1966.

Cooperrider, D. L. "Positive Image, Positive Action: The Affirmative Basis of Organizing." In S. Srivastva, D. L. Cooperrider, and Associates (eds.), *Appreciative Management and*

Leadership: The Power of Positive Thought and Action in Organizations. San Francisco: Jossey-Bass, 1990.

Culbert, S. A. "Training Change Agents for Business and Public Administration." In P. Runkel, R. Harrison, and M. Runkel (eds.), *The Changing College Classroom.* San Francisco: Jossey-Bass, 1969.

Cunningham, I. *The Wisdom of Strategic Learning: The Self Managed Learning Solution.* London: McGraw-Hill, 1994.

Cytrynbaum, S., and Mann, R. D. "Community as Campus-Project Outreach." In P. Runkel, R. Harrison, and M. Runkel (eds.), *The Changing College Classroom.* San Francisco: Jossey-Bass, 1969.

Davis, S. M. "Transforming Organizations: The Key to Strategy Is Context." *Organizational Dynamics,* 1982, *10*(3), 64–80.

Eisler, R. *The Chalice and the Blade: Our History, Our Future.* San Francisco: HarperCollins, 1987.

Eisler, R., and Loye, D. *The Partnership Way: New Tools for Living and Learning: A Practical Companion for "The Chalice and the Blade."* San Francisco: HarperSanFrancisco, 1990.

Emery, M. "Training Search Conference Managers." In M. R. Weisbord and others (eds.), *Discovering Common Ground.* San Francisco: Berrett-Koehler, 1993.

Fink, S. L. "Crisis and Motivation: A Theoretical Model." *Archives of Physical Medicine and Rehabilitation,* Nov. 1967, *43*, 592–597.

Frankl, V. E. *Man's Search for Meaning.* Boston: Beacon Press, 1959.

French, J.R.P., and Raven, B. "The Bases of Social Power." In D. Cartwright (ed.), *Studies in Social Power.* Ann Arbor: University of Michigan, Institute for Social Research, 1959.

Fritz, R. *The Path of Least Resistance.* Walpole, N.H.: Ballentine Books, 1989.

Galbraith, J. *Designing Complex Organizations.* Reading, Mass.: Addison-Wesley, 1978.

Handy, C. *Gods of Management: The Changing Work of Organizations.* (Rev. ed.) London: Pan, 1985.

Harrison, R. "Defenses and the Need to Know." *Human Relations Training News,* 1963, *6*(4), 1–3. (†Chapter Eighteen)

Harrison, R. "Cognitive Models for Interpersonal and Group Behavior: A Theoretical Framework for Research." *Explorations in Human Relations Training and Research.* (Entire issue 2.) Washington, D.C.: National Training Laboratories, 1965a.

Harrison, R. "Defenses and the Need to Know." In P. R. Lawrence, J. A. Seiler, and others (eds.), *Organizational Behavior and Administration.* Homewood, Ill.: Irwin, 1965b. (†Chapter Eighteen)

Harrison, R. "Group Composition Models for Laboratory Design." *The Journal of Applied Behavioral Science,* 1965c, *1*(4), 409–432.

Harrison, R. "Cognitive Change and Participation in a Sensitivity Training Laboratory." *Journal of Consulting Psychology,* 1966, *30*(6), 517–520.

Harrison, R. "Classroom Innovation: A Design Primer." In P. Runkel, R. Harrison, and M. Runkel (eds.), *The Changing College Classroom.* San Francisco: Jossey-Bass, 1969. (†Chapter Twenty)

Harrison, R. "Choosing the Depth of Organizational Intervention." *Journal of Applied Behavioral Science,* 1970, *6*(2), 189–202. (†Chapter Two)

Harrison, R. "Developing Autonomy, Initiative, and Risk Taking Through a Laboratory Design." *European Training,* 1972a, *2*, 100–116. (†Chapter Twenty-One)

Harrison, R. "Understanding Your Organization's Character." *Harvard Business Review.* 1972b *50*(3), 119–128. (†Chapter Ten)

Harrison, R. "When Power Conflicts Trigger Team Spirit." *European Training,* 1972c, *2*, 57–65. (†Chapter Four)

Harrison, R. "Towards a Strategy for Helping Redundant and Retiring Managers." *Management Education and Development,* 1973, *4*, 77–85. (†Chapter Twenty-Three)

Harrison, R. "Diagnosing Organization Ideology." In J. E. Jones and J. W. Pfeiffer (eds.), *The 1975 Annual Handbook for Group Facilitators*. San Diego, Calif.: University Associates, 1975.

Harrison, R. "Self-Directed Learning: A Radical Approach to Educational Design." *Simulation and Games*, 1977, *8*(1), 73–94. (†Chapter Twenty-Two)

Harrison, R. "A Practical Model of Motivation and Character Development." In J. E. Jones and J. W. Pfeiffer (eds.), *The 1979 Annual Handbook for Group Facilitators*. San Diego, Calif.: University Associates, 1979.

Harrison, R. "Organizations and the Planet." *Gaia*, 1981a, *4*(2), 5–6.

Harrison, R. "Startup: The Care and Feeding of Infant Systems." *Organizational Dynamics*, 1981b, *10*(1), 5–29. (†Chapter Five)

Harrison, R. "Strategies for a New Age." *Human Resource Management*, 1983, *22*(3), 209–234. (†Chapter Eleven)

Harrison, R. "Leadership and Strategy for a New Age." In J. D. Adams (ed.), *Transforming Work*. Alexandria, Va.: Miles River Press, 1984. (†Chapter Eleven)

Harrison, R. *Empowerment in Organizations*. Clinton, Wash.: Harrison Associates, 1985.

Harrison, R. "Harnessing Personal Energy: How Companies Can Inspire Employees." *Organizational Dynamics*, 1987a, *16*(2), 4–20. (†Chapter Nine)

Harrison, R. *Organization Culture and Quality of Service: A Strategy for Releasing Love in the Workplace*. (I. Cunningham, ed.) London: Association for Management Education and Development, 1987b. (†Chapter Twelve)

Harrison, R. "Quality of Service: A New Frontier for Integrity in Organizations." In S. Srivastva (ed.), *Executive Integrity*. San Francisco: Jossey-Bass, 1987c.

Harrison, R. *Building an Organization Vision and Mission Statement*. Clinton, Wash.: Harrison Associates, 1988.

Harrison, R. *Culture and Levels of Consciousness in Organizations*. Clinton, Wash.: Harrison Associates, 1990a. (†Chapter Thirteen)

Harrison, R. *Working with Organization Culture: A Workbook*. Clinton, Wash.: Harrison Associates, 1990b.

Harrison, R. *Towards the Learning Organization—Promises and Pitfalls*. Clinton, Wash.: Harrison Associates, 1992.

Harrison, R. *Diagnosing Organizational Culture, Trainer's Manual*. San Diego, Calif.: Pfeiffer, 1993.

Harrison, R. *Consultant's Journey: A Dance of Work and Spirit*. San Francisco: Jossey-Bass, 1995.

Harrison, R., Cooper, J., and Dawes, G. *Humanizing Change: Matching Interventions to Organizational Realities*. Mountain View, Calif.: Harrison Associates, 1991.

Harrison, R., and Dawes, G. "Barriers to Learning in the Organization." In R. Boot, J. Lawrence, and J. Morris (eds.), *Managing the Unknown by Creating New Futures*. London: McGraw-Hill, 1994. (†Chapter Twenty-Four)

Harrison, R., and Hopkins, R. L. "The Design of Cross-Cultural Training: An Alternative to the University Model." *Journal of Applied Behavioral Science*, 1967, *3*, 431–460. (†Chapter Nineteen)

Harrison, R., and Oshry, B. I. "Laboratory Training in Human Relations and Organizational Behavior." *European Training*, 1972, *2*, 189–199.

Harrison, R., and Powell, C. "Organisation Culture and Quality of Service." In R. Benson (ed.), *From Organisation to Organism: A New View of Business and Management*. Forres, Scotland: Findhorn Foundation, 1987.

Harrison, R., and Stokes, H. *Diagnosing Organization Culture*. Berkeley, Calif.: Harrison Associates, 1986.

Harrison, R., and Stokes, H. *Diagnosing Organization Culture*. (Rev. ed.) San Diego, Calif.: Pfeiffer, 1992.

Horn, R. E. "Experiment in Programmed Learning." In P. Runkel, R. Harrison, and M. Runkel (eds.), *The Changing College Classroom*. San Francisco: Jossey-Bass, 1969.

Horsley, J. B. Report on ammonia plant commissioning project, 1973. (Not publicly released.)

James, W. *The Principles of Psychology.* Cambridge, Mass.: Harvard University Press, 1982.

Kelman, H. C. "Compliance, Identification and Internalization: Three Processes of Attitude Change." *Journal of Conflict Resolution,* 1958, *2,* 51–60.

Kelman, H. C. "Processes of Opinion Change." *Public Opinion Quarterly,* 1961, *25,* 57–58.

Kiefer, C. F., and Senge, P. M. "Metanoic Organizations." In J. D. Adams (ed.), *Transforming Work.* Alexandria, Va.: Miles River Press, 1984.

Kolb, D. A., Rubin, I. M., and McIntyre, J. M. *Organizational Psychology: An Experiential Approach.* Englewood Cliffs, N.J.: Prentice Hall, 1971.

Korda, M. *Power! How to Get It, How to Use It.* New York: Random House, 1975.

Kübler-Ross, E. *On Death and Dying.* New York: Macmillan, 1969.

Lawrence, P. R., and Lorsch, J. W. "Differentiation and Integration in Complex Organizations." *Administrative Science Quarterly,* 1967a, *12,* 1–47.

Lawrence, P. R., and Lorsch, J. W. "New Management Job: The Integrator." *Harvard Business Review,* 1967b, *6,* 142–151.

Lehner, G.F.J. "From Job Loss to Career Innovation." Paper presented at the New Technology in Organization Development Conference, Center for Organization Studies, National Training Laboratories Institute for Applied Behavioral Science, New York, 1971.

Louis, A. M. "They're Striking Some Strange Bargains at Diamond Shamrock." *Fortune,* Jan. 1976, pp. 142–156.

Maccoby, M. *The Gamesman: The New Corporate Leaders.* New York: Simon & Schuster, 1976.

Maccoby, M. *The Leader.* New York: Simon & Schuster, 1981.

MacLean, D. *To Hear the Angels Sing.* Issaquah, Wash.: Lorian Society, 1983.

McClelland, D. C. *The Achievement Motive.* New York: Appleton-Century-Crofts, 1953.

McGregor, D. *The Human Side of Enterprise.* New York: McGraw-Hill, 1960.

Maslow, A. H. *Motivation and Personality.* New York: HarperCollins, 1954.

May, R. *Love and Will.* New York: W.W. Norton, 1969.

Naisbitt, J. *Megatrends: Ten New Directions Transforming Our Lives.* New York: Warner Books, 1982.

Noer, D. M. *Healing the Wounds: Overcoming the Trauma of Layoffs and Revitalizing Downsized Organizations.* San Francisco: Jossey-Bass, 1993.

Ouspensky, P. D. *The Fourth Way: A Record of Talks and Answers to Questions Based on the Work of G. I. Gurdjieff.* New York: Knopf, 1957.

Owen, H. *Leadership Is.* Potomac, Md.: Abbott Publishing, 1990.

Pascale, R. *Managing on the Edge.* New York: Simon & Schuster, 1990.

Pascale, R. T, and Athos, A. G. *The Art of Japanese Management.* New York: Warner Books, 1992.

Peck, M. S. *The Different Drum: Community-Making and Peace.* New York: Simon & Schuster, 1987.

Pedler, M., Burgoyne, J., and Boydell, T. *The Learning Company.* London: McGraw-Hill, 1991.

Perrow, C. *Normal Accidents: Living with High-Risk Technologies.* New York: Basic Books, 1984.

Peters, T. J. *Thriving on Chaos: Handbook for a Managerial Revolution.* New York: Knopf, 1987.

Peters, T. J., and Austin, N. *A Passion for Excellence: The Leadership Difference.* New York: Warner Books, 1985.

Peters, T. J., and Waterman, R. H., Jr. *In Search of Excellence: Lessons from America's Best-Run Companies.* New York: HarperCollins, 1982.

Pfeiffer, J. W., and Jones, J. E. (eds.). *A Handbook of Structured Experiences for Human Relations Training.* Vol. I. San Diego, Calif.: University Associates, 1969.

Phillips, M. *The Seven Laws of Money.* New York: Random House, 1974.

Revans, R. W. *Action Learning.* London: Blond & Briggs, 1980.

Rhinehart, L. *The Dice Man.* London: Talmy, Franklin, 1971.

Ringer, R. J. *Winning Through Intimidation.* Los Angeles: Los Angeles Book Publishers, 1974.

Ringer, R. J. *Looking Out for Number One.* Ramsey, N.J.: Funk & Wagnalls, 1977.

Runkel, P. J. "The Campus as a Laboratory." In P. Runkel, R. Harrison, and M. Runkel (eds.), *The Changing College Classroom.* San Francisco: Jossey-Bass, 1969.

Runkel, P., Harrison, R., and Runkel, M. (eds.), *The Changing College Classroom.* San Francisco: Jossey-Bass, 1969.

Schaef, A. W., and Fassel, D. *The Addictive Organization.* New York: HarperCollins, 1988.

Schein, E. H. *Process Consultation: Its Role in Organization Development.* Reading, Mass.: Addison-Wesley, 1969.

Schein, E. H., and Bennis, W. G. *Personal and Organizational Change Through Group Methods: The Laboratory Approach.* New York: Wiley, 1965.

Schön, D. A. *Beyond the Stable State.* London: Temple Smith, 1971.

Schutz, W. G. *FIRO: A Three Dimensional Theory of Interpersonal Behavior.* Troy, Mo.: Holt, Rinehart & Winston, 1958.

Seiler, J. A. "Training Managers in the Laboratory." In P. Runkel, R. Harrison, and M. Runkel (eds.), *The Changing College Classroom.* San Francisco: Jossey-Bass, 1969.

Senge, P. *The Fifth Discipline: The Art and Practice of the Learning Organization.* New York: Doubleday/Currency, 1990.

Shaffer, C. R., and Anundsen, K. *Creating Community Anywhere.* New York: Jeremy P. Tarcher/Perigee, 1993.

Sherwood, J. J. "Creating Work Cultures with Competitive Advantage." *Organizational Dynamics,* 1988, *16*(3), 5–27.

Smith, W. E. "Planning for the Electricity Sector in Columbia." In M. R. Weisbord and others (eds.), *Discovering Common Ground.* San Francisco: Berrett-Koehler, 1993.

South, O. "Creativity for Engineers." In P. Runkel, R. Harrison, and M. Runkel (eds.), *The Changing College Classroom.* San Francisco: Jossey-Bass, 1969.

Spencer, L. *Winning Through Participation.* Dubuque, Iowa.: Kendall/Hunt, 1989.

Tarcher, M. *Leadership and the Power of Ideas.* New York: HarperCollins, 1966.

Torbert, W. R., and Hackman, J. R. "Taking the Fun Out of Outfoxing the System." In P. Runkel, R. Harrison, and M. Runkel (eds.), *The Changing College Classroom.* San Francisco: Jossey-Bass, 1969.

Trist, E. L., and Bamforth, K. W. "Some Social and Psychological Consequences of the Longwall Method of Coal Getting." *Human Relations,* 1951, *4*(1), 3–38.

Vaill, P. B. *Managing as a Performing Art: New Ideas for a World of Chaotic Change.* San Francisco: Jossey-Bass, 1989.

Walton, R. "From Control to Commitment in the Workplace." *Harvard Business Review.* Mar./Apr. 1985, pp. 76–84.

Weisbord, M. R., and Janoff, S. V. *Future Search.* San Francisco: Berrett-Koehler, 1995.

Weisbord, M. R., and others. *Discovering Common Ground.* San Francisco: Berrett-Koehler, 1993.

Wheatley, M. *Leadership and the New Science.* San Francisco: Berrett-Koehler, 1993.

INDEX